D1147365

The

HIDDEN PLACES
of
SCOTLAND

Edited by
David Gerrard

Published by:
Travel Publishing Ltd
7a Apollo House, Calleva Park
Aldermaston, Berks, RG7 8TN

ISBN 1-902-00735-2

© Travel Publishing Ltd 1999

First Published:	*1994*
Second Edition:	*1997*
Third Edition:	*1999*

Regional Titles in the Hidden Places Series:

Cambridgeshire & Lincolnshire	Channel Islands
Cheshire	Chilterns
Cornwall	Devon
Dorset, Hants & Isle of Wight	Essex
Gloucestershire	Heart of England
Highlands & Islands	Kent
Lake District & Cumbria	Lancashire
Norfolk	Northeast Yorkshire
Northumberland & Durham	North Wales
Nottinghamshire	Peak District
Potteries	Somerset
South Wales	Suffolk
Surrey	Sussex
Thames Valley	Warwickshire & W Midlands
Welsh Borders	Wiltshire
Yorkshire Dales	

National Titles in the Hidden Places Series:

England	Ireland
Scotland	Wales

Printing by: Ashford Press, Gosport
Maps by: © MAPS IN MINUTES ™ (1998)
Line Drawings: Rodney Peace
Editor: David Gerrard
Cover Design: Lines & Words, Aldermaston
Cover Photographs: Luss, Loch Lomond; Rothesay Castle, Isle of Bute © Argyll, the Isles, Loch Lomond, Stirling & Trossachs Tourist Board.

FOREWORD

The Hidden Places series is a collection of easy to use travel guides taking you, in this instance, on a relaxed but informative tour of Scotland. The book explores the rich history and culture as well as the wonderful scenery of a country that has been inhabited for thousands of years and which possesses a bewildering variety of landscapes and one of the most impressive coastlines in the world. Scotland is full of *Hidden Places*, which can enrich the visitor's historical knowledge of Scottish heritage and astound the eye with their sheer beauty.

Our books contain a wealth of interesting information on the history, the countryside, the towns and villages and the more established places of interest in the counties. But they also promote the more secluded and little known visitor attractions and places to stay, eat and drink many of which are easy to miss unless you know exactly where you are going.

We include hotels, inns and other types of accommodation, restaurants, public houses, teashops, historic houses, museums, gardens and many other attractions throughout Scotland, all of which are comprehensively indexed. Most places have an attractive line drawing and are cross-referenced to coloured maps found at the rear of the book. We do not award merit marks or rankings but concentrate on describing the more interesting, unusual or unique features of each place with the aim of making the reader's stay in the local area an enjoyable and stimulating experience.

Whether you are visiting the area for business or pleasure or in fact are living in the country we do hope that you enjoy reading and using this book. We are always interested in what readers think of places covered (or not covered) in our guides so please do not hesitate to use the reader comment forms provided to give us your considered views. We also welcome any general comments which will help us improve the guides themselves. Finally if you are planning to visit any other corner of the British Isles we would like to refer you to the list of other *Hidden Places* titles to be found at the rear of the book.

Travel Publishing Ltd

CONTENTS

1 The Borders

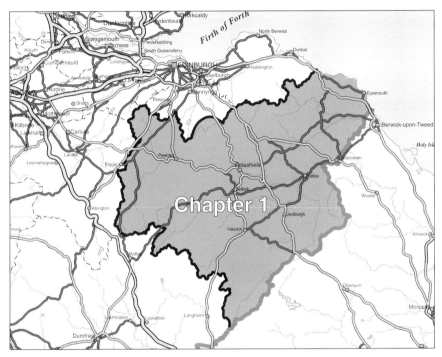

© MAPS IN MINUTES ™ (1998)

Once the bloody cockpit in which for centuries the English and the Scots engaged in interminable warfare, this is now a pastoral, peaceful region dotted with neat little market towns. Its 1800 square miles extends from the rocky Berwickshire coastline with its picturesque fishing villages, through the gentle valley of the River Tweed to rolling hills and moorland in the west.

In medieval times, four great Abbeys dominated the area: Jedburgh, Kelso, Melrose and Dryburgh, all of them now in ruins but magnificent in their shattered glory. The heart of Robert the Bruce is buried at Melrose Abbey; Dryburgh Abbey was the last resting place of Sir Walter Scott whose beloved home, Abbotsford House near Melrose, is still lived in by his descendants. Traquair House, a mile or so south of Innerleithen, boasts an even longer record. The oldest continuously inhabited dwelling in Scotland, it has been lived in by the Maxwell-Stuart family since 1491. Floors Castle at Kelso, the hereditary home of the Dukes of Roxburghe, is a mostly Victorian, mock-medieval extravaganza of turrets and castellations, while by contrast, Paxton House and Mellerstain are gems of 18th century classical restraint, both masterworks the creations of the gifted Adam family. Perhaps the most august of all the great houses is Bowhill, the main Scottish residence of the Duke of Buccleuch, although multi-turreted Thirlestane Castle runs it a close second.

These historic houses are set in an inspiring landscape where grand vistas sweep across the majestic Eildon Hills or the crumpled masses of the Cheviots, broad green valleys unfold and huge tracts of forest shelter a varied wildlife, an unspoilt countryside which generously repays a leisurely exploration. Wherever you travel in the Borders, you will come across memories of the area's most famous son, Sir Walter Scott, who sang its praises in many a poem.

ST ABB'S
Map 3 ref N13

12 miles N of Berwick on the B6348

St Abbs is one of the most picturesque fishing villages on Scotland's east coast, one of the few safe havens along this rocky stretch of coast. Jagged cliffs, some of the highest in Britain, rise 300ft feet above the shore and fishermen's cottages are shoe-horned in wherever they can fit. **Springbank Cottage** enjoys a prime location in this attractive little port, standing close to the harbour's edge. Formerly two fishermen's cottages, Springbank is the home of David and Irene McIntosh who welcome guests for bed & breakfast and also to their charming, sea-facing Tea Garden. This is a real Tea Garden with no seating indoors but, if

Springbank Cottage, The Harbour, St Abbs, Berwickshire TD14 5PW
Tel: 018907 71477

the weather is not so good, the McIntoshs are happy to make up trays for your car and they also provide takeaway facilities. The Tea Garden provides a varied menu and specialises in filled rolls incorporating local seafood delicacies plus a range of home-made scones and tray bakes. Accommodation at Springbank Cottage comprises 3 rooms (1 double, 1 twin, and 1 small double /large single), all of them with colour TV, a washbasin with hot and cold water, tea and coffee-making facilities, and a view of the sea. For the active, there are many lovely walks in the vicinity, opportunities for both sea and river fishing, and boat trips from the harbour. Or you may prefer to just relax in the tea garden, observing the cormorants, fishermen mending their nets, while keeping an eye open for a sighting of the occasional seal.

The village is named after St Ebba, a 7th century princess of Northumbria who was shipwrecked here. She managed to reach shore and founded a nunnery in gratitude for her escape. Just to the north of the village, **St Abb's Head** is a spectacular promontory, now a National Trust for Scotland Marine Reserve. A lighthouse was built here in 1862 but, because of the height of the cliffs on which it stands, no tower was necessary and keepers actually walk downhill to reach the light.

Three miles to the west of St Abb's Head is one of Scotland's most extraordinary castles. **Fast Castle** is perched precariously on a stack of rock, barely accessible by the steep cliff footpath and best viewed from above. Sir Walter Scott used the castle as his model for Wolf's Crag in his novel *The Bride of Lammermuir.*

EYEMOUTH
MAP 3 REF N13
8 miles N of Berwick-upon-Tweed on the A1107

Still an active little fishing port, Eyemouth has long since abandoned its other main source of income in times past, smuggling. Contraband goods were furtively conveyed to **Gunsgreen House** on the far side of the harbour and thence by way of underground tunnels to eager purchasers in the town itself. The elegant 1750s house, designed by James Adam, has now retrieved its respectable status by becoming the headquarters of the local golf club.

In the **Eyemouth Museum** the most striking exhibit is a contemporary tapestry depicting the traumatic disaster of 1881 when 189 fishermen from this small town perished in one of the worst North Sea storms on record. More upbeat celebrations of the town's maritime history take place in June, with a **Seafood Festival**, and in July with the **Herring Queen Festival**.

AYTON
MAP 3 REF N13
8 miles NW of Berwick-upon-Tweed on the B6355

This small village on the River Eye, only a mile or so from the A1, is dominated by **Ayton Castle**, a faeryland fantasy of pepperpot turrets and crow-stepped gables. The castle was built in 1846 and is still a private residence but open to visitors on Sunday afternoons during the season.

From Ayton, 5 miles of country lanes lead southwards to **Paxton House**, "the most perfect example in Scotland of the style now known as neo-Palladianism". A melancholy tale is attached to this gracious house, designed by the Edinburgh brothers John and James Adam in the 1750s. It was commissioned by Patrick Home, Lord Billie, a rich and personable young man who while visiting Berlin on his Grand Tour of Europe bedazzled the court of King Frederick the Great of Prussia. The king's only acknowledged child, Charlotte de Brandt became besotted with the smooth-talking Scotsman. She absolutely rejected her father's long-laid plans for a politically more useful dynastic connection with a plump and terminally boring Silesian prince. The king, surprisingly, finally agreed to her marriage with the wealthy, handsome but politically insignificant Scottish laird. Patrick gleefully returned to Scotland and spent lavishly on building a noble house at Paxton worthy of his intended royal bride. Charlotte never entered its stately portals or passed through its sublimely-decorated rooms. She died young before the house became habitable; her marriage not yet consecrated.

The sad story of Patrick and Charlotte was to be duplicated a few years later when Patrick became engaged to Jane Graham of Dugaldstone. Their marriage did indeed take place, in Naples in 1771, and the couple spent 3 years touring Europe. Once again, Patrick commissioned Robert Adam to design and build a new marital home, Wedderburn Castle. He returned to it alone: Jane stayed in Europe with a new lover. No wonder the striking portrait of Patrick Home by John Hoppner, on display in Paxton House, depicts an elderly man with a choleric complexion, a set jaw and a sour expression. It is part of a large collection which Patrick bequeathed to his nephew George who was then 77 years old. Despite his age, George enthusiastically set about building what is still the largest private picture gallery of any country house in Scotland. A rich selection of other paintings on display here are on loan from the National Galleries of Scotland, (for whom Paxton House is an outstation), and are changed frequently.

Paxton House is also notable for its outstanding collection of furniture by Chippendale, more than 60 pieces ranging from the entire furnishing of the dining-room, (not just tables and chairs but window-seats, wine-coolers and knife-boxes); pier tables with marvellous marquetry inlays; desks and secretaires; mahogany armchairs and sofas.

Outside, the 80 acres of gardens, parkland and woodland were laid out in the late 1770s in the style of "Capability" Brown and are set within a great loop of the River Tweed which here marks the border between Scotland and England.

A few miles upstream from Paxton House, the ruins of **Norham Castle** stand on the south bank of the Tweed and are therefore in England but the Castle is generally considered one of the Border attractions. Its great Norman Keep, which inspired several landscapes by J.M.W. Turner, is regarded as one of the finest examples in England. Built in the 1150s, Norham was the principal stronghold of the Prince-Bishops of Durham and witnessed many battles before Elizabeth I abandoned it in favour of the newly-fortified Berwick-upon-Tweed.

DUNS   MAP 3 REF N14
15 miles W of Berwick-upon-Tweed on the A6105/A6112

The former county town of Berwickshire, this quiet little market town sits at the foot of **Duns Law** - 714 feet high and well worth the 20-minute walk to the summit for its grand views and to see the **Covenanters' Stone** which marks the spot where Alexander Leslie gathered his troops for an expected battle with Charles I's army. In the event, Charles' troops thought better of it and retreated without a fight. Duns Castle, 14th century with early 19th century extensions, is not normally open to the public but the surrounding **Duns Castle Nature Reserve** offers some pleasant trails for walkers through its 190 acres.

Duns was the birthplace of two well-known figures. The medieval theologian, Duns Scotus was born here around 1265. Those who subscribed to his views were contemptuously called "Dunses", hence the word "dunce". A more contemporary figure is Jim Clark who was twice world motor racing champion in the 1960s. His dazzling career, brutally cut short by a fatal crash on the track at Hockenheim in Germany in 1968, is recalled at the **Jim Clark Room** in Newtown Street.

Just across the road from the Jim Clark Room, in Blackbull Street, the **Black Bull Hotel** stands at the heart of the town. This appealing old hostelry was built

Black Bull Hotel, Blackbull Street, Duns, Border TD11 3AR
Tel: 01361 883379

in the late 1700s as a coaching inn and the former stables still stand alongside. The Black Bull is owned and run by Margaret and Dave Sturrock who offer customers a warm welcome, a comprehensive menu of main meals and snacks, and a good selection of beers and ales, including the locally-brewed Bellhaven Ales. The Black Bull serves food every day, all day, and you can enjoy it either in the atmospheric bar, the separate restaurant or, in good weather, on the lovely secluded patio overlooking the garden. And if you are looking for somewhere to stay in the area, the hotel has 3 pleasant and comfortable letting rooms: a single and a twin with shared facilities, and a single en suite.

Two miles east of Duns on the A6105, **Manderston House** is one of the finest examples of a lavish Edwardian house in Britain. Set in some 50 acres of gardens which are noted for their rhododendrons and azaleas, Manderston was built between 1871 and 1905 for the Miller family who had made their fortune in herrings and hemp. No expense was spared. The architect, John Kinross, installed exquisite plasterwork ceilings, an inlaid marble floor and an immensely costly staircase modelled on one in the Petit Trianon at Versailles, its rails plated in silver.

COLDSTREAM

MAP 3 REF N14

15 miles SW of Berwick-upon-Tweed on the A697

This pleasant little town sits beside the Tweed and is linked to England by the graceful 5-arched **Smeaton's Bridge** built by John Smeaton in 1766 on the site of the original ford by which Edward I had invaded Scotland nearly 5 centuries earlier. Like Gretna Green, Coldstream was a favourite with eloping couples who until 1856 could get married in the Toll House at the Scottish end of the bridge. Robert Burns crossed here on his first visit to England in May 1787, an event commemorated by a plaque on the bridge. Nearby, a huge obelisk erected in 1832 to a little-known MP soars above the town.

Coldstream's name is perhaps best known in connection with the Coldstream Guards. Officially designated the 2nd Regiment of Foot Guards of the British Army, the regiment was formed here in 1659 by General Monck with the intention of marching on London to help restore Charles II to the throne. The Guards' distinguished reputation subsequently is recorded at the Coldstream Museum in the attractive, pedestrianised Market Square.

To the northwest of the town, **The Hirsel** was the home of former Prime Minister Sir Alec Douglas-Home. His family still live here and the house is not open to the public, but visitors have been free to wander through large parts of the 3000-acre estate. On the western edge of the estate, former homestead outhouses have been converted into the **Homestead Museum & Centre for Arts & Crafts**, incorporating craft shops, a tea room and a museum which interprets the management of the estate, past and present.

About 4 miles southeast of Coldstream, near the village of Branxton, is **Flodden Field**, the site of Scotland's most disastrous battle against the English.

On 9 September 1513, at least 10,000 men perished, amongst them the Scottish leader, James IV, and "not a family of note in all Scotland was left without cause to mourn that dreadful day". In 1910, a tall Celtic cross was erected on the hill overlooking the battlefield. It is inscribed simply "Flodden 1513. To the brave of both nations".

LEITHOLM

MAP 3 REF N14

3 miles NW of Coldstream on the B6461

About 3 miles northwest of Coldstream is the small village of Leitholm, well worth seeking out for a very special bed and breakfast establishment. A first view of **Stainrigg** is quite breathtaking. This unique old house is a wonderful medley of turrets and crow-stepped gables, huge mullioned windows and a classical entrance, all constructed in pink and grey Border sandstone. Stainrigg's setting is equally enchanting, - some 30 acres of parkland and superb gardens in which you'll discover a beautifully maintained Victorian walled garden as well as a croquet lawn and boules pitch. Dating back to 1631, the house was enhanced and extended in 1880 by General John Cockburn-Hood who returned

Stainrigg, Leitholm, Berwickshire TD12 4JE
Tel: 01890 885200 Fax: 01890 885220

from service in the Indian Army to marry and bring his new wife to the family home. Today, Stainrigg offers visitors to the Borders a quite outstanding place to stay for bed and breakfast with 8 splendidly furnished en suite rooms available, each with its individual character and decor: from a French sleigh bed to a turret dressing room. Stainrigg's speciality, though, is in hosting house parties for business or private occasions. Your party takes over the whole house, the chef cooks exclusively for you, taking your tastes and preferences fully into account, and the owners, Catherine and Charles Duthie, personally supervise every detail of your programme, including organising recreational activities and guided tours if you so wish.

KIRK YETHOLM
MAP 3 REF N15

5 miles S of Coldstream on the B6352

The tiny conservation village of Kirk Yetholm lies little more than a mile from the Scottish-English border with the mighty Cheviot Hills rising to the south. The village is well-known to serious walkers as a stage on the 65-mile cross-border St Cuthbert's Way and as the northern end of the gruelling 270-mile Pennine Way. For serious lovers of good food and drink, it owes its renown to **The Border Hotel**. This striking, partly-thatched and half-timbered building dates back to the early 1800s when it began dispensing hospitality for the coaches plying between the Border towns and Wooler in Northumberland. In late 1996 Maxine Day, with her late husband, became the new owner of the Border Hotel

The Border Hotel, The Green, Kirk Yetholm, Roxburghshire TD5 8PQ
Tel: 01573 420237 Fax: 01573 420549

and they immediately began a programme of upgrading and extending the property, and the service provided. A split-level restaurant has been created, a games room and a magnificent conservatory added. The 5 bedrooms and one bathroom have been adapted to form the Pennines' and Cheviots' rooms, furnished to a very high standard and with private facilities. They are really more like suites, with huge bathrooms and grand views of the countryside. This outstanding inn has an interesting connection with the gypsy community for it was outside the Border Hotel that the last gypsy Coronation took place in May, 1898. The celebration attracted several thousand spectators and some fascinating photographs of the event are on display in the hotel.

ECCLES

MAP 3 REF N14

5 miles NW of Coldstream on the B6461

Set in 25 acres of parkland, woodlands and gardens, **Eccles House** is a striking Edwardian mansion which provides its guests with a truly unique experience. Not many houses have gardens in which stand the ruins of a 12th century Cistercian Nunnery, St Mary's. Also within the grounds is an unusual Georgian summerhouse, a charming spot to while away a lazy summer afternoon with a good book. The house itself has been lovingly restored by Edythe and George Webster, retaining the charm of its period and the atmosphere of a country house whilst incorporating all of the facilities to be expected today. Attention to detail and a desire to provide the highest levels of hospitality are the Websters continuing aims.

In the elegant dining room, they serve the freshest fruits and vegetables of the season, many of them grown in their kitchen garden, as well as excellent locally produced meats, fish and game. The menu is changed regularly and Edythe is happy to provide for vegetarian or special diets. Guests have the use of the lovely hall and drawing room, both of which retain their antique furniture, and a warm welcome is assured by log fires when the weather is inclement. On fine days, the drawing room offers wonderful views of the Border countryside. Each of the guest bedrooms at Eccles House is individually designed and furnished to incorporate everything you would find in first class accommodation,

Eccles House, Eccles, by Kelso, Roxburghshire, TD5 7QS
Tel: 01890 840205 Fax: 01890 840367

- a private bathroom, central heating, a superbly comfortable bed and colour television. You can make yourself a hot drink, enjoy some home-made biscuits, and you'll also find many other thoughtful touches. For those looking for peace, tranquillity and a place to unwind, Eccles House will certainly not disappoint. The house also lends itself particularly well to exclusive house parties, anniversaries, family reunions and special celebrations.

KELSO   Map 3 ref N14
9 miles SW of Coldstream on the A698

Sir Walter Scott considered Kelso "the most beautiful, if not the most romantic, village in the land". Sir Walter was very familiar with this dignified little town, set around the meeting of the rivers Tweed and Teviot. As a boy he attended the Old Grammar School which was actually based within the melancholy ruins of **Kelso Abbey**. Founded in 1128 by King David it became the richest and most powerful monastery in southern Scotland. Successive English invasions culminated in the Earl of Hertford's merciless attack in 1545 when all the monks were murdered and the Abbey set on fire. The fine Norman and Gothic detail of the remaining transepts and façade give some idea of the glorious building that once stood here.

From Kelso's elegant and spacious **Market Square**, believed to be the largest in Scotland, Bridge Street leads to John Rennie's fine 5-arched bridge over the Tweed. It was built in 1803 and Rennie was clearly pleased with his work since, some 8 years later, he used virtually the same design for his Waterloo Bridge in London.

There are grand views from the bridge of **Junction Pool**, the famous salmon fishing beat where the waters of the Tweed and Teviot mingle. If you want to try your angling skills here you must book years ahead and pay somewhere around £5000 per rod per week.

Back in the Market Square a narrow alley leads to **The Cobbles Inn**, definitely worth seeking out for the quality of the food on offer. When Joan Forrest bought The Cobbles in 1994 it was primarily a drinkers' haunt but she has changed that dramatically and her excellent cuisine now attracts customers from all over the Borders. The menus change regularly but there's always a wide choice of imaginative, freshly-prepared dishes, supplemented by several daily specials. The lunchtime menu ranges from sandwiches to steaks with interesting dishes such as 'Junction Parcel' in between. (Junction Parcel is a delectable confection of smoked salmon, smoked haddock and avocado wrapped in a potato pancake and topped with cheese sauce). The dinner menu is equally appealing and along with more familiar dishes may include offerings such as Medallions of Ostrich in a Red Wine & Raspberry Sauce. On no account should you leave without trying one of the superb home-made desserts. The Cobbles' Wine List offers a well-chosen selection of mostly European wines which, like the meals, are very sensibly priced.

**The Cobbles Inn, 7 Bowmont Street, Kelso, Scottish Borders TD5 7JH
Tel: 01573 223548**

From The Cobbles, take a short walk along Roxburgh Street to another alley
that leads to the delightful Cobby Riverside Walk. A short stroll will bring you
to the breathtaking extravagance of **Floors Castle**, hereditary home of the Dukes
of Roxburghe. Originally a rather austere early-Georgian building, the mansion
was transformed in the 1830s by the Edinburgh architect William Playfair into
a dramatic masterpiece of the Scottish Baronial style, its roofscape fretted with a
panorama of stone pinnacles and turrets crowned by lead-capped domes. This
palatial transformation was undertaken by the 6th Duke who had succeeded to
the title at the age of seven. His father's succession had occurred under rather
unusual circumstances. When the 4th Duke died childless, the inheritance was
disputed between several claimants. After a 7 year legal battle the House of
Lords decided that Sir James Innes held the superior right to the title of 5th
Duke. Sir James was then 76 years old and childless, prompting fears that on his
death the succession would again be contested. Rising nobly to this challenge,
the new Duke married the youthful Harriet Charlewood and became a father
for the first time in his 81st year.

The 6th Duke was a discriminating collector of works of art and the magnificent State Rooms of the Castle display many fine paintings, amongst them
portraits by Gainsborough, Reynolds, and the Scottish artists Allan Ramsay and
Henry Raeburn, a collection that has since been supplemented by modern mas-
ters such as Matisse, Bonnard and Augustus John. Other attractions at Floors

Castle include extensive parklands and grounds, a picnic area overlooking the Tweed, a garden centre, gift shop and licensed restaurant. (For more details, telephone 01573 223333).

JEDBURGH

MAP 3 REF M15

18 miles SW of Coldstream on the A68

Approached along the lovely Jed Valley, Jedburgh's glory is the **Abbey**, magnificent even in its ruined state. Built in glowing red sandstone, the Abbey was founded in 1138 by David I but suffered grievously and often from English attacks during the interminable Border wars. The final blow came in 1523 when the Earl of Surrey ordered it to be burned. Some 40 years later, Scotland's monarch came to the town, a visit commemorated at **Mary, Queen of Scots House**. The name is slightly misleading since Mary didn't own the house but stayed there as the guest of Sir Thomas Kerr. The exhibits include a death mask of the hapless Queen and a rare portrait of her third husband, the Earl of Bothwell. The Queen's host at Jedburgh, Sir Thomas Kerr, lived at **Ferniehurst Castle**, just outside the town, and it is still the family home of his descendant, Lord Lothian. The Castle and **Kerr Museum** are occasionally open to the public.

A winner of the country town prize in the "Beautiful Scotland in Bloom" competition, Jedburgh is a pleasant place to walk around, perhaps following the riverside walk or just lingering in the Abbey precincts.

To the rear of the Abbey stands the **Castlegate Restaurant**, housed in an imposing 3-storey granite building. This stately old house dates back to 1798 when it was built as a summer house for Lord Lothian. The Castlegate is owned and run by Alan and Marian Studholme who have lived and worked in the

**Castlegate Restaurant, 1 Abbey Close, Jedburgh TD8 6BG
Tel: 01835 862552**

Borders for some twenty years and took over here in 1997. They are both superb chefs and they make sure that as much as possible on the menu is home-made, with many of the dishes created from their own recipes. The main meals are changed every day and in the evening the à la carte menu offers more than 15 starters, over 17 main courses, and a tremendous sweet trolley. The Castlegate's reputation for good food has spread far and wide so it's essential to book on summer evenings and at weekends. The restaurant isn't licensed but guests are welcome to bring their own wine and there's no corkage charge. In summer, the restaurant is open from 11.00 to 15.00 and 18.00 until 22.00; in winter, from noon until 14.30pm, and from 18.00 to 21.00. (During January, February and March, the Castlegate is closed on Mondays). If you are thinking of staying in the area, the Castlegate provides an excellent base for holiday-makers with it's splendid town centre location. Alan and Marian have two spacious guest rooms to let: a family room which sleeps 3, and a double room, with shared bathroom between the two rooms. Centrally heated, the rooms are fully equipped, including colour television and tea-making facilities.

Conveniently located in the High Street, **The Cookie Jar** has an inviting green and gold frontage, and a welcoming interior to match. Striped tablecloths, fresh flowers on the tables, and friendly service all add to the appeal. Helen Taylor and Margaret Jackson have been running this popular tea room/café since 1993, serving quality food at value-for-money prices. The wide choice on offer ranges from a simple scone, teacake or traybake, through home-made soup, to hearty main meals cooked to order, such as Gammon & Pineapple. Sandwiches, jacket potatoes and hot filled rolls are also available, as well as vegetarian options, and for children, most items are available in half portions. And don't forget to check the menu board for tasty daily specials, sweets and puddings. Whether you're visiting Jedburgh for business or pleasure, you should make sure you find time to sample the top-quality fare dispensed at The Cookie Jar.

The Cookie Jar, 35 High Street, Jedburgh, Roxburghshire TD8 6AQ Tel: 01835 863982

If you are travelling northwards along the A68 towards Jedburgh, it's the first shop you will see in Scotland; travelling southwards, of course, it's the last. **The First and Last Shop** is housed in a charming stone building erected in 1872 on the site of the old Toll House. It's actually much more than a shop since the owners, Alan and Shelagh Lyall, also offer a good range of snacks and light meals. Both of them are accomplished cooks so the menu includes such treats as home-made scones, cakes, soup, and steak pie. There's a selection of filled baked potatoes and sandwiches, a choice of 2 or 3 daily specials, or you can

First and Last Shop, Kenmore Toll, Jedburgh TD8 6JH
Tel: 01835 862377

simply enjoy a round of buttered toast with a cup of tea or coffee. Children have their own menu and for fairweather days there's a peaceful garden to the rear. Don't leave without browsing around the gift shop which stocks an interesting selection of mementoes, cards and other souvenir items.

ANCRUM   MAP 3 REF M15
4 miles NW of Jedburgh on the B6400

Prettily located beside Ale Water, a tributary of the River Teviot, Ancrum saw one of the last of the major Border conflicts, the **Battle of Ancrum Moor** in 1544. A much later and better-known battle is commemorated by the Waterloo Monument, some 2 miles to the northeast, erected in 1815 by the Marquis of Lothian and his tenants.

In Ancrum itself, lovers of real ale will definitely want to seek out the **Cross Keys Inn** which overlooks the green in this picturesque little village. CAMRA, (the Campaign for Real Ale), lists the Cross Keys as a National Heritage Pub, the only one in the Borders to be so honoured, and one of only eleven in the whole of Scotland. The inn is also listed in the National Inventory of Heritage Pubs, reflecting the Cross Keys' long history which goes back to the days of stage coaches. The old archway through which carts and small carriages passed to the stables at the rear is still in place. David and Susan Arnold own and run this historic pub which in addition to its impressive stock of real ales also offers a

**Cross Keys Inn, The Green, Ancrum, Jedburgh TD8 6XH
Tel: 01835 830344**

good choice of quality food. You might well want to linger a while in this out-standing hostelry. As we go to press, the Arnolds are completely refurbishing their accommodation so, by the time you read this, there should be six letting rooms available, all with up-to-date facilities, all en suite, and all with disabled-friendly features built in.

A mile or so east of Ancrum, **Monteviot House Gardens** on the banks of the River Teviot offers a variety of gardens, a water garden of islands linked by bridges, an arboretum, greenhouses and plant stall. For a perfect family day out, com-bine Monteviot House with a visit to **Harestanes Countryside Visitor Centre** which is almost next door. There are beautiful woodland walks, an outdoor play area, lots of countryside activities throughout the season, a gift shop and tea room.

DENHOLM   MAP 3 REF M15
6 miles W of Jedburgh on the A698

This small village was the birthplace of both John Leyden, the 18th century poet and friend of Walter Scott, and Sir James Murray, editor of the monumental *Oxford English Dictionary*. Leyden is commemorated by an obelisk to his memory and by a plaque on the thatched cottage where he was born. Murray's monument is his ground-breaking dictionary of which millions of copies have been published.

Across the river and about 2 miles to the east, atop Minto Crags, stand the ruins of the curiously named **Fatlips Castle**, built in the 16th century for the Lockhart family.

Denholm village grew up alongside the important bridge over the River Teviot. Close by, overlooking the village green, you'll find the **Auld Cross Keys Inn** which enjoys an exceptional reputation in the area for good food, excellent ales, and top-flight entertainment. The premises were built in 1800 as a bakehouse, later becoming a coaching inn. Today, the Auld Cross Keys is well-known for its real ales, (which have earned it a place in the *CAMRA Good Beer Guide*),

**Auld Cross Keys Inn, Main Street, Denholm, by Hawick, Border TD9 8NU
Tel: 01450 870305 Fax: 01450 870778**

and for its cuisine, (which is praised in the *Good Pub Food Guide)*. The comprehensive menu ranges from dishes such as Creamy Mushroom Crepes, to Denholm Beef Sausages which won the 'Best Beef Sausages in Scotland' award in 1996. Ever-popular dishes such as Border Steak in red wine or fresh Eyemouth Haddock, are supplemented by a choice of daily specials and freshly made desserts. On Sundays, the inn serves a traditional Roast Lunch, (booking advisable), followed by High Teas between 16.00 and 18.30. (Please note that the Kitchen is closed on Mondays).

The Auld Cross Keys stocks a good range of ales, amongst them the local Broughton real ale and an ever-changing guest ale. Peter and Heather Ferguson, who have owned and run the inn since 1987, also provide their customers with an outstanding programme of quality folk music, presenting regular performances every other thursday. Artistes who make their way to this country inn include nationally-known performers as well as local folk-singers. The Inn is also a popular venue for weddings, private parties, conferences and other functions, when guests can enjoy the same high standards of food, drink and service that have earned the Auld Cross Keys its enviable reputation.

HAWICK   Map 3 ref M15
14 miles SW of Jedburgh on the A7/A698

The largest of the Border burghsand, like so many Border towns, Hawick was regularly attacked by the English. There was a particularly violent onslaught in 1570 which left scarcely a building standing. A notable exception was **Drumlanrig's Tower** which, after extensive and sensitive restoration, opened in 1995 as a museum recording the town's turbulent history. The tower also houses Hawick's Tourist Information Centre.

In June, the "Common Riding" ceremony of riding the boundaries commemorates the gallant defence of the town against English raiders in 1514 by the youths of the town. Only the youths, because virtually all Hawick's menfolk had been slain the year before in the frightful carnage of the Battle of Flodden. The "Common Riding" became something of a battle itself in 1996 when two local ladies asserted their right to join the previously all-male ride. They faced bitter opposition but their claim was eventually upheld by the Sheriff Court

The largest of the Border burghs, Hawick, (pronounced Hoyk), is a thriving community, its prosperity based on the manufacture of quality knitwear, clothing and carpets. The town is the home of such names as Pringle of Scotland, Lyle and Scott, Peter Scott, and many other smaller firms producing knitwear in cashmere, lambswool and Shetland yarns. In the heart of the town, housed in a substantial Victorian property built of local granite, you'll find **Nardini's Howegate Cafe** which has been serving the hungry and thirsty for more than 60 years. Today, Lynn and Stephen Murray continue that long tradition, offering their customers an extensive menu that ranges from light snacks to hearty meals, all of which they prepare themselves.

The table menu includes All Day Breakfasts, and the blackboard lists a good choice of hot meals, plus a daily special which is designed to make the most of available seasonal produce. Nardini's opening hours are especially convenient: from 8am in the morning until 7pm in the evening, 7 days a week.

On the edge of the town, the award-winning **Wilton Lodge Park** on the banks of the River Teviot offers a whole range of recreational facilities within its 107 acres, - woodland and riverside walks, tennis, bowling and putting, as well as a walled garden with special floral displays.

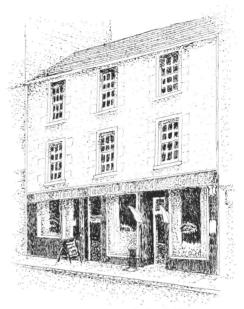

Nadini's Howegate Cafe, 4 Howegate, Hawick, Border TD9 OAA Tel 01450 372688

Nearby, surrounded by the lovely Teviotdale countryside, **Wiltonburn Farm** is nevertheless only a couple of miles from the centre of Hawick. At this 400-acre mixed farm, John and Sheila Shell offer an excellent choice of either bed & breakfast or self-catering accommodation. John and Sheila have lived at Wiltonburn Farm since the late 1970s and started welcoming guests for bed and breakfast in 1987. They have 3 letting rooms upstairs in the main farmhouse, - an en suite family room, a double with private facilities, and a double/twin with shared facilities. All the rooms are well-appointed with many attractive features. If you prefer self-catering, the Shells also have two charming holiday cottages nearby, (as well as a further cottage in Northumberland). The two cottages within the farm sleep 5/6 and 5 people, respectively, and both children and dogs are welcome. Wiltonburn Farm also offers accommodation for horses, very convenient in this popular riding area where you can follow the 18-mile Hawick Circular Riding/Walking Route or tackle the famous Buccleuch Ride which wanders for some 56 miles through the Borders. There is a wonderful 100-acre riverside award-winning park only a mile's walk from Wiltonburn and, for the more energetic, a 200-acre hill to climb with wonderful panoramic views of the town and surrounding countryside. Wiltonburn Farm boasts yet another attraction. Housed in a newly converted barn, Sheila's offers a stylish collection of designer Cashmere knitwear for both ladies and gentlemen, along with gloves, scarves, jackets, socks, and lambswool and cotton products. They are all locally

Wiltonburn Farm, Hawick, Roxburghshire TD9 7LL Tel: 01450 372414
Fax: 01450 378098. e-mail: shell@wiltonburnfarm.u-net.com
http://www.SmoothHound.co.uk/hotels/wiltonbu.html

produced as are the jewellery items, paintings by local artists and country-re-
lated cards. A small selection of hand painted chairs and furnitureadd more
interest in the second phase of developing the spacious barn. Guests staying at
Wiltonburn Farm receive a generous discount on any purchases they make at
the Crafts Shop.

TUSHIELAW INN   Map 3 ref L15
16 miles W of Hawick via the B711/B709

A couple of miles south of Hawick, the B711 strikes off westwards on a wonderfully scenic route that runs alongside Borthwick Water and skirts Craik Forest
before crossing the bridge over Ettrick Water. Turn right here and within a mile
or so you will have arrived at **Tushielaw Inn**. The inn sits in splendid isolation
at the foot of the hill from which it takes its name, overlooking the River Ettrick.
A former coaching stop, Tushielaw Inn was originally built as a drovers' halt
and toll house, with the present building dating back to around 1850. Thank-
fully, the inn has escaped tasteless modernisation and is full of character with
features such as open fires, a vintage cash register and old-fashioned bell ropes
still in operation to summon the staff. The bar is popular with local farmers and
shepherds and whether you're here on a balmy summer evening, taking advantage of the beer patio, or on a chilly winter evening sitting by the real open fire,
the atmosphere is always welcoming and friendly. Gordon and Sarah Harrison
own and run this appealing old hostelry and they place special emphasis on

Tushielaw Inn, Ettrick Valley, Selkirkshire TD7 5HT
Tel/Fax: 01750 62205. e-mail: gordon.harrison@virgin.net

providing quality food using only the best of local produce. Taking over in early 1999, their extensive menu has grown in response to their customers' demands. The Tushielaw Inn has just three bedrooms, so ensuring personal service for all guests. There are two doubles and one twin/family room, all centrally heated with en suite bathrooms and equipped with remote control colour TVs and tea/coffee making facilities. For anyone who enjoys country activities, the Inn is ideally located. Anglers can fish for trout, salmon and sea-trout in the River Ettrick, and still-water trout fishing is offered free to residents on the Inn's own private Clearburn Loch. Salmon fishing, horse-riding, mountain biking and shooting are all available and golfers have a choice of no fewer than 19 courses in the Border area. The hills and valleys surrounding the Tushielaw Inn are perfect for walkers, whether dedicated hill climbers or more relaxed ramblers. The Southern Upland Way is just 4 miles distant and pick-ups can be arranged.

ST MARY'S LOCH
20 miles W of Hawick on the A708

MAP 2 REF L15

As the crow flies, it's a mere 4 miles or so to another fascinating old inn. By road, it's almost three times as far but well worth the journey because few hostelries anywhere can boast such a long and well-recorded history as **Tibbie Shiels Inn**, about 18 miles southwest of Selkirk on the A708. The inn takes its name from Isabella (Tibbie) Shiel, a doughty lady who in 1823 moved with her husband Robert into what was then known as St Mary's Cottage, occupying a lovely situation beside St Mary's Loch. Robert died the following year and Tibbie, de-

**Tibbie Shiels Inn, St Mary's Loch, Selkirk TD7 5LH
Tel: 01750 42231**

termined to support herself and her six bairns, began taking in gentlemen lodgers. Thirteen beds were crowded into what is now the bar and in the attic, but on special occasions such as the 12th of August as many as 35 were accommodated, the extra numbers being "made comfortable" on the floor. During the course of her long life, (she died in 1878 in her 96th year), Tibbie became something of a national treasure, counting Sir Walter Scott amongst her friends and admirers. Her Visitor's Books have survived and they include names such as Robert Louis Stevenson, Thomas Carlyle and William Ewart Gladstone. Since Tibbie's day the inn has been extended but the spirit of the place is unchanged, - low-ceilinged, cosy, full of character, hidden away in a place of incredible beauty and tranquillity.

SELKIRK
MAP 3 REF M15
12 miles N of Hawick on the A7

The twin valleys of Ettrick and Yarrow contain some of the most glorious scenery in the Borders. High on the hillside, the Ancient and Royal Burgh of Selkirk enjoys superb views across Ettrick Water. Sir Walter Scott had close connections with the town, serving as Sheriff of Selkirkshire from 1799 until 1832. There's a striking statue of him in front of the Courthouse where he presided so often and where visitors can see a video recounting the story of Scott's associations with the area and its people.

Another statue in the High Street commemorates Mungo Park, the famous explorer and anti-slavery activist who was born in Selkirkshire in 1777. Two finely-worked bas-reliefs depict his adventures along the River Niger which ended in his death by drowning in 1805.

Selkirk's oldest building, **Halliwell's House**, is now home to the town's Museum and the Robson Gallery (both free), the latter a venue for touring art exhibitions. The museum's most prized possession is the "Flodden Flag". Eighty men of Selkirk marched off to fight in the calamitous Battle of Flodden, only one of them returned. He stumbled into the Market Square bearing a captured English flag. Unable to express his grief, the soldier simply waved the flag towards the ground. His gesture is symbolically re-enacted each year in June during the Common Riding, one of the oldest of the Border Festivals, dating back to the year of Flodden Field, 1513. As many as 400 riders take part in the ceremony.

The town's other visitor attractions include **Selkirk Glass** where you can watch glassmakers at work and purchase the high quality products, factory shops selling the local tweed, and the unusual **Robert Clapperton Daylight Photographic Studio**, an original daylight studio from 1867. There's a small family-owned museum with many photographic artefacts, and a negative archive from which visitors can order prints.

BOWHILL   MAP 3 REF L15
3 miles W of Selkirk off the A708

The principal Scottish residence of the Duke of Buccleuch, Bowhill is a monumental building 437 feet long, most of it built in the first half of the 19th century. The 4th Duke's kinsman and neighbour, Sir Walter Scott, whose own home, Abbotsford, is just 6 miles away, was a frequent visitor to Bowhill and advised on the early stages of the massive new construction. The famous portrait by Henry Raeburn of the affable poet and novelist with his beloved dog "Camp" at his feet hangs in the Scott Room which also contains Sir Walter's plaid and the original manuscript of The Lay of the Last Minstrel.

Bowhill boasts a superlative collection of other works of art, - family portraits by Lely and Reynolds, landscapes by Claude Lorraine and Ruysdael, as well as sumptuous French furniture and priceless displays of Meissen and Sèvres china.

The house alone provides a full and rewarding day but there's also the **Bowhill Country Park** where miles of footpaths and cycle trails criss-cross the estate, there's a very well-designed Adventure Playground, a Victorian Fire Engine Display, a Gift Shop, Courtyard Tea Room, and the thriving Bowhill Little Theatre housed in the former stables.

Apart from visits by educational groups which can be pre-arranged at any time, the house is only open to the public on afternoons during July; the Country Park, afternoons from April to September, (daily during July, closed Fridays during the other months). Disabled visitors have free entry to the house and Little Theatre.

Two miles south of Bowhill, on the B7009, **Aikwood Tower** is the legendary home of Michael Scott the wizard although nowadays occupied by the former Liberal leader (Lord) David Steel. It's a rather austere looking building, its forbidding appearance somewhat softened by the surrounding wooded slopes of the Ettrick Water Valley. In the former byres of the 16th century tower there's an exhibition celebrating the life and work of James Hogg, a self-taught poet and friend of Scott who enjoyed great fame in the late 1700s but whose verse requires sincere dedication from modern readers. The Tower also hosts temporary exhibitions of the work of local artists and sculptors, and there's an interesting garden devoted to medieval plants.

GALASHIELS   Map 3 ref M14
7 miles N of Selkirk on the A7

Lying in the valley of the Gala Water, Galashiels has for centuries been an important centre for wool and cloth-making, so much so that in 1777 the town's textile manufacturers adopted the motto "We dye to live and live to die". The Scottish College of Textiles was established here in 1909 and today the **Lochcarron of Scotland Cashmere & Wool Centre** offers guided tours of their tartan and tweed production from raw yarn to finished product. Within the Mill, Galashiels Museum records the development of the town.

Old Gala House, home of the Lairds of Gala for many generations, is now a Museum & Art Gallery, beautifully set in landscaped gardens. There are more flowers in Bank Street Gardens in the heart of the town, a pleasant spot to linger for a while breathing in the fragrance.

Every year in July, Galashiels hosts the Braw Lads Gathering which, it is claimed, began as a celebration of the marriage of James IV and Margaret Tudor, sister of Henry VIII, in 1503. Whatever its roots, it provides the excuse for a week of ceremonies and events. A "braw lad" of another kind is commemorated by the dramatic statue of a Border Reiver which commands the east end of Bank Street.

Sadly no more is St Trinnean's School which once stood on the edge of the town. Visiting Galashiels in 1941, Ronald Searle met two of the girls from St Trinnean's and their accounts of the pupils' disorderly conduct furnished some memorably comic material for his St Trinian's novels.

Located in a quiet road on the western edge of the town, **Woodlands House Hotel** is a strikingly attractive building in the neo-Tudor style. Built in mid-Victorian times as a family house for the textile magnate, James Sanderson, the gracious old house is now an outstanding hotel where dining is a memorable experience. Whether you take your meal in the elegant dining room, "The Atlas", specialising in continental cuisine, or in the informal lounge bar, the food

**Woodlands House Hotel, Windyknowe Road, Galashiels,
Selkirkshire TD1 1RG Tel: 01896 754722 Fax: 01986 754892**

is lovingly prepared and immaculately presented. During the summer months, visitors can also enjoy an alfresco meal overlooking the lovely gardens. And on Sundays, don't miss out on the 3-course Carvery, served all day from noon until 19.00, and offered at a bargain price. Woodlands has 10 guest rooms, all en suite, and all differently furnished and decorated to give each of them a very individual character. All rooms are well-equipped with colour television, direct dial telephones, trouser press, radio alarm, hairdryer, ironing-board and tea/coffee-making facilities. Out of season, the hotel offers special weekend bargain breaks. If you like ghost stories, Woodlands House will certainly appeal to you. There have been some odd happenings at the hotel over the years, happily none of them very sinister!

Not to be missed by any devotee of Sir Walter Scott is a visit to his home for the last 20 years of his life, **Abbotsford**, a mile or so south of Galashiels. It is a masterpiece of the Scottish Baronial style of architecture, surrounded by trim gardens and looking out to the River Tweed. Inside, visitors pass through a grand barrel-ceilinged Entrance Hall to the galleried and book-lined study where each morning at 6 o'clock Scott would seat himself at the small writing desk made of salvage from the wrecked ships of the Spanish Armada. His chair, his spectacles, the portrait of Rob Roy hanging on the wall, - all remain just as he left them. In the superb Library next door, with a richly moulded ceiling copied from Rosslyn Chapel, are housed the 9000 books he collected during his life-time along with a fascinating assortment of Scottish memorabilia, including Rob Roy's purse and skene dhu (knife), and a lock of Bonnie Prince Charlie's hair. Perhaps the most poignant place in the house is the dining room. In September 1832, his health destroyed by overwork, Sir Walter's bed was placed here so that he could gaze out on his beloved River Tweed. On the 21st, his family was at his bedside, amongst them his son-in-law and biographer, John Lockhart: "It was a beautiful day - so warm that every window was open - and so perfectly still that the sound of all others the most delicious to his ear, the gentle ripple of the Tweed over its pebbles, was distinctly audible as we knelt around his bed, and his eldest son kissed him and closed his eyes".

MELROSE   Map 3 ref M14
3 miles E of Galashiels on the A72

Melrose is an enchanting little town, set beside the River Tweed at the foot of the three peaks of the Eildon Hills. Behind the town square, the noble ruins of **Melrose Abbey** stand in shattered glory. Founded in 1136 by David I, the original building was repeatedly attacked by the English and the present structure dates mostly from the late 1300s. Modelled on the abbeys of northern England, the building reflects the splendidly intricate Gothic style of that age. (Look out for the curious gargoyle of a pig playing the bagpipes).

For centuries, tradition asserted that the heart of Robert the Bruce was buried near the Abbey's high altar. In 1996, the legend was proved true when a casket was uncovered containing a withered heart. Two years later, the casket was ceremonially re-buried and a commemorative stone tablet erected.

Next door to the Abbey, the inviting **Priorwood Garden** (National Trust for Scotland) specialises in growing plants suitable for dried flower arranging. The walled garden encloses an apple orchard walk and a picnic area, and there's a shop selling the dried flowers. Also within the Abbey precincts is the 16th century Commendator's House, formerly the "Estate Office" for the Abbey's extensive properties, now housing a curious collection of ecclesiastical artefacts. In the town itself, the Trimontium Exhibition gives an insight into the Roman occupation of the area, while Teddy Melrose is Scotland's first teddy bear museum with displays recording the full history of the British teddy bear.

About 4 miles east of Melrose, on the B6356, **Scott's View** looks across the River Tweed to the Eildon Hills and was one of the great novelist's favourite viewpoints. When the hearse taking him to his final resting place at Dryburgh Abbey reached this point, it's said that the horses stopped of their own accord.

Dryburgh Abbey itself (Historic Scotland) lies a couple of miles to the south, beautifully set within a curve of the River Tweed. Scott and members of his family are buried in St Mary's Aisle and close by is the grave of Field Marshal Earl Haig, Britain's disastrous Commander-in-Chief during World War I. Originally founded during the 12th century, like its sister Abbeys in the Borders Dryburgh was repeatedly attacked by the English and little of the Abbey Church remains. But the cloister buildings are remarkably well-preserved and the lovely surroundings create a sense of deep peace.

EARLSTON

MAP 3 REF M14

8 miles E of Galashiels on the A68/A6105

Dating back to 1845, **Broomfield House** is an attractive traditional building with a front garden ablaze in summer with flowers and hanging baskets. Lorraine Richardson bought the house in 1994 and now welcomes guests for bed and breakfast accommodation. Her home has a wonderfully welcoming family atmosphere with real fires in the breakfast room and residents' lounge, and a relaxed home-from-home feeling. Lorraine has 5 letting rooms, one of them on the ground floor and en suite. All the rooms are spacious and well-equipped with extra facilities such as trouser-press and video player, two en suite and the others have their own private bathrooms. The upstairs rooms also have pleasant views over the Border countryside. A generous breakfast is included in the

Broomfield House, Thorn Street, Earlston, Borders TD4 6DR
Tel/Fax: 01896 848084

tariff and packed lunches are available on request. Children are welcome and Broomfield House has convenient off-road private parking. All in all, an ideal base from which to explore the Borders and the metropolitan attractions of Edinburgh.

Just south of Earlston, the ruined **Rhymers Tower** is the reputed home of Thomas the Rhymer, a 13th century poet and visionary. According to legend he was carried off by the Fairy Queen riding a white steed. Returning 7 years later, he penned his prophecies in verse and many allegedly came to pass. Thomas is also commemorated in the churchyard where a stone bears the inscription "Auld Rymers tace, lies in this place". (Tace comes from the Latin word for "is silent").

LAUDER

MAP 3 REF M14

12 miles N of Galashiels on the A68

The main town in Lauderdale, the Royal Burgh of Lauder nevertheless has a population of little more than a thousand people. Surrounded on three sides by the gentle Lammermuir Hills, the town has preserved its medieval plan with a single main street widening into a Market Place dominated by the quaint old Tolbooth. **Lauder's Parish Church** of 1673 is decidedly unusual, built in the form of a Greek cross with the pulpit in the centre under the octagonal bell tower. The original box pews are still in place.

Set in the heart of this picturesque conservation village, **The Lauderdale Hotel** is a small privately owned country hotel with a friendly and relaxed atmosphere and an emphasis on good food and quality service. Meals and snacks are available from the bar/grill and in the evenings guests can choose from an extensive dinner menu that includes local specialities such as fresh trout, salmon or game. The Lauderdale opened about a century ago as The Temperance Hotel but nowadays, fortunately, there's a good wine list to accompany the restaurant

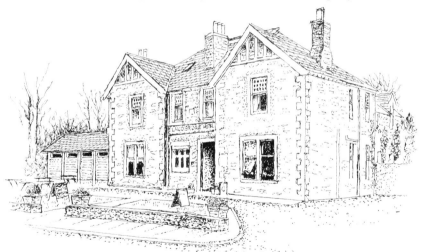

The Lauderdale Hotel, 1 Edinburgh Road, Lauder TD2 6TU
Tel: 01578 722231/Fax: 718642

and bar menus, real ales on tap, and morning coffee and afternoon teas are also available. Accommodation at The Lauderdale is of a very high standard, - all bedrooms are en suite and equipped with direct dial telephone, Sky television and tea/coffee-making facilities. The hotel also has a large function suite with seating for 180 people, making it ideal for parties, meetings and weddings. Attractions in the area include stately Thirlestane Castle nearby, some 16 golf courses within easy reach, salmon fishing in the famous Tweed and trout fishing in the many surrounding lochs and rivers.

A short walk from the centre of the town brings you to the imposing pile of **Thirlestane Castle**. The castle was built in the 1670s for John Maitland, 1st (and only) Duke of Lauderdale. A close confidant of Charles II and a member of the notorious Cabal, the Duke's power was such that he was regarded as the uncrowned King of Scotland. In those days, political power meant rich pickings by way of bribes, and the Duke spared no expense on the building, decorating and furnishing of his opulent castle. The famous English plasterer, George Dunsterfield, was commissioned to create the marvellous ceilings, most notably in the Red Drawing Room where garlands of leaves and flowers cascade from the ceiling as if obeying the pull of gravity. The Castle's other attractions include a wonderful collection of historic toys which children are actually *encouraged* to play with, a Border Country Life exhibition, and a superb park where the Scottish Championship Horse Trials are held in late August.

OXTON   MAP 3 REF M14
16 miles N of Galashiels on minor road off the A68

It's believed that St Cuthbert (635-687) was born and spent his early years in this area. The little parish church of Channelkirk is dedicated to the saint and a church bearing his name is known to have stood on this site long before there are any written records of its existence.

Located in this peaceful village close to Leader Water, **The Tower Hotel**, built in 1903, is a charming, black and white painted building with a curious pepperpot turret from which it presumably gained its name. Three members of

The Tower Hotel, Oxton, nr Lauder TD2 6PN
Tel: 01578 750235

the Gair family are involved in running the hotel: Eleanor, her daughters Fay and Kirstie, along with partners Jean and Raymond. Together they have created a genuinely welcoming atmosphere and have also gained a glowing (and grow-ing) reputation for the quality food on offer. The regular menu is supplemented by at least 3 main dishes listed on the daily specials board and there's also a menu for children. Meals can be enjoyed either in the separate dining room, (please book), in the lounge, or in the bar. This quiet village is a desirable place to stay and The Tower Hotel has 3 letting rooms which by the time you read this should all be en suite. Children are welcome, with cots and high chairs available if required. Eleanor has lived in the village for some 20 years so she possesses lots of "local knowledge" and can direct you to the many attractions in the neighbourhood. Thirlestane Castle is just 4 miles down the road, the Lammermuir Hills roll off to the east and, if you enjoy walking, you could join the Southern Uplands Path for part of its 212-mile coast-to-coast length.

INNERLEITHEN   Map 3 ref L14
12 miles W of Galashiels on A72

The Rivers Tweed and Leithen meet in this charming little town which has a famous watering place known as St Ronan's Wells (free) whose sulphurous wa-ters were once regularly sampled by Sir Walter Scott. In the High Street, Robert Smail's Printing Works (National Trust for Scotland) is popular with children who are allowed to try their hand at typesetting using the original 19th century machinery.

Innerleithen's premier attraction though is undoubtedly historic **Traquair House**, a mile or so to the south of the town. Traquair is the oldest house in Scotland to have been continuously inhabited by the same family, the first of the line being James Stuart who took up residence in 1491. More than 500 years later, James' descendants, the Maxwell Stuarts still live here. The family were staunch Catholics and suffered grievously for their adherence to the Old Reli-gion. A succession of priests lived in hiding in the claustrophobic Priest's Room and during the Jacobite rebellions the Stuarts, now Earls of Traquair, compounded their problems by supporting Bonnie Prince Charlie. The 5th Earl was host to the Prince at Traquair in the autumn of 1745 and when his guest was leaving escorted him to the famous "Bear Gates" guarding the entrance. As the Prince passed through, the Earl vowed that "The gates of Traquair wad be opened nevermair till a Stuart king was crooned in London". They have remained firmly closed ever since.

The long and romantic history of the Stuarts of Traquair comes alive in every part of this fascinating house, - in the exquisite 18th century Library, in the corkscrewing stone staircases and in family mementoes like the list compiled by the 4th Earl's wife detailing the 17 children, including 2 sets of twins, with which she presented her husband over a period of 14 years.

PEEBLES   MAP 2 REF L14
18 miles W of Galashiels on the A72/A703

The Royal Burgh of Peebles enjoys a superb position, surrounded by hills and
with the River Tweed running through its centre. Spacious parklands extend
along the river banks and the town itself has a genteel, almost demure, charm,
its houses presenting a pleasing medley of architectural styles.

Located in the heart of this appealing little town, **The Silver
Spoon**, which was built in 1996, is
a delightful tea room where customers can enjoy the very best kind of
home baking. Anne Symonds prepares and cooks everything herself
and each day an assortment of her
cakes and slices is displayed on the
centre table and very inviting it
looks. The Silver Spoon's menu includes some imaginative sandwich
combinations, - Cream Cheese &
Date, for example, or Ham, Peach
& Cream Cheese, as well as a daily
choice of home-made soups. In addition, there's always a Light Lunch
of the day and a special selection
for small children. Quality teas and
gourmet coffees complement the
excellent food. Smiling waitresses
serve you at your table and the
whole atmosphere is genuinely welcoming.

The Silver Spoon, Innerleithen Road,
Peebles EH45 8AB Tel: 01721 724477

Also set in the heart of this attractive old town, **The Green Tree Hotel** is well
known for its good food and quality accommodation. Whether you are looking
for a light lunch or a hearty 4-course meal, the Green Tree's food is always fresh
and prepared on the premises, using local produce wherever possible. Mervyn
and Christine Edge, who have owned and run the hotel since 1987, pride themselves on their fine selection of ales, wines and spirits. The *Good Beer Guide* has
awarded the Green Tree its coveted seal of approval for three consecutive years.
The hotel has 8 bedrooms, all of which are centrally heated, en suite and with
TV and tea/coffee making facilities. There's also a separate, self-catering bungalow which can be utilised to accommodate large parties. The Edges offer special
rates for golf and fishing parties, and fly casting and teaching weekends are
available with instruction from local ghillie Andrew Dickison. The Green Tree is
also an ideal hotel for weddings and family gatherings of all kinds with a service

The Green Tree Hotel, 41 Eastgate, Peebles, Tweeddale EH45 8AD
Tel/Fax: 01721 720582

that includes a wide range of wedding menus and organising all the arrangements for the great day.

Occupying a magnificent location on the north bank of the River Tweed, **Minniebank Guest House** is a spacious Victorian building of 1895 where guests can be assured of a warm welcome from Ken and Brenda Bowie. The house faces south, overlooking the Minister's Pool (known locally as the Minnie), and has superb views of the river, the town and the countryside beyond. Although within two minutes walk of the shops in the Old Town and less than 5 from the High Street, Minniebank enjoys a quiet position in an area of natural scenic beauty. A

Minniebank Guest House, Greenside, Peebles EH45 8JA
Tel: 01721 722093

short walk along the rear brings you to Hay Lodge Park and the house is only minutes away from Peebles golf course and the local swimming pool. Minniebank has a 4-star rating from the Scottish Tourist Board, an award reflected in the attractive furnishings of the 3 guest bedrooms, one of which is on the ground floor. All rooms have showers and there's also a bathroom if you want a good long soak. A hearty Scottish breakfast is served in the dining room which has lovely views over the garden and river and where, if you wish, you can also have an evening meal.

Natives of the town are known locally as "gutterbluids" and they include William and Robert Chambers, creators of the famous encyclopaedia. In 1859, the brothers presented the town with the Chambers Institute which today houses **The Tweeddale Museum & Picture Gallery**.

Peebles folk also have their own word for a visitor or incomer to the town, - "stooryfit" (dusty-footed). Amongst stooryfits who made Peebles their home are Robert Louis Stevenson, John Buchan, the novelist, soldier and politician, and his sister, the novelist O. Douglas, and the celebrated explorer of Africa, Mungo Park.

A mile to the west of Peebles, **Neidpath Castle** stands dramatically on a steep bluff overlooking the River Tweed. Its 14th century walls are more than 10 feet thick but when Cromwell's artillery relentlessly pounded them with cannon, the castle's owner, the Earl of Tweeddale, was forced to surrender. The castle later passed to the Douglas family, Dukes of Queensberry. In 1795, the 2nd Duke found himself strapped for cash he ordered the felling of every marketable tree on the estate. This spectacular act of environmental vandalism resulted in the Duke becoming the target of a wrathful sonnet by William Wordsworth which begins with the words "Degenerate Douglas...."

2 Dumfries and Galloway

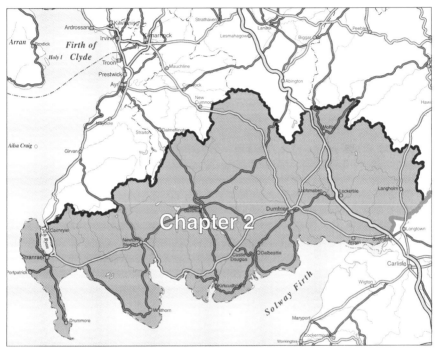

© MAPS IN MINUTES ™ (1998)

Turn west off the M74 at Gretna Green and discover what the local Tourist Board calls "Scotland's best-kept secret". Well, they would say that, wouldn't they? But it's true that most visitors press on northwards and miss one of the most beautiful and unspoiled areas of the country.

Over 200 miles of superb coastline offer an infinite variety of beaches, bays and inlets. Inland stretch the vast expanses of the Galloway Forest Park where a patient observer may well spot a peregrine falcon or golden eagle, and just within the Dumfries and Galloway border is the highest village in Scotland, Wanlockhead, 1500 feet above sea level.

The towns of Dumfries and Moffat are as appealing as any in Scotland and the region boasts more than its fair share of historic buildings, most notably romantic Sweetheart Abbey, the mighty medieval fortress of Caerlaverock Castle, and the palatial 17th century Drumlanrig Castle, Dumfriesshire home of the Duke of Buccleuch.

The area also has strong literary connections. Thomas Carlyle was born at Ecclefechan and the even more illustrious Robert Burns spent the last 8 years of his life in and around Dumfries which is where we begin our tour of the area.

DUMFRIES

It was in this pleasant little town set beside the River Nith that Robbie Burns wrote some of his most famous songs, amongst them *Auld Lang Syne* and *Ye Banks and Braes o' Bonnie Doon*. The poet had arrived in the town in 1791 to take up the improbable post of Excise Officer in charge of tobacco duties. To begin with, Burns lodged in a house in Bank Street, at that time a noisome alley leading down to the river, which he nicknamed "Stinking Vennel". He then moved to a more salubrious dwelling in Mill Street on the edge of town. The road has been re-named Burns Street and **Burns' House** (free) is now a museum containing his manuscripts and other memorabilia.

It was here that Burns died of rheumatic heart disease in 1796 at the age of 37. He was buried in a simple grave in the churchyard of nearby St Michael's Church, a Georgian building only a few years older than himself. Twenty years later, his body was exhumed and re-interred in a splendid, columned Mausoleum which also shelters a finely-executed statue of Scotland's national bard communing with the Muse of Poetry.

Another statue was erected to his memory in the Market Square, (also renamed as **Burns' Statue Square**). This statue is a sentimental Victorian presentation of the roisterer and libertine as a clean-cut young fellow, clutching a posy of flowers in one hand and with a faithful canine curled around his feet.

A more authentic image of the partying poet is conjured up at the Globe Inn in the High Street, a down-to-earth hostelry established in 1610 and one of Burns' most favoured drinking dens, or "howffs" as they were called then. His preferred armchair is still in place but, before settling down in it, be warned that anyone who does so can be called upon to buy a round of drinks for everyone present.

The most comprehensive record of Burns' five year residence in the town can be found at the **Robert Burns Centre** (free), located on the west bank of the River Nith and housed in an old water mill.

Another mill, an 18th century windmill perched on the hill above the Robert Burns Centre, is devoted to the many other years when the celebrated poet *wasn't* living here. **The Dumfries Museum** (free) contains an interesting series of exhibits recording the town's long history and, on its top floor, there's a *camera obscura* of the 1830s which provides fascinating panoramic views over the town.

Four bridges span the River Nith at Dumfries. The most appealing of them is **Devorgilla Bridge**, originally built by the 13th century Princess Devorgilla of

Galloway whose poignant story of deep love and grievous loss is recounted later in this book under the entry for New Abbey. Now only open to pedestrians, this six-arched bridge was in medieval times the main thoroughfare for anyone travelling to or from the remote communities of south-west Scotland.

Dumfries boasts many handsome Georgian buildings. One of the most interesting is **Midsteeple** which dominates the High Street and was erected in 1707 as town hall, courthouse and prison. Sadly, you can't go inside but on the outside you can see two curious features. On its southern wall is incised a line 37 inches long, an "ell", the centuries old standard for measuring lengths of cloth. And a table of distances from Dumfries rather surprisingly includes the small town of Huntingdon in Cambridgeshire. During the 18th century, Huntingdon was the cattle mart where Scottish drovers sold their stock. Huntingdon traders then herded the beasts down the Great North Road to the lucrative meat markets of London. Why the Scottish cattle-men didn't travel the extra 40 miles or so themselves remains a mystery.

Enjoying a splendid position overlooking Dumfries, **The Birkhill Hotel** is a striking early 19th century building with typical crow-stepped gables and a pepperpot turret over the entrance. The hotel is a small family-run establishment "where informality takes precedence" say the owners, Haig and Jessie McCulloch, who assure visitors of a warm welcome and as much assistance as you require. They have added a charming conservatory to the house which provides an excellent place to enjoy a meal from the varied menus of good

The Birkhill Hotel, 16 St Mary's Street, Dumfries DG1 1LZ
Tel/Fax: 01387 253418

down-to-earth food which is also available in the bar. The Birkhill is disabled-friendly with special toilets and ramps installed where necessary. (And the hotel is also dog-friendly). One of the Birkhill's letting rooms is on the ground floor and there are 3 more upstairs, all of them en suite, spacious, and fully-equipped. Another major attraction here is the programme of free live entertainment provided each evening from Thursday to Sunday. On Thursdays, there's a session night when local musicians entertain informally; on Friday and Saturday evenings local bands play a wide range of music, - anything from country to Scottish to chart music, and on Sundays the local jazz club provides the entertainment. This outstanding hotel offers everything from a simple cup of coffee to catering for major functions and as if that weren't enough, you can even get married here.

A fine old detached Victorian villa standing in its own grounds, **Hazeldean Guest House** is a quite exceptional bed & breakfast establishment as its 4-star rating from the Scottish Tourist Board bears witness. Just five minutes walk from the town centre and the railway station, Hazeldean is surrounded by a lovely garden which has won many awards. The house itself is furnished and decorated to a very high standard with full gas central heating, residents' lounge with TV and video, and six charming guest rooms, all en suite and equipped with welcome extras such as trouser presses and hairdriers. Hazeldean is the

Hazeldean Guest House, 4 Moffat Road, Dumfries DG1 1NJ
Tel: 01387 266178

home of Billy and Wilma Harper who take great pride in the service they offer and ensure that providing value for money is their first priority, offering generous reductions for children for example. A hearty Scottish, or Continental breakfast is included in the tariff and non-smokers will be pleased to know that the house is completely non-smoking.

NORTH AND EAST OF DUMFRIES

CAERLAVEROCK

Map 2 ref K17

8 miles SE of Dumfries on the B725

Caerlaverock Castle (Historic Scotland) meets everyone's idea of a medieval fortress with its moat and mighty gatehouse flanked blank-walled towers. In fact, Caerlaverock's ground plan is untypical of castles of the period since the design is triangular. Edward I made a ferocious attack on the castle in 1300 and held it for 11 years. The king's balladeer, Walter of Exeter, considered that "You will never see a more finely situated castle". Parts of the original structure of 1270 have survived but most of the present building dates from the 15th century, with Renaissance additions by the 1st Earl of Nithsdale in 1634. Six years later, the castle surrendered to the Covenanters after a 13-week siege. They did their best to make Caerlaverock militarily useless and the castle has not been inhabited since. Attractions include a model siege engine, children's adventure park, a nature trail and, during July and August visitors can visit the archaeological dig.

About 3 miles to the west of the castle, the 1,350 acres of the **Caerlaverock Wildfowl and Wetlands Trust** attract thousands of barnacle geese and other birds which can be seen from well-located hides and observation towers. In summer, nature trails meander through flower meadows alive with wildlife and you may even catch sight of a rare natterjack toad. There are free Wildlife Safaris starting at 14.00 each day during the summer months.

Continuing westwards to the village of **Ruthwell**, pick up the keys to the church (free) for a view of the magnificent **Ruthwell Cross**. Eighteen feet high, this internationally famous stone cross dates to around AD 680, its marvellously preserved surface decorated with intricate carvings illustrating episodes from the Gospel stories. Around its edge runs a poem written in both runic symbols and Northumbrian dialect.

BRYDEKIRK

Map 2 ref K17

17 miles SE of Dumfries on minor road off the B723

The colourful cherry-and-cream frontage of the **Brig Inn** adds a cheerful note to the main street of this pleasant little village of just 300 souls. Set alongside the River Annan this welcoming hostelry is owned and run by Gillian and Ken

**Brig Inn, 5 Bridge Street, Brydekirk, Annan DG12 5NQ
Tel: 01461 202155**

Aitken, both of them born locally and both farmers until they bought this inviting old inn. The Brig Inn is a popular haunt for local farmers and fishermen, often joined by ramblers taking a break from the lovely riverside walks skirting the River Annan. Along with well-tended beers, Gillian and Ken offer their customers a choice of tasty, home-made traditional dishes, all of them prepared as far as possible from fresh, local produce. As we go to press, their new dining-room overlooking the river is nearing completion so it may well be functioning by the time you read this. The original house, nearly 200 years old, has enjoyed a rather chequered history. It was built as a private house, opened as a pub in 1904, reverted to being a private residence, finally settling down as the Brig Inn some 20 years ago.

EASTRIGGS   Map 2 ref L17
18 miles SE of Dumfries off the B721

St John's Church in this small village just east of Annan contains an unusual reference to "The Devil's Porridge". This was the name given to explosives by the 30,000 men and women who made explosives at the Ordnance Factory in Gretna during World War I. The tribute acknowledges their once-secret work in this hazardous occupation.

Not many pubs can boast a bowling green amongst their attractions but the **Graham Arms** at Eastriggs has just that. Philip Hornby has owned this welcoming pub-cum-bowling green since 1994 and runs it with the help of his daughters Rachel and Nichola. If you are at all picky about what you drink you will have no problem at the Graham Arms. Along with a good selection of Tennants and

Graham Arms, The Rand, Eastriggs, Annan DG12 6NL
Tel: 01461 40244

other ales, Philip stocks some 60 different malts and spirits, a total choice of 109 different brands. By the time you read this, a spacious new restaurant should be functioning but the inn's 10 comfortable bedrooms are definitely available now. The Graham Arms dates back to 1936 when it was designed by Harry Redfearn, the famous London-based architect. It enjoys wonderful views across the Solway Firth to the mountains of Cumbria; the busy little town of Annan is about 3 miles to the west and, if you are thinking of eloping with someone, Gretna Green is just a few miles to the east.

GRETNA GREEN
24 miles SE of Dumfries off the A75

MAP 2 REF L17

Scottish matrimonial law in the 18th century merely required a declaration by the couple in front of any two witnesses for the marriage to be legal. This relaxed attitude attracted many English runaway couples and since Gretna Green was the first village across the Scottish borders, and the blacksmith's shop the closest dwelling the stage-coach stop, it was here that most of them "solemnised" their marriages. Scottish law was changed in 1856, requiring that at least one of the partners had resided in Scotland for 3 weeks before the marriage.

At the Blacksmith's Shop you can enter the original Marriage Room where weddings still take place today, follow the Gretna Green Story in an interesting exhibition, visit the Coach Museum, buy a range of souvenirs in the Gift Shop, and refresh yourself in the Conservatory Bar or the restaurant. There's also a sculpture park, arts centre, and animal park.

ECCLEFECHAN   Map 2 ref K17
15 miles E of Dumfries by Exit 19 of the A74(M)

This trim little hamlet was the birthplace in 1795 of Thomas Carlyle, a towering figure in the literary life of 19th century Britain. Carlyle's strict Calvinist upbringing imbued his prolific writings with a stern moralism which together with his intellectual rigour and often pedantic prose do not endear him to modern readers. He was born in **The Arched House**, now Carlyle's Birthplace (National Trust for Scotland), which has been furnished to reflect domestic life in his time and has an interesting collection of portraits and personal memorabilia.

LOCKERBIE   Map 2 ref K16
12 miles NE of Dumfries on the A709

For generations the Lamb Fair held at Lockerbie in August was Annandale's premier festival and as many as 70,000 animals were gathered in this small town. Its successor is the **Dumfries and Lockerbie Agricultural Show** which is also held in August but nowadays in Dumfries. But Lockerbie also hosts its own events. In June there's the Lockerbie Gala and Riding of the Marches; a Book Festival in September, followed by the Lockerbie Hot Jazz Festival in October.

The town is tranquil enough today but in the 16th and 17th centuries it was often riven by the bitter disputes between the Maxwells from Nithsdale and the Johnstones and Jardines from Annandale. The animosity culminated in a full-scale battle on nearby Dryfe Sands in 1593 when the Maxwells were decisively routed and 700 of them killed.

Tragedy of another order struck Lockerbie on Wednesday, December 21st, 1988 when Pan Am Flight 101 exploded in mid-air. Its fuselage crashed into the town killing eleven residents. A Remembrance Garden on the edge of the town has been planted in memory of all those innocent victims.

Situated at the southern end of the town with easy access from the M74 and only half a mile from the station, **Rosehill Guest House** is a spacious Victorian residence built in 1871, - the first house to be built on this side of the town. It's set in half an acre of lovely garden where there are splendid yew trees more than 120 years old. Ronnie and Gwyneth Callander have been welcoming bed and breakfast visitors to their home for almost 30 years. Both born and bred in Lockerbie, they are an extremely friendly and welcoming couple. Their commodious house has 5 newly-decorated bedrooms, all en suite and all equipped with central heating, colour television and in-room tea and coffee. Guests have the use of a comfortable residents' lounge and a full Scottish breakfast is included in

Rosehill Guest House, 9 Carlisle Road, Lockerbie
Dumfries & Galloway DG11 2DR Tel: 01576 202378

the tariff. Lockerbie itself is a handy base for a holiday with good walking country nearby, an 18-hole golf course, fishing on the River Annan, and visitor attractions nearby invoking historical memories, such as Bruce's Castle, Burns House, Caerlaverock Castle with its Wildfowl and Wetlands reserve, Thomas Carlyle's Birthplace and more poignantly, the memorial commemorating a more recent event, that of the Lockerbie air disaster; or on a happier note, the Tibetan monastery Samye Ling with its garden walks, cafe and shops.

NEWTON WAMPHRAY
MAP 2 REF K16

17 miles NE of Dumfries on minor road off the A74

If you follow the old Carlisle road from Moffat, signposted Newton Wamphray, and turn right at the crossroads in the village, this will lead you to the **Red House Hotel**, the home of Val and Derrick Wilson since 1995. A traditional country house in a peaceful farmland setting, the Red House is a comfortable, family-run licensed hotel with bar meals always available and a wholesome dinner is served by arrangement. The bar is well-stocked with a full selection of beers and a good choice of malt whiskies. Guests have a choice of accommodation. In the hotel itself there are 3 letting rooms, including one double en suite, and an inviting guest lounge with a traditional open log fire. A self-contained detached cottage with double bedroom is also available. There's ample parking space and the centrally heated cottage also has a well-equipped kitchen and a

**Red House Hotel, Newton Wamphray, nr Moffat
Dumfries & Galloway DG10 9NF Tel: 01576 470470**

comfortable lounge/dining-room. Newton Wamphray is a perfect place from which to enjoy touring the locality, walking, bird-watching, and fishing with permits available for 9 miles of the River Annan. These can be used for the trout season from April 15th to September 15th, with a good run of sea trout in June and July. Salmon fishing takes place from February 25th to November 15th, the best time being from September to November.

MOFFAT   MAP 2 REF K16

21 miles NE of Dumfries on the A701

Boasting one of the broadest High Streets in Scotland, Moffat is also one of the most pleasing small towns in the country. It stands beside the River Annan, surrounded by Lowland hills, at the heart of a thriving sheep-farming district. The town's dependence on sheep is symbolised by the striking **Colvin Fountain** at the top of the High Street. It is surmounted by a bronze sculpture of a sturdy ram although unfortunately it was accidentally cast without any ears.

Moffat has been attracting visitors ever since Rachel Whiteford, the minister's daughter, discovered Moffat Well in 1633 and its history as a spa town began. A steady stream of distinguished visitors sampled the 'magic waters', amongst them Robert Burns and James Boswell who came in 1766 "to wash off a few scurvy spots which the warmer climate of europe had brought out on my skin".

In 1878 the grandiose Moffat Hydropathic was built. At its peak, the 300-bedroomed hotel was welcoming some 25,000 guests each year but sadly the Hydro was totally destroyed by fire in 1921 and Moffat's status as a spa town never recovered.

The local tourist information centre has details of some excellent walks in and around the town, whether you just want a gentle riverside stroll or a brisk climb to the top of **Gallow Hill** where there are wonderful views over Annandale.

Only half a mile from the centre of Moffat, **Morlich House** is an award-winning, family-run licensed guest house set in half an acre of garden and sheltered by mature lime, copper beech and sycamore trees. Standing on the hillside, Morlich House enjoys splendid views of the town and surrounding hills. Senga and William Wells are the owners of this grand old house and their philosophy regarding guests is that "whilst you are in Morlich House you should regard it as your home, and we would like you to treat it just like that". Their imposing house was built around 1840 by a Glasgow mill owner as his country residence and later served as a school for many years before reverting to private ownership. The impressive entrance hall features a beautiful pitch pine stair-

Morlich House, Ballplay Road, Moffat, Dumfriesshire DG10 9JU
Tel: 01683 220589

case winding majestically up to the bedrooms. All the 5 letting rooms are en suite, with the exception of the single room which has a private toilet/shower. All are well-equipped with additional features such as radio/alarms, direct dial telephone, and private bar, and all have good views of the Dumfries country-side. Downstairs, the residents' lounge and the Garden Restaurant overlook the well-kept gardens. A generous Scottish breakfast is included in the tariff and although evening meals at Morlich House are optional, it would be foolish to miss out on Senga's first-class cooking!

WANLOCKHEAD
MAP 2 REF J15

30 miles N of Dumfries on the B797

You would naturally expect the highest village in Scotland to be somewhere in the Highlands. In fact, it's here at Wanlockhead in Dumfries & Galloway. The village stands 1500 feet above sea level so that makes Trevor and Senga Palmer's **Mountain Lodge Hotel** the highest hotel in Scotland. Standards here are equally high, with excellent food served in the bar lounge or in the separate restaurant. There's also a games room and, if you want to boast that you have slept in one of the highest beds in the country, the Palmers have 3 twin letting rooms available. Small though the village is there's plenty here to keep you occupied. The Southern Uplands Way passes right through Wanlockhead and the Scottish Lead

**The Mountain Lodge Hotel, Wanlockhead, by Biggar
South Lanarkshire ML12 6UT Tel: 01659 74368**

Mining Museum tells the story of an industry that goes back to at least Roman times. Guided tours of Loch Nell Mine take place every half-hour and provide a chilling insight into the conditions under which the lead miners worked. As well as lead, there's also gold in "them thar hills" and the British, European and World Gold Panning Championships are all held in the village. Why not bring a pan along and try your luck?

At the nearby hamlet of **Leadhills** is the **Allan Ramsay Library**, founded in 1741 by lead miners employed by the Scots Mining Company. It is believed to be the first subscription library established in Britain and many of the books which have survived are rare outside private collections. The library also houses detailed records of mining operations from 1739 until 1854 and a fascinating photographic collection includes many pictures of the Leadhills and Wanlockhead Light Railway which had a precarious existence between 1901 and 1938. The library was named after the poet Allan Ramsay who was born in the village around 1685 and whose son, also Allan, was to become one of Scotland's greatest painters. The Library is usually open on weekend afternoons between May and September.

SANQUHAR
MAP 2 REF J15

26 miles NW of Dumfries on the A76

This little town on the River Nith has the distinction of being a Royal Burgh and boasts a Tolbooth of 1735, now a museum dedicated to local history. Even more venerable is the building of 1712 which houses the oldest working Post Office in Britain and is also home to the town's Tourist Information Centre. Just 30 yards away is Joyce and Billy McLeod's **Caledonian Café and Tea Rooms**, offering a varied menu that includes Billy's delicious home-made doughnuts and cakes, a range of hot and cold snacks, a tasty haggis of course, wonderful fish

**Caledonian Café & Tea Rooms, 3/4 Harvies Wynd, Sanquhar
Dumfriesshire DG4 6DP Tel: 01659 50955**

suppers, and much more. Soccer fans will remember Billy as a professional footballer with Ipswich Town from 1976 to 1980, and later with Partick Thistle and Queen of the South. This friendly and welcoming tea room is decorated with interesting paintings and vintage postcards of the town, fascinating to browse through. The Caledonian is open from 9.30 until 20.00 during the season, every day, but closes between 14.30 and 16.30 in the winter.

SOUTH AND WEST OF DUMFRIES

One of the most satisfying drives in the region is the 80-mile circular route from Dumfries, leaving southwards by the A710. It takes in Sweetheart Abbey, Arbigland Gardens and the Colvend Coast with its superb sandy beaches, then curves northwards to the gleaming grey granite town of Dalbeattie. Southwards again along the A711, past the Orchardton Tower to the East Stewartry Coast and on to the "irreproachable" little harbour town of Kirkcudbright. Northwards now, past Threave Garden and Threave Castle, to Castle Douglas and back to Dumfries.

NEW ABBEY
Map 2 ref K17
8 miles S of Dumfries on the A710

The story of **Sweetheart Abbey** and Lady Devorgilla has been told many times but remains as touching as ever. In 1230, Devorgilla, daughter of Alan, last of the Kings of Galloway, married John Balliol, a marriage that by all accounts was supremely happy. There were a few setbacks. John Balliol managed to offend the powerful Prince-Bishop of Durham and as part of his penance was required to finance a hostel for students at Oxford, a modest establishment that his widow was later to expand into Balliol College.

John died in 1268 and Devorgilla, grief-stricken, had his heart embalmed and for the 21 years of her widowhood carried it with her in a casket of silver and ivory. She was now one of the richest women in Europe, owning most of Galloway along with estates in England and Normandy. She spent lavishly on founding several religious houses in memory of her husband, amongst them *Dulce Cor*, Sweet Heart, at New Abbey and it was here, in 1289, that she was buried beneath the High Altar together with her husband's heart. Sweetheart Abbey today is one of the finest sights in the country, a romantic ruin of rose-red stone that seems to glow in the setting sun.

New Abbey has been described as "the most perfect unspoiled village in Galloway". Take time to walk to the lovely bridge built in 1715 and then up through the avenue of Scots pines planted between 1775 and 1780 to enjoy the classically romantic view over the beck to Sweetheart Abbey.

Nearby is a restored 18th century **Corn Mill**, fully operational and with regular demonstrations during the summer months. Just outside the village, the **Museum of Costume** at Shambellie House provides an absorbing record of our sartorial fads, fancies and extravagances over the centuries.

About 6 miles south of New Abbey, follow the signs to **Arbigland Gardens** - especially if you are American. These famous semi-tropical gardens set around a secluded bay were originally laid out in the 1730s by a gardener named John Paul. One of his sons, also named John, was a lively youth who became a sailor boy at the age of 11 and later spent 5 years on an American slave ship. In Tobago he managed to get himself charged with murder and to avoid arrest changed his name to John Paul Jones, the name by which he is honoured in the United States as the "Father of the US Navy". The tiny white-washed cottage where he was born in 1747 is now the **John Paul Jones Birthplace Museum**, restored to its mid-18th century appearance and housing some fascinating exhibits connected with the Admiral's life. Outside stand 2 flagpoles, one flying the Stars and Stripes, the other carrying Scotland's St Andrew's Cross. The latter, incidentally, is identical to the Empress Catherine of Russia's flag under which the restless John Paul Jones sailed as Admiral of her Black Sea Fleet during the Russo-Turkish war of 1788-89.

COLVEND
MAP 2 REF J18

21 miles SW of Dumfries on the A710

Beautifully set beside the White Loch, Colvend formed part of what the Victorians called "The Scottish Riviera", the lovely stretch of the Solway Coast between Southerness and Rascarrel blessed with fine beaches and ravishing scenery.

It was near Colvend in 1793 that Robert Burns, as an Excise Officer, led an armed attack on a French smuggling ship that had run aground near Gillis Craig and was waiting for the next tide. Whatever credit Burns received from his employers was soon dissipated: they took grave exception when Burns went to the auction of the smugglers' confiscated property and bought their guns with the intention of despatching them to France to assist the revolutionaries.

About a mile to the north-west of Colvend stands **Clonyard House Hotel**, situated in 7 acres of mature gardens and woodlands in a wonderfully secluded position on the Solway Coast. Clonyard House is a small, friendly, family-run hotel where Nick Thompson and his mother Joan welcome visitors to the area and the many local guests who call in for meals or drinks. Bar meals, served both at lunch-time and in the evening, are deservedly popular, and for a truly memorable meal the elegant restaurant serves the very best of local produce:

Clonyard House Hotel, Colvend, Dalbeattie, Kirkcudbrightshire DG5 4QW
Tel: 01556 630372 Fax: 01556 630422

Solway salmon, Kirkcudbright 'queenies' (scallops), Galloway beef or lamb, or tasty venison. Clonyard House also offers a choice of excellent accommodation. In the main house there are traditional, large well-furnished rooms while the Garden Wing has modern, comfortable ground floor rooms, each with its own small patio to catch the sun, and overlooking a quiet area of the garden. One of the rooms is specially equipped for those with limited mobility. The comfortable Lounge Bar is well-stocked with a wide selection of whiskies and ales, - yet another attraction of this relaxing country house retreat.

DALBEATTIE   MAP 2 REF J17
14 miles SW of Dumfries on the A711

Lying in the wooded valley of Urr Water, Dalbeattie is almost entirely built of the local granite, a shining grey stone which has been shipped all over the world and used in building London's Embankment, the Bank of England and Manchester Town Hall. A mile or so outside the town, Old Buittle Tower is a 16th century **Lairds Tower House** with displays of arms and armour plus mounted displays of Border Reivers. The Tower is only open on occasional weekends or by appointment.

About 5 miles south-east of Dalbeattie, on the B793, stands **Auchenskeoch Lodge**, a Victorian shooting lodge set in 20-acre grounds in an enchantingly

Auchenskeoch Lodge, by Dalbeattie, Kirkcudbrightshire DG5 4PG
Tel/Fax: 01387 780277

unspoilt corner of the Galloway countryside. The Lodge is the home of Christopher and Mary Broom-Smith who welcome guests to their outstanding house, the only premises in Dumfries & Galloway to have received the AA's 5-Diamonds Premier Selected rating, along with a Scottish Tourist Board 4-star award. The house is centrally heated and has a comfortable sitting room, elegant dining room, and a billiard room with full size table. The traditional furnishings, log fires, interesting collection of books, paintings, and sculpture all add to the individual character and charm of the house. The attractive gardens include a productive vegetable garden, croquet lawn, small fishing loch, and a turf and gravel maze. There are 3 spacious, comfortably furnished bedrooms, all en suite, with one bedroom on the ground floor and suitable for disabled guests. The elegant dining room features a long oak table at which guests can enjoy sumptuous breakfasts and leisurely dinners. The set 4-course dinner makes full use of the excellent local meat and fish and, wherever possible, produce from the Lodge's own garden.

About 4 miles south of Dalbeattie, a signposted lane off the A711 leads to the **Orchardton Tower** (Historic Scotland, free), a late 15th-century tower house in an idyllic setting. It is built in cylindrical style, a design unique in Scotland although common in Ireland.

KIRKCUDBRIGHT
MAP 2 REF I18

32 miles SW of Dumfries on the A711

"An irreproachable Scottish town...one of the most picturesque and fascinating Lowland towns I have seen". So enthused the travel writer H.V. Morton after visiting this enchanting little town (pronounced "Kir-coo-brit") set beside the River Dee. Morton was especially impressed by the ruins of **MacLellans Castle** which towers over the tiny harbour. Built between 1569 and 1582, it was designed not for defensive purposes but as a private house for Sir Thomas MacLellan. Its Great Hall is particularly striking and there's a curious feature in the enormous lintel over the fireplace. A spy-hole has been cut into the lintel and there's a small room behind it, a primitive but no doubt effective variant of today's bugging devices.

Just across the road, **Broughton House** is a handsome Georgian building which in the late 19th century was the home of the artist Edward Hornel, a major figure in the group calling themselves The Glasgow Boys. Some of their Impressionist-style work is on display here, including several of Hornel's paintings of Japan, a country he found mesmerising. So much so that he designed and built a lovely Japanese Garden in the grounds of Broughton House.

At the corner of the L-shaped High Street stands the 16th/17th century Tolbooth, now an Art Centre featuring more of The Glasgow Boys' paintings, and with studios on the upper floor occupied by contemporary artists and craftworkers.

Not far from the picturesque harbour, in the old part of this artists' colony, **Baytree House** is a beautifully restored Georgian town house offering exceptionally stylish bed & breakfast accommodation. Since opening in February 1997, Jackie and Robert have worked hard, both on the house itself and in the lovely, extremely large garden. There's also a separate vegetable garden which supplies fresh ingredients for Jackie's marvellous cooking, supplementing fish straight from the harbour or high quality local meats. The Baytree is not licensed but

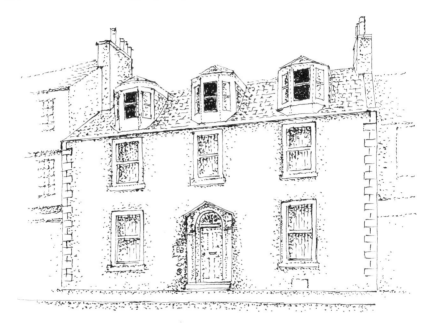

**Baytree House, 110 High Street, Kirkcudbright
Dumfries & Galloway DG6 4JQ Tel: 01557 330824**

feel free to bring along your beverage of choice, (and you *will* be offered a complimentary glass of sherry on arrival just to make you feel at home!)

There are 3 letting rooms, exquisitely furnished with antiques and collectables. On the ground floor there's a large twin room and, for romantics, there's a charming room complete with 4-poster bed. Guests also have the use of a huge drawing room on the first floor where there's an open fire for cold winter days. Breakfast at the Baytree is, naturally, rather special, with delicacies such as Smoked Creetown Kippers and home-made Clootie Dumpling among the tempting options. Jackie and Robert also provide evening meals and are the proud recipients of an AA Dinner Award.

Just along the road from Baytree House is the Selkirk Arms Hotel, an essential port of call for any devotee of Robert Burns. The poet stayed at the hotel in

1794 and it was here that he penned his much-quoted 'Selkirk Grace':

'Some hae meat and canna eat,
And some wad eat that want it,
But we hae meat and we can eat,
And sae the Lord be thanket'.

Conveniently located in Kirkcudbright's main street, **The Belfry** is a very popular café and tea room owned and run by Caroline Ironmonger and Linda McDermid. It has been in their family for quite some time and they share the cooking and serving with another member of the family, Christine. Together,

The Belfry, 39 St Mary Street, Kirkcudbright
Dumfries & Galloway DG6 4DU Tel: 01557 330861

they offer their customers a comprehensive menu which ranges from filled rolls to scampi dishes and all day breakfasts. In addition, there are always a couple of tasty daily specials on offer. This friendly café welcomes children and has good access for the disabled. The Belfry has a wonderfully relaxed atmosphere with no one being rushed. It's open 7 days a week, from 8.00 until 17.00 from Monday to Saturday, and from 10.30 until 17.00 on Sunday. During the season, The Belfry stays open later. Just along the road from the café, the Stewartry Museum is also well worth a visit for its huge collection of exhibits reflecting the life and times of the Solway Coast.

CASTLE DOUGLAS
18 miles SW of Dumfries off the A75

MAP 2 REF J17

In the late 18th century when it was still possible for the rich to purchase whole villages, Sir William Douglas spent £14,000 on a cluster of settlements around Carlingwark Loch and proceeded to create his very own town, Castle Douglas. Sir William had made his fortune in what was murkily described as "the American trade", a term that covered anything from slave trading to straightforward piracy, but his new town was founded on the highest principles.

The result was a triumph of town planning. The 3 main streets running parallel and joined by 5 intersecting roads gave an orderly pattern to the town and some fine Georgian buildings enhanced its appearance. Today, Castle Douglas remains one of the most pleasing towns in the country and in addition enjoys a reputation for being home to some of the best food shops, especially butchers, in Scotland.

Located in the heart of this popular little town, the **Scottish Pantry** is well-known for the excellent food it offers, specialising as its name suggests in

**Scottish Pantry, 184 King Street, Castle Douglas, Dumfries & Galloway
DG7 1DA Tel: 01556 502232**

traditional Scottish cuisine. The owners, Alistair and Sheila Bannerman are both qualified chefs with many years experience between them. They bought the Scottish Pantry in 1994 and completely refurbished the premises to create a warm and inviting atmosphere in which visitors can enjoy their outstanding food. The comprehensive menu includes everything from porridge to curries, fish dishes and Scottish steaks and grills. There's also a wonderful selection of home-made cakes, sponges and other tea-time treats. The Pantry is disabled-friendly, there's a baby-changing room and high chairs, and another indication of the Bannermans' concern for customer satisfaction is their policy on opening hours. They open every day at 7.00 and stay open until late in the evening, not closing the doors until after the last customer has left. Throughout that time, everything listed on the menu or on the specials board is available. Service indeed!

A mile southwest of Castle Douglas, **Threave Garden & Estate** (National Trust for Scotland) is decidedly a garden for all seasons. It's best known for a spectacular spring-time display of some 200 varieties of daffodil but there are also lots of colour summer displays and striking autumn tints in trees and the heather garden. The garden is also home to the National Trust for Scotland's School of Horticulture.

A visit to **Threave Castle**, is something of an experience. It begins with a delightful 10-minute walk to the River Dee where the massive tower stands on an island. Visitors ring a brass bell and the castle custodian rows over to ferry them to the island. A forbidding building, the castle was built in the late 1300s by Archibald the Grim, one of the notorious "Black Douglases". The family earned its nickname by exhibiting a blood-thirstiness that was appalling even by the standards of that barbarous age. The stories of the clan's reign of terror throughout the area fit well with the brooding, gloomy fortress.

CROSSMICHAEL

Map 2 ref J17

20 miles SW of Dumfries on the A731

Located on the shore of Loch Ken (actually a man-made reservoir), this sizeable village is well worth seeking out in order to visit **The Thistle Inn** in Main Street. There was a time in the 1950s when the Lady of the Manor had the inn's licence revoked and the village was dry for several years. Happily, those days are long past and mine host Jim McLelland can offer visitors a good selection of well-kept ales and a staggering choice of more than 150 different whiskies. Jim has owned and run the Inn for some 22 years and has a well-earned reputation for providing quality food every lunchtime and evening. There's a separate dining area but you can eat throughout the inn. The menu is supplemented by daily specials and children are very welcome.

Crossmichael village lies roughly half-way between the superb sandy beaches at Southerness and the unspoilt acres of the **Galloway Forest Park**. A handy

The Thistle Inn, Main Street, Crossmichael, by Castle Douglas
Dumfries & Galloway DG7 3AU Tel: 01556 670203

place to stay, therefore, and Jim has 2 self-catering holiday flats available, situated next to the inn and both sleeping up to 4 people.

NEW GALLOWAY   MAP 2 REF I17
25 miles W of Dumfries on the A725

With a population of just over 300, New Galloway holds the undisputed title of "Smallest Royal Burgh in Scotland". Little more than a single street of neat and attractive stone cottages, the village lies on the River Ken, noted for its fine angling. There's also a church which is well worth visiting for its unusual tombstones, an intriguing collection of curious carvings and strange epitaphs. A mile or so south of New Galloway the river flows into scenic Loch Ken, noted for its excellent bird-watching opportunities, coarse fishing and watersport facilities.

"One of Galloway's finest tea rooms" is the claim made by **Kittys Tea Room** in the High Street, and anyone who has ever visited Kittys will agree wholeheartedly. The premises started life as a Temperance Hotel back in 1850 and whoever panelled the interior walls with old ship's timbers was a master craftsman whose work is a delight to see. Even more delightful is the superb home-made fare on offer, all cooked by Sylvia Brown who together with her husband Gordon owns this outstanding tea room. In addition to her memorable tea-time treats, Sylvia's menu includes legendary home-made soups, "siren salads" (guaranteed love at first bite!), and a choice of succulent, savoury hot dishes. "End your meal with a little ooh-la-la" Sylvia's menu urges. "Dare you sample 'Luscious Lucy', (a light lemon cheesecake), chance your luck with 'Mata

Kittys Tea Room, High Street, New Galloway DG7 3RJ
Tel: 01644 420246

Hari' (sticky date cake served warm with butterscotch sauce & ice cream), or rise above it all with 'Angel's Wings' (light meringues filled with fresh cream)". Whatever else you miss in Galloway, make sure you pay a visit to Kittys.

NEWTON STEWART
MAP 2 REF H17
42 miles W of Dumfries on the A712

Running southwest from New Galloway to Newton Stewart, the 19-mile Queen's Way Tourist Route along the A712 passes through the rugged beauty of the Galloway Forest Park and provides some interesting locations along the way. First, 6 miles from New Galloway, there's **Bruce's Stone**, a massive boulder which marks the spot where Robert the Bruce defeated the English in 1307. Nearby is the **Clatteringshaws Forest Wildlife Centre**, an informative indoor display of forest wildlife, and a couple of miles further the **Galloway Deer Range** where visitors can walk among red deer, handle them and take photographs close up. Near Newton Stewart, the **Kirroughtree Visitor Centre** offers a state-of-the-art children's play area, waymarked trails, cycle routes and a forest drive.

South and west of Newton Stewart stretches the area known as the **Rhins and Machars of Galloway**, a peaceful peninsula of gentle farmland and broad landscapes culminating in the craggy coastline forming Scotland's most southerly point. (Burrow Head's latitude is actually several miles south of Durham in England). Peaceful though it is now, the region did not escape unscathed from the horrors of the Covenanter years. At **Wigtown**, a stone obelisk near the tidal sands of Wigtown Bay commemorates the Wigtown Martyrs, Margaret Machauchlan, aged 63, and Margaret Wilson, 18. In 1685, they were convicted of attending meetings of their sect, tied to stakes in the estuary and left to drown in the rising tide.

WHAUPHILL
MAP 2 REF H18

11 miles S of Newton Stewart on the B7005

About 4 miles to the southeast of Wigtown, there's a very good reason for seeking out the little village of Whauphill. As one satisfied visitor said after staying at **Jacob's Ladder**: "Once found, never forgotten". This charming Country House is surrounded by 8 acres of woodland and lovely gardens and offers guests a choice of either bed & breakfast or self-catering accommodation. Bed and breakfast guests stay in the striking old house, built in 1856, which contains many interesting features such as the porticoed entrance, open log fires, and interior doors which were rescued from Ravenstone Castle. The house is the home of Mary McMuldroch whose home cooking is one of the major attractions of a stay at Jacob's Ladder. In addition to her hearty Scottish breakfast, Mary also cooks evening meals by arrangement, and on Sundays serves a memorable Scottish High Tea between 16.30 and 18.00. For those who prefer self-catering, the

Jacob's Ladder, Whauphill, nr Port William, Newton Stewart, Wigtownshire DG8 9BD Tel: 01988 860227

nearby Coach House is an attractive stone building which can accommodate up to 4 people. There are 2 bedrooms, shower room and a comprehensively-equipped kitchen-cum-lounge. Hidden away in the heart of the Galloway countryside, these are properties well worth seeking out.

A couple of miles from Jacob's Ladder, off the B7052 between Whauphill and Sorbie, **Galloway Farmhouse Cheese** at Millairies Farm is run by Mary McMuldroch's daughter and son-in-law. They use milk from their flock of Friesland sheep to produce a range of cheeses which are sold to delicatessens and some of Scotland's top hotels and restaurants. Visitors can taste the cheeses before deciding on their preference, and there's also a good selection of products, all based on a sheep theme. Tel. 01988 850224

WHITHORN
MAP 2 REF I18

18 miles S of Newton Stewart on the A746

For centuries this little town attracted pilgrims from all around the country, with James IV making regular visits. They came to visit the church founded by St Ninian in 397, the first Christian place of worship north of Hadrian's Wall. During the 12th century, a priory was built to meet the needs of the pilgrims. No trace remains of St Ninian's church but there are some remains of the Priory which can be explored with the help of a free guide service. In the nearby museum, **Cradle of Christianity in Scotland** (Historic Scotland), there's an impressive collection of ancient carved stones, amongst them the 7th century St Peter's Stone and 5th century Latinus Stone, possibly the oldest in Scotland.

GLENLUCE
MAP 2 REF H17

15 miles SW of Newton Stewart off the A75

On the western edge of The Machars of Galloway, near Glenluce village, the ruins of **Glenluce Abbey**, founded in 1192 by Roland, Earl of Galloway, occupy a site of great natural beauty. The Abbey's 15th century Chapter House is surprisingly intact and its ribbed vault ceiling creates such an astonishingly clear acoustic that opera singers often practise here. Look out for the carvings of the "green men", always depicted with foliage sprouting from their faces. These pagan symbols of fertility were often incorporated into the fabric of medieval Christian churches - but always on the outer walls as a sign that they had been cast out by Mother Church.

During the late 1200s, the Abbey was the home of Michael Scot, a wizard and alchemist who was widely credited with enticing a plague that was decimating the population of Galloway into a secret vault here and imprisoning it. Scot's fame was such that he features as one of the damned in Dante's *Inferno*.

In the village itself, the **Glenluce Motor Museum** houses a splendid collection of vintage and classic cars, motor cycles, motoring memorabilia and even a vintage garage.

Family-run inns always seem to have a rather special atmosphere and the **Glenluce Hotel** is no exception. An attractive black-and-white building, colourful in summer with hanging baskets, the Glenluce is a listed building dating back to the early 1700s and served as a coaching and post inn when the village's Main Street was indeed the main road between Dumfries and Stranraer. This welcoming hotel is run by Bob and Sandra Hull and their daughter Claire. Bob and Sandra have more than 20 years experience in the trade but only took over the Glenluce in November 1998. They have undertaken an extensive programme of refurbishing and upgrading and the results have made the old hotel a very

**Glenluce Hotel, 67 Main Street, Glenluce, Newton Stewart,
Wigtownshire DG8 0PP Tel: 01581 300581 Fax: 01581 300645
e-mail: claire@glenlucehotel.freeserve.co.uk
Website: http://www.glenluce.org.uk/glenlucehotel.htm**

pleasant place to eat, drink or stay overnight. Sandra rules the kitchen and offers a good choice of traditional dishes which can be enjoyed either in the bar or in the separate, cosy restaurant. There are daily specials and also a menu specially for children. For anyone planning to stay in the area, the Glenluce has 10 quality letting rooms, 2 of which are family rooms, and five are en suite.

STRANRAER   MAP 1 REF G17
25 miles W of Newton Stewart on the A75

This honest-to-goodness working port is well known to travellers by ferry to Belfast or Larne in Northern Ireland. While you're waiting for your boat, you could explore the **Castle of St John**, a late medieval tower which was later pressed into use as a Victorian prison, or drop into the **Stranraer Museum** in the Old Town Hall which has displays on Wigtownshire farming, folklife and archaeology.

Back in the 1950s, the citizens of Stranraer had a brilliant idea. Each would contribute a plant to help create a colourful public open space to be known as the **Friendship Gardens**. Almost half a century later, the Gardens are a splendid sight in summer, a living monument to the town's community spirit. Just across the road from the Gardens stands **Windyridge Villa**, a handsome Edwardian house built in 1912. It's the home of Olive and Bryce Kelly and, standing high on the hill, enjoys incomparable views across the harbour and coast. Olive and Bryce have been welcoming bed & breakfast guests from the around the world for the last five years or so, and they entertain them with true Scottish hospitality. They have 3 beautifully decorated and furnished rooms, all en suite, centrally heated and double glazed, and each offering colour television, tea/coffee-making facilities, hairdriers and a tempting courtesy tray of home-baked goodies. And Windyridge Villa's breakfast menu sets a model that puts many expensive

Windyridge Villa, 5 Royal Crescent, Stranraer, Galloway DG9 8HB
Tel: 01776 889900

hotels with their rubbery, astronomically-priced 'buffet breakfasts' to shame. Just complete the little green form, leave it on the hall table, and at the hour you prescribe you'll be served with your choice of the freshly prepared dishes amongst which are poached local smoked Haddock served with oatcakes, a hearty Scottish breakfast complete with a portion of Haggis, and de luxe scrambled eggs with smoked salmon. First class!

STONEYKIRK MAP 1 REF G18

5 miles S of Stranraer on the A716

Set in the heart of the Rhinns of Galloway, the hilly peninsula running south from Stranraer, **The County Hotel** is a handsome old inn well-known for its quality accommodation, food, ale and entertainment. Dessie and Liz Wilson bought the hotel early in 1999 and this lively couple have maintained and built on its high reputation. The County is open all day every day and Liz offers a wide choice of mostly home-cooked food, complemented by a good selection of well-kept ales and lagers. The hotel has 9 superior en suite letting rooms, available all year round, and is especially popular with sportsmen who appreciate

**The County Hotel, Stoneykirk, Stranraer, Galloway DG9 9DH
Tel: 01776 830431 Fax: 01776 830600**

the excellent fishing to be enjoyed in this scenic area. Golfers, too, are exceptionally well-served with no fewer than 5 superb 18-hole golf courses all within easy reach of the hotel. Dessie is happy to arrange package golfing holidays, and the hotel will provide a courtesy bus to and from each of the courses. Another major attraction at The County is its live entertainment on Friday and Saturday evenings when the music ranges from Country & Western, through 60s & 70s evenings, to plangent Irish folk melodies.

Continuing southwards from Stoneykirk, the A716 passes close by two outstanding gardens. **Ardwell Gardens**, near Ardwell village, has splendid displays of daffodils, rock plants, rhododendrons and flowering shrubs in a woodland setting overlooking Luce Bay. South of Ardwell, a minor road leads to **Logan Botanic Garden**, a specialist garden of the Royal Botanic Garden, Edinburgh. Logan is truly a plantsman's paradise, famous for tree ferns, cabbage palms, and many rare, unusual and interesting plants from the southern hemisphere.

PORT LOGAN BAY   Map 1 ref G18
15 miles S of Stranraer on the B7065

Port Logan Bay is one of the most scenic locations on the west coast of the Rhinns of Galloway and the **Port Logan Inn** makes the most of its privileged position overlooking the bay. Stand at the inn's porch and you can enjoy a wonderful view of the sweeping bight and the crescent-shaped beach with scarcely a human habitation (or, for much of the time, even a human being,) in sight. Reg and Pat Coupe are the lucky owners of this wonderfully peaceful and secluded inn, a long, low black-and-white building with a profile rather like an

**The Port Logan Inn, Port Logan Bay, Stranraer, Galloway DG9 9NG
Tel: 01776 860272**

ocean-going tanker. Pat is a terrific cook, adding an indefinable flair to everything she prepares, - from breakfasts to lunches to cream teas to evening meals. Reg seems to have an equally enviable talent for serving up a perfect pint. If you fancy the idea of staying in this idyllic spot, Port Logan Inn can offer you the choice of two family or two double rooms for bed & breakfast guests. This beguiling corner of west Galloway is often overlooked by visitors: do yourself a favour and don't make the same mistake!

3 Ayrshire and Arran

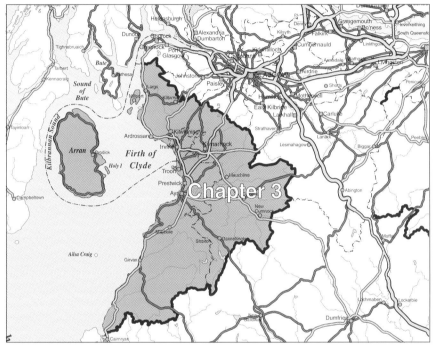

© MAPS IN MINUTES ™ (1998)

Within Ayrshire's 1200 square miles there's a marked contrast between north and south. In the north, there's a taste of the untamed Highlands and while the south is more reminiscent of the Borders, with rolling pasture lands and country villages. The long sandy shores and the popular resort of Largs in North Ayrshire, the rural nature of East Ayrshire with its wide open spaces, and the broad beaches, seaside towns and verdant hills of South Ayrshire, all add to the variety.

This is, of course, Robert Burns' homeland and wherever you go you'll almost certainly find that Scotland's national bard has been there before you and usually left behind a good anecdote to prove it. Pride of place in any Burns itinerary must go to the Burns Cottage & Museum, at Alloway near Ayr, where the poet was born. Homes of a statelier kind can be visited at Kelburn Castle, home of the Earls of Glasgow, and Culzean Castle, Ayrshire's top tourist attraction.

On the Isle of Arran, Brodick Castle has a history stretching back some 700 years, as does that of Crossraguel Abbey whose substantial ruins stand beside the A77 in the south of the county. And if you want a change of scenery from the mainland, there are regular ferries to the islands of Arran, Bute and Great Cumbrae.

AYR

For centuries Ayr rivalled Glasgow as a major seaport. When its importance as a trading centre declined, the town's fine beaches provided a new lease of life - as a popular Victorian resort. A whole new town of wide streets, boulevards, imposing public offices such as the **County Buildings**, and an esplanade sprang up making this part of Ayr stand in marked contrast to the narrow lanes and alleys of the Old Town - "Auld Ayr" as Robert Burns put it, "wham ne'er a toun surpasses for honest men and bonnie lasses".

The most notable survivor of medieval buildings in Ayr is the **Auld Brig**, a sturdy 15th century construction made famous by Burns in his poem *Twa Brigs*. Elsewhere, the poet described the bridge as *"a poor narrow footpath of a street where two wheel-barrows tremble when they meet"*. Auld Brig was restored in 1910 and is now only open to pedestrians.

A few yards from the bridge, the **Auld Kirk** was built by Cromwell after he incorporated the original town church into a massive fort he constructed here. (The fort has long since disappeared). Burns was baptised in the Auld Kirk and a plan of the graveyard in the lych gate indicates the resting-places of some of his friends. Also on the wall of the lych gate is an early 19th century "mort-safe", a heavy iron grille placed over newly-dug graves to discourage body snatchers.

The town honours two of Scotland's heroes with statues. Close to the Auld Kirk is **Wallace's Tower**, 113 feet high and built in 1828 on the site of a medieval tower in which, according to legend, William Wallace was imprisoned and from which he made a daring escape. About 400 yards to the south, Burns himself gazes thoughtfully over Burns Statue Square.

ALLOWAY   Map 2 ref H15
2 miles S of Ayr on the B1274

Today it is part of the Ayr suburbs, but Alloway was just a small village when Robert Burns was born here on January 25th, 1759. The long, low thatched cottage built by his father still stands and is now the **Burns Cottage and Museum** housing a wealth of Burns memorabilia including his original manuscript for *Auld Lang Syne*. To the south of the village, the lovely 13th century **Brig O'Doon** still spans the River Doon, a bridge familiar to all Burns' lovers from his poem *Tam O'Shanter*. Also featured in the poem is nearby **Kirk Alloway**, now a roofless but romantic ruin. Burns' father, William Burnes (sic), is buried in the graveyard here.

A few minutes walk from the kirk, the **Burns Monument and Gardens** commemorates the poet with an impressive Grecian-style monument set in attractive gardens. From here, a short stroll brings you to **The Tam O'Shanter Experience**, a 1990s visitor centre where you can watch a film about the life of Scotland's national bard, another telling the story of *Tam O'Shanter*, browse in the extensive gift shop, or sample the fare on offer in the "Taste of Burns Country" restaurant.

TARBOLTON   MAP 2 REF H15
7 miles NE of Ayr on the A719

Anyone following the Burns Trail will want to seek out this small village in order to visit the charming 17th century house known as the **Bachelors' Club** (National Trust for Scotland). Between 1777 and 1784, the Burns family lived at **Lochlea Farm** near Tarbolton and during these years Burns was a leading light of the Bachelors' Club, a debating society where his ardent republican views ensured that discussions were never less than lively. As well as debating, drinking and the pursuit of pretty women, another of Rabbie's passions was dancing. It was in this house that he attended dancing lessons and in 1781 was initiated as a freemason. The thatched, white-washed building contains a small museum of material relating to Burns' life in the area.

MAUCHLINE   MAP 2 REF I15
11 miles NE of Ayr on the A76

This little town is still vibrant with memories of Robert Burns. Following the death of his father in 1784, the 25-year-old Burns took a lease on nearby Mossgiel Farm which is still a working farm to this day. Robbie was hopelessly incompetent as a farmer and his financial problems with the farm were compounded by a roller-coaster emotional relationship with Jean Armour, a sparky Mauchline lass. Despite these dual tensions, this was a period of extraordinary creativity for Burns and in 1786 his first volume of poems was published. The book became a best-seller and after savouring his literary triumph in the salons of Edinburgh, Burns returned to Mauchline in 1788 to marry Jean.

They set up home in a single room in a house in Castle Street which is now the **Burns House Museum** where a rather meagre collection of memorabilia will enthuse only the most devoted of his fans. Much more rewarding is a visit to the poet's favourite "howff", or watering-hole, **Poosie Nansie's Tavern**, the setting for his cantata *The Jolly Beggars* and still a popular pub in the town. To the north of Mauchline stands **The National Burns Memorial Tower**, an impressive 3-storeyed tower whose first and second floors house an interpretation centre and from whose roof there are panoramic views of the surrounding countryside.

Burns' residence in Mauchline has rather overshadowed the town's two other claims to fame: the production of Curling Stones, made from Ailsa Craig granite, and Mauchline Ware - highly collectable small boxes and other items made from plane or sycamore wood, hand-painted with local scenes and varnished.

TROON   MAP 2 REF H15

8 miles N of Ayr on the B746

As far back as the early 1700s the attractions of coastal towns like Troon were becoming clear to those who lived in the cities and industrial areas. Troon was considered at the time to possess *"an excellent situation for sea bathing"*. In this respect the town has changed little, ~ it's still a small fishing town boasting 2 miles of soft, sandy beaches stretching from either side of the harbour.

The harbour itself is always busy with yachts arriving and berthing, anglers trying their luck, children exploring all the nooks and crannies of the countless rock pools.

Directly opposite the entrance to Troon's municipal Golf Club which offers no fewer than 3 separate courses, **The Tudor Tearoom & Restaurant** is noted for its wonderful home baking, and especially for its scrumptious cakes such as the Chocolate Fudge Cake, served hot or cold with cream or ice cream. There's been a café/restaurant on this site since the 1920s and since 1991 the Tudor Tearoom has been owned and run by Jack and Liz Moore. They offer their customers a vast choice of meals, snacks, high teas and tea-time treats, listed in an 8-page menu and supplemented by daily specials. The menu includes dishes especially for Senior Citizens along with others designed for children. Slimmers are also catered for with a choice of low-calorie open sandwiches and those with a sweet tooth may find it difficult to choose between the tempting desserts. The

**The Tudor Tearoom & Restaurant, 5 Harling Drive, Troon,
Ayrshire KA10 6NF Tel: 01292 318448**

tearoom is open 7 days a week, from 9.00 until 18.00 from Monday to Thursday, and from 9.00 until 19.00 on Friday, Saturday and Sunday. At weekends, you should certainly book ahead.

About 5 miles northeast of Troon, the ruins of **Dundonald Castle** (Historic Scotland) loom over the pretty village of the same name. This hilltop site was occupied well before 2000 BC and a hill fort stood here between 500 and 200 BC. The present castle was built in 1390 by Robert II, the first of the Stuart line of kings who were to rule Scotland and then England for more than three centuries. There's a visitors' centre with a coffee shop, grand views, and an exhibition outlining the castle's history.

IRVINE   MAP 2 REF H14
12 miles N of Ayr off the A71/A78

The largest town in North Ayrshire, Irvine used to be the main port for Glasgow and those busy days are recalled at the **Scottish Maritime Museum** beside the old harbour. Visitors can board the world's oldest Clipper ship, as well as vintage Clyde "puffers" and tugs. Nearby, the **Magnum Centre** is one the largest sports and leisure complexes in Europe, a 250-acre site complete with swimming pools, theatre, cinema, ice rink, bowls hall and much more.

Naturally, the town has connections with Robert Burns. He lived here between 1781 and 1783 at **No. 4 Glasgow Vennel** while learning to dress flax at No.10 in the same street, one of the few old streets in the town to have survived. The town boasts the oldest continuous Burns Club in the world, founded in 1826. At the **Burns Club & Museum**, you can see a collection of original manuscripts prepared for the famous Kilmarnock Edition of his poems. There's also an impressive 9 feet high statue of the poet on the banks of the River Irvine.

Mary Stuart stayed at Irvine in 1563 and her visit is celebrated each year with a week-long **Marymass Festival** in August.

SALTCOATS   MAP 2 REF H14
19 miles N of Ayr on the A728

In the 1500s, King James V dipped into his own pocket to establish the salt panning industry here from which the town takes its name. Saltcoats nowadays is much better known for its picturesque harbour and golden, sandy beaches set around Irvine Bay. Visitors interested in the history of the area will find a comprehensive overview at the **North Ayrshire Museum** which is well worth visiting.

With its superb position on the promenade at Saltcoats, the **Bay Hotel** provides its guests with fantastic views over the Firth of Clyde to Arran. "Just come to enjoy yourself and get away from it all" says the owner, Janet Gimson. "Watch the sun set over Arran as you enjoy a drink in the bar, watch the swans in the bay and the waves rolling along the shoreline. Stroll along the beach before breakfast or in the evening, then come into the hotel to enjoy a meal freshly

**Bay Hotel, 15-16 Winton Circus, Saltcoats, Ayrshire, KA21 5DA
Tel: 01294 462317**

cooked by our loyal chef and his staff". Food is taken seriously at the Bay Hotel, whether it's a tasty bar lunch (chicken breast in cream peppered sauce, for example), afternoon teas and snacks, high tea or dinner. The hotel is happy to arrange special menus for special occasions, has a children's menu for the youngsters and is an ideal place for functions. The relaxed friendly atmosphere of the hotel makes this a perfect base and there are 4 guest bedrooms available, 2 double, 1 twin, 1 family/double/twin, all of them en suite with bathroom or shower. And if you are visiting on a Friday or Saturday evening, you can join in the Bay's popular quizzes and maybe even win a valuable prize!

FAIRLIE   MAP 2 REF H14
26 miles N of Ayr on the A78

This picturesque village boasts a sandy beach, a pier and not just one but two castles. Standing in a glen to the east, **Fairlie Castle** was built in 1521 and is now a ruin. **Kelburn Castle & Gardens**, 2 miles north of the town, on the other hand is very much lived in, the historic home of the Earls of Glasgow. The castle has a late 16th century tower attached to a house of 1700 and is open to visitors during the summer months. The park is open from Easter to October and offers woodland walks, pony treks, a secret forest, crocodile swamp and much more.

Just south of Fairlie, between the seaside resort of Largs and the Isle of Arran ferryport of Ardrossan, is Fencefoot Farm, well-known for the **Fencebay Fisheries & Food Court**. Once a busy fishing village, Fairlie overlooks the Cumbrae Islands in the Firth of Clyde and was renowned as the home of Fyfe's yacht-building yard - one of Sir Tommy Lipton's great Americas Cup challengers, "Shamrock I", was built here. Bernard and Jill Thain took Fencefoot over in

**Fencebay Fisheries & Food Court, Fairlie, Largs, KA29 0EG
Tel: 01475 568918**

1985 to revive the fish-smoking industry which had also brought fame to the village in the past. A wide variety of fresh and smoked fish, and shellfish, is sold in Fencefoot's Farm Shop, its smoked salmon winning several awards for flavour and quality. Its popularity has led to the conversion of the farm's byre into a delightful fish restaurant, "Fins", and the old stables into a specialist craft and cookshop called "Octopus". Fins Restaurant serves only the freshest fish and shellfish, much of which is landed by local fishing boats and the food is beautifully presented in comfortable and friendly surroundings. Fins has won several awards, including the much-coveted Taste of Scotland "Macallan 25" award, identifying it as one of Scotland's top 25 places to eat. Octopus, with its off licence, crafts and cookshop, complements this haven for food-lovers by selling everything for your dinner party - from the pans to cook it in, the plates to serve it on, and the wine to serve with it, as well as a multitude of useful gadgets and local crafts. All Fencebay products are available by mail order, (just write or phone for a price list), or through their web site: www.fencebay.co.uk. And if you take along this copy of Hidden Places, you will be eligible for a 5% discount at the Farm Shop, "Fins" and "Octopus".

LARGS   Map 2 ref H13
30 miles N of Ayr on the A78

Set against a spectacular backdrop of spreading woodland and hills rising up to 1500 feet, Largs has been a popular seaside resort for many years and was recently voted Scotland's Top Tourism Town. Just a few yards from the harbour, the superb **Skelmorlie Aisle** (Historic Scotland, free) is all that remains of the former parish church. In 1636, the aisle was converted into a mausoleum for Sir Robert Montgomerie and its elaborately painted barrel-vaulted ceiling and

Montgomerie's intricately carved tomb are masterpieces of Renaissance art.

Amongst the town's many visitor attractions, a relative newcomer is **Vikingar!** which start-of-the-art multi-media technology tells the story of the Vikings from their first raids in west Scotland to their defeat at the Battle of Largs in 1263. That victory is celebrated every year with a Viking Festival held during August and September and, to the south of Largs, the site of the battle is marked by the elegant **Pencil Monument**, reached by a coastal footpath.

Just 5 minutes by ferry from Largs, **Great Cumbrae Island** is worth visiting for its fine beaches, splendid views and peaceful countryside. Rather surprisingly, the island, just 4 miles long and 2 miles wide, boasts a **Cathedral of the Isles,** located in its one and only town, Millport. Completed in 1851 to a design by the Gothic revival architect William Butterfield, it is the smallest cathedral in Europe. Another major attraction on Great Cumbrae is the **Marine Life Museum**, operated by Glasgow and London Universities, which houses a magnificent aquarium.

KILMARNOCK
Map 2 ref H14
12 miles NE of Ayr on the A77

It was back in 1820 that a Kilmarnock grocer named Johnnie Walker began blending his own whisky at his shop on King Street. Today, the whisky bottling business he founded is the largest in the world and one of Kilmarnock's major industries along with the manufacture of carpets and footwear.

Conveniently located in the heart of the town, **The Chimes Coffee Shop** is very much a family run business. Margaret Duncan is assisted by her two daughters Sheila and Julie-Ann, as well as by her mum Marlene and two friends, Sally and Anne. When Margaret and her husband Malcolm bought the coffee shop in 1994 it had been standing empty for some 3 years. They set about a total refurbishment and created an attractive dining room, pleasantly furnished and with vintage memorabilia decorating the walls. They also put together an extensive menu of quality food

The Chimes Coffee Shop, 8 Fowlds Street, Kilmarnock KA1 3DG Tel: 01563 574165

which, together with the smiling service and very reasonable prices, have made The Chimes a popular venue with locals and visitors alike. There's a hearty All Day Breakfast and a huge choice of hot or cold filled rolls, toasted sandwiches, baked potatoes with side salad, as well as a "Kids Corner" and a selection of tea-time treats such as scones, biscuits, slices and cakes. Chimes is open every day except Sunday, from 9.00 until 17.00, and if you are visiting Kilmarnock between those hours, you will be doing yourself a favour if you call in!

The town also has strong connections with Robert Burns. The first edition of his poems was published here in 1796 and an original copy is on display in the museum attached to the red-sandstone **Burns Monument** in Key Park. Amongst other memorabilia is the announcement of the poet's death on 21 July 1796 as printed in the *Kilmarnock Standard*.

A short walk from the Monument, the **Dick Institute** is noted for its impressive collections of Geology, Scottish Archaeology, Natural History and reminders of bygone history. The Institute also offers a varied programme of contemporary art and other exhibitions.

Situated in one of the oldest streets in Kilmarnock, **The Coffee Club** is one of the town's most longstanding, and popular, places of refreshment. Svend Kamming opened his original coffee shop in 1959. The building has changed

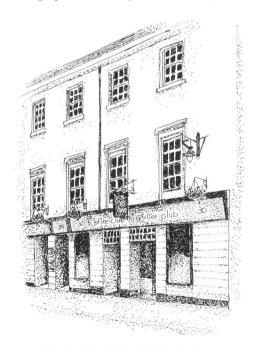

considerably since then and now has a striking frontage, approved and grant-aided by Historic Scotland. Inside there are two separate restaurants: a ground floor counter service dining area and, downstairs, an intimate restaurant with waitress service. The Coffee Club menu offers a huge choice, ranging from steaks to vegetarian options, Mexican dishes to all day breakfasts, from traditional Scottish fare such as Haggis, Tatties & Neeps, to tea-time treats all of which are baked on the premises. The Coffee Club really is like a club, producing regular newsletters which keep customers up to date on its many services - services such as its party plans, jazz evenings, special

The Coffee Club, 30 Bank Street, Kilmarnock KA1 1HA Tel: 01563 522048

Christmas evenings with live entertainment, take-away service and much more. A quite unique experience, the Coffee Club should not be missed.

On the northern edge of the town **Dean Castle Country Park** extends to 200 acres and facilities include a ranger service, children's zoo, riding centre and visitor centre. The massive 14th century Castle Keep houses an excellent collection of armour, tapestries and early European musical instruments. Children love exploring the dingy dungeons. Guided tours of the Keep and the adjacent 15th century Palace are available, culminating in superb views from the battlements.

GALSTON
Map 2 ref I14
13 miles N of Ayr off the A71

Lying in wooded country in the valley of the River Irvine, Galston has a thriving textile industry established in the 17th century by Dutch and Huguenot immigrants. Visitors can see lace tablecloths and curtains being made at some of the mills. Nineteenth century designs are still in production and visitors are welcome to purchase souvenirs from the factory shops.

Built in 1890, **The Maxwood Hotel** at Galston has been recently refurbished and extended by the addition of an attractive Restaurant which offers customers a wide choice of quality food and drink. A measure of the hotel's reputation for excellent food is the fact that you would be well-advised to book ahead for

The Maxwood Hotel, 12 Maxwood Road, Galston, Ayrshire KA4 8JN
Tel: 01563 821699 Fax: 01563 822285

weekend meals. Children are welcome at The Maxwood and on Sundays they eat free if accompanied by two adults buying meals. Bar snacks are also available every day. Dorothy McCallum, who runs the Maxwood Hotel, believes in providing service as and when customers want it, which is why the hotel stays open until midnight from Sunday to Thursday, and until 1am on Friday and Saturday when she also lays on musical entertainment. Galston is a convenient base from which to explore southwest Scotland and if you are thinking of staying in the area, the Maxwood Hotel has four comfortable letting rooms, 2 twins en suite and 2 doubles with private bathrooms.

On the edge of the town **Loudoun Gowf Club** is unique in retaining the game's old Scots spelling. The course is open to visitors on weekdays. Nearby **Loudoun Castle** is notable as the location where the Act of Union between Scotland and England was signed in 1707. Most of the present building is 19th century although a 15th century tower has survived. The castle's 500-acre grounds are now home to the **Loudoun Castle Theme Park** which claims to be the largest in Scotland. Along with stomach-churning roller coaster rides, the park also offers a wide variety of amusements for all the family, including pony rides, a kids farm, log flume and much more. There's an à la carte restaurant in the former coachhouse, and fast food outlets such as the William Wallace Food Court, named after the Scottish patriot who won a resounding victory over the English in 1297 at nearby Loudoun Hill.

MUIRKIRK
MAP 2 REF I15

26 miles E of Ayr on the A70

Set beside the River Ayr, the village of Muirkirk has a parish church dating from 1650, one of the few to have been built during the Commonwealth period.

As its name suggests, **The Coach House Inn** was once a stables, serving a large hotel just across the road which has since disappeared. Dating back to the

**The Coach House Inn, 1-3 Furnace Road, Muirkirk, Ayrshire KA18 3RE
Tel: 01290 661257**

late 1700s, it has been an inn for more than a century under the name of the Black Bull. It received its present name when Dave and Alison Peebles bought the impressive building in 1995. They have created a charming dining room, elegantly furnished and decorated, which offers a good choice of main meals and snacks, along with a children's menu. Visitors can also eat in the lounge area, and both restaurant and lounge have good wheelchair access.

Upstairs, there's a good-sized function suite, complete with its own bar. The Inn has 3 letting rooms, (2 twin, 1 single), all with excellent decor and furnishing, and smart, clean bathrooms. Children and pets are welcome by arrangement. An additional bonus is the grand view from the rear of the Inn to Cairn Table hill, some 1950 feet high, so named because of the prehistoric cairns that crown its summit.

PATNA
MAP 2 REF H15

8 miles SE of Ayr on the A713

For those who like their bed and breakfast accommodation to have some character, the place to seek out is **Parsons Lodge** in the small village of Patna. As the name indicates, the house was formerly the residence of the minister of the United Free Church of Scotland whose church stands right alongside. Parsons Lodge is a spacious Edwardian building, now the home of Sheila Campbell. Sheila has been welcoming bed and breakfast guests since 1990, many of them returning for repeat visits. The Lodge has 3 letting rooms, all either en suite or with private bathrooms. A particular attraction here is the downstairs licensed Bistro where Sheila serves a tempting choice of traditional food for lunches, high teas, dinners and suppers every day for residents, but closed on Wednes-

Parsons Lodge, 15 Main Street, Patna, Ayrshire KA6 7LN
Tel: 01292 531306

days for non-residents. Given the former manse's ecclesiastical origins, it seems appropriate that you can get married here - and Sheila will be delighted to cater for parties of up to 30 people. Parsons Lodge is conveniently situated for touring Ayrshire or the Galloway Forest, fishing in the River Doon, or golfing on the many nearby courses.

About a mile south of Patna, at Waterside, **The Dunaskin Experience** stands on the site of the former Dalmellington Iron Works Company. An open-air living museum, The Dunaskin Experience contains Europe's best remaining example of a Victorian Ironworks with more than half its 110 acres listed as a Scheduled Ancinet Monument. Attractions include an audio-visual recreation of Ayrshire life in the late 19th century, a period cottage, Furnace Play Tower, walks through Dunaskin Glen, gift shop and coffee shop.

DALMELLINGTON

MAP 2 REF I16

15 miles SE of Ayr on the A713

Dalmellington lies in the heart of the Doon Valley, once the industrial heartland of Ayrshire. The area's industrial heritage is explored in the **Cathcartston Interpretation Centre** which contains a working loom and interesting displays on weaving, mining and other local industries. **Chapel Row Cottage** has been carefully reconstructed and furnished to reflect the austere life of styles of iron workers during the years of the Great War

Built as a Victorian country house, **The Bellsbank House Hotel** opened in 1997 after being lovingly restored by its owners, Stewart and Barbara McAleese,

**The Bellsbank House Hotel, Bellsbank Road, Dalmellington
East Ayrshire KA6 7PR Tel: 01292 55024 Fax: 01292 550014**

who have retained all the old house's period charm. Situated high on the hill, the hotel has breathtaking views along the Doon valley and across to the Isle of Arran. It's surrounded by a wealth of forest parks, walks and trails, an ideal location for an active holiday as well as a relaxing break away from it all. Stewart, the proprietor chef, takes great pride in preparing delicious meals which can be enjoyed either in the elegant restaurant or in the baronial-style bar. (If you are a connoisseur of desserts, do try the Cranachan, a sumptuous confection of whisky & honey-flavoured cream, topped with toasted oatmeal and served with Scottish raspberries and shortbread). The guest bedrooms at Bellsbank House enjoy grand views across open countryside, are all en suite and equipped with television, direct dial telephones, and hospitality tray. For romantics, the Dalcairny room with its antique four poster bed will have a special appeal!

Dalmellington is set beside the River Doon whose source is **Loch Doon** about 2 miles to the south, a delightful place for walks and picnics. On its shore stand the impressive ruins of **Loch Doon Castle** with walls up to 9 feet thick and 26 feet high. Dating back to the early 14th century, the castle was originally built on an island in the loch but when the Galloway hydro-electric scheme raised the water level in the 1930s, the castle was dismantled stone by stone and re-erected on the shore. The island can still be seen from time to time when water levels are low.

KIRKMICHAEL   MAP 2 REF H15

12 miles S of Ayr on the B7045

Located in the heart of this picturesque village, **Jock's Restaurant** takes its name from a local character who was known as a "Jock of All Trades"! Housed in 17th century weavers' cottages, Jock's has a really atmospheric interior with stone

Jock's Restaurant, 24 Patna Road, Kirkmichael, Ayrshire KA19 7PJ
Tel: 01655 750499

walls and real fires along with quality furnishings and decoration. It has been a restaurant since 1982, for the last couple of years owned and run by Rosalind McIlwraith and Bob Russell, ably supported by chef Bill Baira and baker Marian Sloan. Together, they offer customers an exceptional choice of excellent food, served from 11.00 until last orders at 21.00, every day except Tuesday. The lunch and supper menus include a good range of starters, main courses and wonderful sweets such as Orange and Mango Bavarois. For the afternoon teas, Marian's bakery items come into their own, and there's a wide choice of fish, meat and poultry dishes on the dinner menu which is available from Wednesday to Sunday - all lovingly prepared to order and served with tasty fresh vegetables. Jock's is licensed so you can also enjoy a glass of wine with your meal.

CROSSHILL   MAP 2 REF H16
12 miles S of Ayr on the B7023

Nestled in the heart of Burns Country, in the picturesque conservation village of Crosshill, is a Hidden Place that certainly deserves seeking out. **The Pippins Hotel** is a family run inn offering quality food, drink and accommodation in a relaxed and friendly atmosphere. Iain Colquhoun, his son, also Iain, and daughter Fiona, provide the kind of old-fashioned hospitality that is as rare as it is welcome. Expert chef Dougie McEwen presents customers with a varied selection of dishes, all made using prime quality ingredients. There's a table d'hôte or à la carte choice, served in the restaurant which enjoys stunning views across the lovely Ayrshire countryside, and bar snacks are also available. If you appreciate wine with your meal, Pippins can offer you a good selection at reasonable prices.

The Pippins Hotel, 2 Dalhowan Street, Crosshill, Ayrshire KA19 7RN
Tel/Fax: 01655 740547

The hotel has 6 letting rooms, all of them en suite, tastefully decorated and fully equipped with colour television and tea/coffee making facilities. For that very special event, Pippins also has a spacious function room capable of accommodating up to 200 guests.

MAYBOLE   MAP 2 REF H15
9 miles S of Ayr on the A77

In the centre of Maybole, across the road from the Town Hall, the **Dairy Corner Tearoom** is just the place for a light snack and a refreshing pot of tea or coffee. As the name suggests, this early 18th century building has been a dairy and also a baker's. The baking tra-dition is continued today by Samantha Lowrie who offers her customers a wonderful choice of home-made cakes and sweets. Her menu also includes a good choice of sand-wiches or baguettes, hot filled rolls, baked pota-toes and, until 11.00, a hearty Big Breakfast. This friendly and welcoming tearoom is beautifully decorated and furnished, very different from how it was when Samantha took over here. A display of photographs on one of the walls records the mammoth task of resto-ration and refurbishment she had to undertake. Also on

Dairy Corner Tearoom, 82 High Street, Maybole, Ayrshire KA19 7BZ Tel: 01655 884188

display is an interesting collection of gifts and crafts for sale. The Dairy Corner Tearoom is open 7 days a week in summer, (closed Sundays in winter), from 9.00 until 16.30pm.

Maybole is the fifth largest town in Ayrshire and formerly the capital of the Carrick area. It is notable for its restored 17th century **Maybole Castle**, a pictur-esque building with turrets and oriel windows. It was formerly the town house of the Earls of Cassillis, leaders of the powerful Lowland Kennedy family, who now live at Cassillis House (private) about 4 miles to the northeast. It was the

Kennedys who established a **Collegiate Church** at Maybole in 1371 and the roofless ruin of the 15th century church can be seen in the old graveyard in Abbot Street.

In the High Street, a clock tower is all that remains of the ancient **Tolbooth** which was originally the town house of the Lairds of Blairquhan. It stands next door to Maybole's 19th century Town Hall forming the Town Buildings.

About 4 miles west of Maybole, **Culzean Castle** (National Trust for Scotland) is Ayrshire's premier tourist attraction. Magnificently furnished, the castle was designed by Robert Adam in 1777 and built around an ancient tower of the Kennedys. The work took 15 years to complete but the result is one of Adam's finest creations, marked by dazzling features such as the oval staircase and circular saloon. A small exhibition commemorates the life and times of Dwight D. Eisenhower who stayed here several times during World War II. The top floor was presented to him for life by the castle's owners at that time, the Kennedys.

Culzean overlooks the Firth of Clyde and stands in 565 acres of grounds set alongside the shore. Guided tours are available, there's a Reception & Interpretation Centre, swan pond, deer park, picnic sites, restaurant and tea rooms. Definitely not to be missed.

Two miles southwest of Maybole, the substantial ruins of **Crossraguel Abbey** (Historic Scotland) include a mighty gatehouse and a sturdy tower house. Founded in 1244, the present remains mostly date back to 1400s and are a fine example of that glorious period of church architecture. The Abbey's funnel-shaped **Dovecote** is remarkably well-preserved, with 240 nesting boxes for the birds which provided the monks with a reliable year-round source of food.

KIRKOSWALD
MAP 2 REF H15

13 miles SW of Ayr on the A77

Two of Burns' best-loved characters lie buried in the churchyard at Kirkoswald. Douglas Graham of Shanter was the model for Tam O'Shanter, and his crony, the village cobbler John Davidson, inspired the character of Souter Johnnie in the same poem. **Souter Johnnie's Cottage** (National Trust for Scotland), built in 1785, stands across the road from the churchyard and has been furnished with contemporary furniture, including items used by the Souter's family, a cobbler's chair that was almost certainly his, and various Burns memorabilia. In the garden are life-size stone figures of a jovial-looking Souter Johnnie and other characters from *Tam O'Shanter*. They were carved in 1802 and exhibited around Scotland and England before being brought to the house in 1924.

COLMONELL
MAP 1 REF G16

35 miles S of Ayr on the B734

This pretty village is set in the lovely valley of the River Stichnar and boasts a graceful late 18th century parish church. Standing high on the hillside, **The**

Queens Hotel enjoys outstanding views along the valley. The hotel's owners, Pieter and Liz Cross, took over here in 1998 but the building itself dates back to the 1820s. Floor to ceiling wood panelling and a real fire make the interior very welcoming and anyone interested in country sports will be fascinated by the display in the main bar. As well as providing information on local fishing opportunities, it includes a collection of various kinds of fishing rods, another of

**The Queens Hotel, 21 Main Street, Colmonell, Ayrshire KA26 0SD
Tel: 01465 881213**

ornamental guns and hunting horns, along with fencing swords and even a stuffed boar's head. The hotel is well-known for its varied menu of quality food, its well-kept ales, and its regular live entertainment every Friday evening. If you are looking for somewhere to stay in this lovely area, The Queens makes a handy base and offers visitors a choice of 6 letting rooms, five of which are doubles.

BALLANTRAE
Map 1 ref G16

34 miles SW of Ayr on the A77

Robert Louis Stevenson visited this attractive little holiday resort in 1876 to see the ruins of Ardstinchar Castle and several years later borrowed its name for his classic novel *The Master of Ballantrae*. The town has a busy little harbour where the River Stinchar flows into the sea. From the harbour, there are boat trips to **Ailsa Craig**, a large rock some 10 miles off-shore which is actually the plug of an extinct volcano. In medieval times, offending monks from Crossraguel Abbey were sent here to contemplate their sins but its only residents nowadays are thousands of gannets, one of the largest colonies in the British Isles.

Occupying a splendid position with superb views over both coast and countryside, **The Royal Hotel** stands off the main road between Girvan and Stranraer. The hotel is owned and run by Rob and Carole Barter who arrived here in October 1997 and quickly acquired a reputation for first class hospitality. The hotel's Poachers Restaurant has earned a "Land o' Burns" recommendation for its excellent food and, if you want something lighter, snacks are available in the bar areas. Visitors will also find a good selection of quality ales. (The restaurant is open daily from Easter to October, weekends only for the rest of the year. Bar

The Royal Hotel, 71 Main Street, Ballantrae, Ayrshire KA26 0NA
Tel: 01465 831555

snacks are always available). The hotel is a popular venue for functions of every kind - wedding, dances, birthday and other celebrations. The Royal also has three comfortable letting rooms - a single and 2 doubles, one of them with shower room, providing a convenient base for exploring this attractive corner of Ayrshire. The pretty seaside village of Ballantrae is nearby where the River Stinchar, well known for its trout and salmon fishing, runs into the sea; there are 3 castles within easy reach; and inland stretch the wide open spaces of the south Ayrshire hills, grand country for walkers.

THE ISLE OF ARRAN

With some justification, Arran is often referred to as "Scotland in Miniature". Twenty miles long and ten miles wide, the island unfolds dramatically from the Highland scenery of the north, capped by **Goat Fell** (2866 feet), to the typically Lowland landscape of farmlands and rolling moors in the south. The island has suffered a turbulent history, having been over-run by the Dalriada Scots who invaded from northern Ireland, then by the Vikings whose links with Arran are still celebrated, and finally by the Scottish Crown. Robert the Bruce stayed here in 1307 before leaving for the mainland to continue his struggle for Scottish independence, a mission he would finally achieve seven years later at the Battle of Bannockburn.

The island is almost entirely owned by the Duke of Hamilton and the National Trust of Scotland. Together they have successfully resisted any inappropriate development, ensuring that Arran is almost completely unspoilt. In addition, the island offers visitors a comprehensive range of recreational possibilities, from a choice of 7 golf courses, to fishing, water-sports, pony-trekking, walking and climbing, as well as medieval castles and a wealth of prehistoric and Iron Age sites.

BRODICK   MAP 1 REF G14
East Coast on the A841

The comings and goings of the ferries which link Brodick to the mainland at Ardrossan provide constant activity in this large village overlooking a broad, sandy bay and backed by granite mountains. Brodick's development as a tourist resort was obstructed for many years by the Dukes of Hamilton who owned the village and much of the surrounding land. Their ancestral home, **Brodick Castle** (National Trust for Scotland), stands to the north of the village crowning a steep bank. The oldest parts date back to the 13th century, with extensions added in 1652 and 1844, the latter in the familiar Scottish baronial style. The interior contains some fine period furniture, notable paintings (by Watteau, Turner and Richardson amongst others), and important collections of silver and porcelain. The castle grounds are particularly attractive. There's a formal walled garden which was first laid out in 1710, and a woodland garden covering some 60 acres, which was established in 1923 by the Duchess of Montrose, daughter of the 12th Duke of Hamilton. The magnificent collection of rhododendrons is widely regarded as one of the finest in Britain. The two gardens form part of **Brodick Country Park** which also includes the mountain of **Goat Fell** (2618 feet): a popular walk is the path leading to its summit where the views are quite staggering. The castle is open daily from Easter to October; the grounds are open daily throughout the year, from 10 a.m. to dusk.

In Brodick itself, the **Arran Heritage Museum** is housed in an 18th century crofter's farm and among its exhibits are a working smithy, an Arran cottage and a wide range of agricultural tools. The museum is open weekdays from Easter to October.

LAMLASH
MAP 1 REF G15

4 miles S of Brodick on the A841

The second largest village on the island after Brodick, Lamlash enjoys an unusually mild climate and its mainly Edwardian architecture bestows a pleasing kind of period charm. The village's curious name is actually a corruption of Eilean Mo-Laise, or St Molaise's Island, and originally the name applied to what is now called **Holy Island**, where the 6th century saint lived in a cave. The island, 2 miles from Lamlash, is currently owned by a group of Scottish Buddhists who have established a meditation centre there, but visitors are welcome to the island and there are regular ferries during the season.

4 Central Scotland

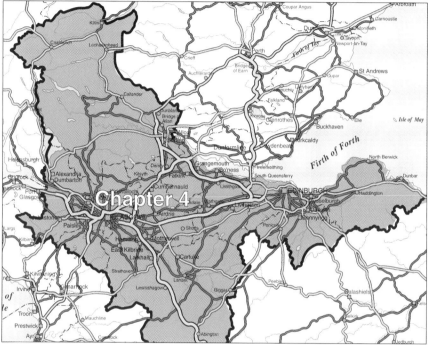

© MAPS IN MINUTES ™ (1998)

Scotland's most populous region by far, the area around the Firths of Forth and Clyde contains the country's largest city, Glasgow; one of its most atmospheric, Stirling; and the cosmopolitan capital, Edinburgh. It was in this region that the 14th century struggle for independence raged, culminating in Robert the Bruce's decisive victory at the Battle of Bannockburn near Stirling in 1327.

The area boasts a wealth of castles, palaces and stately houses. Linlithgow Palace, where Mary, Queen of Scots was born; Stirling Castle, set on a soaring crag high above the central lowlands; and Hopetoun House, a William Adam masterpiece, are just a few of the places that should figure on every visitor's itinerary.

Both Edinburgh and Glasgow offer an incredible range of cultural attractions, with the treasures of Glasgow's Burrell Collection alone sufficient to occupy several days. And the countless events staged during Edinburgh's famed International Festival will satiate even the most voracious culture vulture.

EDINBURGH

One of the world's great cities, Edinburgh is also one of the most attractive. Dramatically sited overlooking the Firth of Forth, like Rome, the city drapes itself across 7 hills. The most prominent of these is **Castle Rock**, a craggy outcrop which has been fortified since Stone Age times.

The present **Castle** dates back to 1230 although there have been many additions and alterations. The oldest part is **St Margaret's Chapel**, an austere Norman place of worship which for 300 years was used as a powder magazine. Its original purpose was recognised in 1845 and the chapel was finally re-consecrated in 1924. The castle is part fortress, part Renaissance palace. In the palace, visitors can see the room in which Mary, Queen of Scots gave birth to James VI (later James I of England), and view the **Honours of Scotland**, the Scottish equivalent of England's Crown Jewels. The dazzling display includes the Crown, Sceptre and Sword of State and, lying rather incongruously in the midst of such splendour, the **Stone of Destiny**, the plain sandstone slab on which 47 kings of Scotland were crowned.

The Castle stands at the western end of the **Royal Mile**, the backbone of the medieval city. In herringbone fashion, narrow wynds and alleys skitter off this main road which is stacked for most of its length with lofty tenements. One of these, the 6-storey **Gladstone's Land** (NTS), is a splendid and authentic example of an early 17th century merchant's house. The Gladestan family occupied part of the tenement and rented out the remainder. If you are looking for a rather unusual holiday location, it's still possible to rent one of the floors.

Allow plenty of time for exploring the Royal Mile. Its places of interest are too numerous to detail here, but not to be missed are the **High Kirk of St Giles** with its magnificent spire, **Outlook Tower** whose *camera obscura* has been delighting visitors ever since it was installed in 1853, **John Knox's House** where the fiery reformer lived for a while, and the **Museum of Childhood** which, paradoxically, was created by a man who hated children. He dedicated his museum to King Herod.

At the eastern end of the Royal Mile stands the **Palace of Holyroodhouse**, most of which was built in the 1660s as a Scottish residence for Charles II who never in fact visited his elegant northern home. Of the medieval palace, only the Tower House remains, ingeniously incorporated into the present building. Here visitors can see Mary, Queen of Scots' private rooms, amongst them the study in which her private secretary, David Rizzio, was murdered. A group of Scottish noblemen, incited by Mary's husband, Lord Darnley, burst into the study, stabbed Rizzio 56 times, and dragged his body through her bedchamber.

Within the Palace grounds stand the romantic ruins of **Holyrood Abbey**, founded by David I in 1238. Most of it was destroyed in 1547 by English troops on the orders of Henry VIII when the Scots refused his demand to hand over the infant Mary, Queen of Scots.

When King David built his Abbey here, it was surrounded by open countryside. Astonishingly, it still is. **Holyrood Park** covers 5 square miles of fields and lochs, moorland and hills, all dominated by **Arthur's Seat**. The crest of an extinct volcano, Arthur's 823 feet are easily scaled and the views from the summit are breathtaking.

By the 1790s the old town, or "Royalty", had become so grossly overcrowded, decayed and dangerously insanitary that a New Town was started on land to the north. With its leafy squares and handsome boulevards, Edinburgh's New Town was an inspired masterpiece of town planning. Stately neo-classical public buildings blend happily with elegant Georgian terraces and the main thoroughfare, Princes Street, was deliberately built up along one side only so as not to obstruct the dramatic view of the Castle, high above. Some 40 years later, the town's planners even managed to make the huge expanse of Waverley railway station almost invisible by tucking it in against the hillside.

A stroll along Princes Street begins at **Register House** (free), a noble neo-classical building designed by Robert Adam in the 1770s to house Scotland's historic documents and records. It still does. A little further west, the 200 feet high **Scott Monument** celebrates the country's greatest novelist with the largest memorial to a writer anywhere in the world. The monument's Gothic details echo the architecture of Scott's beloved Melrose Abbey.

The **Royal Scottish Academy** is a grand Doric building which hosts temporary art exhibitions throughout the year and the annual Academy Exhibition from April to July. The Academy was designed by William Playfair who was also the architect for the nearby **National Gallery of Scotland** (free) which houses a mouth-watering display of masterworks. They range from Hugo van der Goes' lovely mid-15th century altarpiece, the "Trinity Panels", through exquisite Renaissance and 17th century European works, to a comprehensive collection of Scottish paintings. Adding to the charm of this famous street, (also renowned for its shopping opportunities), are the green open spaces of the extensive gardens which border its length. There always seem to be public entertainers here, especially during the last 3 weeks of August when the **Edinburgh Festival** attracts around one million visitors to the city. If you plan to be one of those visitors, book your accommodation well in advance.

As in the old town, the New Town has too many attractions to list in full here. But you certainly shouldn't leave the city before sampling the **Scottish National Portrait Gallery** (free), housed in a curious building modelled on the Doge's Palace in Venice, and the **Georgian House**, restored by the National Trust for Scotland to its late-18th century elegance, complete with furniture of that time and some fine paintings by Ramsay and Raeburn.

Several of the city's most popular attractions are to be found in the suburbs. **Edinburgh Zoo** is Scotland's top wildlife venue, home to some 1500 animals, many of them endangered species, and the world's largest number of penguins in captivity.

Also well worth a foray into the suburbs are the **Royal Observatory Visitor Centre** on Blackford Hill for an informative introduction to the mysteries of the skies, and the **Royal Botanic Gardens** (free), within whose 70 acres of beautifully landscaped grounds you will find the largest collection of Chinese wild plants outside China itself.

Another suburb, **Leith**, was formerly Scotland's major east coast port. Most of that maritime traffic has long since moved elsewhere, but Leith's harbour area has been regenerated in the past few years and is now busy with potential patrons sussing out its stylish cafés, bistros and restaurants. In 1997, against fierce competition, Leith also managed to acquire a prime attraction, the former **royal yacht** *Britannia*. Visitors to the *Britannia* follow an audio-led tour around its 4 main decks which, as you might expect, reveals a distinct difference between the royal apartments and those accorded to the crew.

Finally, and rather unexpectedly, Edinburgh also has a beach, at **Portobello**, once a stylish seaside resort but now somewhat down at heel.

SOUTH QUEENSFERRY   MAP 2 REF K13
7 miles E of Edinburgh off the A90

At times the town lies literally in the shadow of the mighty **Forth Rail Bridge** which passes directly overhead. Completed in 1890, the cantilevered bridge is one of the greatest engineering triumphs of the Victorian age. A mile and a half long and 360 feet high, its construction absorbed more than 50,000 tons of steel. Close by, the **Forth Road Bridge** is a graceful suspension structure whose opening in 1964 put an end to the ferry service which had operated from here for almost a millennium. But there are still regular boat trips from Hawes Pier along the Firth of Forth and to the little island of **Inchcolm** with its lovely ruined Abbey.

About 3 miles east of South Queensferry, **Dalmeny House** has been the home of the Primrose family, Earls of Rosebery, for more than three centuries. The splendid Tudor Gothic house seen today was built in 1815 by the English architect William Wilkins. Along with a hammerbeam roofed hall, vaulted corridors and classical main rooms, the interior also features some excellent family portraits, works by Reynolds, Gainsborough and Lawrence, tapestries, fine 18th century French furniture, porcelain from the Rothschild Mentmore collection and Napoleonic memorabilia. In the grounds, there's a delightful 4-mile walk along the shoreline.

Flanking South Queensferry to the west, **Hopetoun House** lives up to its claim of being "Scotland's Finest Stately Home". Back in the late 1600s, the 1st Earl of Hopetoun built a grand house overlooking the Forth and a mere 20 years later commissioned William Adam to extend it enormously. Adam rose to the challenge magnificently, adding a colossal curved façade and two huge wings. The interior, completed after his death by his two sons, has all the elegance and panache one associates with this gifted family. Their ebullient decor is enhanced by some superb 17th century tapestries, Meissen porcelain, and an outstanding collection of paintings which includes portraits by Gainsborough, Ramsay and Raeburn. The grounds are magnificent too.

LINLITHGOW

Map 2 ref K13

17 miles W of Edinburgh on the A706/A803

The glory of this little town is the partly-ruined **Linlithgow Palace** whose origins go back to the 1200s. The oldest surviving parts date from 1424 when James I began rebuilding after a catastrophic fire and his successors continued to extend the palace over the next two centuries. The palace has many royal associations. Mary, Queen of Scots was born here in 1542 and her father, James V, was married to Mary of Guise in a sumptuous ceremony when the elaborate octagonal Fountain in the inner court flowed with wine. Cromwell made Linlithgow his headquarters for a while and Bonnie Prince Charlie visited during the rebellion of 1745. The cavernous medieval kitchen is still in place, as is the downstairs brewery which must have been a busy place: old records show that an allowance of 24 gallons per day per person was considered just about adequate in the 1500s.

Adjoining the palace, **St Michael's Church** is a splendid medieval building, one of the largest in Scotland. Inside, there is some outstanding woodcarving around the pulpit.

In the town itself, the **Linlithgow Story** tells the story of its royal, industrial and social past and the **Canal Museum** (free) presents the history of the Union Canal which was built in 1822 linking Edinburgh to the Forth-Clyde canal near Falkirk. The museum is located at the Manse Road Basin where you can also board a replica Victorian steam packet for trips along the canal.

Linlithgow's MP, Tam Dalyell, lives a few miles outside the town at the **House of the Binns** (NTS) which has been occupied by the Dalyell family for more than 350 years. It was built in the early 1600s by another Tam Dalyell, one of the band of "hungrie Scottis" who accompanied James VI southwards to his coronation as James I of England. Less than a decade later, Tam returned to Scotland an exceedingly wealthy man.

The outstanding feature of the tall, grey 3-storeyed house he built is the artistry of the ornate plaster ceilings. They were created in 1630 when it was hoped that Charles I would stay at The Binns before his coronation at Holyrood as King of Scotland.

It was Tam's son, General Tam Dalyell, who added the 4 corner turrets, a design feature apparently instigated by the Devil. The fearsome General was reputed to have frequent *"trookings (dealings) wi' the deil"*. During one of these trookings, the Devil threatened to *"blow down your house upon you"*, to which Tam retorted *"I will build me a turret at every corner to pin down the walls"*.

One of the great charms of the House of the Binns is the wealth of family memorabilia which has been amassed over the years and displayed informally around the house. Outside, there are extensive grounds and a folly Tower affording panoramic views over the Forth Valley.

ROSLIN   MAP 2 REF L13
8 miles S of Edinburgh off the A701

This quiet village in the Esk Valley is notable for the unique **Rosslyn Chapel**, a fantastic medley of pinnacles, towers, flying buttresses and gargoyles. The chapel is best known for the number and quality of the stone carvings inside. Amongst allegorical figures such as the Seven Deadly Sins are carvings of plants from the New World which pre-date Columbus' arrival in America by more than a century. They tend to confirm the legend that the daring navigator Prince Henry of Orkney, grandfather of the Prince of Orkney who founded the chapel, did indeed set foot in America. The most famous of the carvings is the **Prentice Pillar** which tradition asserts was crafted by an apprentice. When his master saw the finished work he murdered the lad in a fit of jealousy.

DALKEITH   MAP 3 REF L13
8 miles SE of Edinburgh on the A68

This busy little town has an unusually wide High Street at the eastern end of which are the gates of **Dalkeith Country Park**. This lovely wooded estate surrounds Dalkeith Palace, home of the Dukes of Buccleuch, a fine early-18th century mansion which can only be seen from the outside. Its former chapel, built in 1843 and now the parish **Church of St Mary**, is open however and well worth visiting to see its exceptionally fine furnishings and the only water-powered Hamilton organ in Scotland!

About a mile to the south of Dalkeith, the former Lady Victoria Colliery has been converted into the **Scottish Mining Museum** which offers guided tours by former miners, award-winning "talking tableaux", a visitor centre, tea room and gift shop. Visitors can also marvel at the massive proportions of the largest steam engine in Scotland. It used to power the winding machinery which lowered workers down the mine shaft, 1625 feet deep.

ARNISTON   MAP 3 REF L13
11 miles SE of Edinburgh on the B6372

Standing just outside this small village **Arniston House** is by common consent one of William Adam's finest buildings. It's a noble and dignified house built in a local sandstone that blushes pink in the clear Midlothian sun. The mansion was commissioned by Robert Dundas, Lord President of the Court of Session, and a singularly unprepossessing person *"with small, ferret eyes, round shoulders, and a harsh croaking voice"*. But Dundas was also a fine example of that 18th century ideal - a Man of Taste and Judgement. Building at Arniston began in 1726 but four years later financial problems brought the work to a halt with one third of the house unfinished. More than twenty years passed before a judicious marriage to an heiress allowed it to be resumed by which time both Dundas and William Adam were dead. The building was eventually completed in 1754 by William's son, John.

Most of William Adam's glorious interiors have survived intact along with some excellent period furniture and one of the most appealing features of the house is its comprehensive collection of family portraits, including several by Allan Ramsay.

DIRLETON   Map 3 ref M12
23 miles NE of Edinburgh off the A168

Many visitors consider Dirleton the prettiest village in Scotland. It is certainly a charming sight. Mellow 17th century cottages with red pantiled roofs nestle in well tended gardens, there's a pretty, corbelled church, and the ruins of the 13th century **Dirleton Castle** provide a romantic backdrop to its own herbaceous borders and carefully tended gardens first laid out in the 1500s. An unusual, honeypot-shaped dovecot built with 1,100 nests stands beyond the colourful borders, and the geometric gardens provide a wonderful summer display.

NORTH BERWICK   Map 3 ref M12
26 miles NE of Edinburgh on the A168

For grand views across the town and the Firth of Forth, follow the undemanding path to the top of **North Berwick Law** (612 feet). On top of this prominent hill stands a Watchtower built during the Napoleonic wars and an archway made from the jawbone of a whale which was first set up in the early 1700s.

A few miles offshore rises the towering bulk of the **Bass Rock**, a volcanic outcrop which is now home to millions of seabirds, mostly gannets but with colonies of puffins, fulmars, terns and razorbills. During the season, weather permitting, there are regular boat trips around the rock, but be prepared for the noise. Some 500 years ago the poet William Dunbar described the air near the rock as dark with birds that came *"With shrykking, shrieking, skymming scowlis / And meikle noyis and showtes"*.

North Berwick town, which likes to describe itself as the *"Biarritz of the North"*, is a popular family resort with safe, sandy beaches and a rather genteel atmosphere inherited from the mid-1800s when it was first developed as a holiday destination. Down by the shore stand the ruins of **Old Kirk**, where in 1590 a gathering of witches and wizards negotiated with the Devil (actually the Earl of Bothwell in disguise) to bring about the death of James VI. Despite completing the ceremony by kissing the Devil's bare buttocks, *("as cold as ice and hard as iron")*, the coven's efforts were in vain. Ninety-four witches and 6 wizards were tried and tortured. They were not executed however, James taking the view that their failure, even when in league with the Devil, demonstrated his invincibility.

The only beach front hotel in this popular resort is the **Tantallon Inn,** a sturdy Victorian building of 1860 whose frontage provides stunning views of the ancient Bass Rock with its world-famous gannet colony. Colin and Karen Chalmers bought the hotel in 1994 and have built up an enviable reputation for their freshly prepared and exquisitely cooked local produce. Colin has been a top class chef for some 28 years and has had the honour and experience of

The Tantallon Inn, Marine Parade, North Berwick, East Lothian EH39 4LD
Tel: 01620 892238 Fax: 01620 895313

working with a Culinary Olympics Gold Medal Chef. His outstanding cuisine is served in the attractive wood-panelled restaurant which is candlelit in the evenings. Karen has 19 years experience in hotel management and "front of house" organisation, ensuring that guests receive a warm welcome and courteous, efficient service. The hotel lounge bar, with its open log fire and relaxed atmosphere, provides an inviting resting place at the end of a tiring day and the hotel's 4 guest bedrooms, 3 of them en suite, complete the sense of peace and tranquillity. The Tantallon has an ideal location. Step from the hotel in one direction and you are on the beach, in another on the first tee of the Glen Golf Course. Attractions such as Tantallon and Dirleton Castles, magnificent Gosford House, and the John Muir Country Park are all within easy reach.

The inn takes its name from **Tantallon Castle**, three miles to the east of North Berwick. Spectacularly sited on a sheer-sided crag and surrounded by the sea on three sides, Tantallon was a fortress of the Douglas family for centuries until it was destroyed by General Monck in 1651. Only an imposing 50 feet high tower and a curtain wall 14 feet thick have survived. Together with the dramatic location and the Bass Rock in the background, Tantallon provides a good photo opportunity but otherwise there is little to see within the ruins.

DUNBAR
MAP 3 REF M13

25 miles E of Edinburgh on the A1057

A Royal Burgh since 1370, Dunbar has a broad High Street, a ruined Castle, picturesque harbour, excellent beaches and more sunshine hours to enjoy them than anywhere else in Scotland. One of the oldest buildings in Dunbar is the 16th century **Town House**, once a prison but now housing a small museum of local history and archaeology. Americans especially will be interested in **John Muir House** in the High Street, where the explorer, naturalist and founder of the American conservation movement was born in 1838. His family emigrated to America when John was 11 years old and he was later instrumental in the establishment of the Yosemite National Park, the first in the United States. Appropriately, Dunbar commemorates its most famous son with the **John Muir Country Park**, located on a beautiful stretch of coastline.

EAST LINTON
MAP 3 REF M13

23 miles E of Edinburgh off the A1

This pleasant little town is well known because of **Preston Mill and Phantassie Doo'cot** (NTS, free). Standing picturesquely beside its duck pond, the 18th century Mill has been carefully restored and visitors can watch one of the oldest mechanically intact water-driven meal mills at work. A short walk away, Phantassie Doo'cot, or dovecote, was once home to 500 birds. Just outside the town, **Hailes Castle** is a beautifully sited ruin incorporating a 13th century fortified manor. Mary Stuart was brought here by the Earl of Bothwell, her 3rd husband, on her flight from Borthwick Castle in 1567.

In the old days, East Linton was a regular resting-point for drovers herding their prime Scottish cattle southwards to the markets of northern England. That's how **The Drovers Inn** acquired its name. This sturdy stone-built hostelry still evokes the olde-worlde atmosphere of that long-gone era in its characterful bar and bistro but the excellent food and drink on offer definitely belong to the present day. Michelle and Nicola Findlay tempt their customers with a bar/bistro lunchtime menu which includes at least 8 starters (seafood bisque finished with cream & brandy, for example); main courses such as seasonal game casserole with sweet red cabbage; and desserts to die for. The dinner menu is if anything even more beguiling: a starter of stir-fried tiger prawns with vegeta-

The Drovers Inn, 5 Bridge Street, East Linton, East Lothian EH40 3AG
Tel: 01620 860298

bles and Chinese oyster sauce, say, or a main course of Rabbit Saddle with roasted root vegetables & tarragon gravy. The food is superb, the service charming and courteous, the ambience delightful. Definitely a place to seek out.

About 4 miles northwest of East Linton, the **Museum of Flight** houses a massive collection of aircraft and related items. Displayed in cavernous World War II hangars, the planes on show include a Tigermoth, a Spitfire, a Comet and a Vulcan bomber. The museum is open daily during the season.

HADDINGTON   MAP 3 REF M13
18 miles E of Edinburgh off the A1

Fortunately, the A1 by-passed Haddington as long ago as 1920 and so allowed its picturesque market place, elegant streets and dignified buildings to remain unspoilt. More than 200 buildings in the town centre are listed. The classical **Court House**, designed by William Burn, dominates Court Street and, close by, the **Jane Welsh Carlyle House** was the childhood home of the girl who later married Thomas Carlyle. Only the dining-room and garden are open to the public and both have been preserved much as she would have known them.

Jane's sudden death in 1866 left Carlyle grief-stricken. His touching words mourning the loss of *"the light of his life"* can be seen on a plain slab in the choir of **St Mary's Church**. The largest parish church in Scotland, the "Lamp of Lothian" is also notable for the sumptuous alabaster tombs in the Lauderdale Aisle, for its concerts and art exhibitions of international standard and for providing the unusual amenity of an excellent tea-room.

Also well worth seeking out is **Mitchell's Close**, a picturesque 17th century corner of the town where the houses with their crow-stepped roofs and cramped staircases have recently been restored.

Just around the corner from Mitchell's Close and set in the heart of the old town conservation area, **Hamilton's** is an early-Victorian building offering quality bed & breakfast accommodation. It's owned and run by Vivien and Ian Hamilton who provide a warm and friendly welcome, comfortable lodging and hearty Scottish breakfasts to their visitors. Vivien is an accomplished creator of patchwork items, an interest reflected in the individually designed bedrooms furnished with such pieces as colourful patchwork quilts. There are 3 letting rooms, all on the first floor - a family room and a double, both with hot and cold water, and a single room. All rooms are fully equipped with central heating, colour televi-

**Hamilton's, 28 Market Street, Haddington, East Lothian EH41 3JE
Tel: 01620 822465 Fax: 01620 825613**

sion, clock radio and hospitality tray. Breakfast at Hamilton's is something to look forward to, with a choice that includes home-made preserves and freshly-baked rolls, croissants and butteries. The town's location means that Edinburgh is easily accessible, both by car and regular bus service - especially convenient during the period of the Edinburgh Festival. (Please note that guests at Hamilton's are requested not to smoke).

A mile south of the town, **Lennoxlove House**, home of the Dukes of Hamilton, is an impressive sight with its 14th century tower house and the interior is equally splendid. The Hamilton collection of fine and applied art includes some striking family portraits, French furniture, and porcelain. One of the Maitland family was secretary to Mary Stuart at the time of her execution and it was he who obtained the death mask of the Queen and one of her rings, both of which are on display. Lennoxlove House acquired its name from one of its former owners, the Duchess of Lennox, otherwise known as *La Belle Stewart*. An outstanding beauty, the Duchess was the model for the figure of Britannia on British coinage. On her death in 1672 she bequeathed the house to Lord Blantyre, stipulating that it should be re-named in memory of her love for her husband.

GIFFORD   MAP 3 REF M13
18 miles E of Edinburgh on the B6355/B6369

Set at the foot of the Lammermuir Hills, this pretty village was mostly laid out in the early 1700s when the then Earl of Tweeddale began building a new residence. The settlement of Bothans lay too close to Yester House so Bothans was demolished and its inhabitants resettled at the hamlet of Gifford.

One of the most charming buildings in this picturesque village is the **Tweeddale Arms Hotel**. It's a lovely white-painted, pantiled building overlooking the village green and the 300-year-old avenue of lime trees leading to the

Tweeddale Arms Hotel, High Street, Gifford, East Lothian EH41 4QU
Tel: 01620 810240 Fax: 01620 810488

gates of Yester House, formerly the home of the Marquesses of Tweeddale. The hotel is also probably the oldest building in the village, referred to in a title deed of 1687 as the "Great Inn at Gifford". The Tweeddale Arms is family-run and traditional hospitality here goes side by side with modern facilities. All 16 letting rooms have a bathroom en suite and are comprehensively equipped with colour TV, clock-radio, direct dial telephone, trouser press and tea/coffee-making facilities. Children under 5 sharing their parents' room are accommodated free, a charge is only made for meals taken. The comfortable and restful residents' lounge has a welcoming open log fire and there are two bars where you'll find a wide range of refreshments, including bar lunches. The hotel restaurant offers table d'hôte menus at all times, and an à la carte menu in the evening. And if you enjoy Real Ale, you'll be pleased to know that these are always available and have earned the Tweeddale Arms an entry in the *Good Beer Guide*.

GLASGOW & THE CLYDE VALLEY

"The River Clyde" still conjures up an outdated image of interminable miles of shipbuilding yards and multi-storey warehouses. In fact, for most of its 106 miles the river passes through unspoilt countryside. There's a particularly lovely stretch near Lanark where the river drops 250 feet in 4 miles over a spectacular series of waterfalls, the **Falls of Clyde**.

Glasgow itself vies with Edinburgh for the title of cultural capital of Scotland. Glasgow's claim is greatly strengthened by being the home town of Charles Rennie Mackintosh whose Art Nouveau architecture provides some of the city's most distinctive buildings. It is also home to the stupendous Burrell Collection, a dazzling assemblage of works of art from all around the world.

Amongst the many places of historic interest in the area, two in particular stand out. One is the humble tenement at Blantyre in which David Livingstone spent his childhood years; the other, the fascinating community of **New Lanark** where, in the early 19th century, Robert Owen managed to translate his Utopian ideas of a socialist "village of unity" into practice.

GLASGOW

With its traditional industries of iron, steel and shipbuilding no longer significant, Glasgow has re-invented itself as a vibrant, self-confident city. High points in the process came in 1990 when it enjoyed the year-long title of European City of Culture, and most recently in 1999 with its designation as City of Architecture and Design.

At the time, Glasgow's role as City of Culture provoked amused comment from those who only knew the city as the home of the Gorbals, (the worst slums in Europe), and as the originator of the "Glasgow Hallo", (a head butt). In fact, Glasgow has enjoyed a long history of cultural vitality, most notably during the Art Nouveau period when the architect and interior designer Charles Rennie Mackintosh (1868-1928) brought great prestige to the city.

His career took off in 1896 when he won a competition to design the **Glasgow School of Art**, generally considered one of Mackintosh's most impressive buildings. (Student-led guided tours are available). His most popular creation though was the **Willow Tea Rooms** in Sauchiehall Street for which he also designed the furniture, fixtures and fittings, cutlery and even the menu cards. The original building of 1908 closed in 1930 but half a century later Mackintosh enthusiasts funded a reconstruction faithful in every detail and standing on the original site. Mackintosh was also the architect for the Glasgow Herald building off Argyle Street, the **Queens Cross Church** in the northwest of the city, and **Scotland Street School** which stands near another of Glasgow's premier attractions, **The Burrell Collection** (free).

The shipping magnate Sir William Burrell (1861-1958) was a lifelong collector of works of art and his interests ranged from 4000 year old antiquities such as the splendid Mesopotamian lion's head, through Oriental art to mainstream European painting. Unlike his close contemporary, William Randolph Hearst, Burrell was a discriminating collector, acquiring pieces because he admired them rather in deference to current fashions. In 1943, Burrell offered his fabulous collection to the city stipulating only that it should be housed in a rural setting, away from the then heavily polluted city centre. It wasn't until the 1960s that his conditions could be met only in 1983 that the purpose built gallery was opened. For many, the Burrell Collection is in itself worth a journey to Glasgow.

Art lovers will find it easy to overdose in the City of Culture. In addition to the inexhaustible treasures of the Burrell Collection, there are also outstanding collections at the **Kelvingrove Museum & Art Gallery** (free), a huge Victorian pile containing a wide range of European paintings, and at the **Hunterian Museum & Art Gallery** which majors on Scottish painters and the work of the US-born James McNeill Whistler.

It may seem that Glasgow is just one huge art gallery but there are, of course, many other places of interest. **Glasgow Cathedral** is a splendid Gothic building dating in parts to the 12th century. Here, in a superb medieval tomb, lie the remains of St Mungo, the 6th century evangelist and reputed founder of the city. Adjoining the Cathedral, the **Necropolis** is a wonderfully atmospheric wonderland of funerary extravagances. It was designed in 1833 by John Strong who modelled it on the Père Lachaise cemetery in Paris.

Across from the Cathedral, in Cathedral Square, stands the oldest house in the city, **Provand's Lordship** (free), built around 1470 and originally a clerical residence. The rooms contain furniture of the period and outside there's a fragrant medieval herb garden, a peaceful retreat from the busy city.

Glasgow's visitor attractions are too numerous to detail in full here, but two more must be mentioned. **The People's Palace** (free) opened as a social history museum as long ago as 1898 and, more than a century later, remains as innovative as ever with inventive inter-active displays and lively exhibits evoking the city's colourful story. Also not to be missed is the time capsule of **Tenement House** (NTS). Agnes Toward moved in here with her mother in 1911 and for more than half a century its decor and furnishings remained unchanged. Agnes was something of a magpie so the rooms contain a marvellously random collection of ephemera such as ration books, framed religious mottoes and monochrome holiday snaps.

PAISLEY   Map 2 ref I13
5 miles W of Glasgow on the A761

This famous textile manufacturing town grew up around its 12th century **Abbey** which was destroyed by Edward I in 1307 but rebuilt 7 years later after the Scottish victory at the Battle of Bannockburn. Victorian restorers also gave the Abbey a mauling but the interior with its beautiful stained glass and fine stone-vaulted roof is still impressive.

Victorian builders made a much better job of the **Thomas Coats Memorial Church**, a grand red sandstone masterpiece which is generally considered the finest Baptist church in Europe. The Coats family, local textile magnates, also furnished the town with the **Coats Observatory** (free) where, on winter evenings, visitors can use its ten-inch telescopes to view the night sky.

The colourful Paisley "tear-drop" design is known around the world and one of the displays at the town's **Museum & Art Gallery** follows its development from simple design to the elaborate pattern now so familiar.

DUMBARTON   Map 2 ref H13
14 miles NW of Glasgow off the A82

Dumbarton is an unlovely concrete town but, a mile or so to the southeast, **Dumbarton Castle** stands proudly atop a volcanic plug, guarding the Clyde estuary. For 2000 years this strategic site has been fortified and the present castle's remarkably well-preserved medieval structure provides visitors with superb views across the Firth of Clyde.

A few miles to the north of Dumbarton, the beauty of **Loch Lomond**, the largest expanse of fresh water in Britain, just about manages to survive the busy A82 which runs along its western shore. There are much more peaceful views of the famed loch from the **Balloch Castle Country Park** which is owned and run by Glasgow City Council.

LUSS   Map 2 ref H12
24 miles NW of Glasgow off the A82

This 19th century estate village has a fine beach and enjoys mesmerising views over the loch. The **Loch Lomond Park Centre** offers audio-visual presentations on both the natural and human influences on the area and has a gift shop selling locally-produced crafts.

Occupying a wonderful position on this west bank of Lomond, with panoramic views over the loch and surrounding countryside, **Shantron Farm** offers outstanding bed and breakfast accommodation, while nearby **Shemore Cottage** is ideal for those who prefer self-catering. Both stand within the 5000 acres, mainly devoted to sheep and beef cows, farmed by Anne and Bobby Lennox whose family has lived in the farm since 1750. Visitors are welcome to walk anywhere on the farm, help gather the sheep in, feed the pet lambs, observe the abundant wildlife, or marvel at the spectacular 100 feet deep Gorge where a

Shantron Farm, Luss, Alexandria, Dumbartonshire G83 8RH
Tel/Fax: 01389 850231

Colquhoun leapt to safety while fleeing from the MacGregors after the battle of Glen Fruin. The property also includes the site of an Iron Age Fort and there's a Cup and Ring marked stone from the time of the Druids. The farm and surrounding area of Luss is regularly used for the filming of the TV series High Road, with the back door of Shantron Farmhouse serving as the entrance of Morag's Croft. Bed and breakfast guests stay at Shantron Farm where there are 3 en suite rooms, available from March to November. (During the winter months, these rooms are available on a self-catering basis). Breakfast is served in the spacious living-room with its large picture window looking out across to Loch Lomond. Anne and Bobby do not provide evening meals but there is a variety of eating places within easy reach. They can give you full details along with copious information about the many other attractions in the area. Self-catering guests stay at Shemore Cottage which is available to rent all year round and offers comfortable accommodation for 6 plus a baby. As at Shantron Farm, a barbecue is available, along with garden chairs and furniture for those long summer nights.

THE CLYDE VALLEY

BLANTYRE
MAP 2 REF I13

8 miles SE of Glasgow on the A724

Blantyre is now a suburb of Hamilton but was just a quiet village beside the River Clyde when David Livingstone was born here in 1813. His family lived in a one-room apartment in a tenement block which is now the spruce white-painted **David Livingstone Centre**. Visitors can see the cramped room in which he was brought up; other rooms have displays on the great explorer and missionary's life and work, including of course the legendary meeting with Henry Stanley. Outside, there's a themed garden, African playground and riverside walks.

About a mile north of Blantyre, **Bothwell Castle** is considered by many to be the finest 13th century fortress in Scotland. The mighty ruin stands dramatically on a hill above a loop in the river, its walls 15 feet thick. Built in the 1200s by the Douglas family, the oldest part is the great circular donjon, or keep, 65 feet in diameter and 90 feet tall. Well worth a visit.

HAMILTON
MAP 2 REF J14

9 miles SE of Glasgow on the A724

This former coal mining town is mostly notable for the colossal **Hamilton Mausoleum**, burial place of the Dukes of Hamilton. It was built by the eccentric 10th Duke in the 1850s and cost the huge sum of £150,000. A large portion of this sum was spent on the floor alone, a wheel mosaic containing almost every known variety of marble. The building is famous for its 15-second echo which made using it as a chapel, the original intention, impossible.

Hamilton's other historic building of interest is **Chatelherault**, a former hunting lodge designed by William Adam in 1732, also for the Hamilton family. The lodge is set in the beautiful surroundings of Chatelherault Park (free) where there are some pleasant riverside walks.

GLASSFORD
MAP 2 REF J14

17 miles SE of Glasgow on minor road off the A71 or A723

This small village hidden away in the South Lanarkshire countryside has become something of a magnet for gourmets because one thing you can certainly be assured of at the **Steayban at the Glassford Inn** is fine dining. Its owner and

Steayban at the Glassford Inn, Jackson Street, Glassford, nr Strathaven, South Lanarkshire ML10 6TQ Tel: 01357 521324 Fax: 01357 523400

controller of the kitchen is Steven Sanderson, a fully-trained chef who regularly lectures on the subject of creating culinary masterpieces at nearby Anniesland College. His menus are changing all the time but amongst the starters you may well find a Haggis Gateau - layered haggis, neeps and tatties suffused with a redolent Drambuie sauce. Steven's main dishes are based on prime Scottish produce, presented with an extra flourish: Fillet of Beef, for example, cooked to your taste and accompanied by caramelised onions and Madeira jus. And how about a Delice for dessert - lemon and apple bavarois delice with apple tuille? The Steayban is an attractively designed extension to the Glassford Inn and although it only opened in 1998 already attracts a regular clientele from as far afield as Glasgow, East Kilbride and Hamilton. Clearly, Steven's ambition to provide fine dining in a stylish and relaxed environment has been triumphantly realised. The Steayban is open from Wednesday to Saturday evenings from 17.00 until midnight, also at Sunday lunchtimes form 12:30 to 17:00, and Steven is always happy to cater for any special dietary needs.

STRATHAVEN
MAP 2 REF J14

18 miles SE of Glasgow on the A723

Pronounced "Straiven", this former weaving centre has its own ruined castle and a fine Georgian church of 1777. The **John Hastie Museum** contains displays on local history, handloom weaving, agriculture and the history of the Covenanters. The town's premier amenity is the 300-acre **Calderglen Country Park** which has a boating pond, bowling green, mini-railway, children's playground and many waymarked woodland and riverside walks.

On the outskirts of the town and approached by a tree-lined drive, **The Strathaven Hotel** is one of the most impressive hotels in central Scotland. Designed by the famous architect Robert Adam, it was built as a private residence in 1797 for a Glasgow merchant and is now a Category B listed building with many of its original features still intact. The hotel is privately owned and managed by the Macintyre family, friendly and experienced hosts who provide a warm welcome, first class service, and superb food and accommodation. The guest lounges are comfortable and elegant, and, with the recently completed

The Strathaven Hotel, Hamilton Road, Strathaven, Lanarkshire ML10 6SZ Tel: 01357 521778 Fax: 01357 520789 e-mail: sthotel@globalnet.co.uk. http://www.users.globalnet.co.uk/~sthotel

12-room extension, there are now 22 well-appointed rooms, all with en suite facilities, direct dial telephone, satellite TV, tea/coffee-making facilities, trouser press, hair-dryer, basket of fresh fruit, toiletries and a private mini-bar. (Non-smoking rooms are also available). The award-winning, non-smoking, Avon Restaurant is renowned for its cuisine and serves the finest Scottish and Continental dishes using fresh local produce wherever possible. Consolidating its position as the area's premier hotel, The Strathaven is a popular venue for business meetings, private functions and wedding receptions with a newly refurbished Strathaven Suite capable of accommodating up to 180 people. The Macintyres have a Grand Ball planned for Hogmanay and are also offering a 3-day residential package for the Millennium weekend which should certainly be something to remember.

Conveniently located on the A71 about 5 miles southwest of Strathaven, **Baxter's Country Inn** offers first class bed & breakfast accommodation, an excellent restaurant and a large, well-stocked gift shop which offers a wide range

**Baxter's Country Inn, Darvel Road, by Strathaven, Lanarkshire ML10 6QR
Tel/Fax: 01357 440341**

of gifts, including a selection of stylish Scottish Heritage items. Ideal for a place with plenty of local history. Situated close to the Ayrshire border and surrounded by beautiful countryside, the Inn makes the ideal base for touring, or a relaxing interlude in any journey. There are 10 lodge type bedrooms, all of them en suite and one suitable for disabled guests. The attractive, fully licensed restaurant serves an excellent choice of snacks and hot and cold meals, all prepared with locally sourced fresh produce, throughout the day. Children are well-provided for with an indoor soft play area which has easy access to the outdoor play area where there is plenty of space and excellent play equipment.

CROSSFORD
MAP 2 REF J14

21 miles SE of Glasgow on the A72

Set on the banks of the River Clyde, the Clyde Valley Country Estate offers a variety of visitor attractions, amongst them the **Conservatory Coffee Shop.** Owned and run by Colin Cursiter, with the assistance of a young and very friendly staff, the coffee shop, as you might expect from the name, is indeed located in a light and airy conservatory building. Visitors will find a wide ranging menu on offer, using predominantly quality local produce, with all meals freshly made to order. In addition there is a large selection of deliciously tempting snacks and home baking, to go with the high quality tea and coffee. Also in the Country Estate complex you'll find a garden centre, pony stables, a narrow gauge railway, hat shop and gift shop and an attractive courtyard. Access to the Clyde Valley Country Estate is by way of the B7506, off the A72 or A73. A visit

Conservatory Coffee Shop, Clyde Valley Country Estate, Crossford, Carluke, South Lanarkshire ML8 5NJ Tel: 01555 860203

to the Estate can be combined with an hour or two at nearby Craignethan Castle. Located in a picturesque setting overlooking the River Nethan, the castle was the 16th century home of the Hamilton family and is an outstanding example of military fortification.

LANARK   MAP 2 REF J14
25 miles SE of Glasgow on the A72/A73

Lanark is one of the original 4 Royal Burghs of Scotland created by David I who also built a castle here in the 12th century. It was at Lanark Castle that William Wallace began the war of independence by successfully attacking the English garrison here. Wallace is commemorated by a statue in front of St Nicholas' Church which is itself notable for possessing the world's oldest bell, cast in 1130.

Lanark sits on hills high above the Clyde; in the valley below is the fascinating village of **New Lanark**, a nominated world heritage site. This model village was founded in 1785 by David Dale and Richard Arkwright for their cotton-spinning business. The Palladian-style mills and the workers' houses, by the standards of the time, approached the luxurious. But it was Dale's son-in-law, Robert Owen who had the vision of creating a "village of unity". Fair wages, decent homes, health care, with free education for adults and children, a co-operative shop, and even the world's first day nursery would prove that a happy workforce was a productive workforce.

Visitors can wander through the three huge mills, take a chair-ride through the **Annie McLeod Experience** which re-creates the life and times of a young mill girl in 1820, and see Robert Owen's house with its Georgian-style furnished rooms. The focus of the village in Owen's time was the neo-classical building of 1816 he called The Institute for the Formation of Character, now the Visitor Centre. The high-minded name didn't exclude the provision of a dance hall along with its library, chapel and meeting rooms.

Also within the village, housed in the former dyeworks, **The Scottish Wildlife Trust Visitor Centre** which has copious information about the nearby Falls of Clyde Wildlife Reserve. A lovely riverside walk from the village leads to the famous **Falls of Clyde**, a series of picturesque waterfalls with drops ranging from the 30 feet fall at Bonnington, to Cora Linn's 90 feet descent in three scenic cascades.

BIGGAR   Map 2 ref K14

37 miles SE of Glasgow on the A702

This colourful market town boasts no fewer than six museums featuring a wide diversity of interests. They range from the history of Upper Clydesdale at the **Moat Park Heritage Centre** through the **Greenhill Covenanters' Museum** to the **Biggar Puppet Museum** which puts on large scale puppet shows in its Victorian-style 100-seat theatre. **Gladstone Court Museum** contains a "real" Victorian street complete with bootmaker's, dressmaker's and even a schoolroom, while at the **Biggar Gasworks Museum** in the town's former gasworks visitors can follow the process of extracting gas from coal.

Just outside the town is the but an ben (2-roomed cottage) in which the Scottish poet Hugh MacDiarmid lived with his wife Valda from 1951 until his death in 1978. The cottage has been restored to exactly as it was and is now the base for a writer-in-residence. As the house is very small it can be visited by appointment only.

WALSTON   Map 2 ref K14

14 miles E of Lanark on minor road off the A721 5 miles from Biggar

Staying for bed and breakfast at a farmhouse always seems to have a rather special quality about it and that's certainly true of **Walston Mansion Farm House**. The house is almost 200 years old and stands on the site of the former mansion house some of whose ancient doors have been incorporated into the present building. It's the family home of Margaret Kirby who has been welcoming visitors here since 1989. Margaret serves evening meals by arrangement and these should not be missed since she uses home-grown organic produce wherever possible. And at breakfast you may well find a choice of free-range eggs that includes duck, goose, guinea-fowl and peahen! An interesting feature of the house is the half-turn staircase that leads to the 3 letting rooms, (1 double, 1 twin, 1 family room), 2 of which are en suite. All are immaculately decorated and furnished, and well-equipped with features such as television and video

**Walston Mansion Farm House, Walston, Carnwath, by Biggar,
South Lanarkshire ML11 8NF Tel: 01899 810338 Fax: 01899 810338**

player. An additional romantic touch is the splendid 4-poster bed in the double
room. Downstairs there's a residents' lounge, complete with blazing log fire in
winter, and a separate comfortable dining-room. Walston village is a peaceful
spot, surrounded by open rolling hills and woodland - ideal for a relaxing break

STIRLING, FALKIRK & CLACKMANNANSHIRE

East of Loch Lomond lies the area known as the **Central Lowlands**. It is certainly
central but not all that low-lying. Some 700 years ago, this was the cockpit in
which Scottish folk-heroes such as William Wallace and Robert the Bruce fought
ferociously against the English to establish the independence of their homeland,
an ambition they finally achieved with the decisive defeat of Edward II at the
Battle of Bannockburn, near Stirling, in 1314.

Echoes of that epic struggle still resound. Mel Gibson's 1997 film, *Braveheart,*
displayed the customary Hollywood disregard for historical facts in telling the
story of William Wallace but his well-crafted film brought many Scottish cinema audiences to their feet, applauding, and the film has been credited with
boosting the triumphs of the Scottish Nationalist Party in recent elections.

STIRLING
Map 2 ref J12

28 miles NE of Glasgow on A872

Stirling is one of the most atmospheric of Scottish towns. Its imposing **Castle** (National Trust for Scotland) gives the appearance of growing naturally from the 250 feet high crag on which it stands. Long before the present castle was built, this bottleneck in the only feasible route in ancient times between southern and northern Scotland across the River Forth demanded a military presence. Iron Age warriors established a garrison at Stirling: the Stuart kings of Scotland from James I onwards also recognised the importance of the town's dominating position.

So did the English. During the 13th and 14th centuries, the neighbour nations fought savagely for control of this crucial river-crossing. In a famous victory in 1297, William Wallace recaptured Stirling from the English. Edward I seized it back in 1304, and the aggressive to-and-fro only ended when Robert the Bruce finally routed the English army at the Battle of Bannockburn in 1314. **Bannockburn Field**, to the east of the town and now in the care of the National Trust for Scotland, is dominated by a striking equestrian statue of the Bruce and an audio-visual interpretation of the battle can be seen in the **Heritage Centre**.

Stirling Castle enjoyed its greatest glory during the reigns of the Stuart monarchs. The castle's magnificent, 125 feet long **Great Hall**, one of the finest medieval structures in Scotland, was built by James IV between 1500-1503. James V added the superb **Renaissance Palace** with its exterior of richly carved figures, while James VI had the old chapel demolished and replaced in 1594 by the sumptuously decorated **Chapel Royal.** In the restored **Castle Kitchens** there is a fascinating re-creation of the lavish banquet given by Mary Stuart to celebrate the baptism of her son, James VI, (later James I of England).

The castle also houses the **Regimental Museum of the Argyll & Sutherland Highlanders** which explores the annals of the 200 year old regiment, while outside on the Castle Esplanade, the **Royal Burgh of Stirling Visitor Centre** offers a multi-lingual audio-visual tour through 1000 years of the town's history.

Just outside the castle gates stands the fine medieval **Church of the Holy Rude** where Mary, Queen of Scots and, later, her son James VI were crowned, both of them babies at the time.

A short walk from the castle, **Argyll's Lodging** (Historic Scotland) is a charming 17th century building, once the home of the Marquis of Argyll. A prominent Scottish nobleman, it was Argyll who in 1651 crowned Charles II as King of Scotland 9 years before he was restored to his English throne.

History, wholesome home-baking and great Scottish hospitality all come together at the **Darnley Coffee House**, situated in the heart of Stirling's Old Town. It enjoys a unique setting for a coffee shop - the barrel-vaulted cellars of the 16th century "Darnley's House". According to tradition, these were the cellars of the Town House of Lord Darnley, husband of Mary, Queen of Scots, and

Darnley Coffee House, 18 Broad Street, Stirling FK8 1BS Tel: 01786 474468

the nursery home of their son, James VI. In these atmospheric surroundings the owners, Maureen and Rob Pleace, serve an excellent selection of light meals and wonderful home-made soups. There's always a choice of at least two soups and Maureen and Rob reckon that since they arrived here in 1997 they have produced more than 240 different varieties. Also enormously popular is the array of home baking displayed on the cake trolley along with other home-made treats such as scones and Millionaire's Shortbread. Or you might prefer one of the sumptuous ice cream confections bearing names such as "Bothwell's Surprise" and "Darnley's Revenge". The Coffee Shop is licensed and its full menu is available all day with everything prepared freshly to order and served at your table by friendly staff. With its historic surroundings and first class food, the Darnley Coffee House provides an experience not to be missed.

Before leaving the Old Town, a visit to the forbidding **Old Town Jail** provides a chilling experience with presentations by costumed actors of old-style prison life. Stirling's medieval hangman is on site to explain the mysteries of his craft and the displays include such correctional hardware as the "Crank", a lever which prisoners had to turn pointlessly 14,400 times a day.

To the north of the town, rises the extraordinary, many-turreted **Wallace Monument**, erected in the 1860s during a surge of Scottish nationalism. Commemorating Wallace's victory over the English at the Battle of Stirling Bridge in 1297, the tower stands on top of 360 feet high Abbey Craig and is itself 220 feet high. Inside, the exhibits include what is claimed to be Wallace's own sword, and the **Hall of Heroes** features models of famous Scotsmen ranging from Adam Smith to John Knox.

Another unusual structure can be seen at Dunmore Park, about 8 miles south-east of Stirling. If you enjoy curiosities, you will really relish **The Pineapple** (National Trust for Scotland, free). This extraordinary folly, 37 feet high, was erected in 1761 as a wedding present from the 4th Earl of Dunmore to his new bride. If you fancy spending more time close to the exotic fruit, the attached outhouse, which sleeps 4, can be rented from the Landmark Trust.

DOLLAR   Map 4 ref K12
12 miles E of Stirling on the A91

Just above the town, the spectacular ravine of Dollar Glen is dominated by the imposing bulk of **Castle Campbell**, formerly and still popularly known as Castle Gloom. Visiting the town in the 1920s, the travel writer H.V. Morton was told "that in ancient times, the Castle was called Castle Gloom (from the Gaelic *Gloume*), beside the waters of Griff (or Grief), in the Glen of Care, in the village of Dollar, or Dolour, surely the most miserable addresses on earth". Morton could have added that, for good measure, one of the mountain streams rushing down to the river Devon is called the Burn of Sorrow, completing a clutch of lugubrious names that seem totally inappropriate for such a superbly scenic corner of Clackmannanshire

Hidden away in the lower slopes of the Ochil Hills, **The Strathallan Hotel** is well worth seeking out. It's an attractive old building, architecturally interesting

The Strathallan Hotel, Chapel Place, Dollar FK14 7DW
Tel: 01259 742205 Fax: 01259 743720

with its dormer and double-arched windows, and creeper-clad walls. (One of the windows, on the stairway, contains a dazzling heraldic device in modern stained glass). The owners, Nick Green and Phillip McKinlay, are both accomplished chefs so the food here is reliably excellent. So is the choice of real ales, amongst them Harviestain Ale which is actually brewed in Dollar. The Strathallan's menu changes daily, always offering plenty of choice, and you can enjoy your meal either in the characterful and cosy Bistro, (closed Monday & Tuesday lunchtimes), in the atmospheric bar or, if you're lucky with the weather, on the patio in the beer garden - a real sun trap. The hotel has 3 top of the range guest rooms, all decorated and furnished to a very high standard. One is a lovely double room, the other two form a suite with its own bathroom, ideal for families. The welcoming atmosphere, the outstanding food and the superior accommodation ensure that a visit here will be something to be remembered with pleasure.

MUCKHART

MAP 4 REF K12

17 miles NE of Stirling on the A91

Tucked away in this pleasant little village, **The Inn at Muckhart** looks as pretty as a picture. Long and low, its white-washed walls, black window surrounds and red pantiled roof offer an irresistible invitation to step inside. The interior of this late 18th century building is just as welcoming, as are its hosts, Derek and Lorna Graham who have been here since 1994. The beers they serve are rather special ones. Lorna's father owns the Mansfield Arms at Sauchie where he operates a micro-brewery producing a full range of real ales, named Devon Ales. To accompany your home-brewed drink, the Grahams offer a good selection of food, available every day from noon onwards. Everything is freshly cooked to order and the choice ranges from spicy vegetable pasta bake to Roast Pork or

**The Inn at Muckhart, Muckhart, Clackmannanshire FK14 7JN
Tel: 01259 781324**

Lam dishes. There's a special menu for children and additional dishes are usually available in the evening.

FALKIRK
8 miles SE of Stirling on the A803

MAP 2 REF J13

Around AD 140 the Romans made a doomed attempt to quell the rebellious Picts by building the **Antonine Wall** which ran through Falkirk. They abandoned the enterprise some 20 years later but stretches of the brick and turf construction can be seen in the grounds of **Callendar House** and, 5 miles to the west at Bonnybridge, **Rough Castle** is a well-preserved example of one of the forts established along the wall at 2-mile intervals. Callendar House was the home of the Livingston family, loyal Jacobites, and is notable for its marvellous Georgian kitchens which are complete with steaming cauldrons, a mechanised spit, and a kitchen maid in costume who explains it all. Falkirk boomed during the Industrial Revolution when a network of canals was constructed linking the town to Edinburgh and Glasgow. These provide plenty of scope for walks, boating and canoeing. A major millennium project, currently under way, will eventually restore the old canal routes providing a through route from the North Sea to the Atlantic.

CARRONBRIDGE
6 miles SW of Stirling on the B818

MAP 2 REF J12

The Carronbridge Hotel stands on the B818, once an important drovers' road between Argyll and Falkirk, now a quiet road passing through lovely open coun-

Carronbridge Hotel, Carronbridge, by Denny, Stirling FK6 5JG
Tel: 01324 823459

tryside. The hotel occupies a superb position in this tiny hamlet, its spacious patio enjoying tranquil views across the River Carron and green pastures to the wooded hills beyond. The hotel itself dates back to the early 1600s and since 1991 has been owned and run by Jacqueline Bisset. Open all year round, The Carronbridge has 3 letting rooms, (2 twins, 1 family), all of which are en suite with excellent facilities and enjoying those wonderful views. Children are very welcome and will be fascinated by the resident animals - Jacob's sheep, a Highland cow, chickens, geese, rabbits and a well-stocked aviary. During the summer months, quality meals are available all day from 11.00 until 19.00, (17.00 until 19.00 in winter). For a peaceful, relaxing, away-from-it-all holiday, the Carronbridge is hard to beat.

KIPPEN
MAP 2 REF I12

10 miles W of Stirling off the A822

A delightful village overlooking the fertile Carse of Stirling, Kippen once had its own king. John Buchanan, the local laird in the 1520s, styled himself King of Kippen which seems somewhat foolhardy since the real king, James V, lived just down the road at Stirling Castle. James however was merely amused by the laird's pretensions and on several occasions invited his "royal brother" to dine at the castle.

This pleasing village possesses an equally appealing hostelry, **The Crown Hotel**, a long, white-painted building adjoining the parish church. A traditional village inn, some 200 years old, The Crown has been fully modernised and equipped with all the facilities you would expect. Its owner, Grace Glen, prides

The Crown Hotel, Fore Road, Kippen, Stirling FK8 3DT
Tel: 01786 870216

herself on offering a genuine welcome to customers, first-class service and real value for money. The bar menu, available every day at lunchtime and in the evening, provides a good choice of traditional dishes along with tasty starters such as Baked Brie & Cranberry Dip, vegetarian options and a full children's menu. Smaller portions are always available if required. In the evening, the Huntsman Restaurant is open for à la carte meals from 7.00 until 19.30. The hotel also has 4 attractive guest rooms, (3 doubles and 1 family room), each with tea/coffee-making facilities and colour television. A full Scottish breakfast is served in the Restaurant each morning. In addition, The Crown Hotel's Function Suite can accommodate 80 guests and provides an ideal setting for Weddings, Christenings, Birthday and Anniversary celebrations.

CALLANDER   Map 4 ref I12
17 miles NW of Stirling on the A84

This popular holiday centre has Sir Walter Scott to thank for putting Callander on the map. He first visited the town in 1806 when he rode through the dramatic **Pass of Leny** and gazed entranced at the raging **Falls of Leny**. He travelled westwards to **Loch Katrine** whose mystical beauty inspired his best-selling poem, *The Lady of the Lake*. And Scott absorbed like a blotter the colourful stories of Rob Roy Macgregor, cattle rustler, freebooter and local folk-hero. He romanticised the latter-day Robin Hood in his novel *Rob Roy* (1818), a book which prompted an immediate tourist interest in Rob Roy's home territory, the Trossach Hills. The novelist's championship of the area is reflected in the naming of the vintage steamship, the **SS Sir Walter Scott** which has been navigating the waters of Loch Katrine since 1900 and still sails forth 3 times a day during the season.

Rob Roy's chequered career is explored at the **Rob Roy & Trossachs Visitor Centre** in Callander which poses the question "Rob Roy - hero or villain?", presents a wealth of evidence on either side, and invites visitors to decide for themselves. In the mid-20th century, Callander benefited from the work of another popular author, A.J. Cronin, whose books about a local GP named Dr Finlay cast Callander in the starring role of "Tannochbrae".

Devotees of the popular BBC-TV series *Dr Finlay's Casebook* will immediately recognise **Arden House** as the home of Drs Finlay and Cameron and their housekeeper, Janet. Built in 1872 as a private residence, Arden House is situated in one of the finest positions in Callander, standing peacefully in its own attractive gardens overlooking the village, with marvellous panoramic views of nearby Ben Ledi and the surrounding countryside and hills. There is attractive parkland to one side and woods at the rear. All 6 bedrooms (each named after a cast member of the TV series) have en suite facilities, central heating, colour television, radio, a tea and coffee-making tray, and other thoughtful extras. Two of the bedrooms are on the ground floor, as is the comfortable sitting room. Arden

Arden House, Bracklinn Road, Callander, Perthshire FK17 8EQ
Tel/Fax: 01877 330235

House is open from Easter to November but the owners, Ian Mitchell and William Jackson, regret that the house is not suitable for pets or children under 14 years of age and, for the comfort of all house guests, it is a non-smoking residence.

One can only reach for superlatives in order to describe the manifold attractions of **The Roman Camp Country House Hotel.** The hotel stands on the site of a 1st century Roman camp, the present buildings displaying a wonderful architectural medley which spans almost four centuries and happily incorporates conical towers, dormer windows and a 1930s circular restaurant, the whole

The Roman Camp Country House Hotel, Callander, Perthshire FK17 8BG
Tel: 01877 330003 Fax: 01877 331533

rambling complex harmonised by walls painted an attractive light pink. The house became a hotel in 1939 and fifty years later Eric and Marion Brown found themselves in proud possession of this enchanting property - a wedding present from Eric's parents. "We try to keep the house with a 'Come into our home' feeling, using an abundance of freshly cut flowers from the garden" Marion says. Imagine staying at a gracious country house; taking tea in an elegant drawing-room overlooking the unhurrying River Teith; sampling exquisitely-prepared food in a dining-room hung with tapestries; settling down in a panelled library to enjoy your coffee and a good book beside a real fire; and then retiring to an individually-designed bedroom enjoying peaceful views across the 20 acres of gardens. "We hope that the Roman Camp becomes *your* favourite country retreat" Eric and Marion say, and it's difficult to imagine that, once you have stayed here, anywhere else could displace it from your affections.

MILTON, NR ABERFOYLE
17 miles NW of Stirling off the A821

MAP 4 REF I12

Lovely Loch Ard broadens away to the west and the wooded hills of the Queen Elizabeth Forest Park encircle the tiny village of Milton, one mile outside Aberfoyle. Whoever built **Creag-Ard House** in the 1890s certainly knew how to make the best of this picturesque location. This handsome old house, ("mansion" might be a better description), is now the home of Cara and David Wilson who welcome guests in search of a peaceful and relaxing break, far away in place and spirit from the relentless stress of turn-of-the-century Britain. It's easy

Creag-Ard House, Milton, nr Aberfoyle, Stirling FK8 3TQ
Tel: 01877 382297

to wind down here - whether you are casting a line from Creag-Ard's own fishing preserve; gently exploring the loch in one of the boats available for hire; or settling down in the evening to sample one of Cara's virtuoso preparations of prime Scottish produce. You don't have to take dinner at Creag-Ard since you can stay on either a bed & breakfast, or a dinner, bed & breakfast arrangement but anyone who has once tasted the evening meal here will surely opt for the latter.

KILMAHOG
MAP 4 REF I11

18 miles NW of Stirling on the A84/A821

From Callander, the road to Loch Katrine passes through the village of Kilmahog, on the edge of the Queen Elizabeth Forest Park. At the **Kilmahog Woollen Mill** visitors can watch work in progress in a traditional weaving shed, observe a working waterwheel in action, browse through the mill shop offering a wide selection of knitwear, clan tartans and gifts, or sample the fare on offer in the Coffee Shop.

Just outside the village and occupying a lovely countryside location, **The Lade Inn** is quite outstanding both for its food and its Real Ales. There's always a choice of at least 4 and these include the unusual "Fraoch" Heather Ale, an ancient brew which has been drunk since at least 2000 BC. It's made by boiling the flowering tips of heather with Scottish malts and wild myrtle to extract their flavour and nectar. The hot ale is then poured over a filter bed of heather tips where it picks up its unique aroma - "sweeter far than honey, stronger far

The Lade Inn, Kilmahog, Callander, Perthshire FK17 8HD
Tel: 01877 330152

than wine" wrote Robert Louis Stevenson. The Lade Inn is very much a family-run business, its owners Angela and Paul Roebuck supported by their son Jon and daughter-in-law Helene. Angela and top chef Louis Moir offer customers a choice of two menus, "A Taste of Scotland" and "Wayside Feast". The former includes Scottish specialities such as Roast Perthshire Venison or Tartan Chicken - a supreme of chicken stuffed with haggis, pan fried and served with a whisky and grain mustard sauce. The "Wayside Feast" includes traditional favourites such as home-made Steak Pie along with vegetarian options. In addition there are at least 4 daily main course specials and children have their own selection of meals. The wine list offers a good choice of wines from around the world as well as French house wines available by the glass or half-litre carafe. Food is available every lunchtime and evening, charmingly served by waitresses wearing kilts of the Lindsay Clan. There's a delightful beer garden outside with three fish ponds and wonderful views across to the Menteith Hills.

STRATHYRE

Map 4 ref I11

20 miles NW of Stirling on the A84

The name means "sheltered valley" and the development of **Strathyre Forest** has made the description even more appropriate. Walter Scott wrote apprecia-tively about the area and his enthusiasm is shared by modern visitors who come to this quiet resort close to Loch Lubraig for its lovely scenery and tranquil walks.

The term "peaceful retreat" might well have been coined specifically to de-scribe **Ardoch Lodge,** an early-Victorian Scottish country house set in 12 acres of surpassingly beautiful countryside surrounded by the Queen Elizabeth Country

Ardoch Lodge, Strathyre, Perthshire FK18 8NF
Tel: 01877 384666

Park. Guests can wander across smooth-cropped lawns, through a water meadow, along the banks of the Balvaig River, or explore the tranquil walled garden that slopes towards the river's edge. Ardoch Lodge is the home of Yvonne and John Howes who since 1989 have been welcoming guests here, many of whom return year after year. One can understand why. Whether you stay in the Lodge itself, where each of the 3 bedrooms enjoys outstanding views of the mountains, or in the stylish log cabins nestling amongst woodland, you'll find that Yvonne and John have provided almost every amenity you can think of. You don't have to take the evening meal but you will be missing a real treat if you do not: the best of fresh Scottish fish, seafood and meat, together with local cheeses, combine to make dinner at Ardoch Lodge a memorable experience.

BALQUHIDDER
MAP 4 REF I11

24 miles NW of Stirling on minor road off the A84

About 4 miles northwest of Strathyre is the attractive little village of Balquhidder. Here, in the graveyard of the ruined church, the "Highland Rogue" himself, Rob Roy, is buried alongside his wife and two of his sons. The **Grave of Rob Roy** is marked by a rough-hewn stone on which is carved a sword, a cross and a man with a dog. Despite a sometimes violent career - at one point there was a Government bounty of £1000 on his head - Rob Roy died peacefully in his bed at Balquhidder in 1734 at what was in those days the ripe old age of 65.

The outlaw's story is well told at the Rob Roy Centre in Callander, so the **Bygones Museum & Balquhidder Visitor Centre** concentrates instead on a collection of everyday items and curios from the past, all displayed in a former Laird's mansion which is also home to the **Clan Ferguson Centre**.

LOCHEARNHEAD
MAP 4 REF I11

25 miles NW of Stirling on the A85/A84

Set at the western end of Loch Earn, Lochearnhead is one of Scotland's premier venues for water sports, anything from kayaking to windsurfing. Walkers too are happy here since there's a delightful circular walk (about 12 miles long) around the shore of the loch.

Occupying a glorious position on the banks of Loch Earn, the **Lochearnhead Hotel** brilliantly combines the style of a fine old Scottish manor, visually in accord with its splendid surroundings, along with the provision of modern and efficient amenities. "Tradition we love - but progress we pursue" say Angus and Ollie Cameron who bought the hotel in 1984 and together with Angus' mother, Anne, have made it a popular base for visitors exploring the Rob Roy country. The hotel itself has 12 letting rooms, 8 of them en suite, and guests have the choice of staying either on a bed & breakfast, or a dinner, bed & breakfast basis. For those who prefer a self-catering holiday, there are 8 attractive Danish-design villas and lodges set in the hotel grounds, overlooking the loch. All the hotel

Lochearnhead Hotel, Lochearnhead, Perthshire FK19 8PU
Tel: 01567 830229 Fax: 01567 830364

facilities are at your disposal, including its superb à la carte restaurant and excellent bar food menu. Guests who bring their own boat also have free use of the hotel's private slipway, jetty and moorings. Prime fishing is available locally and no fewer than 8 golf courses lie within a half-hour drive.

From Lochearnhead, the road cuts northwards through **Glen Ogle**, a wild domain with heathery hillsides slashed by lines of rocky cliffs. Queen Victoria dubbed this dramatic landscape "Scotland's Khyber Pass"; nowadays it is known by the less romantic name of "The A84".

KILLIN   MAP 4 REF I10
32 miles NW of Sterling on the A827

At the western end of Loch Tay, the Breadalbane Mountains provide a spectacular backdrop to the picturesque little town of Killin where the River Dochart rushes through its centre, tumbling on its way down the foaming **Falls of Dochart**. Opposite the Falls, the **Breadalbane Folklore Centre** presents the old tales and legends of Breadalbane, (pronounced Bread-_al_-bane), which was one of the country's founding earldoms. Its Gaelic name means "High Country of Scotland".

In the main street of this little town **Breadalbane House** offers excellent bed and breakfast accommodation in comfortable and attractive rooms. It's the home of John and Isabel Carnochan and if you detect a certain Oriental influence in the furniture and decorations that's because they spent some 25 years working in the Far East before settling in Killin late in 1998. There are 5 letting rooms, all en suite and all well-equipped with comfort-making features like double-glazing along with thoughtful little extras such as shampoos. For wheelchair users, there's a ground floor room which overlooks the pleasant garden. Guests have the use of a relaxing residents' lounge with plenty of books and games available.

Breadalbane House, Main Street, Killin, Perthshire FK21 8UT
Tel: 01567 820134 Fax: 01567 820798
e-mail: stay@breadalbane48.freeserve.co.uk

The Carnochans will happily provide evening meals if required, (served in the elegant dining room), and packed lunches are also available. Children are welcome in this strictly non smoking guest house and there's ample parking. This inviting establishment is open from February until November.

MORENISH   MAP 4 REF I10
34 miles NW of Sterling on the A827

A couple of miles northeast of Killin, the village of Morenish sits beside Loch Tay with Perthshire's loftiest mountain, **Ben Lawers,** 3980 feet high, looming over its shoulder. The Visitor Centre here provides copious information about the natural history of the area. From its doorstep, a quite strenuous trail leads to the summit where the dedicated hill-walker will be rewarded with views which, on a clear day, extend from the North Sea to the Atlantic.

Nestling in the shadow of Ben Lawers and commanding magnificent views over Loch Tay, **Morenish Lodge Hotel** enjoys a peaceful setting in approximately four acres of grounds. Originally built around 1750 as a shooting lodge for the Earl of Breadalbane, Morenish Lodge blends comfort and amenity with the inviting character of a Highland hotel. Lorna and Carew Thomas bought the hotel in 1996 after a number of years abroad running luxury yachts in many parts of the world. Carew was the captain and Lorna catered for the guests and they both enjoy bringing the same high standards of service to their visi-

Morenish Lodge Hotel, by Killin, Perthshire FK21 8TX
Tel/Fax: 01567 820258

tors at Morenish Lodge. In the lovely dining-room with its panoramic view across the loch, they offer friendly service and delicious Scottish and international cuisine using, wherever possible, local products such as trout, salmon, venison and prime Scottish beef. The cosy "Laird's Bar" stocks an interesting selection of wines and some of the finest malt whiskies to be had. All rooms at the Morenish Lodge are en suite with the exception of one, which has private facilities. Of the 13 bedrooms, two are on the ground floor, convenient for those who may have trouble with stairs. There is also a 2-bedroom family suite available, ideal for two single persons travelling together.

TYNDRUM   MAP 4 REF H11
41 miles NW of Sterling on the A82/A85

Surrounded by the sky-scraping summits of Beinn Odhar, Ben Lui and Ben Udlaidh, this modestly-sized village has been described as a "fulcrum of Highland communications". In other words, two main roads strike off from the village: the A85 westwards to Oban; the A82 northwestwards to Fort William or southwards to Glasgow. Two railway lines, with two separate stations, also set off in different directions to those same destinations, both of them adored by lovers of Great Railway Journeys. (The two routes have, in fact, been featured in the television series of the same name).

The **West Highlander Restaurant & Pine Trees Leisure Park** is a great place to base all your touring and exploration of such a spectacular area. This scenic site was developed by the owner, Ruaraidh Johnston in 1988 and provides visitors not just with value for money accommodation but also a quality restaurant, and a pleasant country park where there are many beautiful forest and moun-

West Highlander Restaurant & Pine Trees Leisure Park, Tyndrum, Perthshire FK20 8RY Tel: 01838 400243 Fax: 01838 400314

tain walks, including a stretch of the West Highland Way. The park's West Highlander Restaurant, built in warm-coloured pine, offers a large and delicious selection of home-baked dishes and vegetarian meals along with an All Day Highland Breakfast which is guaranteed to satisfy the heartiest of appetites. The restaurant is fully licensed to sell both beers and wines, and is disabled-friendly with ramps leading to the entrance. Next door is a well-stocked craft shop filled with a wide range of quality gifts, ceramics, glassware, books and some attractive hand-carvings. The caravan and camping park is a well-run, clean and tidy site with a children's play area, games room, and a heated indoor swimming pool which includes a sauna and showers. Other on-site facilities include electric hook-ups, water points, wash-up sinks, launderette, chemical disposal, drying room, toilets and free shower facilities. The park has 90 pitches for either caravans or tents and there's also a centrally-heated pine bunkhouse which sleeps 16 in 2-bunk bedrooms, ideal for skiers and walkers alike. Also on site is an all-day shop selling a wide range of groceries, camping equipment, camera films, newspapers, and all those bits and pieces we always forget to pack. And if you're feeling energetic, you can also hire a mountain bike here.

5 Argyll & Bute

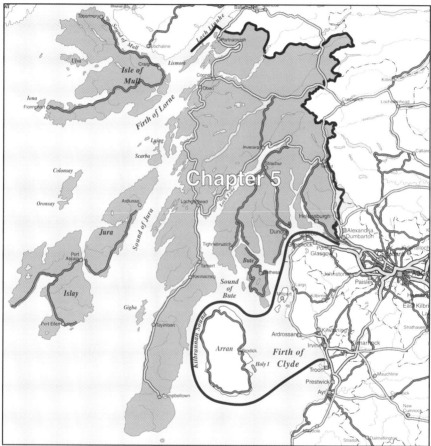

This huge area with a population less than that of the City of York attracts large numbers of visitors in the summer months but apart from a few "honey-pot" centres Argyll is wonderfully empty and peaceful. Oban is the undisputed holiday centre with excellent road and rail communications and a generous choice of regular car and passenger ferries serving the main islands of the Inner Hebrides, as well as seasonal day trips to many of the smaller islands. The town stands at the heart of what was the 5th century Kingdom of Lorn, supposedly founded by the legendary Irish Celt of that name. Lorn later formed part of the great early Kingdom of Dalriada, whose kings were inducted at Dunstaffnage Castle, just north of Oban, on the hallowed "Stone of Destiny", later known as the Stone of Scone.

The area's main attraction, of course, is its magnificent coastal and mountain scenery, but the formidable Duart Castle on the Isle of Mull should be on every visitor's itinerary, the holy island of Iona has a very special mystical charm, and anyone with an interest in Scotland's industrial heritage will want to visit the Bonawe Iron Furnace near Taynuilt. We begin this tour of the area at its western edge, on the Isle of Mull.

THE ISLE OF MULL

For ten months of the year, from September until June, the 3000 residents of Mull virtually have its 370 square miles to themselves - a spectacular landscape of moorland dominated by the massive bulk of **Ben More** (3170 feet), with a west coast gouged by two deep sea-lochs, and an east coast unusually well-wooded for the Hebrides. During July and August, it's quite a different story as visitors flock to this unspoilt island. Its charming "capital", the little port of Tobermory, becomes crowded and the narrow roads congested. But as always in the Highlands, one only has to travel a mile or so from the popular venues to find perfect peace and quiet. Getting away from the pestilent swarms of summer midges may not be quite so easy.

Some 200 years ago, there were more than three times as many permanent residents on the island, but the infamous Highland Clearances of the early 19th century saw a constant stream of the destitute and dispossessed pass through Tobermory, boarding ships which would take them to an uncertain future in the slums of Glasgow or on the distant shores of America, Canada, and Australia. The island is still littered with the ruins of the crofts from which these refugees were driven or, quite often, even smoked out.

Today, Mull is well-served by vehicle and passenger ferries from Oban, either by the 40-minute crossing to Craignure on the southeastern tip of the island, or to Tobermory in the northeast. In this survey of Mull, we begin at Craignure and then travel more or less anti-clockwise around the island, with an excursion from Tobermory to the Ardnamurchan peninsula, finally ending up at the pilgrim destination of Iona.

CRAIGNURE   MAP 8 REF F10
East coast of Mull on A848

As one approaches Craignure on the ferry from Oban, the great fortress on *dubh ard*, the "black height", becomes ever more imposing. **Duart Castle**, with its huge curtain wall 30 feet high and 10 feet thick, was built in the 13th century by the Macleans of Duart to protect them from their inveterate enemies, the

Campbells. A century later, around 1360, they added the massive Keep that still stands today.

Like most of the clans at that time, the Macleans were a pretty blood-thirsty bunch, but the behaviour of one of their early-16th century Chiefs appalled even his contemporaries. Lachlan Maclean had taken as his second wife, Catherine, sister of the powerful Earl of Argyll. When Catherine failed to produce an heir, Lachlan decided to dispose of her. One night, he bound her, took her to a rock in the Sound of Mull that becomes submerged at high water, and abandoned her there. The next day, he informed her brother of Catherine's death by drowning. In fact, she had been rescued by fishermen and taken to the Earl's castle at Inverary. A few days later the grieving Lachlan arrived at the castle with his "late" wife's coffin and was ushered into the Great Hall to find Catherine sitting at the head of the table. Throughout the meal that followed no-one made mention of her amazing resurrection, but later that year, 1523, Catherine's family had their revenge. Lachlan was visiting Edinburgh when he was surprised by her uncle, the Thane of Cawdor, and stabbed to death in his bed.

At low water, the skerry on which Catherine was marooned, now known as **The Lady Rock,** can be clearly seen from the Sea Room at Duart Castle. The splendid vista takes in Lismore lighthouse, the town of Oban and, on a clear day, the lumpy profile of Ben Nevis, some thirty miles distant.

In the Macleans' long connection with the castle there is a huge gap of more than 200 years. In 1691, Duart was sacked by their relentless enemies, the Campbells; after the Battle of Culloden, the Maclean estates were confiscated by the Crown and the castle was allowed to become increasingly dilapidated. Then in 1911, Sir Fitzroy Maclean, 10th Baronet and 26th Chief of the Clan Maclean, was able to buy Duart and begin the daunting work of restoration. To his eternal credit, Sir Fitzroy disdained any fake medieval additions - none of the extraneous castellations and pepper-pot turrets favoured by most Victorian and Edwardian restorers. When he died here at the age of 101 in 1936, he left behind a castle that was faithful in essentials to the uncompromising spirit of his forefathers who had laid its foundations some 700 years earlier.

Craignure village itself offers a number of guest-houses, an inn, and a part-time Tourist Information Centre, but perhaps its most popular attraction is the **Mull and West Highland Railway**, a miniature-gauge line which runs southwards for a couple of miles to **Duart Bay** and **Torosay Castle.** The ancestral home of the Guthrie family, Torosay Castle is an extravagant 19th century mansion, a full-blooded example of the Scottish Baronial style of architecture. The opulent Edwardian interior contains an interesting collection of family portraits by artists such as Sargent and de Laszlo, and wildlife paintings by Landseer, Thorburn and Peter Scott. Even more impressive are the magnificent terraced gardens which include a Japanese garden area and an avenue lined with 19 elegant life-size statues by the 18th century Venetian sculptor, Antonio Bonazza.

TOBERMORY
MAP 8 REF E10

21 miles NW of Craignure on the A848

This picture-postcard little town, (population 700), is set around an amphithea-tre of hills which cradle one of the safest anchorages on Scotland's west coast. Oddly, Tobermory's potential as a port was not recognised until 1786 when the British Society for the Encouragement of Fisheries decided to develop the har-bour and build a quay. Despite the Society's encouragement, the fishing industry never really prospered. (Lacking modern aids, the fishermen were baffled by the arbitrary movements of the herring shoals).

The British Society's development of Tobermory port did, however, leave behind a charming legacy of (now) brightly-painted, elegant Georgian houses ranged along the quayside. Combined with the multi-coloured pleasure craft thronging the harbour, they help to create an atmosphere that is almost Conti-nental: bright, cheerful and relaxed. The town's other attractions include its recently-opened arts centre, **An Tobar**, which stages exhibitions and live events; the tiny **Tobermory Distillery** where visitors are offered a guided tour and a complimentary dram of its famed single malt whisky; and the **Mull Museum** on Main Street where one of the exhibits is devoted to the most dramatic inci-dent ever recorded on the island.

It occurred in 1588 when a galleon of the routed Spanish Armada sought shelter in Tobermory harbour. The Spaniards were received with Highland cour-tesy; their requests for fresh water and victuals amply fulfilled. At some point, though, the people of Tobermory suspected that their guests intended to sail away without paying the bill for these provisions. Donald Maclean of Duart was deputed to go on board the Spanish ship and demand immediate payment. The Spaniards promptly locked him up and set sail towards their homeland. The ingenious Donald somehow managed to release himself, find his way to the ship's magazine, blow it up, and consign himself, the crew and the ship's ru-moured cargo of fabulous amounts of gold bullion to the deep. Ever since then, strenuous efforts have been made to locate this watery Eldorado of Spanish gold. So far, all the divers have been rewarded with is a few salt-pocked cannon and a handful of coins.

During the summer months, a vehicle ferry plies the 35-minute crossing from Tobermory to Kilchoan on the wild Ardnamurchan peninsula, famed for its abundance of birds, animals and wildflowers. (The area can also be reached by road from Fort William). From Kilchoan, with its ruined 13th century Mingary Castle dramatically sited on the cliff top, a five mile drive will bring you to **Ardnamurchan Point**, the most westerly point in mainland Britain, offering some grand views across to the islands of Coll, Mull and Tiree. The unmanned lighthouse here is not normally open to the public but there's a café, gift shop, children's play area and a Visitor Centre dedicated to the theme of lighthouses and lighthouse people. Two of the keepers' cottages have also been converted into self-catering accommodation.

Just a few minutes walk from the busy harbour, **Highland Cottage Hotel** is a charming small hotel of quality located in the quiet elegance of Upper Tobermory's Conservation Area. In the hotel's restaurant, excellent food is served in an attractively informal ambience - top-quality fresh, local ingredients, imaginatively cooked and impeccably presented. The restaurant has been awarded an AA Rosette for the second year running and has now been accepted into the prestigious "Taste of Scotland" scheme for the use of quality local products. After your meal, you can relax with a post-prandial liqueur or a dram of the famed Tobermory single malt whisky, and perhaps settle down with a good book from one of the hundreds on display throughout the hotel. And so to bed. The extremely well-appointed bedrooms all have an "Island" theme and thoughtful extra little touches which should help to ensure a good night's sleep. David and Josephine Currie are the owner/managers of this friendly and welcoming hostelry and will do everything they can to make sure that you return home with very pleasant memories of your stay in Tobermory.

Highland Cottage Hotel, Breadalbane Street, Tobermory, Isle of Mull, Argyll PA75 6PD Tel: 01688 302030 Fax: 01688 302727

DERVAIG   MAP 8 REF E10

6 miles SW of Tobermory on the B8073

From Tobermory, the B8073 to Dervaig follows a tortuously twisting route through dramatic scenery - one of the more demanding stretches of the annual round-the-island **Mull Rally** held in October. Nestling at the head of Loch a'Chumhainn, Dervaig itself is a pretty village of white-washed houses set in pairs along the main road. It's best known perhaps for being the home of the **Mull Little Theatre**. Housed in a former cow byre, this is the smallest professional theatre in Britain with just 43 seats for the audience. Each season, nevertheless, it stages a varied programme of plays, some of which have to be adapted for the small number of resident actors.

An attractive white-painted building, the **Ballachroy Hotel** dates back to 1608 and is believed the oldest continuously inhabited dwelling on the island. It was originally a drovers' inn but nowadays it's an inviting hotel, set in its own

Ballachroy Hotel, Dervaig, Isle of Mull, Argyll PA75 6QW
Tel: 01688 400314

grounds, where visitors receive a warm welcome from the owners David and Karen Gervers who have been here since 1992. Karen does most of the cooking, offering mainly bar food served either in the welcoming bar (an excellent place to retreat if the weather is unkind), or in the Dining Room. The regular menu is supplemented by daily lunch-time specials. Ballachroy has 7 comfortable guest rooms, 4 of them en suite, all pleasantly furnished, with TV and lovely views of the river and Ben Moor, and there's a cosy residents' lounge to relax in during the evening. Dog lovers will be pleased to know that David and Karen have a dog of their own and visitors' dogs are made more than welcome! Located in the centre of the village, the Ballachroy is within easy reach of Dervaig's famous Mull Little Theatre and just a little further away is the well-known Old Byre Heritage Centre.

About a mile south of Dervaig, **The Old Byre Heritage Centre**, housed in a lovely old building of variously-coloured stone, has become an essential stop on any visitor's tour of the island. The Centre explores the history of the island's inhabitants and dwellings, from the first settlers to the present day, with the help of over 25 specially created models. These striking models also feature in a 30-minute film presentation, "The Story of Mull and Iona", with a commentary accompanied by specially composed music played on the Clarsach, or Celtic harp.

Five miles west of Dervaig, still on the B8073, the tiny village of **Calgary** has one of the best sandy beaches on the island and enjoys enchanting views across to Coll and Tiree. Calgary has been known as an ideal holiday spot for generations, and one of its earliest visitors was a certain J.F. McLeod. Later, as a Colonel in Canada's North West Mounted Police, he founded what later became the capital of the province of Alberta and christened the new settlement with the name of this remote Scottish village. Twenty miles further along this road, just after it joins the B8035 at Gruline, another famous founder is commemorated at the **Macquarie Mausoleum** (NTS). This is the burial place of Lachlan Macquarie, the "Father of Australia", who served as Governor of New South Wales for 12 years from 1809 when he was appointed to succeed the highly unpopular William Bligh, former captain of *HMS Bounty*. Macquarie's simple tomb looks across Loch na Keal to the island of Ulva where he was born in 1761.

Travelling southwestwards from the Mausoleum, along the B8035, there is a spectacularly scenic drive as the road runs between the edge of the loch on one side, and mighty **Ben More** (3170 feet), an extinct volcano, rises in terraced slopes on the other. Then, as the road swings south, it passes beneath the formidable, overhanging **Gribun Rocks**. Some years ago, one of them tumbled down the hillside and smashed through the hamlet of Gribun, demolishing one of the houses. The boulder is still there.

After another 8 miles or so, the B8035 joins the A849. Turn right here, and you now enter the **Ross of Mull**, a 20-mile narrow, rocky promontory.

PENNYGHAEL   MAP 8 REF E11
20 miles SW of Craignure on the A849

Situated on the shores of Loch Scridain, a deep inlet on Mull's western coast, **Pennyghael Hotel** (Scottish Tourist Board 3 star and AA 2 star rating) commands magnificent views ranging from Ben More to Iona. On summer evenings, the pleasure of your evening meal in the dining room overlooking the loch may well be made even more memorable by a breathtaking sunset. The food here is all home-cooked, using local produce wherever possible, such as wild salmon, scallops, Mull cheese and venison. The hotel has 6 bedrooms, (4 double, and 2 twins on the ground floor), all with private bathrooms, colour TV, direct-dial telephones, and tea/coffee making facilities. Tony and Sandra Read, who own and run this attractive, white-painted hostelry, also have 3 self-contained holi-

The Pennyghael Hotel, Pennyghael, Isle of Mull, Argyll PA70 6HB
Tel: 01681 704288 Fax: 01681 704205

day cottages to let. Oak Cottage, a detached stone building, has the unusual history of having served first as a barn, then as the village cinema, until being converted to its present use in the 1980s. Clansman Cottage and Pine Cottage are semi-detached stone cottages which have been converted to provide spacious self-catering accommodation for up to 4 people. The Scottish Tourist Board's rating for Pine Cottage is currently awaited: the other two cottages enjoy an STB 4 Crowns Commended award. The hotel and the cottages are open from Easter to the end of October.

A short drive from Pennyghael across the peninsula will bring you to **Carsaig**, a small village noted for its scenic setting, picturesque old stone pier, and the **Carsaig Arches**, dramatic columns of basalt some 750 feet high which have been sculpted by the sea into fantastic caves and arches. Returning to the A849 and continuing southwestwards, we pass the **Angora Rabbit Farm** (seasonal) where children can stroke these appealing floppy-eared creatures, and watch their fur being clipped and then spun. About 7 miles further, the A849 ends at the village of Fionnphort.

FIONNPHORT

MAP 8 REF D11

37 miles SW of Craignure on the A848

Pronounced Finnyfort, Fionnphort is busy during the summer with ferries plying the one-mile crossing to the pilgrim island of Iona, or the 20-mile round trip to the Isle of Staffa to see the celebrated **Fingal's Cave**. In the village itself, the **St Columba Centre** has a small museum telling the story of the saint's life with the help of audio-visual effects and original artefacts. Opened in 1997 to celebrate the 1400th anniversary of his death, the centre is open daily throughout the year. A mile or so south of Fionnphort, there is a superb beach at **Fidden**, looking across to the Isle of Erraid where Robert Louis Stevenson stayed when he was writing *Kidnapped*. (He even had the hero of the book, David Balfour, shipwrecked here).

OBAN

Back on the mainland, the handsome and lively Victorian port of Oban is always busy with boat traffic criss-crossing between the islands of the Inner and Outer Hebrides. Protected by the length of the island of Kerrera, Oban's harbour is the finest on the west coast, with three piers and plenty of room for its still-active fishing fleet, a multitude of holiday craft, and the ever-busy ferries. Tourism is by far Oban's most important industry, but the town does have its own distillery, founded in 1794, and the producer of the famous **Oban West Highland Malt.** Forty-minute tours of the distillery are available during the season. The tours conclude with a free dram and your admission fee is refunded if you buy a bottle of their product.

Another local industry is glass, and **Oban Glass,** part of the Caithness Glass group, also welcomes visitors to watch the process of glass-making from the selection of the raw materials to finished articles such as elegant paperweights. Samples of their products are on sale in the factory shop. On the North Pier, **World in Miniature** displays some 50 minuscule "dolls' house" rooms in a variety of historical styles, including two furnished in the manner of Charles Rennie Mackintosh and, like the others, built to a scale of one-twelfth.

The most striking feature of Oban however is a completely useless building. High on the hillside overlooking the town stands one of Britain's most unforgettable follies, **McCaig's Tower,** erected by John McCaig between 1897 and 1900. On the foundation stone McCaig describes himself as "Art Critic, Philosophical Essayist, and Banker". He was motivated by a wish to provide work for unemployed masons in the area and, while a less romantic man might have built a Town Hall or a school, McCaig decided to build a replica of the Colosseum of Rome which he had admired on a visit there. His enormously costly project was designed from memory and its similarities to the original building are general rather than precise. McCaig had intended that a museum and art gallery would also form part of the complex and that large statues of his family would be stationed around the rim. None of this came to pass. He died in 1902 and his sister Catherine, who inherited his fortune, didn't share her brother's taste for such a grandiose monument. John McCaig's Colosseum remained a dramatically empty granite shell, a wonderful sight when floodlit and adding an oddly Mediterranean aspect to this picturesque town.

What could be more pleasant than settling down to a well-prepared meal in a setting where you can gaze out across a sheltered harbour to distant hills and islands? **The Spinnaker Restaurant** on George Street offers just that, with candlelit dinners (guaranteed), and stunning sunsets (not quite so reliable, but certainly frequent), thrown in for good measure. In the four years or so they have run The Spinnaker, business partners John Stewart and George MacDonald have made this harbourside restaurant first choice in the town for anyone who appreciates good food served in an enchanting setting. George is the chef and his extensive menu is designed to appeal to every palate, offering steaks, fish dishes, vegetarian options and desserts such as Clootie Dumpling made to a famous Argyll recipe. In a stuffier kind of restaurant, John would be known as the maître d': here, he's a friendly presence unobtrusively making sure that your meal is one you will remember for all the right reasons. Their appealing restaurant is decorated with a discreet maritime theme with pride of place given to a superb model of a grand 3-master ship, its spinnaker sail billowing out.

The Spinnaker Restaurant, 28 George Street, Oban, Argyll PH34 5SB Tel: 01631 562225

Overlooking Oban Bay, the **Kings Knoll Hotel** enjoys a magnificent situation standing in its own grounds. It is easily located as the first hotel visitors meet when driving down into Oban on the A85. Standing on "The King's High-

Kings Knoll Hotel, Dunollie Road, Oban, Argyll PA34 5JH
Tel: 01631 562536 Fax: 01631 566101

way", the "Bealach-an-Righ", where the bodies of the ancient kings of Scotland are reputed to have been carried on their way to burial on Iona, The Kings Knoll is only 5 minutes' walk from the town centre. Your hosts at this former Manse are Archie and Margaret MacDonald and from the moment guests arrive at reception they are fully aware of the genuine hospitality that Scotland is so famous for. In the Kings Knoll Restaurant with its maritime theme, a bright airy feel has been created with its high-beamed ceiling and picture windows enjoying delightful views over the town. The cuisine is outstanding, making the best use of fresh, local west coast seafood, venison and Angus steaks, all complemented by a select wine list. All 15 bedrooms at The Kings Knoll are attractively furnished to a high standard, with the majority offering full en suite facilities and one with a splendid 4-poster bed. Guests will also appreciate the elegant King's Rest lounge bar with its wide selection of malt whiskies, the comfortable residents' lounge and the attractive garden and patio.

Oban is set in a natural amphitheatre overlooking the Bay and in this theatre **La Cala** enjoys a particularly good seat! There are breathtaking views across the beautifully maintained gardens to the islands of Lismore, Mull, Kerrera and the Mountains of Morvern. This spacious, luxuriously appointed, 2-storey Georgian-style house is situated on the northern outskirts of the town in a quiet residential area directly opposite Little Ganavan Beach and just over a mile from the town centre. La Cala has been the home of Mairi Jackson and her husband

La Cala, Ganavan Road, Oban, Argyll PA34 5TU
Tel/Fax: 01631 562741

for more than 20 years and they have made the house delightful with polished wooden floors throughout, antique furniture and stylish decoration. They offer both bed & breakfast or self-catering accommodation. The house itself has 3 guest rooms, (1 double, 1 twin, 1 single), all of them tastefully decorated and provided with every luxury for your comfort. For those who prefer self-catering, there's a 2-bedroomed self-contained flat with its own patio looking across to the sandy beach and sea. (Please note that La Cala has a non-smoking policy and that pets are not allowed in the house).

The **Rare Breeds Farm Park,** 2 miles east of Oban, has been a winner of the Scottish Tourist Boards "Tourism Oscar" and is very popular as a family day out. In its 30 acres of attractive countryside, visitors can meet a large number of rare, but mostly indigenous, species of deer, goats, cattle and sheep. There's a children's corner where kids can meet the baby animals at close quarters, a woodland walk, conservation centre, and tea room.

Just to the north of Oban stand the ruins of **Dunollie Castle**, much admired by both Sir Walter Scott and William Wordsworth. It was once the seat of the MacDougalls, Lords of Lorne, who still live nearby at Dunollie House (private), but little remains of the castle now apart from an impressive ivy-covered Keep rising majestically from a crag. **Dunstaffnage Castle** (Historic Scotland), a couple of miles further north, also sits atop a crag, and offers some superb views across the Lynn of Lorne to the island of Lismore. Substantial parts of the castle's 13th century fabric have survived, including walls 66 feet high and 10 feet thick in places, a curtain wall with 3 round towers, a large well surrounded by four small turrets, and a ruined chapel. As mentioned earlier, the castle was the original home of the Stone of Scone.

Over to the east, near Taynuilt, stands **Bonawe Iron Furnace** (Historic Scotland), the well-preserved remains of a charcoal furnace, or "bloomery", for iron smelting. Built in 1753, it was in operation until 1876, "the longest-lived blast furnace in the Scottish Highlands".

PORT APPIN   MAP 8 REF F10
25 miles N of Oban on minor road off the A828

From the A828 north of Oban, a single-track road snakes its way to the shore of Loch Linnhe and the pretty village of Port Appin. Settle down on the patio of **The Pierhouse Hotel & Seafood Restaurant** and savour the breath-taking view that includes the bare, furrowed hills of Sunart across the loch, a candy-striped lighthouse to the north, and Castle Stalker on its small mid-loch island looking eerily like the conning-tower of a submarine. It's a magical setting for an outstanding restaurant which is widely-known for its superb fish cuisine. Fish and crustaceans caught in the loch are kept fresh in its waters until needed and then beautifully prepared and served. Langoustine Thermidor, Smoked Salmon & Prawn Parcels, Seafood Pasta - fish lovers may think they have died and gone to heaven. Once visited, Port Appin is a place you will want to linger in. Fortu-

The Pierhouse Hotel & Seafood Restaurant, Port Appin, Argyll PA38 4DE
Tel: 01631 730302 Fax: 01631 730400

nately, The Pierhouse has 12 comfortable bedrooms, all en suite and many enjoying wonderfully soothing views over the loch. This outstanding hotel/restaurant is owned and run by David and Liz Hamblin, whose 26 years experience as hoteliers is reflected in the high standards of both food and accommodation.

From Port Appin there are regular passenger-only ferries to the **Isle of Lismore**, 12 miles long and never more than two miles wide. (The island can also be reached by car ferry from Oban). In Gaelic *lios mor* means "great garden" and indeed Lismore is one of the most fertile of the Inner Hebrides, albeit virtually treeless. In medieval times, the island was the seat of the Bishops of Argyll whose former cathedral has diminished in status to behind the parish church. With a population of around 150, Lismore is wonderfully peaceful, with gentle walks and cycle routes opening up exhilarating views across to the hills of Morven and the Isle of Mull.

LERAGS   MAP 8 REF F11
2 miles S of Oban off the A816

Lerags is a glen steeped in clan history with the burial ground of the chiefs of the clan MacDougall, the ruins of Kilbride church, and the 16th century **Campbell of Lerags Cross** all within a one mile radius. The Cross, carved in 1526 with a depiction of the Crucifixion, was discovered centuries later lying in three pieces beside the ruined church. The figure of Christ escaped almost undamaged and is still a striking image.

KILMARTIN   MAP 8 REF F12
28 miles S of Oban on the A816

About 27 miles south of Oban, on the A816, **Carnasserie Castle** (Historic Scotland), is an outstanding example of a 16th century fortified house. Although the castle was sacked during the Monmouth rebellion of 1685, enough remains to give a good idea of what the house was like with features such as the huge open fireplace in the kitchen, large enough to roast a whole ox.

Two miles south of the castle, Kilmartin is well-known to archaeologists for the astonishing number of prehistoric chambered cairns, stone circles, burial cists, and rocks inscribed with ritual cup-and-ring signs, all concentrated to the west and south of the village. The most ancient and impressive is the **Nether Lairg South Cairn**, some 5000 years old, where visitors can enter the large chambered tomb with its stone-slabbed roof. A little further south, the two **Stone Circles** at Templewood, excavated as recently as the 1970s, appear to have been the main centre for burials from Neolithic times to the Bronze Age. The various sites are well-signposted, have useful information boards, and are normally open throughout the daylight hours. The village of Kilmartin is itself notable for the early Christian crosses in the church, some medieval grave slabs in the churchyard, and a ruined 16th century tower which was once the home of the rectors.

The Cairn Restaurant stands opposite the museum of Ancient Culture in the heart of this tiny village. The house was built in Victorian times as a Grocers and Drapers and was subsequently converted into a restaurant in 1972 by Ian and Marion Thomson who are now assisted by their daughter Gillian. Over the years The Cairn has become well known for its high standard of cooking, a standard recognised by the AA which has showered the restaurant with a steady stream of Rosettes every year since 1991. Marion is queen of the kitchen and her menu offers a tempting choice of traditional Scottish and European dishes,

The Cairn, Kilmartin, Argyll PA31 8RQ
Tel: 01546 510254

all prepared from fresh local produce and all at affordable prices. Seasonal dishes, including vegetarian, pasta and seafood, are prepared individually and cooked to order, and The Cairn will also cater for special dietary requirements on request. Open every day except Tuesday, the restaurant serves lunch between noon and 15.00, and dinner from 18.30 onwards. The Cairn's reputation is such that bookings are advisable in the evenings, and essential at weekends.

KILMICHAEL GLASSARY
MAP 1 REF F12
32 miles S of Oban on minor road off the A816

About 5 miles south of Kilmartin, there are yet more prehistoric remains, some of the most important in the country. The rocky outcrop of **Dunadd Fort** was the seat of power in western Scotland from around AD 500 - the capital of the Pictish Kingdom of Dalriada. Here, generations of Scottish kings were crowned, one of them, Aidan, by St Columba, and the ceremonies are recorded in some remarkable stone carvings along with an inscription in the ancient Irish language of Ogham. Dunadd thrived for nearly 4 centuries, until 873, when Kenneth McAlpin conquered the Picts and moved his capital to Scone, near Perth.

Kilmichael Glassary takes its name from yet another prehistoric survival, a rock inscribed with the typical cup and ring markings of that period.

TAYVALLICH
MAP 1 REF F12
45 miles S of Oban via the A816/B8025

Considering its glorious position on the shore of Loch Sween it's not surprising that the **Tayvallich Inn's** speciality is fresh seafood - Loch Sween Moules

The Tayvallich Inn, Tayvallich, by Lochgilphead, Argyll PA31 8PL
Tel: 01546 870282 Fax: 01546 870333 e-mail: tayvallich.inn@virgin.net

Marinières or Oysters, for example, locally smoked Salmon with a hint of rum, or pan-fried Sound of Jura Scallops, (just to get your mouth watering). Jilly and Andrew Wilson, and Andrew's sister Alyson, took over this lochside restaurant in early 1999 and have already made it a popular and well recommended place to eat and drink. Andrew is the chef and in addition to the wonderful fish dishes also offers meat, poultry and vegetarian options. Snack lunches are served from noon until 14.00, bar suppers between 18.00 and 20.00, and dinner from 19.00. Booking for the restaurant, especially at weekends and during the main season, is essential. (Please note that the Inn is closed on Mondays in winter). The Tayvallich is an attractive building with clean-cut lines and large windows overlooking the loch so it's incredible to learn that it was actually built 40 years ago as a bus garage, only becoming an Inn some 20 years later.

LOCHGILPHEAD   Map 1 ref F12
37 miles S of Oban on the A82

This little town overlooking Loch Gilp is, rather surprisingly, the administrative centre for the sprawling district of Argyll & Bute. The main visitor attraction is **Kilmory Woodland Park** boasting gardens which were originally laid out in 1770 and during the season delight the eye with a dazzling display of more than 100 varieties of rhododendrons.

TARBERT   Map 1 ref F13
32 miles N of Campbeltown, on the A83

At Tarbert an isthmus, just one mile long, links the Kintyre Peninsula to the mainland. A venerable, but true, story recounts that in 1093 the wily Viking King Magnus Barefoot made a surprise attack on the west coast while the Scottish king, Malcolm Canmore, was away fighting the English. Malcolm was forced to cede the Hebrides, but seeking to keep Magnus off the mainland, he stipulated that the 20-year-old invader might only retain any island he could navigate his ship around. Magnus coveted Kintyre, at that time much more fertile than the Hebridean islands, so he mounted his galley on wooden rollers and "sailed" his ship across the isthmus near Tarbert thus claiming the whole of the peninsula.

More than three centuries later, Robert the Bruce performed an identical manoeuvre while establishing his supremacy over the region. The Bruce was also responsible for building a **Castle** at this strategic point, but today only the ivy-covered ruins of the Keep remain, standing atop a 100 feet mound. This appealing little town, backed by low green hills, was once a busy fishing port but nowadays it is pleasure craft which throng the harbour, particularly during the last week in May when the yacht races in the Rover series take place. They are followed the next week by the powerboat Grand Prix.

GLENBARR

MAP 1 REF E14

24 miles S of Tarbert, on the A83

From Tarbert, the A83 skirts the rugged coastline, providing some excellent views of the islands of Jura and Islay, and if you are lucky, sightings of Atlantic grey seals, Britain's largest wild animals, draped across the offshore rocks. There are no settlements of any size along this route until you come to Glenbarr which has been described as "the most pleasing village of south Kintyre".

Visitors to Scotland are understandably fascinated by the clan system, and at **Glenbarr Abbey** they can enjoy a privileged insight into this unique element of Scottish society, as notable for its ferocious loyalties as for its sometimes barbarous feuds. The family seat of the Macalisters of Glenbarr, Glenbarr Abbey was built in the late 18th century and then greatly enlarged around 1815 with the addition of a striking west wing in the Gothic Revival style. This beautiful house is the home of Angus, 5th Laird of Macalister, and his wife, Jeanne, who personally conduct visitors around its many treasures. Guided by the people who know and love them best, you will be introduced to a veritable wealth of exhibits: antique toys, an original Spode dinner service, a collection of Sevres and Derby china, family jewellery, 19th century fashions, wonderful patchworks, a unique thimble collection, and even a pair of gloves worn by Mary, Queen of Scots. You can also learn about the Macalister Clan's long history, with its origins dating back to the 13th century and to Alasdair Mor, brother of Angus Mor of the Isles. There are still many Macalisters living in this area of Kintyre, but the 5th Laird

Glenbarr Abbey, Glenbarr, by Tarbert, Argyll PA29 6UT
Tel: 01583 421247

is the only major landowner. In 1984, he gifted Glenbarr Abbey and its contents to a charitable trust to create this **Macalister Clan Visitor Centre**, where in addition to exploring the grand old house itself, visitors can also wander through the lovely grounds with its riverside and woodlands walks, browse in the Gift Shop, and enjoy refreshments in its tearoom. (Admission fee on entry).

CAMPBELTOWN   MAP 1 REF F15
38 miles S of Tarbert on the A83

Campbeltown enjoys a very scenic position at the head of a deep bay sheltered by Davaar Island and surrounded by hills. In its 19th century heyday, when Campbeltown boasted a large fishing fleet and a thriving shipbuilding industry, it was said that there were 34 distilleries and almost as many churches in the town. A glance at the skyline here shows that most of the churches seem to have survived, although not necessarily for religious purposes. The former Longrow Church for example is now the **Campbeltown Heritage Centre** and where the altar once stood there's now a beautifully crafted wooden skiff constructed in 1906. There are displays on the area's whisky industry, and exhibits relating to the 6th century St Kieran, the "Apostle of Kintyre". Kieran lived in a nearby cave which can still be visited at low tide. The saint believed in self-abnegation of an extreme kind. His food consisted of three equal parts of bread, herbs and sand; he heaped his body with heavy chains, and slept in the open air with a flat stone for his pillow. One is not surprised to learn that, after sleeping outside during a snowfall, St Kieran died of jaundice at the age of 33.

Of Campbeltown's numerous distilleries which, it was claimed, produced such a powerful aroma that boats could find their way through thick fog to the harbour by following its bouquet, only two remain: Glen Scotia and Springback. They produce a malt which is quite distinctive from those made at nearby Islay or at any other of the Highland and Lowland distilleries. The family-owned **Springback Distillery** has tours by appointment.

The most striking feature of the town is the **Campbeltown Cross** overlooking the harbour.The 15th century cross is carved with highly intricate ornamentation of Biblical figures and Celtic designs.

A popular outing from Campbeltown is to **Davaar Island** which at low tide is linked to the mainland by a mile long causeway. The uninhabited island is used for grazing, (so no dogs are allowed), and its main attraction is a cave in which a wall-painting of the Crucifixion mysteriously appeared in 1887. Years later, in 1934, a local artist, Archibald MacKinnon, admitted that the painting was his work, and in the following year, at the age of 85, he returned to renovate it.

Ten miles south of Campbeltown, **Keil**, just to the west of Southend, is best known as the spot where St Columba first landed in Scotland, in AD 563. It's claimed that two footprints carved into a rock mark his first steps ashore, and that the ruined medieval chapel stands on the site of the one he founded here.

Beyond Keil, a minor road leads to the most southwesterly point of the peninsula, the **Mull of Kintyre**. The road ends a mile short of the lighthouse of 1788 which stands 300 feet above sea level, exposed to the full force of Atlantic gales. It's a bleak, wild spot, but on a clear day worth the trek for the views across to Ireland, just 12 miles away.

INVERARAY

Map 4 ref G11

35 miles SE of Oban on the A819/A83

A striking example of a planned "new town", Inveraray was built in the mid-1700s by the 3rd Duke of Argyll, chief of the powerful Clan Campbell. He demolished the old settlement to build his grand new Castle and rehoused the villagers in the attractive Georgian houses lining Main Street. The Duke also provided them with an elegant neo-classical church, **All Saints**, which was originally divided into two parts: one for services in English, the other for Gaelic speakers. A later addition, erected as a memorial to Campbells who fell in World War I, is the free-standing **Bell Tower**, equipped with ten bells which are reputedly the second heaviest in the world. During the summer season, the tower is open to visitors and there are splendid panoramic views from the top.

One of the most popular attractions in the area is **Inveraray Jail**, yet another of the 3rd Duke's benefactions to the town. The stately Georgian courthouse and the bleak prison cells were last used in the 1930s and have since been converted into an award-winning and imaginative museum where costumed actors re-create the horrors of prison life in the past. Visitors can also seat themselves in the semi-circular courtroom and listen to excerpts from real-life trials that took place here.

A few minutes walk from the Jail stands the grand neo-Gothic **Inveraray Castle,** still the family home of the Duke of Argyll whose ancestor, the 3rd Duke, began building it in 1746. Despite two major fires, in 1877 and 1975, the most important treasures survived and include portraits by Gainsborough, Ramsay and Raeburn, superb furniture, and a mind-boggling array of weaponry which includes the dirk, or traditional Highland dagger, used by Rob Roy. Outside, the grounds are extensive with many pretty walks, some by waterfalls on the River Aray, and the old stables now house the **Combined Operations Museum** which recalls the period leading up to the D-Day landings when some quarter of a million Allied soldiers were trained in amphibious warfare on Loch Fyne.

THE COWAL PENINSULA

Bounded by Loch Long and Loch Fyne, the Cowal Peninsula is like a three-taloned claw with the Isle of Bute clutched in its grip. (The name Cowal is believed to come from an old Norse word meaning a forked piece of land). In this comparatively small area there's a wide variety of scenery, from the extensive forests smothering the Highland peaks of the north, to the low-lying coastline of the southwest. Apart from the area around Dunoon, where two-third's of the peninsula's 16,500 population live, Cowal is sparsely-populated with an abundance of wildlife untroubled by too much human disturbance. The area is particularly popular with bird-watchers. In addition to the prolific variety of indigenous species, including hawks, buzzards and eagles, there are even more exotic birds to be seen at the Cowal Bird Garden, near Dunoon.

CAIRNDOW
Map 4 ref G11

39 miles N of Tarbert on the A83

Standing at the head of Loch Fyne, Cairndow is a small village with a curiously shaped white-washed church. Built in 1816, the church is hexagonal in shape with Gothic-style windows in pairs and a tower crowned by an elaborately carved parapet and four turrets. Just behind the village, **Ardkinglas Woodland Garden** boasts the tallest trees in Britain - conifers more than 200 feet high, and hundreds of other attractive trees and shrubs, including many exotic rhododendrons. Dominating a promontory overlooking Loch Fyne, **Castle Lachlan** was first mentioned in a charter of 1314 and was the ancient home of the MacLachlan of MacLachlan. Today the clan Chief, Madam Maclachlan of Maclachlan, lives in a nearby 18th century castle/mansion and if you are a member of the MacLachlan clan you are welcome to visit by appointment.

REST AND BE THANKFUL
Map 4 ref H12

6 miles SE of Cairndow on the A83

The modern A83 makes easy work of the pass through Glen Coe along which William and Dorothy Wordsworth struggled "doubling and doubling with laborious walk" in 1803. As they reached the summit, 860 feet above sea level, the Wordsworths noted with approval the plaque inscribed "Rest-and-be-thankful", placed here by the army troops when they repaired the old stone road in 1743. The viewpoint provides superb vistas of **Beinn an Lochain** (2,992 feet) to the west, and **Ben Ime** (3,318 feet) to the east.

LOCHGOILHEAD
Map 4 ref H12

10 miles S of Cairndow on the B839

From Rest-and-be-Thankful, the B828 climbs to almost 1,000 feet, drops sharply down into Glen Mor and then passes through the **Argyll Forest Park** before reaching this little town set in a lovely position at the head of Loch Goil. The town is mostly a resort centre offering a wide range of watersport activities, but if you follow the lochside road southwards it will bring you to the ruins of **Carrick Castle**. A classic tower house castle, built around 1400, it was used as a hunting lodge by James IV. A stronghold of the Argylls, the castle was burned by their enemies, the Atholls, in 1685, but the lofty rectangular great hall is still imposing in its solitary setting beside the loch.

From Lochgoilhead, return along the B839 to the A815 near Cairndow. The last four miles of this route traverses the narrow **Hell's Pass**, a lonely, rockstrewn landscape ideal for the footpads and highwaymen who earned the pass its name. At the junction with the A815, look out for the **Wedding Ring**, a group of inset white stones in the shape of a heart marking the spot where the gypsies of Argyll once solemnised their marriages. Southwestwards from this point, the A815 runs alongside Loch Fyne, where seals are a common sight, to Strachur, a straggling village where the road forks. The A886 runs down the western side of the peninsula, the A815 leads to the area's major town, Dunoon, on the east coast. We begin by following the latter which passes through more than 20 miles of the Argyll Forest Park before reaching the village of Kilmun. En route it passes the celebrated **Younger Botanic Gardens** at Benmore. They were established in the late 1800s by the Younger family who bequeathed them to the Royal Botanic Gardens, Edinburgh, in 1928. The 120 acres of gardens contain a staggering collection of shrubs and trees, most notably some 250 species of rhododendron, azaleas, giant Californian redwoods, and more than 200 varieties of conifers, about one third of all those in existence. One of them, a fir tree, now stands at more than 180 feet high, (although there's an even loftier one near Cairndow which exceeds 200 feet).

KILMUN
MAP 1 REF G12
8 miles N of Dunoon on the A880

Kilmun stands on the shore of **Holy Loch** which, according to tradition, was given its name when a ship carrying earth from the Holy Land, destined for the foundations of Glasgow Cathedral, was wrecked here. It was taken for granted that the exotic soil had sanctified the loch, hence its name. The village itself was an important early Christian site, with a chapel founded here around AD 620 by St Mun, a contemporary of St Columba. The present church was built in 1816, but looming behind it is the domed **Mausoleum** of 1794 which contains the earthly remains of all the Earls and Dukes of Argyll since 1442. Amongst them are the Earl Archibald who died at the Battle of Flodden, and the 8th Earl who was beheaded in 1661. In the church's graveyard running up the hillside is the grave of Dr Elizabeth Blackwell (1821-1910), who struck an early blow for Women's Lib by becoming the first woman doctor registered in Britain. Just to the west of the village, the Forestry Commission's **Arboretum** will appeal to anyone who loves trees, and its Information Centre can provide copious details of the many forest walks throughout the Argyll Forest Park.

DUNOON
MAP 1 REF G13
29 miles S of Cairndow on the A818

A popular resort in the 19th century for Glaswegians, (it was, and still is, linked to Clydeside by a regular ferry), Dunoon is by far the largest town in Argyll, with some 13,000 inhabitants. In the years following World War II, the town benefited greatly from the establishment of a US nuclear submarine base on nearby Holy Loch, and later suffered badly from the economic effects of the base's closure in 1992. But Dunoon is once again a lively resort, well-known for the **Cowal Highland Games**, Scotland's largest, which take place on the last Friday and Saturday of August and completely take over the town. Upwards of 150 bands, more than 2000 pipers and drummers, take part in the centrepiece march past, and some 40,000 visitors come to watch the spectacle.

On Castle Hill are some sparse remains of the 12th century **Dunoon Castle**, notorious as the setting for a grisly massacre in 1646 when the Marquis of Argyll had scores of his Lamont prisoners hanged from "a lively, fresh-growing ash tree" and their bodies tossed into a shallow communal grave. The grave was rediscovered in the 19th century during construction of a new road and a memorial now marks the site. Forty years after that massacre, the castle was burnt down and remained derelict until 1822 when James Ewing, Provost of Glasgow, cannibalised its stone to build **Castle House,** a castellated "marine villa" which is currently used as council offices.

At the foot of Castle Hill is an appealing **Statue of Mary Campbell**, the Dunoon-born lass who became one of Robert Burns' many lovers. It was an intense affair and, despite being already married, Burns became engaged to Mary. At that time he was obsessed with the idea of emigrating to the West Indies and poems such as *Will you go to the Indies, my Mary?* make it clear that the poet's

Cowal Bird Garden, Dunoon

then-pregnant wife was not his preferred partner in the enterprise. Mary died at the age of 22, officially of a fever, but there has been persistent speculation that she died giving birth to a stillborn baby. **Dunoon Grammar School** merits a special mention since it is second only to Eton in the number of its former pupils who have become Members of Parliament, amongst them Ken Livingstone, Virginia Bottomley, Brian Wilson and the late leader of the Labour Party, John Smith.

Less than a mile to the north of the town, on the A885, the **Cowal Bird Garden** makes an ideal venue for a family outing. Set in some 10 acres of oak and birch woods, this award-winning attraction is home to a fascinating variety of exotic birds, amongst them macaws and parrots who, if they're feeling like it, may well croak back a "Hello!" in response to yours; brightly-hued budgerigars; kakarikis from Australia, and many other species.

THE ISLE OF BUTE

A short ferry crossing from Colintraive will take you to the Island of Bute, an island which displays something of a split personality. Its sheltered east coast has been a popular holiday venue for Clydesiders since Victorian times; the west coast, however, never more than 5 miles distant, is sparsely populated, its most northerly minor road coming to a halt some 8 miles short of the northern tip of the island. Fortunately, there's no difficulty in getting to the mile-long sands of Ettrick Bay, regarded by many as the most beautiful place on the island.

ROTHESAY   Map 1 ref G13
East coast of Bute on A886

The largest community on Bute is Rothesay, an attractive small town which displays its legacy as a popular Victorian resort for Clydesiders in its tall colour-washed houses, trim public gardens, and pedestrianised esplanade. Long before the paddle-steamers brought 19th century holiday-makers here, Rothesay was a favourite refuge for Scottish kings in need of rest and recuperation. They would lodge at **Rothesay Castle** (Historic Scotland), built in the early 1200s and generally regarded as one of the finest medieval castles in the country. A picturesque moat surrounds the huge circular walls, (unique in Scotland), which in turn enclose the well-preserved Great Hall built by James IV. The Argylls sacked the castle in 1685 but did a less thorough job than usual, leaving much of it intact. Some 200 years later, the castle's hereditary guardians, the Marquesses of Bute, tidied the place up, opened it to the public, and Rothesay Castle has been one of the region's major tourist attractions ever since.

Rothesay has a definite taste for festivals. On the last weekend in August it hosts its own **Highland Games**, when the guest of honour may well be the Duke of Rothesay, a distinguished personage much better-known as heir to the throne, Prince Charles. During the third weekend in July, there's an **International Folk Festival**, and on May Day Bank Holiday the town resounds to the upbeat rhythms of a **Jazz Festival**.

For a comprehensive insight into the island's history, archaeology and natural history, a visit to the **Bute Museum** across from the Castle in Stuart Street, is essential and very rewarding. The museum houses exhibits from every period of Bute's history, from early stone tools to Clyde steamers.

Before you leave the town, do pay a visit to the celebrated **Victorian toilets** on the pier installed by Twyfords in 1899.

6 Perthshire

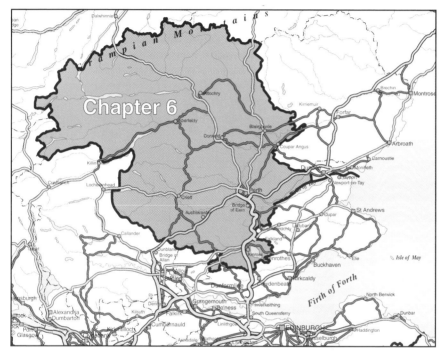

© MAPS IN MINUTES ™ (1998)

"Perthshire forms the fairest portion of the northern kingdom - the most varied and the most beautiful". That was Sir Walter Scott's opinion and few visitors to "Scotland in Miniature" would disagree.

It's an area renowned for the splendour of its noble mountains and romantic lochs. The country's tumultuous past is reflected in historic sites such as Loch Leven Castle, where Mary Stuart made a famous escape, ruined Dunkeld Abbey and Scone Palace where all 42 of Scotland's kings were crowned. Perth itself is one of the stateliest towns in the realm, and the great open spaces make the county ideal for a wealth of outdoor pursuits, shooting, fishing, skiing and, naturally, golf, with a total of 38 courses to choose from.

For lovers of good food, Perthshire represents a lavishly stocked outdoor larder full of prime ingredients - salmon, trout, beef, game and venison.

PERTH

For a hundred years until 1437 the "Fair City of Perth" was Scotland's capital and it still carries an air of distinction. A regular winner of the "Britain in Bloom" competition it has also received the accolade of "Best Quality of Life in Britain".

Beautifully set beside the River Tay, the compact city centre is framed by two extensive parks, the **North Inch** and **South Inch**. The North Inch was the site of a bloody tournament in 1396 which became known as the Battle of the Clans and later provided the background to Scott's novel *The Fair Maid of Perth*. The historical Fair Maid was Catherine Glover who lived in a house in Northport, the oldest dwelling in the city. **The Fair Maid's House** was restored in 1893 but can only be viewed from the outside.

Just around the corner from the Fair Maid's House, the city's imposing **Art Gallery & Museum** has displays on Perth's history and local industries. Prominent amongst these is whisky since 3 major producers all had their origins here - Dewar's, Bells and Famous Grouse. There's more industrial history at **Lower City Mills** where a massive working waterwheel still grinds out one of Scotland's staple foods, oatmeal. (You can also see quality glass being made at **Caithness Glass** on the outskirts of the city).

In the heart of the city stands the striking medieval **St John's Kirk**. It was here, in 1559, that John Knox preached a rabble-rousing sermon that provoked an anti-Catholic riot in which 4 monasteries were razed to the ground, including the historic Abbey at Scone, 2 miles north of the town. It was a defining moment in the movement for Church reform in Scotland. South of St John's, the splendid **Fergusson Gallery** is a must for art lovers. Housed in the former Perth Waterworks (now a Grade A Listed Building), the Gallery boasts the largest single collection of works by Scotland's foremost "Colourist" painter, J. D. Fergusson.

When **Balhousie Castle** was built in the 1400s, it stood well outside the city but now stands rather uncomfortably on the edge of a residential area. The Castle was formerly the home of the Earls of Kinnoull but is now devoted to the **Black Watch Museum**, celebrating the exploits of the historic regiment founded in 1739.

Conveniently located on the edge of the city centre, **The New County Hotel** is an impressive looking building which dates back to the early 1800s. Owen and Sarah Boyle only took over here in early 1999 but they have both been in the hotel and catering business all their lives, mainly in Ireland, so they certainly understand all about hospitality. They have created a newly-refurbished bar and bistro, called Chapters, and also Gavin's Bistro Restaurant. The hotel is open for quality food all day, starting at 7.00 for breakfast (until 9.30), followed by morning coffee, bar menu and lunchtime specials, afternoon teas, high teas, and dinners between 18.00 and 21.00. Children are welcome and there's good access and toilets for the disabled. The hotel has 23 letting rooms, all en suite

The New County Hotel, 26 County Place, Perth PH2 8EE
Tel: 01738 623355 Fax: 01738 628969

and all equipped with double glazing and modern facilities, including one with a gracious 4-poster bed. For families, there are specially designed family rooms accommodating from 3 to 6 people, and the hotel also offers special rates for weekend breaks. With its excellent location, personal service and high standards of cuisine and accommodation, the County is an ideal venue for either an overnight stay or a longer holiday.

The area around Perth has a rich agricultural heritage which is explored with the aid of an audio-visual presentation at the **Perth Mart Visitor Centre**, next door to the Auction Market which sells more pedigree beef cattle than anywhere else in Europe. Children will love the Highland animals in the Mart's Animal Farm, and just outside Perth, they can also marvel at the majestic Clydesdales at the **Fairways Heavy Horse Centre**.

One of Perth's hidden places that is definitely worth seeking out is the delightful **Kinnoull Hill Tearoom**. From the city centre, go across either Queen's Bridge or Perth Bridge and follow the signs for Kinnoull Hill Woodland Walk. From the car park at the top you can see the tearoom, housed in a white-painted former drover's cottage which dates back to 1745 and was once a smugglers' retreat. In this traditional tearoom with its colourful tablecloths and flowers on every table, Allison Armstrong offers her customers a wide selection of home baking and refreshments. Her mum, Lorna, and best friend Alison Rivett do the baking - truly wonderful scones, cakes and sponges. There's a pretty garden

Kinnoull Hill Tearoom, Corsiehill, Perth PH2 7BN
Tel: 01738 638000

where you can enjoy both the delicious food and superb views over Perth to the mountains beyond. The tearoom is also a visitor centre for the Woodland Walk, providing an excellent choice of maps, brochures, books and information for walkers. During the summer, the tearoom is open from 10.00 until 17.00; 11.00 to 16.00 in winter, but is closed on Mondays. Good disabled access.

To the west of Perth, **Huntingtower Castle** (Historic Scotland) was the scene of the Earl of Gowrie's kidnapping of James VI in 1582. The Earl invited the 16-year-old king to his stern-looking 15th century castellated mansion and held him prisoner there for 9 months. The conspirators had planned to coerce him into dismissing his favourites. The plot failed and Gowrie was later beheaded. Today, Huntingtower is notable for its richly painted walls and ceilings.

Two miles north of Perth, **Scone Palace** is one of the most historic sites in the country. Between AD 840 and 1296, all 42 of Scotland's kings were "made", (not "crowned"), on the Stone of Scone. The Stone, also known as the Stone of Destiny, was brought here by the first King of All Scotland, Kenneth McAlpin. Kenneth had acquired the throne by the rather sneaky method of inviting his Pictish enemies to a feast at Scone, waiting until they were helpless with drink, and then massacring the lot of them. An odd feature of the King-making at Scone was that all the nobles in attendance carried some earth from their own lands inside their boots. The mound on which the later Abbey stood was supposedly formed as they emptied their footwear after the ceremony. The Abbey no longer stands. It was one of those destroyed by the Perth mob after John Knox's inflammatory sermon in 1559. Strangely, the rioters spared the Bishop's Palace and this forms the core of the present building. Since 1604, the Palace has been the home of the Murray family, now Earls of Mansfield. It was the 3rd Earl who, in 1802, began enlarging the house in the Gothic style popular at the time, creating what Queen Victoria called *"A fine-looking house of reddish stone"*.

Scone's treasures include a priceless collection of Meissen and Sèvres porcelain accumulated by the 2nd Earl during his assignments as Ambassador to Dresden, Vienna and Paris, along with exquisite sets from Chelsea, Derby and Worcester. With such a huge collection, the Earl was able to ensure that distinguished guests never dined twice off the same service. In the Ambassador's Room stands the magnificent bed presented to the Earl by George III, its rich crimson hangings liberally sprinkled with the royal cypher and coats of arms. Nearby hangs Zoffany's enchanting portrait, *Lady Elizabeth Murray with Dido*. Elizabeth was the 1st Earl's daughter, Dido a black slave girl he had freed. His unprecedented action helped spark off the Anti-Slavery Movement. Other fine paintings in the Palace include major works by Reynolds and Allan Ramsay. The extensive grounds at Scone include a 100-acre Wild Garden, a historic pinetum nearly 200 years old containing the original British Douglas Fir, a Maze, Adventure Playground, picnic park, gift shop and coffee shop.

GUILDTOWN MAP 5 REF K11
5 miles N of Perth on A93

Situated on the edge of the Scone Palace Estate, the **Anglers Inn** provides Scottish hospitality at its best. There's been an inn here since the days of stage coaches, although the present building dates back a mere (!) hundred years. It has a wonderfully warm and friendly atmosphere, largely due to the welcoming

Anglers Inn, Main Road, Guildtown, Perthshire PH2 6BS
Tel/Fax: 01821 640329

personalities of the owners Rhoda and Gordon Brodie who have been here since 1994. They have made The Anglers renowned for its outstanding cuisine - imaginative menus created from the finest Scottish produce and served in an informal, unhurried ambience to the accompaniment of blazing log fires and fine malt whiskies. The Inn's 4 guest rooms (1 double, 3 twins) have been recently refurbished to a high standard and are fully equipped with all the usual amenities as well as providing useful extras such as hairdryers. The Anglers Inn is ideal for a completely relaxing holiday but, if you want to be out and about, the Brodies have produced a useful leaflet listing many activities for both adults and children, all available within a short drive.

If you continue northeastwards from Guildtown along the A93 towards Blairgowrie, look out for the **Meikleour Beech Hedge,** an extraordinary feature which has earned itself an entry in the *Guinness Book of Records*. Planted in 1746, the hedge is now some 750 feet long and more than 90 feet high.

WOODSIDE   MAP 5 REF K10
11 miles NE of Perth on the A94

Just south of the hedge, a minor road leads to the village of Woodside where you'll find the excellent **The Woodside Inn.** During its hundred-year history, the Inn has served as a convalescent home for World War I casualties and as a doctor's surgery before finally finding its proper role as a friendly and relaxing hostelry. Roy and Helen Jacobs bought this attractive white-painted building in 1997 and quickly established a reputation for serving top quality food along with well-kept Real Ales. There are always 3 or 4 Real Ales available and they change frequently so that during the course of a single year patrons of The Woodside Inn will have had the opportunity of sampling up to 150 different

The Woodside Inn, Main Street, Woodside, Perthshire PH13 9NP
Tel: 01828 670254

brews. An interesting feature of the inn's decor is a colourful display of all the beer mats associated with these real ales, smothering the old beams and now spreading across the walls. Before the Jacobs bought the pub, Roy was chef here and his cooking is the other reason why The Woodside Inn is so popular. A glance through the menu explains it all. Haggis and Drambuie Cream amongst the starters, Suprème of Scottish Salmon, Thai Spicy Chicken, and a Mixed Grill "for the hungry only!!!" amongst the main dishes, with a choice of wonderful sweets to follow. It's no surprise to discover that if you plan to eat here over the weekend you would be well-advised to book in advance.

MEIGLE
Map 5 ref L10

19 miles NE of Perth off the A94

Tucked away at the foot of the Sidlaw Hills, the tiny village of Meigle has become a place of pilgrimage for anyone interested in Scotland's distant past. In the little churchyard here were found no fewer than thirty of the most remarkable early Christian and Pictish inscribed stones ever discovered in Scotland. They date from the seventh to the tenth centuries and it remains a mystery why so many of them should have been erected at Meigle. The most impressive of them all is a 7 feet high cross, delicately carved with both Biblical characters and mythological creatures. According to tradition, this graceful memorial ~ red sandstone at its base, merging into grey at the top - is the gravestone of Queen Guinevere, but the meaning of the enigmatic symbols has yet to be deciphered. This striking collection is now housed in the **Meigle Museum**.

When the railway still ran through Meigle, the **Belmont Arms Hotel**, right next to the station, thrived by providing travellers with hospitality. The memory of that railway connection is kept alive inside the inn by its unusual dining

Belmont Arms Hotel, Meigle, Blairgowrie, Perthshire PH12 8TJ
Tel: 01828 640232

room which is modelled on a Pullman railway coach. Lots of vintage photographs and a striking mural depicting a steam train add to the Railway Age atmosphere. This characterful hotel is a family-run business, with owner Sandra Milne ably supported by daughter Emma and son Eric. Sandra is the chef, responsible for the outstanding choice of wonderful home-cooked dishes on offer in the extensive menu of tasty main meals, snacks and delicious home-made desserts. There are special dishes for children and vegetarians, Scottish High Teas are served between 16.30 and 16.30 and a traditional roast lunch on Sundays. Friday night at the Belmont Arms is karaoke night and from time to time Sandra arranges quizzes or live entertainment. This lively inn also offers visitors 4 attractively-decorated letting rooms, all of them en suite, one of them a romantic honeymoon suite.

Just off the A94 to the west of Meigle, **Stripside** is a picture postcard property reached by a long driveway. It's the home of Ray and May Eskdale who have been welcoming bed & breakfast guests here since 1991. Parts of the old farmhouse date back to Georgian times but it has been sympathetically modernised and few residents would suspect that the comfortable lounge was once the carrot shed. Stripside has a 4-star rating from the Scottish Tourist Board, a

Stripside, Meigle, Perthshire, PH12 8QX
Tel: 01828 640388 Mobile: 0780 3691066

high standard which is reflected in the delightful guest bedrooms. The 3 rooms are all en suite, spacious and with top of the range furnishings. The two upstairs rooms enjoy lovely views over extensive gardens which are beautifully laid out and maintained with no fewer than 3 ornamental ponds. Stripside is non-smoking, offers its guests a well-stocked library, and if you are looking for peace and quiet in attractive, comfortable surroundings, this is the right place for you. Meigle's other great attraction of course is the famous Sculptured Stone Museum, housed in the former schoolhouse, which contains Scotland's most important collection of Pictish and Christian inscribed stones. There are thirty of them, all dating from the 7th to the 10th century, and all found in the nearby churchyard. The most impressive stands 7 feet high, a beautifully carved stone which is reputed to be the gravestone of Queen Guinevere.

ERROL   MAP 5 REF L11
11 miles E of Perth on minor road off the A90

This quiet village overlooking the Firth of Tay and enjoying lovely views across to the hills of Fife managed to support a working blacksmith until the mid-1970s. Today his former workshop, **The Old Smiddy**, is a convivial restaurant, invested with great character by the many features of the old blacksmith's shop which have been sympathetically preserved. The forge itself is still in place, along with a huge set of bellows, (its broad circular top conveniently serving as a table), and fascinating memorabilia of the blacksmith's craft is displayed around

**The Old Smiddy, The Cross, Errol, Carse of Gowrie, Perthshire PH2 7QW
Tel: 01821 642888**

the walls and along the ancient beams. This intriguing eating-place is owned and run by Sandy Knight and the extensive menu he offers is just as interesting as the location. How about a starter of Black Pudding Bites with a banana & sherry sauce, a main course of a home-made Smiddy Beef Curry, with a Berry Fruit Brulée to follow? If those aren't quite what you want, there are plenty more choices of good traditional cooking available including vegetarian dishes and children's choices, along with small portions and bar snacks for those with smaller appetites. And to complement your meal, Sandy offers an excellent selection of wines and malt whiskies. Definitely a Hidden Place worth seeking out.

Railway buffs will find an additional attraction in the village. The **Errol Railway Heritage Centre** has taken over the old station and re-created a typical country station of the 1920s, complete with lots of railway memorabilia and a slide show. The centre is only open on Sundays during the season.

RHYND　　　　　　　　　　　　　　　　　　　　　MAP 5 REF K11

4 miles SE of Perth on minor road off the A912

Whether your preference is for bed & breakfast or for self-catering accommodation, **Fingask Farm** provides the perfect answer. Bed & breakfast guests stay in the spacious old farmhouse, the welcoming home of Sandy and Libby Stirrat who also run the surrounding 750-acre farm. Their charming house enjoys lovely views across the River Tay to the hills beyond and in summer you can play croquet on the lawn or just settle down in one of the many seats scattered around the garden. There's a large residents' sitting-room/dining-room, complete with TV/Video and a log fire for cooler evenings. The guest bedrooms, (1

Fingask Farm, Rhynd, nr Perth PH2 8QF
Tel: 01738 812220 Fax: 01738 813325

twin with private bathroom, a double and a single with shared bathroom), are all well-appointed with thoughtful extras such as electric blankets also provided. Self-catering accommodation is available in two former farm cottages. They are fully furnished to a high standard and sit on an elevated position on a grass bank above the farm. Rowanbank is the larger, sleeping up to 4 adults plus 2 children in 2 bedrooms, while Oatmeal cottage is ideal for 2 people. Evening meals in the farmhouse are available if you wish and the farm is easily accessible from the M90.

KINROSS   Map 5 ref K12
15 miles S of Perth off the M90 (Exit 6)

Once the capital of one of Scotland's smallest counties, Kinross-shire, the town grew up beside Loch Leven, now a National Nature Reserve and the most important freshwater lake in Britain for migratory and breeding waterfowl.

Overlooking the loch is **Kinross House**, a fine late-17th century mansion whose enchanting gardens are open to the public during the summer. From the nearby pier, a 5-minute ferry trip takes visitors to the island on which stand the ruins of **Loch Leven Castle**. Mary Stuart was imprisoned here for 11 months in 1567-8 but managed to escape with the sole help of an 18 year old lad, William Douglas. He stole the castle keys, arranged a boat and, as they rowed away threw the keys into the loch. Three centuries later, a bunch of keys was recovered from the loch floor near the castle.

ABERNETHY   Map 5 ref K11
10 miles SE of Perth on the A913

Once an important Pictish centre, this little village is now best-known for its 12th century Irish-style Round Tower, one of only two such towers in Scotland. The tower was part of a Saxon church where, according to tradition, Malcolm Canmore swore fealty to William the Conqueror.

AUCHTERARDER   Map 4 ref K11
12 miles SW of Perth via the A9/A824

"A city set on a hill cannot be hid" says the promotional brochure for Auchterarder, and although it's an 800 year old Royal Burgh rather than a city, the town certainly enjoys an elevated position with the stunning scenery of the Grampian Mountains as a backdrop. Auchterarder is known locally as The Lang Toon because of its lengthy High Street. Here you will find the **Star Hotel**, a striking black and white painted building with a history going back some 600 years. A coaching and post inn in centuries past, the Star is now a friendly old-style hostelry offering good food and traditional Scottish ales, comfortable accommodation and a great atmosphere. The Star has been owned by Lloyd Young's family since 1977; he and his wife Julie took it over in 1994 and have continued to build on its popularity. Both of them are keen golfers and are happy to arrange a round for their visitors at any one of the 30(!) courses that lie

The Star Hotel, 113 High Street, Auchterarder, Perthshire PH3 1AA
Tel: 01764 662782 Fax: 01764 662407

within 22 miles of the hotel. They can also offer you a choice of 8 letting rooms. Three of them are in the hotel itself, the other 5 are in another ancient property just a couple of doors away. Evening meals are available on request and at weekends both the Bar Lounge and Public Bar stay open until 23.45 allowing plenty of time to savour a couple of choice malts after your dinner!

GLENEAGLES   MAP 4 REF J11
16 miles SW of Perth off the A9/A823

In Perthshire, golf is a way of life with almost every town and village seeming to have its own golf links. Some of the best known are the 4 picturesque courses at Gleneagles, although these are reserved for club members and hotel residents only. Elsewhere, visitors are welcome and are often pleasantly surprised by the modest green fees and the fact that, even in summer, most courses are quiet.

Close to Gleneagles course and set in 27 acres of magnificent grounds with scenic views in every direction, the **Duchally House Hotel** dates back to July 28th 1838. Exactly. The date is known so precisely because during alterations at the house a sealed bottle was found under the foundations of the porch. It contained a written statement by the Laird, Alexander Monteath, a brief history of his family, a silver medallion recording the accession of Queen Victoria, and

**Duchally House Hotel, Gleneagles, Auchterarder, Perthshire PH3 1PN
Tel: 01764 663071 Fax: 01764 662464**

"various coinage". The striking old house with its curious octagonal tower is now owned by Club la Costa but that curious collection of items still lies buried beneath the porch. Duchally House cossets visitors with the ultimate in both comfort and relaxation. The elegantly appointed main restaurant offers a superb range of top quality cuisine created by experienced Head Chef Tony McGraw and there's also an informal bistro. A visit to the tastefully decorated Lounge Bar is ideal for either a convivial pre-dinner drink or a relaxing evening spent beside one of the Duchally's traditional open fires. A special feature of the Duchally House is its Billiard Room, complete with full sized snooker table and the original wood panelling. With its recently refurbished en suite bedrooms and splendid sporting facilities literally on the doorstep, the Duchally House provides the perfect location for short holiday breaks, private functions, small business conferences and courses alike.

BRACO   Map 4 ref J11
21 miles SW of Perth on the A822

Just outside the quiet village of Braco, **Perthshire Falconry Services** offers visitors the opportunity to handle and fly a selection of the most spectacular hawks, owls, falcons and eagles in the world. Sessions range from 1-hour tutorials in basic training to 5-hour safaris in the Perthshire hills pursuing game with your own trained bird.

In the village itself, the **Braco Hotel** is the place to visit for genuine Scottish hospitality. Ken and Doris Coates, are "mine hosts" at this welcoming inn which dates back more than 150 years and was formerly a coaching inn. Ken and Doris only bought the hotel in 1998 but they have placed it firmly on the map for

Braco Hotel, Front Street, Braco, Perthshire FK15 9QN
Tel: 01786 880203 Fax: 01786 880666

anyone who enjoys good food and drink in friendly surroundings. Quality food is available at lunchtimes and evenings with a wide choice of meals from either the regular menu or the daily specials listed on the board. For those planning to stay in the area, the Braco Hotel has 7 letting rooms available all year round, some of which will be fully en suite by the time you read this. Braco is a pleasant little village set beside Knaik Water. In Roman times there was a major garrison of some 40,000 troops quartered here and the well-preserved remains of their great fort are some of the largest in Britain. In the 1920s a hoard of coins from the time of the Emperor Hadrian were discovered in the camp site.

CRIEFF   MAP 4 REF J11
17 miles W of Perth on the A85

It's hard to imagine that the now-peaceful town of Crieff was once the scene of sackings and burnings. Twice in the 18th century this hillside town was attacked and virtually destroyed by rampaging Highlanders, and there are grim tales of dark deeds linked to nearby Drummond Castle.

Clinging to a hillside above the River Earn, Crieff today is a mellow town, with peaceful flower-filled gardens and parks, and streets winding up the steep hill. Once, drovers brought their cattle down from the Highlands to the great market here, and more than 200 years ago, the foundations of a great Scottish tradition were laid when a distillery was established on the banks of the river

Turret. Founded in 1775, **Glenturret** is the oldest whisky distillery in Scotland: it still produces award-winning malt whisky which visitors can sample, free, at their Visitor Centre.

Just a couple of minutes walk from the town centre, **Keppoch House Hotel** is a spacious and attractive Victorian mansion, built in 1877 as a private residence for a local draper. He named it Keppoch after a nearby hamlet which was then a local centre for weavers. Today, this welcoming hotel is well-known locally for the quality of its food, available every lunchtime and evening. The chef's menu changes at least once a week but you'll always find a good choice of tasty and imaginative dishes: Grilled Avocado & Prawns sprinkled with blue cheese and port as a starter, perhaps, a main course of Baked Angel Haddock

Keppoch House Hotel, Perth Road, Crieff, Perthshire PH7 3EQ
Tel: 01764 654341 Fax: 01764 655435

with white wine and rosemary butter, followed by one of the chef's wonderful home-made desserts. Bob and May Brown, who became owners of the hotel in 1989, have been in the hotel business for many years and certainly know to how to make their guests feel at home. They have 5 letting rooms, all of them en suite and well-equipped. The rooms are available on either a bed & breakfast, or dinner, bed & breakfast basis.

Crieff still retains the gracious atmosphere of its days as a spa town, although no-one comes here nowadays to drink the pungent water. There are far more pleasant beverages available at **Heather's Koffee Shoppe** in King Street. Here, Heather Ivey serves a good fresh pot of tea or coffee along with her excellent cooking. Delicious scones are made daily on the premises and Heather's home-

Heather's Koffee Shoppe, 46 King Street, Crieff, Perthshire PH7 3AX
Tel: 01764 652044

made cakes are something to remember. The menu also includes soups, toasties, rolls, sandwiches, along with hearty full breakfasts and main dishes which range from quiches to salads. Home-made daily specials add to the choice. After many years in the catering business, Heather took over here in 1995 and now has a devoted following of regulars who appreciate the wholesome fare on offer and the warm and friendly atmosphere. Children are welcome, there's a no-smoking area, and Heather's Koffee Shoppe is open from 8.30 until 16.00, Monday to Saturday.

Located on the edge of the town, **Stuart Crystal** offers an unusual combination of attractions. Visitors can view the skills involved in the decoration of fine crystal glass, browse in the factory shop, and also watch a free display of trained owls and falcons swooping dramatically in response to the falconer's commands.

A couple of miles south of Crieff, **Drummond Castle Gardens** truthfully claims to be one of the finest formal gardens in Europe. First laid out in the early 1600s, the gardens visitors see today were replanted in the 1950s, preserving features such as the ancient yew hedges and the copper beech trees planted by Queen Victoria to commemorate her visit in 1842. In the centre of the magnificent Victorian parterre stands John Mylne's famous multiple sundial, dating from 1630. As a backdrop to these superb gardens, rise the towers and turrets of Drummond Castle, home of the Earls of Perth and not open to the public.

AMULREE   Map 4 ref J10
28 miles NW of Perth on the A822

From this small village at the foot of **Craig Hulich** (1650 feet), you can strike off along no fewer than 5 different roads winding their way through the magnificent Perthshire countryside. To the south lies Glen Almond, to the north Strath Braan and Glen Cochill, while to the west, two minor roads run along opposite banks of Loch Freuchie.

Before you set off though you should call in at Peter and Carol Parker's **Amulree Tearoom** for a refreshing pot of tea or coffee and a taste of the heavenly home cooking and baking on offer. There's always a good choice of truly delicious home-made cakes and scones as well as an extensive selection of snacks, filled rolls, main meals, and daily home-made specials. The Parkers ensure that the choice includes at least 4 vegetarian dishes and there are also special meals for children. In good weather, you can enjoy your refreshments in the pleasant

Amulree Tea Room, Amulree, Dunkeld, Perthshire PH8 0BZ
Tel: 01350 725200

garden looking across to Craig Hulich. (Ideal for smokers, too, since the tea room itself is non-smoking). The Amulree Tearoom serves as the village Post Office and shop, and also stocks a small selection of interesting crafts. The tearoom is always closed on Thursdays, on Tuesdays as well during the winter. During the season, it's open from 9.00 until 17.00, weekdays, 10.00 to 18.00, weekends, closing one hour earlier in the winter months.

DUNKELD   Map 4 ref K10
15 miles NW of Perth off the A9

Set in idyllic surroundings on the east bank of the Tay, **Dunkeld Cathedral** is one of the noblest and most historic buildings in the country. Back in 850,

Kenneth MacAlpin moved the religious centre of the country to Dunkeld from Iona and the town also became the seat of the royal court. The present Cathedral was built between the 12th and 15th centuries and although its nave is roofless, the Choir remains intact and is still used as the parish church. The leper's squint is still in place and the cathedral generously allowed a striking tomb of the "Wolf of Badenoch" to be installed. Otherwise known as Alexander Stewart, Earl of Buchan, the Wolf was notorious for his lawlessness. His most infamous deed was the sacking of Elgin Cathedral in 1390 as a measured response to the Bishop's criticism of the Earl's marital infidelity.

From this appealing little town with its beautifully-restored 17th century houses, Thomas Telford's lovely 7-arched bridge of 1809 leads to the village of **Birnam** where the **Beatrix Potter Garden** recalls the popular writer who spent many childhood holidays in the area.

Birnam Wood, or its impersonation by Macduff's soldiers, played a crucial part in the downfall of Macbeth according to Shakespeare, and the story of the much-maligned king is presented at **The Macbeth Experience** where visitors can also see the famous Birnam Oak, all that remains of the ancient forest of Birnam Beeches.

ABERFELDY   MAP 4 REF J10
32 miles NW of Perth on the A827/A826

> *Now simmer blinks on flowery braes,*
> *And o'er the crystal streamlet plays;*
> *Come let us spend the lightsome days*
> *In the birks of Aberfeldy.*

Scotland's much-loved poet Robert Burns composed his ballad *The Birks of Aberfeldy* while standing near the dramatic **Falls of Moness** in September 1787. "Birk" means birch, and the beautiful trees he wrote about can still be seen south of this handsome town.

Fifty years before Rabbie Burns came to Aberfeldy and immortalised the silver birches, General Wade was building the distinctive **Wade's Bridge** across the *Fair Tay, flowing by in stately, placid majesty.* Designed by William Adam, architect father of Robert Adam, the 4-arched, humpback bridge was the first to span the river Tay.

Located in the heart of the town, **The Pantry** is a first-class tearoom offering an inviting selection of tasty home-made teatime treats. The emphasis at Christina MacDiarmid's inviting tearoom is on home baking - wonderfully fresh cakes, scones and sponges. Christina has been here since 1994 and with tremendous help from her family, and right hand help Rita, has made The Pantry *the* place to go to for tea in Aberfeldy. The premises were completely refurbished, the door access is wide enough for wheelchairs, and there are separate

The Pantry, 25a Dunkeld Street, Aberfeldy PH15 2AA
Tel: 01887 829722

area for smokers and non-smokers. In good weather, you can enjoy your refreshment in the lovely garden to the rear of the tearoom. The Pantry is open
every day during the season, from 10.00 until 16.00 or 16.30, but is closed on
Sundays during the winter.

Aberfeldy today is a dignified town where you will be greeted in spring by
golden banks of daffodils. **Aberfeldy Distillery**, an impressive building of 1898
with a genuine "turn of the century charm", welcomes visitors for guided tours,
has a well-stocked shop and a pleasant Nature Trail through the native woodland which surrounds the distillery. In the centre of the town, **Aberfeldy Water
Mill** was built in 1825 and after restoration in 1987 its 4 grinding stones, each
weighing 1.5 tons, are still producing oatmeal made in the traditional Scottish
manner. There's an interesting film showing the place of the miller in Scottish
history and visitors can buy stone ground oatmeal straight from the mill.

Set back from the town square and housed in a sturdy stone building, **7 The
Square Café & Bistro** is definitely the place to seek out in Aberfeldy if you
appreciate top quality cooking. Richard Lyth who, together with his wife Kirsteen,
owns and runs this outstanding café/bistro is a gifted chef with many awards

7 The Square Café, 7 The Square, Aberfeldy,
Perthshire PH15 2DD Tel/Fax: 01887 829120

testifying to his skills. Everything served here of course is home-made and that
includes the bread and ice cream, as well as the wonderful sorbets and desserts.
The daytime menu includes a good selection of starters and main dishes while
the evening à la carte menu offers three courses with a choice of three starters,
two main dishes and two desserts, rounded off by a fragrant cup of Italian coffee.

Although Richard and Kirsteen only arrived here in 1998, word has travelled
fast so it's essential to book for the evening. Children are welcome and the café/
bistro is non-smoking. 7 The Square is open Tuesday to Saturday from 10.00
until 15.00, and from 19.00 to 21.30

Located about 5 miles west of Aberfeldy, on the B846, the **Coshieville Inn** is
set amidst the stunning Perthshire hills, an area of outstanding natural beauty.
There has been a hostelry on this site for centuries and the present building is
more than a hundred years old. Dougie and Annemarie Harkness arrived here
in 1990 and have made this appealing old inn a popular venue for anyone who

Coshieville Inn, by Aberfeldy, Perthshire PH15 2NE
Tel: 01887 830319

enjoys good food and drink, comfortable accommodation and a welcoming atmosphere. The inn is fully licensed, with a "Taste of Scotland" restaurant offering the very best of traditional Scottish cuisine prepared from prime quality ingredients. If you are touring the area, the Coshieville Inn makes an ideal base. Its six bedrooms are all en suite and well-equipped with such features as TVs, tea making facilities, and hairdryers. Visitors will find plenty to keep them occupied. Hill-walking, pony-trekking, wildlife safaris, water-sports on Loch Tay, stalking, fishing are all available within easy reach and, as you would expect here in the heart of Scotland, so are a good number of excellent golf courses.

ACHARN   MAP 4 REF J10
8 miles SW of Aberfeldy on minor road off the A827

Back in the mid-1800s, the enlightened Earl of Breadalbane built a cluster of sturdy stone cottages for the workers on his estate. Today, these architecturally interesting buildings have been rebuilt inside and as **Loch Tay Lodges** provide attractive self-catering accommodation. They are situated on the eastern side of the small village of Acharn, close to Loch Tay, in countryside characterised by hill farms and sporting estates. There are majestic views in all seasons, with the tree cover around the Ben Lawers foothills providing breathtaking vistas in Spring and, particularly, in late October and early November. All the lodges are fully equipped and furnished. The pine woodwork blends with the original stonework and colourful furnishings to give a very homely welcome. Four of the lodges enjoy the charm of an open fire with free logs provided. All of them have individual enclosed garden areas, there's a safe play space for children, and one

Loch Tay Lodges, Acharn, near Aberfeldy, Perthshire PH15 2HR
Tel: 01887 830209 Fax: 01887 830802

of the lodges is suitable for accompanied wheelchair users. Cots and high chairs are available on request at no extra cost and pets are welcome. Awarded 4 stars by the Scottish Tourist Board, the lodges are ideally located for fishing in Loch Tay, (trout fishing is free) and there are unsurpassed opportunities for hill walking or gentler rambles through the Tay and Tummel valleys.

Close by, **The Scottish Crannog Centre** offers a fascinating reconstruction of the ancient loch dwellings on stilts used throughout Scotland and Ireland as early as 3000 BC and as late as 1600 AD. The crannogs are appropriately furnished and visitors are invited to try their hand at ancient crafts such as spinning and woodworking.

PITLOCHRY   Map 4 ref J9
28 miles NW of Perth off the A9

This popular resort is set in a particularly beautiful part of the Perthshire Highlands. To the west runs the lovely glen of Strathtummel while to the north the majestic peaks of the Grampians *"pierce the heavens".*

Over the years, Pitlochry has added many other attractions to these natural ones. **The Blair Athol Distillery,** makers of Bell's whisky was founded in 1798 and is one of Scotland's oldest distilleries. Visitors are welcome and can watch the distilling process as crystal clear water from the Allt Dour, the "burn of the otter", is transformed into amber nectar. Guided tours end with a complimentary dram and there is also a whisky and gift shop, coffee shop and bar.

A sight not to be missed is the **Salmon Ladder** at the Pitlochry Power Station and Dam. In the 1950s, the River Tummel was dammed to produce hydro-electric power but in order to permit salmon to pass upstream the ladder was constructed. An underwater viewing chamber allows visitors to watch these noble fish flailing their way up the 1000 feet long tunnel during their annual migration.

Nearby stands the world-famous **Pitlochry Festival Theatre** which from May to October presents a full programme of plays, concerts and other entertainments. In the town itself, the summer season brings pipe band concerts, country dancing displays, ceilidhs and many other events.

Located directly below the Pitlochry Festival Theatre and set on the banks of the River Tummel, the **Portnacraig Inn & Restaurant** is housed in one of the oldest buildings in Pitlochry, Grade B listed and dating back over 300 years. It's also a mere 200 yards downstream from the Hydro Electric Dam and the famous Salmon Ladder. The Inn is owned by Bill and Theresa Bryan, together with their son Andrew who is also the chef. Andrew has created a unique menu, devised with imagination and flair, which uses only the best in quality food, from steak to salmon to after-theatre fare. He's also renowned for his superb home-made

Portnacraig Inn & Restaurant, Pitlochry PH16 5ND
Tel: 01796 472777 Fax: 01796 472931

desserts, Kiwi Pavlova with a passion fruit & raspberry coulis, for example. Intimate candelight dinners are served before or after the theatre and in good weather you can dine on the picturesque riverside patio and enjoy the magnificent scenery - or perhaps the excitement of seeing a fisherman catch a salmon! The Inn has two lovely guest bedrooms, one of them overlooking the river and both en suite. Children are welcome and the Inn is wheelchair accessible. Few restaurants in the country can offer such a winning combination of a stunning location, excellent food, friendly atmosphere and quality accommodation.

Less than a mile from the centre of Pitlochry, **Auchnahyle** is a delightful old farmhouse set in some 16 acres of farmland, offering visitors a choice of both bed & breakfast or self-catering accommodation. This peaceful retreat is the home of Penny and Alistair Howman who use the surrounding fields for grazing sheep and pheasant farming. They also keep a number of fowl and game-birds, mostly running wild, and some ornamental pheasants. Auchnahyle's tally of resident animals also includes a black Labrador called "Waggle", her friend "Pixie", a Cocker Spaniel, and several friendly goats! Bed & breakfast guests stay in the

Auchnahyle, Pitlochry, Perthshire PH16 5JA
Tel: 01796 472318 Fax: 473657

farmhouse itself where there are 3 twin or double rooms, one of them on the ground floor. All are en suite, well-equipped with extras such as hair-drier and trouser-press, and the upstairs rooms also enjoy splendid views across the Perthshire countryside. Self-catering visitors are accommodated in Rowan Tree Cottage, a traditional stone-built cottage just across the courtyard from the main house. This picturesque old cottage has a sitting room with colour TV and plenty of books and games, a dining room, an extremely well-equipped kitchen, bathroom and 2 bedrooms - one with twin bed and a smaller bed, the other with a double bed. Children and dogs of all ages are welcome: a cot and high chair can be provided, but you are asked to bring your own dog bed. There's a pay-phone for outgoing calls and, outside, a small fenced garden with some garden furniture, as well as parking space for at least 2 cars. If you become weary of catering for yourself, it is often possible to arrange to have dinner at the farmhouse; if not, Pitlochry offers a wide choice of pubs and restaurants.

Nestling in the hills a couple of miles east of Pitlochry, **Edradour Distillery** is the smallest in the country, producing just 12 casks of its prized whisky each week. An old distiller's yardstick states that the smaller the still, the finer the taste and the Edradour stills are the smallest allowed under Excise regulations - any smaller, the theory goes, and they'd be hidden away on the hillsides! Guided tours begin with the usual complimentary glass and there's a short video re-counting Edradour's history since it was founded in 1825.

KILLIECRANKIE
3 miles NW of Pitlochry off the A9

MAP 4 REF J9

On 27 July 1689, William of Orange's troops marched through the lovely **Pass of Killiecrankie** to attack the Highland forces massed on the hillside a mile away. A few hours later, the English soldiers were fleeing back through the Pass. The battle at Killiecrankie was the first military encounter of the Jacobite rising and is commemorated at the **Killiecrankie Visitor Centre** (National Trust for Scotland) which also offers guided walks around the area during the summer months.

Originally built as a manse by a local vicar in 1840, **The Killiecrankie Hotel** is now home to the Anderson family who have lived here since 1988. Colin and Carole have striven to create a welcoming and informal ambience - a home away from home. The hotel continues to be recognised for the quality of its food and accommodation in all the leading hotel and food guides. The evening table d'hôte menu uses only the best local produce and is served in the casually elegant dining room with views of the flower garden and surrounding hills. As the hotel's reputation implies, dinner is strongly recommended for those who come to stay at Killiecrankie. The sitting room with its fireplace, books and magazines is a perfect place to enjoy a quiet chat after dinner. It opens on to the

The Killiecrankie Hotel, Killiecrankie, by Pitlochry, Perthshire PH16 5LG
Tel: 01796 473220 Fax: 01796 472451
e-mail: killiecrankie.hotel@internet.com
http://www.btinternet.com/~killiecrankie.hotel/

fine herbaceous garden which is a feature of the grounds. The hotel's ten bedrooms are individually decorated, finished in natural pine by local craftsmen. Each has its own en suite facilities and enjoys views on to the wooded grounds that surround the house. However long you intend to stay, you will find that the Killiecrankie Hotel's tranquil setting, excellent food, informal but comfortable atmosphere, and convenient location will ensure a memorable visit.

BLAIR ATHOLL
Map 4 ref J9

5 miles NW of Pitlochry off the A9

The village of Blair Atholl is dominated by the gleaming white walls and towers of **Blair Castle**, the most visited, privately-owned home in Scotland. The hereditary seat of the Dukes of Atholl, the castle's oldest part is Cummings Tower, built in 1269. The 2nd Duke transformed the castle into a gracious Georgian mansion and a century or so later the 7th Duke remodelled the building in the flamboyant "Scottish Baronial style".

Most of the 32 rooms open to visitors at Blair Castle date from this period - a marvellous sequence of grand apartments containing outstanding collections of furniture, painting, china, lace, tapestries, arms and armour. In the vast Ballroom, where one whole wall is festooned with antlers, look out for the portrait of the 7th Duke. Beneath it lies his walking stick, scored with 749 notches, one for each stag he had killed.

Visitors to the castle may well find themselves greeted by a piper of the Atholl Highlanders, the Duke's "private army". This 80-strong force is unique in Europe, the legacy of a visit to Blair Castle in 1844 by Queen Victoria. Enormously impressed by the Guard of kilted Highlanders assembled for her visit, Victoria conferred on them the right to carry the Queen's Colours, a privilege which also allowed them to bear arms. Every year, in May, they hold their annual parade for the Duke's review and complete the Whitsun weekend with the famous **Atholl Gathering**. These historic Highland Games feature internationally known sportsmen, Highland dancing, traditional caber-tossing and local competitions. In August, the **Blair Castle International Horse Trials**, held in the challenging castle grounds, have become a major event and are followed by Sheep Dog Trials.

In addition to Blair Castle's 32 State Rooms, visitors may also wander through the extensive parklands, which include a Deer Park, a restored 18th century Walled Garden, a gift shop and restaurant.

Only in Scotland it seems can one find superior bed & breakfast accommodation in grand old country houses - and at very reasonable prices. **Ptarmigan House** is a perfect example. It's an impressive, cream-painted property, made architecturally interesting by ranks of gables and lofty windows. The busy A9 is just a few minutes drive away, but at Ptarmigan House all is peace and tranquillity. The house is surrounded by 1 1/2 acres of its own grounds, the adjoining 9-hole golf course provides extra space, and the wild, untamed ranges of the Grampian Mountains stride away to the north and east. This extremely desirable property, almost 100 years old, is the home of Gordon and Lin Muirhead who welcome bed & breakfast visitors in search of a warm Scottish welcome, comfortable accommodation and a hearty breakfast that will set them up for most of the day. After sampling the breakfast you may well want to plan your day. Gordon is a native to this area and will always give advice on routes to take

Ptarmigan House, Blair Atholl, Perthshire PH18 5SZ
Tel/Fax: 01796 481269

for an interesting tour of the Highlands. If you prefer a self-catering holiday, Gordon and Lin can offer a spacious cottage, just 200 yards away, which accommodates up to 8 adults and a child.

STRATHTUMMEL

MAP 4 REF J9

7 miles W of Pitlochry on the B8019

The B8019 running westwards from Pitlochry forms part of the romantic Road to the Isles, and provides magical vistas that are outstanding even in a country where sensational landscapes are almost taken for granted. In 1866 Queen Victoria came to the famous viewpoint in Strathtummel and, like everyone else who has stood here, was enraptured. The astoundingly beautiful view takes in the length of **Loch Tummel** with the conical peak of **Schiehallion** (3457 feet), the "Fairy Mountain", rising above it. The spot is known as **Queens View**, not because of Victoria, but after Queen Margaret, wife of Robert the Bruce.

Few hotels can boast such a spectacular setting as that enjoyed by the **Queens View Hotel.** Standing on wooded slopes overlooking lovely Loch Tummel, it's a magnificent building, dating back to the early 1800s when it was built as a shooting lodge. Traditional crow-stepped gables, witches'-hat turrets and ivy-clad walls all add to the charm. Incredibly, following World War II the building was used for some 20 years as a Youth Hostel, only becoming a hotel in 1972. Norma and Richard Tomlinson bought this wonderful old property in 1995 and completely refurbished the interior, retaining many attractive features such as the intricately carved marble fireplaces. The public rooms offer a range of environments from an elegant drawing room reminiscent of the gracious days of

Queens View Hotel, Strathtummel, by Pitlochry, Perthshire PH16 5NR
Tel: 01796 473291 Fax: 01796 473515
www.queens-view-hotel.co.uk enquiries@queens-view-hotel.co.uk

country living to a cosy bar and restaurant with staggering views along the loch 100 feet below. The guest bedrooms also enjoy these grand views and are stylishly furnished and decorated in keeping with the country house ambience of the hotel. Outside, there are terraced lawns and a path leads to the loch-side where the hotel has fishing rights. Idyllic.

KINLOCH RANNOCH
20 miles W of Pitlochry on the B846

MAP 4 REF I9

This little village at the eastern end of Loch Rannoch is popular with anglers and backpackers setting off for the vast expanses of Rannoch Moor, where there are no roads and only a single railway line. Just south of the village, **Bunrannoch House** is an attractive white-painted building occupying a lovely wooded situation. Built in 1860 as a hunting lodge, it's located on the site of a medieval settlement and stands guard to the "Sleeping Giant" mountain, providing fine views across the surrounding countryside to both Loch Tummel and Loch Rannoch. Jennifer and Keith Skeaping offer visitors a warm welcome to their home where open fires, locally-renowned home cooking and spacious rooms all create the atmosphere for a most pleasant and enjoyable stay. There are 7 letting rooms, most of them en suite, all centrally heated and all enjoying grand views. Accommodation is available either on a Bed & Breakfast, or Dinner, Bed & Breakfast basis. Dinners at Bunrannoch House are heartily recommended -

Bunrannoch House, Kinloch Rannoch, Perthshire PH16 5QB
Tel/Fax: 01882 632407

imaginatively cooked meals prepared with prime ingredients and with a choice of 2 dishes for each course. The hotel is licensed so you can also enjoy a glass or two of wine with your meal. For departing guests, there's an added courtesy ~ a complimentary tray of home baking.

West of Kinloch Rannoch, the B846 runs through the increasingly desolate expanses of Rannoch Moor for 15 miles before coming to a dead end at Rannoch Station on the Glasgow to Fort William line. This is the heart of wilderness country, Perthshire's Empty Quarter, and yet another aspect of the county's varied landscapes.

7 The Kingdom of Fife

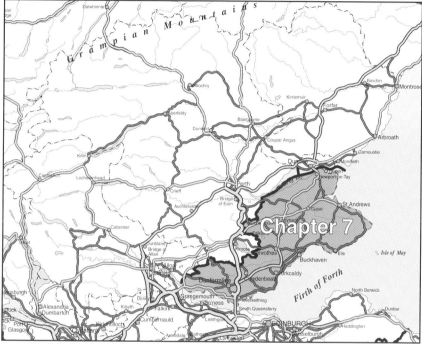

© MAPS IN MINUTES ™ (1998)

Surrounded on 3 sides by water, (the Tay, the Forth and the North Sea), Fife has retained its identity ever since it was established as a Kingdom by the Picts in the 4th century. Its capital, then as now, is the small market town of Cupar set in the fertile Howe of Fife, the pastoral heart of the kingdom. Also in the Howe is Falkland, a charming medieval town with a glorious Renaissance Palace.

Over to the east, the handsome and dignified town of St Andrews is surrounded by unspoilt countryside and a coastline edged with extensive sandy beaches. The most picturesque stretch of coast, however, lies to the south in the area known as the East Neuk of Fife. From Leven to Crail, there's a succession of quaint old fishing villages with distinctive pantiled roofs.

Most of Fife's industrial towns are located in the south but this is where you'll also find the beautifully preserved 16th century village of Culross and historic Dunfermline with its grand old ruined Abbey.

IN AND AROUND DUNFERMLINE

As the Fife Tourist Board points out, in Dunfermline you can walk through 900 years of history in a day. The capital of Scotland for 6 centuries until James VI succeeded to the English throne in 1603, the square mile of Dunfermline town centre is rich in history.

A good place to start your walk is, strangely enough, in Glen Bridge car park where you are just yards from **St Margaret's Cave**. In the late 11th century, the pious Margaret, queen to Malcolm III, frequently came to the cave to pray and here she would also wash the feet of the poor.

Just across from the car park, the **Town House** is a gloriously extravagant building, a heady mixture of Scottish Baronial and French Gothic styles. Nearby rises the impressive **Dunfermline Abbey**, originally founded by Queen Margaret and greatly extended by her equally devout son, David I in the early 1100s. Only the nave of the medieval church has survived, its massive Norman columns reminiscent of Durham Cathedral. Robert the Bruce was buried in the Abbey in 1295 but, astonishingly, his resting-place was "lost" and not rediscovered until 1821 when the new parish church was being built. The body was reburied beneath a fine memorial brass thus ensuring that it would not be mislaid again. (His heart, of course, remains at Melrose Abbey).

Within the Abbey precincts, the 14th century **Abbot House** was formerly the estate office for what was then the richest Benedictine Abbey in Scotland. After being neglected for many years the house has been refurbished and its upper rooms are now dazzlingly colourful with brilliant murals and life-size models illustrating the town's history and people.

Across the road from the Abbey is the entrance to **Pittencroft Park** where a substantial wall, 205 feet long and 60 feet high, is all that remains of the **Royal Palace** in which Charles I was born in 1600. This splendid park, and the Laird's House within it, (now a museum of local history), was a gift to the town from its most famous son, Andrew Carnegie.

Carnegie was born in 1835 in a modest, two up, two down, cottage in Moodie Street which is now the **Andrew Carnegie Birthplace Museum**. As a young man, Carnegie emigrated to the United States where he rose from bobbin boy, telegraph operator and railroad developer to "Steel King of America". When he sold his businesses inn 1901 for $400 million he became the richest man in the world. He lavished most of his huge fortune on endowing schools, colleges and free public libraries. The **Carnegie Library** at Dunfermline was the first of an eventual 3000 such buildings. The various Trusts and Foundations established by Carnegie are still operating and dispensing around £100 every minute.

The New Victoria Restaurant in Bruce Street rightfully claims to be Dunfermline's "Oldest and Newest Restaurant". For many years the Victoria Restaurant and Hotel traded at 63, High Street, now the home of Boots the Chemists, but moved in June 1923 to its present address, renaming itself the

The New Victoria Restaurant, 2 Bruce Street, Dunfermline KY12 7AG
Tel: 01383 724175

New Victoria Restaurant and Hotel. The hotel ceased trading in 1953 but the restaurant continues and has now been New for over 75 years. The McEwan family have owned the business since 1956 with Alistair McEwan today continuing the family tradition. As Dunfermline's most traditional restaurant The Vic, as it's affectionately known, maintains a high standard of Scottish Fare, using fresh produce wherever possible. With a menu providing over 50 choices of main courses, served all day from 10.00 until closing and with prices starting from as little as £3.95, Alistair promises his customers "a well-cooked meal, in pleasant surroundings, on a level above all others, with prices and service to surpass all others". The Vic's comprehensive menu offers Coffees, Teas, Snacks, Lunches, (with a 3-course Lunch Special currently at £5.95), High Teas and Dinners, seven days a week. In a word, Dunfermline's Oldest and Newest Restaurant also has a good claim to be its best!

NORTH QUEENSFERRY
MAP 2 REF K13
6 miles SE of Dunfermline on minor road off the A90

Nestling beneath two soaring bridges, the village of North Queensferry acquired its name from the medieval Queen Margaret who regularly used the ferry on the way to her favourite home at Dunfermline. With the opening of the Forth Road Bridge, the ferry's 800-year-old history came to an abrupt end and North

**Channel Restaurant, 17 Main Street, North Queensferry, Fife KY11 1JG
Tel: 01383 412567**

Queensferry reverted to being a peaceful backwater. It's well worth visiting for its grand views of the Firth and those two magnificent bridges, and also to sample the fare on offer at the **Channel Restaurant**. Its owners, Andrew and Samantha, describe their cuisine as "modern Scottish", an imaginative blend of traditional and innovative dishes. So Samantha's menu always includes old favourites such as Fillet of Scotch beef along with dishes like Seared Sea Bream with west coast mussels, noodles and Thai green curry. Puddings are Andrew's province - a heavenly Ice Armagnac parfait with prunes, for example, or you can settle for a selection of Scottish cheeses and oatcakes. Widely recommended, the Channel Restaurant is open Tuesday to Saturday all year from 19.00 with last orders at 21.30. The restaurant is licensed, children over 12 are welcome, but please note that guests are requested not to smoke until coffee is served.

On the edge of the village, **Deep Sea World** boasts the largest underwater tunnel in the world, some 120 yards long. Its transparent upper half allows visitors excellent close-up views of the more than 3000 fish in the Aquarium, amongst them the largest collection of Sand Tiger Sharks in Europe. A team of experienced divers regularly hand feed the fish and the latest communication technology allows visitors to put questions to the divers. Exhibits include a Touch Tank, where children can touch all kinds of marine species, including small friendly sharks, and an Amazonian Rain Forest display complete with piranhas and a tropical thunderstorm.

LIMEKILNS   MAP 2 REF K12
3 miles SW of Dunfermline on minor road off the A985

The pretty village of Limekilns lies off the main road between the Forth Road
Bridge and the Kincardine Bridge. Once the port for Dunfermline, its oldest
building is the 14th century **King's Cellar** which was formerly a store for the
royal court.

It is well worth a stop at Limekilns to eat at **Il Pescatore Restaurant** which is
housed in a handsome stone building, set off in summer by colourful tubs of
flowers and window-boxes. Celia and Reza Bazazi bought the restaurant in 1993,
completely refurbished it and have also converted the building next door into a
stylish **hotel**. All 6 rooms are en suite and have been decorated and furnished to
an extremely high standard. Satellite television, tea & coffee, and direct dial
telephones are available in every room. The restaurant itself is a striking room
with fluted columns supporting elegant arches and a patterned ceiling. Celia is
an outstanding chef, her cuisine mostly classical Italian but also featuring steaks
and fish dishes, all freshly cooked to order. Reza is renowned for his colourful
personality and waistcoats to match! Both of them provide a sincere welcome
for their guests, many of whom return again and again to enjoy the good food
and great hospitality.

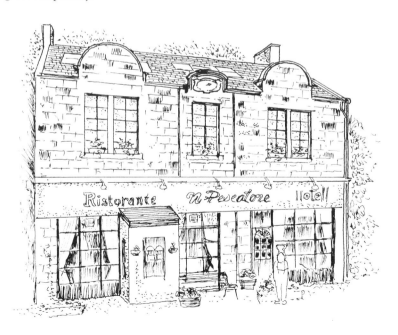

**Il Pescatore Hotel and Ristorante, 40 Main Street, Limekilns,
Fife KY11 3HL Tel: 01383 872999 Fax: 01383 872199**

Overlooking the busy seagoing traffic of the Firth of Forth, **The Ship Inn** is reputed to have welcomed a different kind of trafficking in times gone by. In those days the inn was notorious as a smugglers' haunt; nowadays it's much better known as a welcoming hostelry where you'll find quality food and a well-kept selection of real ales and other beverages. Mine hosts, Hugh and Jane, only bought the Inn back in October 1998 but their reputation is already well-established. Within a short period of time, it is hoped Jane's creative menu of bar food will be supplemented by a top-of-the-range restaurant on the first floor with an experienced chef installed to provide quality cuisine. Bar food is avail-

The Ship Inn, 17 Halkettshall, Limekilns, Fife KY11 3JG
Tel: 01383 872247

able downstairs where the bar has been pleasingly decorated with maritime memorabilia, items such as a mighty helmsman's wheel. This is a good place to be on a Saturday night when you can enjoy live music from 20.00. In good weather, you can settle yourself on one of the benches outside and gaze across the Firth of Firth. From this vantage point outside the Ship Inn you can see Blackness Castle which, because of its unusual galleon-like outline, is often known as the Ship Castle.

CULROSS
MAP 2 REF K12
8 miles W of Dunfermline, on minor road off the A985

Culross, pronounced "Cooross", is an outstanding example of a 16th/17th century town, thanks partly to the National Trust for Scotland which has been looking after its picturesque buildings with their crow-stepped gables and red pantiled roofs since 1932. The Trust's Visitor Centre occupies the 16th century **Town House** which has an exhibition and video presentation outlining the burgh's 400 year old history. The house also contains a tiny prison, complete with built-in manacles.

Culross Palace is an impressive ochre-painted mansion built in the late 1500s for a wealthy coal merchant, Sir George Bruce. Inside, there are some remarkable painted ceilings, superb pine panelling and antique furniture and outside, a garden planted with the kinds of herbs and vegetables appropriate for a 16th century garden.

The cobbled alleyway known as **Back Causeway** has a raised centre which was apparently reserved for the gentry alone. The alley leads to the **Study**, another early 17th century house, which takes its name from a room at the top of the tower reached by a turnpike stair. Nearby stands the **Mercat Cross** of 1610 and, a little further up the hill, the ruins of **Culross Abbey**. Only the choir remains intact and now serves as the parish church. Inside, there's a 10th century Celtic cross and a magnificent tomb with alabaster figures portraying Sir George Bruce, his wife, and their 8 children. A browse around the graveyard reveals some unusual tombstones with carvings depicting the occupations of the late departed - a gardener with a crossed spade and rake for example.

This delightful village receives some 80,000 visitors a year and a goodly number of them find their way to the **Dundonald Arms Hotel** in the cobbled pedestrianised alley known as Midcauseway. The hotel is a sturdy old stone

The Dundonald Arms Hotel, Midcauseway, Culross, Fife KY12 8HS
Tel/Fax: 01383 881137

building dating back to 1640 when this narrow thoroughfare was part of the main Dunfermline to Stirling stage-coach route. It looks a picture in summer with its tubs of flowers and hanging baskets. Inside, the bar has a nautical flavour with lots of maritime memorabilia and paintings in oil and acrylic created by the hotel's talented owner, Michael Batchelor. The hotel is well-known for its quality food, (available every lunchtime and evening), which includes main meals such as Tender Duck in a rich bramble sauce, traditional desserts like the individual Clootie Dumpling, as well as Lite Bites of sandwiches, toasties, baked potatoes or Haggis Creggins with oatcakes. Culross is a gem of a village and also makes a good base for exploring the other attractions of the ancient Kingdom of Fife. If you are thinking of staying in the area, the Dundonald Arms has 7 inviting guest rooms, all of them en suite and comfortably appointed.

ABERDOUR   MAP 2 REF K12
6 miles SE of Dunfermline on the A921

Aberdour is famous for its silver sands and has even been dubbed the "Fife Riviera". The town also boasts a 14th century **Castle** (HS) with an attractive and spacious 17th century garden where there stands an unusual circular dovecote of the same period. Also in the Castle grounds is **St Fillan's Church**, notable for some fine Norman work.

Located on Hawkcraig Point in this picturesque coastal village, the **Forth View Hotel** is a striking, 3-storeyed stone building of 1880. Its Victorian builders positioned the house so that it commands the most impressive views possible across the Firth of Forth to Edinburgh. A private residence for only 20 years, it became a Temperance Hotel in 1900 but since 1977 has been the home of Pauleen Norman. Pauleen welcomes bed and breakfast visitors to this splendid house

Forth View Hotel, Hawkcraig Point, Aberdour, Fife KY3 0TZ
Tel: 01383 860402 Fax: 01383 860262

where there are 5 guest bedrooms, 3 of them en suite, each with a character of its own and each enjoying its share of the glorious views. Evening meals are not served, (there are many good eating places within easy reach), but provision can be made for packed lunches as well as vegetarian breakfasts. Rooms are available from April to October, children are welcome and so too are dogs. From the house, scenic walks lead to the old harbour and the village. Also nearby are the ruins of Aberdour Castle, the famous Silversands beach, and the 12th century St Fillan's church, with its ancient Do'cot, as well as Aberdour's award-winning station.

KELTY
MAP 2 REF K12
8 miles NE of Dunfermline on the A909

Only a few minutes drive from Junction 4 of the M90, **The Clippies Fayre** serves outstanding food throughout the day in a stylish restaurant part of which is a lovely conservatory overlooking a well-tended garden. Owners Kenny and Corriane Sinclair opened their elegant restaurant in November 1998 and word spread fast - it's already necessary to book for Saturday nights. The fayre on offer is the creation of talented chef Ceri Davies who begins the day by serving hearty Scottish breakfasts. Light snacks are always available, there's a lunchtime menu of traditional dishes such as Steak & Ale Pie or Haggis, Neeps and Tatties, High Teas are served from 16.00 until 18.00, and these are followed by the night-time dinner menu. There's always a choice of vegetarian dishes and special meals for

The Clippies Fayre, Kelty Crossroads, Kelty, Fife KY4 0AA
Tel: 01383 839544/831423

pensioners and kiddies are also available daily. This excellent restaurant shares a very imposing town centre building with a pub bearing the unusual name of "The No. 1 Goth". The pub was built in the 1890s by a co-operative of local miners and other workers calling itself The No.1 Gothenburg Society which also provided a swimming pool for the town.

GLENROTHES   Map 5 ref L12
15 miles NE of Dunfermline on the A92

About 2 miles east from the unlovely 20th century architecture of the New Town of Glenrothes, **Balgonie Castle** is a survivor of a more attractive style of building. With its mighty 14th century Keep, the castle is the home of the Laird and Lady of Balgonie and as likely as not it will be one of them who guides you around the partly restored castle. The informative tour provides interesting details about the castle's construction, and its history, which includes a visit by Rob Roy and 200 of his clansmen who were quartered at Balgonie in 1716.

FALKLAND   Map 5 ref L12
22 miles NE of Dunfermline on the A912

Set in the Howe (Plain) of Fife, Falkland is a perfect gem, an unspoilt little town which grew up around a superb Renaissance mansion, **Falkland Palace** (NTS). Built between 1501-41, the palace was a favourite seat of the Stuart kings from the time of James V. He extended the building considerably, adding the beautiful Chapel Royal and also a Royal Tennis court in 1539. Both are still in use, and the tennis court is believed to be the oldest in the world.

James was on his deathbed at Falkland when he received news of the birth of his daughter, Mary Stuart. His two sons had died in infancy: now his turbulent kingdom would pass to a woman. He was filled with foreboding: the throne, he said "cam wi' a lass and it will gang wi' a lass". Six days later he was dead and Mary began her ill-fated reign.

Mary, whose experience of castles and palaces was generally pretty melancholy, seems to have spent a happy childhood here, often playing in the splendid gardens which have recently been restored, and frequently returned in later years to ride through the Leven hills.

This enchanting little town was the first in Scotland to be designated a Conservation Area. Concern for protecting Falkland's unique character has even extended to hiding its electricity sub-station in an ordinary house, an idea that could usefully be copied elsewhere.

A stroll around the old town reveals some interesting features such as the "fore-stairs", outside stairs leading to an upper floor, and "marriage lintels" over front doors inscribed with the initials of the newly-wed householders and the year of their marriage.

LEVEN   MAP 5 REF L12
24 miles NE of Dunfermline on the A955

The area to the east of Leven is known as the East Neuk (nook, or corner) of Fife. Its coastline is dotted with pretty villages and there's a long stretch of excellent sandy beaches around the broad curve of Largo Bay. Leven is the largest of the towns on the bay, popular with holiday-makers enjoying its fine beach, lively Promenade offering all the usual seaside attractions, and two peaceful public parks.

Located in the heart of this busy little resort, the **Krazy Corner Café** offers customers anything from a simple cuppa to a hearty main meal, tasty dishes such as Scotch Pie or Chicken Cutlets. Especially popular are the home-made puddings but you'll also find delicious cakes, stovies, all day breakfasts, toasties and hot and cold filled rolls. Sheila Paterson is the owner of this friendly café which she runs with the capable assistance of her daughter Shona. Their emphasis is on home cooking and baking and together they have created a "cracking" atmosphere where locals and visitors often find themselves chatting together like old friends. In good weather, you can enjoy your refreshments on the patio at the rear of the café. The Krazy Korner is open Monday to Saturday from 9.00 to 17.00, children are welcome and there's good access for the disa-

Krazy Korner Café, 2 Mitchell Street, Leven, Fife KY8 4HJ
Tel: 01333 439292

bled. While you are in the town, you should take a look at Mr Bissett's Bus. A late resident of Leven, Mr Bissett was obsessed with seashells as decorative objects. A good example is his bus, every inch of which, apart from the windows, is adorned with crustaceans.

LOWER LARGO
MAP 5 REF L12
26 miles NE of Dunfermline on minor road off the A915

The "real" Robinson Crusoe, Alexander Selkirk, was born in this attractive seaside town in 1676. At the age of 19, he ran away to sea and a few years later was master of a pirate ship operating in the South Seas. After a dispute with his captain, William Dampier, Selkirk was put ashore on the uninhabited island of Juan Fernandez. He stayed there for 4 years and 4 months, never seeing another soul. (Man Friday was Daniel Defoe's fictional addition). Then Dampier returned and rescued him. Lower Largo's most famous son is commemorated by a statue near the harbour showing Selkirk dressed as a castaway.

Fife has many hidden attractions but there can be few more attractive than **The Crusoe Hotel** in this beautiful backwater. The comfortable hotel, nestling on the rocks beside the harbour, exudes an atmosphere of relaxed continental charm. With its 16 en suite bedrooms the hotel also provides an unbeatable base from which to explore the East Neuk of Fife. The food served in the Crusoe Hotel is unmistakably stamped with the confident and highly skilled signature of the owner's son, who is the Head Chef. He honed his talents in top establishments in London and Edinburgh before coming home to the Crusoe and is passionate about his food which has to be honest and accessible. While the

The Crusoe Hotel, Lower Largo, Fife KY8 6BT Tel: 01333 320759
Fax: 01333 320865 e-mail: info@crusoe-hotel.co.uk
Website: www.spr.co.uk/users/crusoe-hotel

Castaway Restaurant offers modern British food with French influence of which every part of the dish - vegetables, rice, pasta, cous cous or potatoes, fish or meat - is designed to marry together in a well defined way; the new Juan Fernandez Bistro reflects the growing tendency towards more relaxed eating out. Aside from the view across Largo Bay, another advantage of being so close to the water is the fresh crab and lobster delivered literally to the hotel's front door from local lobster boats which are still based at the harbour. What better reason could there be for choosing the Crusoe Hotel for a break away from daily hustle and bustle?

IN AND AROUND ST ANDREWS

A measure of the historic importance of this elegant town is the fact that almost the whole of its town centre enjoys the protection of Listed Building status. The most striking of these buildings is the ruined magnificence of **St Andrews Cathedral**. Masons started to build it in 1160; their descendants finally completed the largest church ever built in Scotland in 1318. Robert the Bruce attended its consecration in that same year. Two and a half centuries later, this beacon of Christian faith was effectively snuffed out when John Knox arrived in St Andrews. On the 5th of June, 1559, Knox delivered a rabble-rousing sermon inciting his Protestant congregation to attack the Catholic church. The mob stripped St Andrew's Cathedral of its treasures (never recovered), and enthusiastically mutilated any stone image of saints and prophets within reach of their axes. The people of St Andrews never found the heart, money or will to restore their desecrated Cathedral.

Standing alongside the ruins of the Cathedral is **St Rule's Tower**, an extraordinary survival from 1130 when, according to legend, it was built to house the sacred relics of St Andrew. No-one knows where those relics are nowadays. Within St Rule's tower, a 174-step corkscrew staircase leads to a platform from which there are grand views across the town and surrounding countryside.

The tower was part of the Augustinian Priory that once stood on this site and the only other building to survive is the massive 14th century gatehouse known as **The Pends**. From here, it's just a short walk to the rocky coastline and the ruins of **St Andrews Castle** surrounded by the sea on three sides, by a moat on the fourth. The castle witnessed some grim scenes during the turbulent years of the Reformation. In 1546 the Protestant reformer George Wishart was burnt at the stake in front of the castle while the Bishop of St Andrews, Cardinal Beaton, seated himself on the balcony *"to feed and glut his eyes with the sight of it"*. Less than 3 months later, Knox's supporters stabbed the Cardinal to death and hung his body from the castle wall. Later, it was dumped into the "bottle dungeon", a 24 feet deep pit gouged out of solid rock which can be seen in the Sea Tower.

Many of the impressive buildings in the city centre are part of St Andrews University, founded in 1410 and the oldest in Scotland. Two of the college quads are open to the public, **St Salvator's** and **St Mary's**, and during the summer vacation guided tours are available.

For golfers around the world St Andrews is a holy place. Back in 1754 the Society of St Andrews Golfers was formed to organise an annual competition on the natural links to the west of the town. Eighty years later it became the Royal & Ancient Golf Club, now the governing body for the rules of golf in most countries. In all, St Andrews has 6 golf courses and visitors can book a round on any of them at the **Golf Information Centre** or find out more about the game and its history at the British Golf Museum.

St Andrews also boasts one of Scotland's best beaches at **West Sands** where scenes for *Chariots of Fire* were filmed. And the **Botanic Garden**, now a hundred years old, is renowned for its collections of cacti and other exotic plants.

If you are looking for superior, en suite, bed & breakfast accommodation in the St Andrews area, **Whitecroft Guest Lodges** have the very thing. They are located just a 5-minute drive from the centre of the town but are surrounded by peaceful, well-tended gardens and enjoy spectacular views over the Fife countryside. The owners, Linda and Bill Horn, have 5 guest rooms, 2 of them in the

Whitecroft Guest Lodges, 33 Strathkinness High Road, St Andrews, Fife KY16 9UA Tel/Fax: 01334 474448

east wing. The other 3 are lodge rooms with private entrances, tastefully converted from a 1950s laundry with a modern extension. The rooms are outstanding - beautifully furnished and well-equipped with lots of little extras supplied, and breakfasts here are equally impressive. Bill is a keen golfer and will happily arrange bookings at any of the local courses. He and Linda are also very familiar with the area and can guide you to its many other attractions - golden beaches, historic houses and castles, scenic walks and rides, and much more. And St Andrews itself of course is one of the most historically interesting and attractive towns in the country, distinguished by a wealth of ancient buildings.

COLINSBURGH
Map 5 ref M12

12 miles S of St Andrews on the B942

The **Balcarres Arms Hotel** is one of those friendly places where, if you don't see your favourite dish listed on the menu, just say what you would like and if the kitchen has the ingredients available they will cook it for you. This kind of flexibility is typical of Ian and Anne Cooper's welcoming hostelry, a delightful old 18th century coaching inn still complete with its arched entrance leading to the stables at the rear. (The neighbouring building is a former Army barracks, its dungeon and morgue still intact although happily neither is still in use!) Ian and Anne arrived at the Balcarres Arms in September 1996 as managers, became its owners in May 1999 and, while they are constantly improving the inn's amenities, are careful to preserve its unique charm and character. Tasty bar snacks

Balcarres Arms Hotel, 59 Main Street, Colinsburgh, Fife KY9 1LS
Tel: 01333 340600

are available throughout the day until around 21.00 and the good selection of beverages includes a heady "Scrumpy Jack". Children are welcome inside until 20.00, there's a lovely beer garden to the rear, and every other Saturday customers are entertained with live music, or entertain each other with a lively karaoke.

PITTENWEEM   MAP 5 REF M12
12 miles SE of St Andrews on the A917

Many of the small houses in this coastal village have been restored by the National Trust for Scotland and the quiet streets and lanes leading up from the harbour invite a leisurely exploration. Pittenweem's unusual name is derived from an ancient term for sea caves and, sure enough, here is **St Fillan's Cave**. Once the retreat of the early Christian missionary, the cave has for the most part been respected as a shrine, although at one time fishermen used it to store their nets. The cave was re-dedicated in the 1930s and services are still held in this unconventional setting.

A couple of miles inland, **Kellie Castle & Garden** (NTS) is an outstanding example of Lowland domestic architecture. Dating from the 14th century, the castle was sympathetically restored by the Lorimer family in the late 1800s. The castle contains magnificent plaster ceilings and painted panelling, as well as fine furniture designed by Sir Robert Lorimer.

The Victorian nursery and kitchen are both fascinating and the late-Victorian garden features a collection of organically cultivated old-fashioned roses and herbaceous plants.

ANSTRUTHER   MAP 5 REF M12
11 miles SE of St Andrews on the A917

Fifty years ago, the picturesque port of Anstruther was so busy with fishing boats it was possible to walk from one side of the wide harbour to the other by stepping from boat to boat. Then the North Sea herring shoals which had brought prosperity to the town for centuries mysteriously disappeared and the vessels now rocking gently in the harbour are mostly pleasure craft.

The town's long association with the sea is vividly brought to life at the **Scottish Fisheries Museum** beside the harbour. Lovingly restored craft stand beached in the paved courtyard, with a huge anchor alongside. Inside, tableaux, reconstructions, models and paintings give a comprehensive overview of the local fishing industry. On a more poignant note, there's a room devoted to a Memorial to Scottish Fishermen Lost at Sea.

About 4 miles offshore, on the **Isle of May**, stands a lighthouse built in 1816 by Robert Louis Stevenson's grandfather, and also the ruins of the country's first lighthouse, erected in 1636. The island is now a bird sanctuary with thousands of puffins and eider ducks in permanent residence. Transient birds stopping off have boosted the number of different species spotted here to more than 200.

There are regular boat trips to the island during the season.

In Anstruther itself, collectors of curiosities will be pleased with Buckie House. Its former owner decorated it outside and inside with buckies, or shells, and as a final touch stipulated that he should be buried in a shell-encrusted coffin.

CRAIL
Map 5 ref M12

10 miles SE of St Andrews on the A917

The most ancient Royal Burgh in the East Neuk of Fife, Crail also has one of the most photographed harbours in Scotland. Artists, too, love to make paintings of the red-tiled houses cascading down to the shore. Pretty as it is, this picture-postcard village is still a working port, home to Fife's crab and lobster fleet.

About halfway between Crail and St Andrews, at Troywood, is one of Fife's most offbeat visitor attractions: **Scotland's Secret Bunker**. Hidden 100 feet underground and encased in concrete walls 15 feet thick, the bunker was built during the Cold War of the 1950s as a headquarters refuge for government and military officials in the event of a nuclear war. The otherwise austere complex was provided with 2 cinemas to entertain the expected 300 reluctant residents. These now show government information films of the time which, in the style of Harry Enfield, advised ludicrously inadequate protective measures for civilians to follow when the 4-minute warning of a nuclear bomb attack had been activated.

CUPAR
Map 5 ref L11

10 miles W of St Andrews on the A91

The capital of Fife, Cupar sits beside the River Eden in the heart of the fertile Howe of Fife for which it serves as the market centre and hosts a regular livestock auction each week. The town is desperately in need of a by-pass to divert the busy A91 which runs through its centre and destroys its medieval character. The 17th century **Mercat Cross** has already been knocked over once by a lorry and the fragments re-assembled.

Two miles south of the town, the **Hill of Tarvit Mansionhouse & Garden** (NTS) is well worth a visit. The house is an Edwardian country mansion designed by Sir Robert Lorimer for a Dundee industrialist, Frederick Bonar Sharp. Sharp was a noted art collector and the house provides a perfect setting for paintings by Raeburn, Ramsay and Dutch artists, as well as superb French, Chippendale and vernacular furniture. In the delightful grounds, there's a restored Edwardian laundry and also **Scotstarvit Tower**, an outstanding example of a late 16th century fortified tower house.

Also within easy reach of Cupar are two family attractions that children in particular will enjoy. The **Scottish Deer Centre** specialises in the rearing of red deer but also raises species of silka, fallow and reindeer. Some of the animals are tame enough to be stroked. The Centre also puts on falconry displays three times a day. Stranger creatures occupy the **Ostrich Kingdom** beside Birnie Loch Nature Reserve. As well as these huge birds, the children's farm is stocked with goats, chickens and pot-bellied pigs.

DUNDEE & ANGUS

The glorious glens of Angus, carving their way through the southern Grampian mountains, are amongst the grandest sights in Scotland. Just a few scattered villages are dotted along the quiet minor roads which, for the most part, end at the foot of some unscalable crag. The area includes no fewer than 10 Munros, mountains of 3000 feet or more, but it is also great walking country where there's a good likelihood of seeing wild deer, golden eagles or ptarmigan.

The Angus coastline offers some fine beaches east of Dundee and there's a fine stretch of cliffs and bays between Arbroath and Montrose. Ruined Arbroath Abbey was the setting in 1320 for the signing of the Scotland's declaration of independence from England, and there's more history to be savoured at Glamis Castle where, according to Shakespeare, Macbeth murdered King Duncan.

In the south, Scotland's 4th largest city, Dundee, has weathered the loss of its traditional industries and re-emerged as a lively, progressive university city.

DUNDEE   MAP 5 REF L11
13 miles NW of St Andrews on the A92

Approached by either the road or rail bridges over the Tay, Dundee presents a splendid panorama with the city sprawling across the twin hills of Balgay and Law, framed by the often snow-capped Grampians in the distance. The **Tay Rail Bridge**, incidentally, stretches for 2 miles making it the longest rail bridge in Europe. It replaced the one which collapsed during a storm in December 1879 sending 75 passengers and crew to their deaths. The disaster inspired an out of work actor named William MacGonagall to write *Railway Bridge of the Silvery Tay*. Despite the poem's blithe disregard for metre and its banal sentiments, MacGonagall was lionised in Edinburgh's literary salons and his work still gives enormous pleasure to every new generation of readers.

Any visitor to Dundee will soon hear the term "The Three Js", a reference to the three pillars on which the city's past prosperity was founded - jute, jam and journalism. In the 19th century, it was Britain's leading producer of jute which was then widely used in the manufacture of coarse sacking, canvas and rope. Dundee's textile heritage is presented in a lively way at **Verdant Works** with the help of vintage working machinery and up-to-the-minute interactive technology.

The association with jam began when a Dundee grocer named Keiller bought a cargo of oranges from a ship taking refuge from a storm. Keiller's wife made marmalade from them and a sweet-tasting success story followed.

The third J, journalism, is still flourishing with D. C. Thomson's ever-popular *Beano* and *Dandy* comics still delighting children with such characters as Desperate Dan and Dennis the Menace.

Thomson's headquarters stand in Albert Square, across from the city's most imposing Victorian building, the **McManus Art Galleries and Museum** (free). Dundee's 19th century prosperity allowed its citizens to endow the museum with a remarkable collection of Pre-Raphaelite and Scottish paintings. The Museum has a significant display of material from Ancient Egypt and, closer to home, also has the table on which the Duke of Cumberland signed the death warrants of Jacobites captured at the Battle of Culloden.

One of the city's most popular visitor attractions is the **RRS Discovery** which was built at Dundee in 1901 and used by Captain Scott in his expedition to the Antarctic in 1901-1904. The ship lies alongside **Discovery Point**, an award-winning centre where visitors watch an informative film about life on board the Discovery, (crewmen were permitted one bath every 47 days, for example), before stepping on to the ship with its gleaming brass and scrubbed deck.

A short walk along the waterside brings visitors to another remarkable ship. **HM Frigate Unicorn**, a 46-gun wooden warship, was launched at Chatham in 1824 and is now the oldest British-built ship still afloat. The ship has been restored to her original appearance and provides a fascinating insight into what life was like for its 300 officers and crew just 19 years after the Battle of Trafalgar.

One of the city's unusual attractions is the **Mills Observatory** (free), the only full-time public observatory in Britain. Located in picturesque wooded surroundings on Balgay Hill, it houses a 10 inch refracting telescope and displays illustrating the history of space exploration and astronomy. The best time to visit is during the winter months when the mysteries of the night sky are explained by the resident astronomer.

Four miles to the east, **Broughty Castle Museum** (free) is an impressive 15th century fort overlooking the Firth of Tay. General Monck "slighted" the castle, (made it militarily useless), during the Civil War but it was restored in 1861 as part of Britain's coastal defences. It now houses interesting displays on local history, arms and armour, seashore life and Dundee's whaling history.

CARNOUSTIE
MAP 5 REF M10
11 miles NE of Dundee on the A930

Carnoustie is internationally famed as host to the British Open Golf Championship, most recently in July 1999, and many other major golfing events. Every street in this coastal town seems to lead down to a fairway and a bunker is in the foreground of almost every sea view. Carnoustie's sweeping bay, fringed with fine sandy beaches, has also made it a popular holiday town. There are lovely coastal walks, tennis courts, a bowling green, yachting club, water sports facilities, a leisure centre, as well as two country parks within easy reach.

A mere 5 minutes walk from the 1st tee of Carnoustie's famous golf course, **Joseph's** hotel and restaurant is also renowned. Although it stands only a few yards from the town's main street, Joseph's has its own spacious and attractive garden, complete with children's play area. The hotel itself is one of Carnoustie's oldest buildings and later extensions give it an interesting character all of its own. Joseph and Alison Martin, who own and run this exceptional establishment, have had many years experience of the hotel and catering business. They have worked for international hotel groups in Australia, Hong Kong and Malaysia, and before coming to Carnoustie had their own restaurant in Melbourne. Joseph is the culinary wizard and he brings a magical touch to his beautifully

Joseph's, 13 Philip Street, Carnoustie, Angus DD7 6ED
Tel: 01241 852182 Fax: 01241 855440

prepared dishes and wonderful desserts (which include a heavenly home-made ice cream). The menu changes every 2 or 3 days; the quality always remains first-class. Joseph's restaurant, with its crisp white linen tablecloths and vases of flowers on each table, is open for lunch and dinner every day. Such is the restaurant's popularity, you are strongly advised to book ahead for weekends. Carnoustie is a handy base for exploring the charms of this interesting corner of the country and Joseph's can offer visitors to the area a choice of 7 superior guest bedrooms, one of which is on the ground floor.

Ideally situated in the centre of the town, within easy reach of the railway station, shops, the beach and the Championship Golf Course, the **Kinloch Arms Hotel** is perfect for a short stopover or a longer family or golfing holiday in this popular seaside resort. Liz Ross has been running this welcoming hotel since 1991 and, together with her friendly staff, ("always smiling" noted one visitor, appreciatively), makes the Kinloch Arms a particularly pleasant place to stay. There are two bars: a large saloon, decorated in Victorian style, which provides a warm, welcoming atmosphere, and a cocktail bar which tends to attract a

Kinloch Arms Hotel, 27-29 High Street, Carnoustie, Angus DD7 6AN
Tel: 01241 853127 Fax: 01241 855183

more mature clientele. Excellent home-made food from the varied lunch and supper menus is served in both bars during the day with coffee available through-out the day. There's also a superb restaurant, Rannoch's, offering an impressive selection of Scottish and international dishes - Aberdeen Angus steaks, Jeda Chicken, Shanghai Beef or Pork Mexicana for example. (Make sure to book ahead if you want to eat here over the weekend). All the guest rooms at The Kinloch Arms are furnished to a high standard, complete with satellite TV, hospitality tray and even a video-player. An additional, popular attraction here is the live entertainment presented on Sunday evenings once a month.

Two miles west of Carnoustie, **Barry Mill** (NTS) was in continuous use from the 18th century to the early 1980s and its huge waterwheel is now fully func-tioning once again. The intriguing machinery - fanners, elevators, sieves and sack hoist, are also all still operating. From the Mill, there's a delightful walk alongside the lade, or mill-race, to a small apple orchard and picnic area.

ARBROATH   MAP 5 REF M10
17 miles NE of Dundee on the A92

Arbroath holds a special place of affection in the hearts of Scottish nationalists. Back in 1320, it was at **Arbroath Abbey** that Robert the Bruce signed the Decla-ration of Arbroath asserting Scotland's independence from England. The Abbey was then one of the wealthiest and grandest churches in the country. Today, the pink sandstone ruins of the Abbey are a melancholy sight but the remnants of its massively proportioned West Front, the Abbot's House and the Gatehouse testify to its former glory. Dr Johnson described the ruins as *"fragments of magnificence"*.

Anyone with the slightest interest in food will immediately link the name of Arbroath with "smokies". These uniquely tasty delicacies of haddock smoked over oak chips are produced in tiny smokehouses around the picturesque harbour.

Arbroath's name was originally Aberbrothock which is why Kevin and Julie Smith have called their outstanding eating place the **Aberbrothock Restaurant**. It stands alongside the mouth of the Brothock Burn and from the upstairs part of the restaurant there are grand views over the busy little harbour. Kevin is an experienced Chef of some 20 years standing and he offers a tempting menu of home-made dishes, most of them with a very Scottish flavour. You'll find

Aberbrothock Restaurant, 61 Ladybridge Street, Arbroath, Angus DD11 1AX Tel: 01241 871267

steaks of the finest Angus beef, tasty fish, chicken and pasta dishes, as well as vegetarian options and a children's menu. You shouldn't leave without sampling Kevin's home-made truffles or his shortbread made to a secret recipe! The restaurant is licensed and the wine list offers an interesting selection of New World varieties as well as House Wine available by the glass, and in half-litre or litre carafes. During the summer, the restaurant is open daily from 10.00 until 22.00 and it's wise to book ahead at weekends. During the winter months, the Aberbrothock is closed on Mondays and Tuesdays.

Conveniently located in the centre of the town, **Scotties Café** is housed in a rather grand building smothered with pilasters, architraves, mouldings and arches. Happily, there's a much more homely atmosphere inside Catherine Whitton's friendly and attractively decorated café where local patrons are on first name terms with the staff and visitors find themselves equally welcome. Catherine's menu offers a good choice of light meals and snacks: filled baguettes, baked potatoes, toasties, hot or cold rolls and sandwiches, as well as more substantial dishes such as deep-fried haddock or a hearty Full Scottish Breakfast. In addition, there are daily specials, (stovies, Cream of Leek soup, and Lasagne, perhaps), and as Scotties is licensed you can also enjoy a glass of wine with your meal if you wish. The specials board also lists two Sweets of the Day. These are freshly made each day and should certainly not be overlooked. Scotties is open all year round, Monday to Saturday from 8.30 until 16.30.

Scotties Café, 90 High Street, Arbroath, Angus DD11 1HL Tel: 01241 870725

AUCHMITHIE   MAP 5 REF M10
13 miles S of Montrose on minor road off the A92

Four miles northeast of Arbroath, Auchmithie is perched unbelievably high on the cliffs, practically tumbling into the North Sea. The residents of this minuscule fishing village claim that it was here that the famous "smokie" was first produced. But the village has never had a proper harbour so most of the haddock catches were landed at Arbroath and cured there. If you want to be popular in Auchmithie, refer to the celebrated dish as an "Auchmithie Smokie".

Amongst lovers of good food and wine this tiny coastal village is best known for **The But 'n' Ben**, an outstanding licensed restaurant specialising in delicious Scottish cuisine and seafood. The curious name means "two room cottage" and the attractive black-and-white painted building is indeed a pair of fishermen's cottages, about 250 years old. Iain and Margaret Horn have owned and run the restaurant since 1976 and their son Angus is the chef, responsible for the wonderful cooking. The menu features Arbroath (Auchmithie) Smokies of course,

**The But 'n' Ben, Auchmithie, by Arbroath, Angus DD11 5SQ
Tel: 01241 877223**

along with a superb choice of fresh fish dishes, steaks, venison, salads and much more. Definitely not to be missed. The But 'n' Ben is open all year round, except on Tuesdays, with lunch served from 12 noon until 14.30, then afternoon teas, High Teas from 16.00, and evening meals from 19.00. (Last orders 21.00). The Horn family also own **The Fishermen's Inn** in nearby Arbroath where another son, Ralph, is the chef, competing with his brother for the cooking honours. The Fishermen's Inn serves food from 12 noon until 14.30, again from 17.30 until 20.00, and on Saturday evenings there's live entertainment from 20.30.

MONTROSE   MAP 5 REF N9

30 miles NE of Dundee on the A92

Montrose stands on a bulbous peninsula with the North Sea washing into its natural harbour on the east, and the 2-mile wide **Montrose Lagoon** defining its western boundary. The Lagoon is a wildlife sanctuary of international importance, its mussel and reed beds providing a nature reserve for migrant birds. Seals, thousands of ducks and geese are regular visitors; osprey and kingfishers have also been spotted here. At the **Montrose Basin Wildlife Centre** you can join one of the regular guided walks or view the wildlife through powerful binoculars and on live remote-control television.

The town's natural harbour has been its focal point for generations. Skins, hides and cured salmon were the earliest exports, contraband goods flooded in during the great days of smuggling, and currently the port services the North Sea oil industry. It was from Montrose that the Old Pretender sailed for France after the failure of the 1715 rising.

Montrose Museum (free), built in 1841, is one of the oldest in Scotland. The stately neo-classical building contains comprehensive displays on local life as well as an interesting collection of Napoleonic items, include a cast of the Emperor's death mask. Also within the museum is the **William Lamb Sculpture Studio** commemorating the town's best known artist. Born in 1893, Lamb was famous for making sculpture with subjects such as the Queen and Princess Margaret when they were children. The studio, designed by Lamb himself, has been preserved as it would have been when the artist worked there.

Just off the High Street, **The Limes** is a handsome Georgian house with an impressive crenellated semi-circular tower through which visitors enter. Margaret and William Dick have lived here since 1974 and it's hard to believe that this welcoming and comfortable guest house was virtually derelict when they bought it. They spent 6 months of hard labour restoring the building and have since

The Limes, 15 King Street, Montrose, Angus DD10 8NL
Tel/Fax: 01674 677236

added a charming conservatory overlooking the pleasant front garden. The Limes is a spacious house with 12 letting rooms, some fully en suite, some with an en suite shower and toilets opposite. There's a large comfortable residents' lounge with television and a mini-library of books to browse through. Excellent breakfasts are served in the attractive dining-room which has a relaxing home-from-home atmosphere. Margaret and William do not provide evening meals but they can advise you on the many good eating places within easy reach. The Limes has a 3-star rating from the Scottish Tourist Board and, if you are planning to stay in the area, provides a welcoming and convenient base.

Three miles west of Montrose, the **House of Dun** (NTS) is an imposing Georgian mansion designed by William Adam and built in 1730 for David Erskine, Lord Dun. Outside, the house has an elegant and restrained appearance but inside there's a riot of baroque plasterwork and sumptuous furnishings. One of William IV's daughters lived here and the house contains many royal mementoes. Within the grounds there's an attractive Victorian walled garden, a miniature theatre, a handloom weaving workshop, icehouses and fine parkland with woodland walks.

BRECHIN   MAP 5 REF M9
9 miles W of Montrose on the A935

At Brechin the valley of Strathmore meets the rugged Grampian mountains and the old city is itself set on a hill. Standing at the heart of this small city, **Brechin Cathedral** was founded in the 1100s but time has not been kind to it and most of the structure is the result of extensive restoration in 1900. Pre-dating the Cathedral is the fascinating **Round Tower** of 990 AD, some 80 feet tall. It was built as a refuge for the clergy in times of invasion, which is why its doorway stands 6 feet above the ground.

Devotees of steam railways will surely want to take a trip on the **Caledonian Railway** which operates a regular summer timetable of passenger trains on the 4-mile route from Brechin to Bridge of Dun. The Brechin Railway Society have also restored the station building with its superb glass canopy and opened a small but growing museum in the former telegraph office.

Founded as a coaching inn in the early 1800s, the **Northern Hotel** has a long tradition of dispensing hospitality to travellers in the Angus area. It enjoys an ideal location in the heart of this quaint old historic burgh and the resident owners, Donald and Jan Macintyre, assure visitors of a warm welcome and a comfortable stay at their charming, family-run hotel. The hotel's Manor Restaurant provides a very pleasant setting for all meals, with its stylish decor and real fire. An eye-catching café/bar offers a more informal location for coffee, snacks and lunches. There's also a separate cocktail bar for that pre- or after-dinner drink, and a residents' lounge. The Northern Hotel has 17 guest bedrooms, all of them offering en suite facilities, remote control colour television, direct dial telephone, and tea-making facilities. Seven of the rooms are on the ground floor and one room is disabled-friendly. Children are welcome; bed & breakfast, or dinner, bed & breakfast tariffs are available, and so are packed lunches if required. The Northern can also cater for conferences and functions of all kinds in either the Glamis Suite which can accommodate up to 100 people and has its own bar, or the Macintyre Suite for smaller parties.

Standing on the banks of the South Esk River, Brechin has long been a centre for visitors wishing to explore this historic corner of Scotland. The city itself is notable for the unusual round tower standing next to the Cathedral. One of only 2 such towers in Scotland, it dates back to the 10th century when it was

The Northern Hotel, 2-4 Clerk Street, Brechin, Angus DD9 6AE
Tel: 01356 625505 Fax: 01356 622714

built as a refuge from Viking raids. Magical Glamis Castle, childhood home of the Queen Mother, is only 15 miles away, and steam railway enthusiasts can enjoy a trip on the Caledonian Railway Company trains which ply between Brechin's Victorian station and Bridge of Dun during the summer months.

Located a couple of miles north of Brechin, **Brathinch Farm** is a quite outstanding place to stay for bed and breakfast. It's the home of Rosemary and Billy

Brathinch Farm, by Brechin, Angus DD9 7QX
Tel: 01356 648292 Fax: 01356 648003

Beatty and their sons who have farmed the 485 acres of mixed farming here for some 7 years. The farmhouse itself is more than a hundred years old, a charming building with a conservatory housing a flower vine which has been growing for well over half a century. Inside, the house is beautifully furnished and decorated, with wooden floors, lots of antiques and quality furniture.

There are 3 letting rooms at Brathinch Farm, two of them en suite, the third with its own private bathroom. All of them enjoy superb views over the immaculate gardens and the lovely Angus countryside. As you might expect, breakfast at Brathinch Farm is in the great tradition of Scottish farmhouse hospitality, generous enough to satisfy the most ravenous appetite! If you are touring the area, the farm is conveniently close to the A90, (just a mile or so away), and within easy reach of the area's many attractions. Edzell Castle and Gardens are just a few miles to the north; the stately Georgian "House of Dun" about the same distance to the east. The Kincardine coast with its sheltered beaches is only a couple of miles further, while inland stretch the spectacular ranges of the Grampian Mountains.

EDZELL   MAP 5 REF M9
11 miles NE of Montrose on the B966

Described as the "jewel in the crown of Angus", this pretty village right on the Grampian border is always winning "best-kept village" awards. It's approached through the much-photographed **Dalhousie Arch**, erected in 1887 to the memory of the 13th Earl of Dalhousie and his Countess who died within a few hours of each other.

Edzell itself is an estate village, created in the 1840s to a regular plan and with trim Victorian houses lining the straight-as-an-arrow main road. About a mile to the west stand the ruins of **Edzell Castle** (HS) an important 15th century tower visited by Mary Stuart and James VI and also used by Cromwell's troops as a garrison. Much of the 16th century castle is ruined, but the beautiful walled garden has survived for more than 350 years and is one of Scotland's unique sights. It was created in 1604 by Sir David Lindsay, Lord Edzell: enclosed by the rosy-coloured sandstone walls of the **Pleasaunce** it still retains its elegant symmetry with sculptured stone panels on the walls and an immaculate box hedge spelling out the family motto: *Dum spiro spero* - "While I breathe I hope".

Northwards from Edzell runs **Glen Esk**, the most easterly and the longest of the Angus Glens. A minor road follows the course of the River North Esk through stunning mountain scenery to The Retreat, a typical glen shooting lodge which houses the **Glenesk Folk Museum**. The museum was founded in 1955 by Mrs Greta Michie and her vast collection of artefacts and records provide an encyclopaedic overview of past life in Glen Esk. There's also a tea room and craft gift shop.

FORFAR MAP 5 REF L10

14 miles N of Dundee off the A90

Forfar, the county town of Angus, stands on what was once the centre of the kingdom of the Picts and the surrounding countryside is scattered with solitary stones carved deep with mysterious shapes. Some of them, along with Neolithic and Celtic examples, are on display at the **Meffan Gallery & Museum** (free) in the High Street which also has an interactive computer archive logging every known Pictish stone in Angus. Other attractions include some inventive simulations of historic street scenes amongst which is a re-creation of a witch hunt. (Forfar was the only town in Angus where witches were executed).

A more pleasant aspect of the town is the 93-acre park surrounding **Forfar Loch** where rangers organise guided tours and events throughout the year. If you are picnicking here, don't forget to take one of the famous Forfar Bridies, the local equivalent of a Cornish pasty. It was created by Mrs Bridie, a farmer's wife, so that the farmworkers could eat it with work-soiled hands. The crust was simply thrown away.

Back in the town and just a short walk from the centre stands a handsome old inn, the **Volunteer Arms,** so named because in 1896, it was here that volunteers for the Boer War signed up for the Army. Under different names, the hostelry

Volunteer Arms, 1 Arbroath Road, Forfar, Angus DD8 2HS
Tel: 01307 462056

has a history stretching back to the early 1700s when it served as a post horse station where the teams were changed and the adjacent blacksmith's attended to any re-shoeing necessary. The old stables still stand intact to the rear of the inn. Inside, the Volunteers Arms has retained its largely Victorian decor, together with a welcoming and friendly atmosphere. Mine host, Graham Stirling, offers customers a fine choice of ales, and quality food is available at lunchtimes from Monday to Saturday. Children are welcome and the pub has good access for the disabled. This lively pub becomes even livelier on Friday and Saturday nights when there's a disco from 22.00 until 01.00.

Two miles northeast of Forfar rise the substantial remains of secluded **Restenneth Priory** (free), mostly 12th century and standing on the site of a Pictish place of worship. It has a striking square tower surmounted by a shapely brooch spire.

RESCOBIE   Map 5 ref M10
4 miles E of Forfar on the B9113

Farmhouse holidays have a special appeal and **West Mains of Turin** offers excellent accommodation, either in the charming old 19th century farmhouse or in a bungalow about 100 yards away. West Mains of Turin takes its name from the nearby hill on which stand the ruins of Kemp's Castle Fort which are actually within the boundaries of the 300-acre working farm owned and run by Catherine and Eric Jolly. They offer bed & breakfast visitors and holiday-makers a warm welcome, good food and a high standard of comfortable accommoda-

West Mains of Turin, Rescobie, by Forfar, Angus DD8 2TE
Tel/Fax: 01307 830229

tion, with the scenic Angus countryside as an extra bonus. Their farmhouse overlooks the lovely Rescobie Loch and the 3 guest bedrooms enjoy enchanting views either over the loch or across to the hills. The comfortable lounge offers colour television and an open fire, and superb home cooking and baking is served in the dining room where guests may also have an evening meal if they wish. The farmhouse rooms can accommodate up to 6 guests, as can the centrally-heated Bungalow which also has wonderful views. One of the rooms is equipped with en suite facilities for disabled visitors. Guests are welcome to enjoy the large gardens adjoining the farmhouse, and both snooker and croquet are available for evening entertainment.

GLAMIS

MAP 5 REF L10

5 miles SW of Forfar on the A94/A928

With its Disneyesque towers and turrets, cupolas and bartizans, **Glamis Castle** has an enchanting fairy-tale look about it. The name, (pronounced Glahms), is indissolubly linked with Macbeth's murder of Duncan as presented in Shakespeare's play. In fact, the Bard was playing fast and loose with history since Macbeth actually killed his cousin in a battle near Elgin, some 50 miles away.

All the same, when you step into the 15th century Dunce's Hall, among the oldest and eeriest parts of the castle, it seems an appropriately grim setting for such a dreadful deed. Glamis continued to have close associations with royalty right up to the present day. Mary Stuart stayed in August 1562 and "never merrier", and her son James VI became a close friend of the 9th Lord Glamis whom he elevated to the rank of Earl of Kinghorne.

The Lyon family, now Earls of Strathmore and Kinghorne, have lived at Glamis since 1372. It was to be the childhood home of their most famous descendant, the present Queen Mother, 2nd daughter of the 14th Earl. After her marriage to the Duke of York in 1923, the royal couple spent much of their time at Glamis and it was here that Princess Margaret was born.

The richly furnished Royal Apartments in which the Yorks lived are open to the public and contain notable collections of Dutch and Chinese porcelain, and a dazzling portrait by de Laszlo of the young Duchess of York which hangs in the Queen Mother's Bedroom.

It was the 3rd Earl in the mid-1600s who did most to give Glamis its present appearance, inspired by his love of French chateaux architecture. He transformed the 15th century Great Hall into a sumptuous Drawing Room, still the most splendid apartment in the castle, 60 feet long and 22 feet wide with a fine arched ceiling of delicate plasterwork. A complete west wing was added, and a lovely Chapel whose ceiling and walls are covered with devotional paintings. A generation later, when the Old Pretender, James VIII, was staying at Glamis he came to this Chapel to touch people against the "King's Evil", or scrofula. All those whom the king touched, it was reported, were cured.

The 3rd Earl also laid out the lovely gardens where the formal vistas are enhanced by some fine statuary and a huge baroque sundial with 84 faces. There are delightful walks and a Nature Trail through the extensive landscaped Park, and other attractions include an "Elizabeth of Glamis Exhibition", gift shops and restaurant.

KIRRIEMUIR
MAP 5 REF L10

6 miles NW of Forfar on the A926/A928

This handsome little town is often called the "Gateway to the Glens" and roads lead directly from Kirriemuir to the magnificent scenery of Glen Clova and Glen Prosen. Another, Glen Isla, was frequently visited by Kirrie's most famous son - the creator of the eternally youthful Peter Pan, J.M. Barrie who was born here in 1860. **Barrie's Birthplace** (NTS) is a modest terraced cottage at 9, Brechin Road where from an early age Barrie dragooned his brothers and sisters into performing his "plays" in the family wash-house. The wash-house is still there, looking much the same as it did more than 130 years ago. Barrie was later to use it as the model for the house that Peter Pan built for Wendy in Never-Never-Land.

Barrie's most famous creation is commemorated in the little town square by a winsome **Statue of Peter Pan**. Towards the end of his life, Barrie presented his home town with the rather unorthodox gift of a cricket pavilion with a camera obscura within it. It stands on Kirriemuir Hill and provides some grand views across Strathmore and along the Glens.

Although Barrie was offered burial in Westminster Abbey, he chose to be interred in Kirrie's St Mary's Episcopal Church, just along the road from the house where he was born.

A few hundred yards from the town square, the **Aviation Museum** houses the private collection of Richard Moss who has amassed a wealth of wartime photographs, uniforms, medals, models and other World War II memorabilia. The museum is open to the public every day in summer: admission is free but donations for local charities are welcome.

LINTRATHEN BY KIRRIEMUIR
MAP 5 REF L10

6 miles W of Kirriemuir off the B951

In Glen Isla, at the foot of the Knock of Formal, by the waters of the Loch of Lintrathen, hard by the waterfall of Reekie Linn that tumbles eighty feet into a deep pool known as the Black Dub..... The place names of Glen Isla are as entrancing as the magical views.

Glen Isla is the most westerly of the lovely Glens of Angus and **Purgavie Farm** is located at its foot with wonderful views of this captivatingly scenic area. David Clark's grandfather came to Purgavie in 1902 and the family has farmed here ever since, with potatoes and barley now the main crops, while

Purgavie Farm, Lintrathen by Kirriemuir, Angus DD8 5HZ
Tel/Fax: 01575 560213 e-mail: purgavie@aol.com

cattle and sheep graze on the hill. Purgavie Farm is a marvellously peaceful place to stay and visitors have a choice of either bed & breakfast or self-catering accommodation. David and his wife Moira welcome bed & breakfast guests to their spacious old farmhouse where there are 3 large comfortable bedrooms, all en suite and all enjoying glorious views. The hospitality here is wonderful. The generous Scottish breakfast makes lunch unnecessary and evening meals are made especially tasty with fresh, in season vegetables. (Feel free to bring your own wine). If you prefer self-catering, Brankam Cottage, looking across to Brankam Hill, is a pleasing 2-bedroomed cottage equipped with just about every amenity you can think of. Alternatively, the 3-bedroomed "Tipperwhig" is a recently built log house which, like the farmhouse rooms, has been accorded a 4-star rating by the Scottish Tourist Board.

BRIDGEND OF LINTRATHEN
MAP 5 REF L10
6 miles W of Kirriemuir off the B951

This tiny hamlet overlooking Lintrathen Loch offers visitors not just entrancing scenery but also a unique "restaurant with rooms": the **Lochside Lodge and Roundhouse Restaurant.** The circular restaurant used to be a grinding room where a tethered horse would walk round and round, hour after hour, turning the millstone to grind corn. Lochside's proprietors, Stephen and Jackie Robertson

Lochside Lodge and Roundhouse Restaurant, Bridgend of Lintrathen, by Kirriemuir DD8 5JJ Tel: 01575 560340 Fax: 01575 560202

have transformed it into a bright and stylish restaurant which offers a daily-changing menu incorporating the finest local produce. A quick sample of the fare on offer starts the mouth watering. Amongst the lunchtime starters, for example, there might be a Thinly Sliced Caramelised Duck Breast with Apple Salad and a Cranberry & Thyme Sauce. At dinnertime, the main courses might include Seared Wild Venison with Root Vegetable Puree and a Juniper & Tarragon Sauce perhaps, while amongst the desserts you may well find an Iced Terrine of Lemon, Vodka and Poppyseed Parfait on a Passionfruit Sauce. Enough said. The Lochside Lodge maintains similarly high standards for accommodation. Each of the 2 letting rooms is individually furnished in keeping with the coomed ceilings and quaint barn windows of the old hay loft. A meal and overnight stay here is something visitors do not forget very quickly.

KIRKTON OF GLENISLA   Map 5 ref L9
13 miles NW of Kirriemuir on the B951

About ten miles along the glen, the attractive little village of Kirkton of Glenisla stands beside the River Isla, framed on all sides by superb scenery. Here you will find the appealing **Glenisla Hotel**, a cosy old hostelry with beamed ceilings and a roaring open fire. Owned and run by Steve and Shona, the Glenisla is believed to have been in existence since before 1750. Wall paintings discovered during refurbishment and analysed by Dundee University indicate this date and some of them have been preserved under glass at the hotel. Glenisla Hotel enjoys a glowing reputation for its excellent food, all home-made from the very best of

Glenisla Hotel, Kirkton of Glenisla, by Blairgowrie, PH11 8PH
Tel: 01575 582223 Fax: 01575 582203

fresh produce. Chefs Heather and Gyll offer customers separate lunch and dinner menus, although their award-winning Haggis with neeps and tatties understandably appears on both. Tasty main dishes such as Mrs Nicol's Glamis Breast of Chicken in a mild curry sauce, or local Aberdeen Angus steaks, can be followed by one of the delicious home-made puddings listed on the blackboard. Diners can complement their meal with wine, fine ales from the Inveralmond Brewery at Perth, or Cairn o'Mohr Fruit Wines produced at Errol, near Perth. But take care, some of them have an alcohol strength of 14%! With your after-dinner Fair Trade coffee, served with Scottish shortbread or mints, you might like to sample one of the Glenisla's quality malt whiskys - there are more than 80 to choose from. If you are staying in the area, the hotel can offer you a choice of bed & breakfast or self-catering accommodation, an ideal base for exploring the spectacular mountain scenery of the Grampians, or for visiting the popular resort of Pitlochry and its famous Festival Theatre. Closer to Glenisla, about 4 miles further up the glen, stand the ruins of Forter Castle, once a stronghold of the Ogilvie Clan and currently being restored.

8 The Grampian Highlands

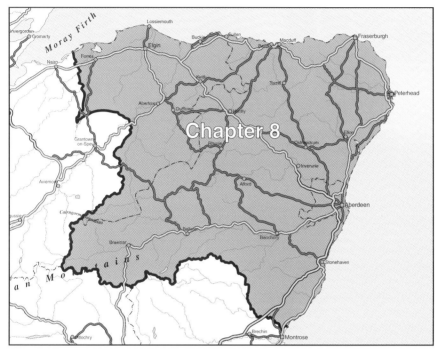

© MAPS IN MINUTES ™ (1998)

The Grampian region falls fairly neatly into five distinct areas. Firstly, there's the City of Aberdeen, Scotland's third largest city, a prosperous port and holiday resort. To the south of the region, Royal Deeside is rich in associations with Queen Victoria who moved into Balmoral in 1852, visited regularly each year, stayed longer and longer each time, and left with increasing reluctance.

The rural heartlands are astonishingly rich in castles, more than a dozen of them, set in a pastoral landscape of rolling hills and farmland. Around Inverurie, is a cluster of prehistoric sites, most notably the East Aquharthies Stone Circle. The northeast corner, historically known as Buchan, includes the fishing ports of Peterhead and Fraserburgh and a rugged coastline dotted with picturesque villages. No castles here but Duff House, near Macduff, is one of Grampian's "must-see" attractions, a flamboyant exercise in Georgian baroque architecture built for the Earl of Fife. He refused to set foot in it.

Finally, there's the former county of Moray which stretches from the Moray Firth, famed for its bottlenose dolphins, to the foothills of the Cairngorms. The clear mountain streams provide an essential ingredient of Moray's most renowned product - whisky. Altogether there are more than 50 distilleries within its borders.

ABERDEEN

Aberdeen is well-known as the Granite City which makes it sound rather dour but in fact the granite is of a rather special kind. In sunlight, the millions of specks of mica embedded in each block add a distinctive sparkle to the city's handsome buildings. Another quirk of nature has endowed the area with the kind of soil beloved by roses. You see them everywhere in the city, in the splendid parks, brightening up the roadsides, filling private gardens. No wonder Aberdeen has been barred from the "Britain in Bloom" competition - it was winning too regularly!

One of the most striking floral displays can be seen in the Old Town, at the University's **Cruickshank Botanic Gardens,** laid out in 1898. The gardens provide a superb foreground to **St Machar's Cathedral** which was reputedly founded by Machar, a follower of St Columba, in 580. The present 15th century building, part church, part fortress, is notable for its sumptuous stained glass windows and the equally colourful nave whose oak roof is ablaze with heraldic coats of arms. Nearby, **King's College Chapel** is the oldest of the University's buildings, completed in 1495. The chapel contains a wealth of exquisite medieval woodcarving, with especially fine work in the rood screen and the canopied stalls.

South of the Old Town, the city centre is a model example of good town planning. In 1800, Aberdeen embarked on an ambitious programme of development, so ambitious that it was nearly bankrupted. Fortunately, a boom in ship construction, particularly of the famous Tea Clippers, saved the Town Fathers from disaster.

Amongst the older buildings, **Provost Skene's House** (free) dates from 1545 and is now a museum illustrating the life and times of the rich Aberdonian merchant, Sir George Skene, who lived here in the late 1600s. The **Tolbooth Museum** (free) is also 17th century. Formerly the city jail, the exhibits displayed in its claustrophobic rooms and corridors reflect the barbarous penal systems of the past.

Aberdeen's myriad attractions are too numerous to list in full here but two of them must definitely not be overlooked. The **Art Gallery** (free) houses an outstanding collection of mostly British paintings from the 18th to the 20th century along with some important Impressionist works; there's a Sculpture Court with works by Barbara Hepworth and Paolozzi; and the display of prints and drawings ranges from a 15th century Flemish illuminated manuscript to water-colours by Edward Lear.

Also not to be missed is the **Maritime Museum** (free) in the harbour district. Aberdeen is still an important fishing port and the museum explores its history from the days of herring fishing to the era of North Sea oil and gas exploration. Incorporated within the museum is **Old Provost Ross's House**, built around 1590 and the oldest surviving dwelling in the city.

Aberdeen once claimed the title of Scotland's largest seaside holiday resort and its 2 miles of sandy beaches, (which continue for miles further up the coast), are backed by a huge range of attractions. Amongst them there's another "largest in Scotland" claim for the permanent fun fair, **Codona's Amusement Park**.

KINGSWELLS   MAP 5 REF N8
4 miles W of Aberdeen off the A944

Four Mile House is so named because it is indeed 4 miles from the centre of Aberdeen, located in this tiny village off the A944. A long low building, its most striking feature is the spacious conservatory, light, airy and stylishly furnished. It can seat some 70+ diners but such is its popularity you would be well-advised to book ahead for Fridays and weekends. If you have left it too late, there's still

Four Mile House, Kingswells, Aberdeen AB15 8QA
Tel: 01224 740318 Fax: 01224 749886

plenty of room in the restaurant and lounge areas, both serving the same high quality food that has made Four Mile House such a popular venue for Aberdonians and visitors alike. There's an extensive menu which not only offers the best of Scottish traditional food but also exotic dishes from Mexico, China and Thailand, along with vegetarian options and Healthy Eating choices. In addition, there's a daily Carvery with a choice of 3 roasts, and a Chef's Special of the Day. A particularly attractive feature of Shirley Shirreffs' outstanding hostelry is its "Courtesy of Choice" policy which reflects the centuries- old philosophy that acknowledges differences while allowing them to exist together in har-

mony. Accordingly, Four Mile House accommodates the preferences of indi-
viduals by offering both smoking and non-smoking areas "in the spirit of
conviviality and mutual respect".

ROYAL DEESIDE & THE MEARNS

Queen Victoria made her first visit to Scotland in 1842 and was immediately
captivated by the scenery - *"so wild and grand"* she wrote. She was to return as
often as her numerous pregnancies permitted and in later life spent so much
time at Balmoral that her ministers became increasingly fretful that she chose
to spend up to 4 months of each year 500 miles away from the capital.

In the early years, Victoria was an indefatigable explorer, braving storms and
mountains passes with equanimity. In her diary she noted *"I seldom walk less
than four hours a day, and when I come in I feel as if I want to go out again"*. Victoria's, and her successors', close association with Deeside is reflected in the many
"By Royal Appointment" signs proudly displayed throughout the region.

BRAEMAR   MAP 5 REF K8
67 miles W of Aberdeen on the A93

The **Braemar Gathering**, or Highland Games, has its origins in the athletic
contests initiated by Malcolm III (1031-93) to find *"his hardiest soldiers and fleetest
messengers"*. The Games lapsed in medieval times but in 1834 were revived and
featured such traditional contests as Putting the Stone, Throwing the Hammer
and, the most distinctive of the Highland Games, Tossing the Caber - a 20 feet
long pole of stripped pine weighing 132 lbs. The Gathering is held on the first
Saturday in September but if you want to attend, make sure you get a ticket well
in advance.

The event takes place close to **Braemar Castle**, a small but forbidding fortress occupying a strategic position where three mountain passes meet. Built in
1628, it was badly damaged during the first Jacobite rising of 1689, re-fortified
by the English in the wake of the '45 Rebellion, and in 1797 passed to the
Farquharson family, now Lairds of Invercauld.

They began converting the castle into a family home and the result is an
intriguing blend of uncompromising military architecture and elegant features
such as Heppelwhite chairs and Chippendale mirrors.

In the heart of the village, **Gordon's Restaurant** offers a wide range of tempting dishes, with the emphasis on Scottish specialities such as Orkney Salmon
Steak and Scottish Rainbow Trout. Campbell and Margaret Carr, who own and
run this highly recommended restaurant, spent many years in Durban, South
Africa, running a coffee house/restaurant there. Campbell is the chef and his
menu also includes offerings such as Thai Vegetable Schnitzel, steaks from the
griddle bar, and a good choice of "lite bites". During the summer months, there's

**Gordon's Restaurant, 20 Mar Road, Braemar, Royal Deeside AB35 5YL
Tel: 013397 41247**

also a High Tea menu, and there's always a special menu for children. Campbell is a baker/confectioner by trade so you can count on finding an excellent selection of wonderful desserts. Another appealing feature of this friendly restaurant is the fact that guests are served by waitresses wearing the authentic Gordon tartan. Gordon's Restaurant, which is non-smoking, is open from 10.30 until 17.00, (21.00 during the season), but closed during January and early February.

CRATHIE   MAP 5 REF L8
58 miles W of Aberdeen on the A93

This neat and tidy village has 'model' cottages built by Victoria and Albert for workers on the Balmoral Estate and a church of 1895 whose building was funded by the proceeds of a bazaar held at Balmoral Castle. The grey granite church is familiar to television viewers since it is regularly attended by the royals when they are in residence. Victoria's favourite ghillie, John Brown, is buried in the graveyard, Princess Anne married her second husband here and, following the death of their mother, Princes William and Harry made their first appearance at its gates.

   Balmoral Castle nearby is a full-blooded example of the Scottish Baronial style of architecture, beautifully set in a wooded landscape beside the River Dee with **Lochnagar** (3786 feet) rising to the south. Victoria and Albert bought the estate in 1852 for £31,000, demolished the rather poky mansion that stood there, and a gracious building of white granite, dominated by a tower 80 feet high, rose in its place. Royalists will be disappointed to discover that access to Balmoral Castle is restricted to the Ballroom and grounds - and only in May, June and July.

BALLATER   Map 5 ref L8
17 miles NE of Braemar on the A93

Victoria was particularly fond of the valley of Glen Muick (pronounced "Mick") which runs southwest from Ballater and it's still popular with walkers and cyclists. But whichever direction you travel from this trim little town, the River Dee and the pine-clad hills provide superb vistas at every turn. Victoria often arrived by train at Ballater, although she vetoed plans to extend the railway closer to Balmoral itself. The railway service petered out many years ago but the elegant station still stands, part of it now housing a tearoom.

A traditional Scottish dwelling set in its own grounds, **Morvada House** enjoys a peaceful and picturesque location at the foot of Craigendarroch - "The Hill of the Oaks". Built in 1886, Morvada House is the home of Allan and Thea Campbell who assure their guests of a warm and friendly stay in a home-from-home atmosphere. All the attractively furnished rooms are well equipped, with en suite facilities, colour television, electric blankets and tea/coffee trolley. If stairs are a difficulty, one of the rooms is located on the ground floor. Guests

**Morvada House, 28 Braemar Road, Ballater, Aberdeenshire AB35 5RL
Tel: 013397 56334**

have the use of a comfortable lounge and the healthy grilled breakfast is served in the spacious dining room. The Campbells do not serve evening meals but there are many good eating and drinking places in this historic and peaceful village, all of them within easy walking distance. Morvada House is open all year; children over 12 are welcome, but smoking is not!

Built in the early 1900s, **Balgonie Country House** lies on the outskirts of the village in the heart of one of the most beautiful and unspoilt areas of Scotland. It is unsurpassed for privacy, with no passing traffic - a haven for those who enjoy peace and tranquillity in a traditional setting. This Edwardian-style Country House is set within four acres of mature gardens and commands truly superb views overlooking Ballater Golf Course to the hills of Glen Muick beyond. The resident proprietors, John and Priscilla Finnie, aim to make your stay,

**Balgonie Country House, Braemar Place, Ballater
Royal Deeside AB35 5NQ Tel: 013397 55482**

however long or short, both enjoyable and memorable. They regard the Dining-room as the heart of Balgonie, providing outstanding Scottish cuisine using the best of local produce - fresh salmon from the River Dee, marvellous local game, high-quality Aberdeen Angus beef, and excellent seafood fresh from the East Coast and Orkney, all complemented by the carefully selected wine list. Balgonie has 9 guest bedrooms, each individually decorated and furnished, and equipped with en suite bathroom, colour television and direct dial telephone. All but one share the extensive views towards Glen Muick. Not surprisingly, the hotel has been showered with awards, amongst them the Taste of Scotland Award for "Country House of the Year Award" in 1993, the AA Inspectors' Selected Hotel of the Year in Scotland, 1994, and has also been awarded 2 AA Rosettes for its restaurant.

CORGARFF   MAP 5 REF L8
52 miles W of Aberdeen on the A939

From Ballater, the scenic A939 leads northwards to Corgaff village and the bleak
fortress of **Corgarff Castle** (Historic Scotland). It's an unusual building with the
main house enclosed within a star-shaped wall. There was a gruesome incident
here in 1571 when its owners, the Forbes family, were massacred by the Gordons.
The English commandeered the castle after the Battle of Culloden, using it as a
barracks, and in the mid-1800s English soldiers were again quartered at Corgarff,
charged with the hopeless task of detecting and destroying the countless illicit
whisky stills hidden away in the hills.

Overlooking Corgarff Castle and nestling in the rolling foothills of the Grampians, on the north bank of the upper River Don, the **Allargue Arms Hotel**
enjoys a splendid position. The hotel is owned by Carolyn and Phil Herbert
who came to know it because it was their "local". When the 200-year-old property was put up for sale in May 1998, they decided to buy it. The Allargue Arms

Allargue Arms Hotel, Corgarff, Strathdon, Aberdeenshire AB36 8YP
Tel: 019756 51410 Fax: 51465 e-mail:herbert@allargue.demon.co.uk

is an ideal base for a whole range of activities. Skiers are attracted here during
the winter since the Lecht Ski Centre is just a couple of miles to the north;
fishermen can take advantage of the hotel's own 6-mile stretch of the upper
Don which offers excellent fishing for wild brown trout and the occasional
salmon; and hill walkers, mountain bikers and ornithologists all find their interests well-catered for. The food served at the Allargue Arms is just as satisfying,

with a comprehensive bar menu catering for all tastes, including a selection of vegetarian dishes. The hotel also offers 7 comfortable rooms, most en suite, providing excellent facilities and all as warm as toast!

STRATHDON
MAP 5 REF L7

45 miles W of Aberdeen on the A97

The road from Corgaff to Strathdon follows the lovely valley of the River Don. En route, it passes **Candacraig Gardens**, home of Anita Roddick, founder of the Body Shop, and much-photographed signs to the village of Lost. It's well worth popping into the village itself to visit **The Lost Gallery** which hosts excellent, and eclectic, exhibitions of paintings, sculpture and photographs.

Pretty as a picture itself, **Buchaam Farmhouse** offers visitors to this lovely corner of the country a good choice of either bed & breakfast or self-catering accommodation. Mr and Mrs Ogg welcome bed & breakfast guests to their 19th century centrally-heated farmhouse set in 650 acres of open fields and woods. Families with children will appreciate the safe play areas and the 18-hole putting green. During the season, guests also have the use of a full-size badminton court, table tennis is available, as well as an area for indoor football and other ball games. All the necessary equipment is provided. The Farmhouse has three comfortable and attractively furnished letting rooms, (1 double, 1 family, 1 twin), with two shared bathrooms. One of the rooms is on the ground floor, the other two upstairs. A hearty breakfast is included in the tariff but the Oggs do not

Buchaam Farm, Strathdon, Aberdeenshire AB36 8TN
Tel/Fax: 019756 51238

provide evening meals and they regret that pets are not allowed in the farm-house. If you prefer self-catering, there are 2 attractive cottages on Buchaam Farm to rent, and a house on Deskry Farm, about half a mile to the west. All of these properties are stone built, fully equipped and with double glazing through-out. They sleep 7/8 people, with a cot available if required, and all enjoy open views of peaceful countryside. Heating is by coal or stick fires (which help to heat the water), storage heaters and electric fires. If you are arriving out of sea-son, the heating will have been on to give you a warm welcome. The kitchens are all-electric and well-equipped with fridge, immersion heater, automatic wash-ing machine, and microwave. Colour TV is also provided. Around each property there are woodland and hill walks, and quiet glens offering a perfect setting for a country picnic. With so much to offer, it's not surprising that Buchaam Farm-house has been a runner-up in the Scottish Farmhouse of the Year Award.

DINNET   MAP 5 REF M8
34 miles W of Aberdeen on the A93

Victoria Tea Rooms lies in the heart of Royal Deeside, on the Queen Victoria Heritage Trail. This quaint and lovely tea room, owned and run by Maureen and Douglas Fiddes, ably assisted by their daughter Jennifer, offers widely acclaimed home baking - huge, light, creamy Meringues, Pancakes with Maple Syrup, Ap-ple & Cinnamon or Banoffee Cream, Cream Teas or the Traditional Victorian

Victoria Tea Rooms, Dinnet, Aboyne, Aberdeenshire AB34 5JY
Tel: 01339 885337

Afternoon Tea complete with laden cake stand. The menu is extensive, including Cold Platters; Hot Savoury dishes; All day Breakfast; Low Calorie options; with Daily Specials adding to the selection. Children are welcome and there are facilities for the disabled. There are attractive Arts and Crafts and Bric à Brac for sale, and accommodation is also available if, like Queen Victoria, you would like to stay and explore this "Dear Paradise".

Just outside the village and a few miles from the famous ski resorts of the Lecht and Glenshee, **Loch Kinord Hotel** stands amidst the beautiful scenery of Royal Deeside. This friendly, family-run hotel is ideally situated for both summer and winter sporting holidays. Deeside is a golfers' paradise with the hotel centrally located between no fewer than six courses; fishing on nearby Loch Kinord is recommended for its pike and perch; water skiing can be enjoyed at Aboyne Loch, and Deeside Gliding Club is just a five minute drive away. Andrew and Jenny Cox, who own and run the Loch Kinord Hotel, offer their guests

Loch Kinord Hotel, Ballater Road, Dinnet, Royal Deeside AB34 5JY
Tel: 013398 85229 Fax: 013398 87007

excellent cuisine, whether you are enjoying an informal bar meal or choosing from the table d'hôte menu. Families are welcome, with childrens portions available. The accommodation includes a splendid Honeymoon Suite with 4-poster bed, en suite bathroom and adjoining sauna and jacuzzi. All bedrooms are furnished to a high standard, including colour television, tea & coffee-making facilities and many bedrooms also have an en suite shower room. Even if you are not staying in the area, the Loch Kinord makes an excellent place to stop for morning coffee, afternoon tea or light snacks throughout the day.

ABOYNE
MAP 5 REF M8

30 miles SW of Aberdeen off the A93

Quietly situated in two acres of grounds just half a mile from the village centre, **Struan Hall** is one of the very few bed & breakfast establishments to have been awarded the Scottish Tourist Board's top 5-star rating. The charming old house has had a curious history. It was originally built, around 1820, about 5 miles east of here and was known as Tillydrine House. Then in 1904 a wealthy Glasgow merchant had it removed, stone by stone, to its present location. Phyllis and Michael Ingham bought the house in 1989 and after substantial but sympathetic refurbishment began welcoming bed & breakfast guests in 1991. Their

Struan Hall, Aboyne, Aberdeenshire AB34 5HY
Tel/Fax: 013398 87241 e-mail: struanhall@zetnet.co.uk

aim has been to provide modern facilities in traditional surroundings so all bedrooms have private bathrooms, central heating, TV, and tea/coffee-making facilities. A spacious Lounge and Dining Room overlook the pleasant front garden. Phyllis is very knowledgeable about this historic area and can guide you to its many attractions, whether your interest is in Castles, National Trust properties, Gardens, Distilleries, Highland Games or wildlife. (Please note that Struan Hall is open from March to October and is totally non-smoking).

LUMPHANAN
MAP 5 REF M8

25 miles W of Aberdeen on the A980

Macbeth's Cairn to the north of Lumphanan is said to mark the spot where Macbeth made his last stand in 1057. He was immediately executed and his head was taken to Malcolm at Kincardine Castle near Fettercairn. Shakespeare's play compresses Macbeth's reign into a matter of months but in fact he ruled for more than a decade and was neither more nor less bloodthirsty than his contemporaries.

Lumphanan itself is an attractive place and when the railway still served the village, the Station Hotel provided quality refreshment and accommodation for travellers. Now re-named the **Macbeth Arms Hotel,** Henry and Carol-Anne Wright's welcoming establishment performs the same service for modern visitors. If you are looking for fine ales, good food and comfortable accommodation in the area, look no further. The well-kept ales include McEwans Export and

Macbeth Arms Hotel, 1 Station Square, Lumphanan, Banchory Aberdeenshire AB31 4TE Tel: 013398 83236 Fax: 013398 83421

John Smiths; the excellent menu is available all day; and the 3 letting rooms are all en suite, very comfortable, and furnished with colour television and telephone. Amongst the interesting places to visit in the neighbourhood are Craigievar Castle, a few miles to the north, which is an extraordinary fantasy castle built in the 1600s; the prehistoric structures of Peel Ring, (5 minutes walk from the hotel), and Tornaverrie Stone Circle, a few miles to the west.

BANCHORY

MAP 5 REF M8

18 miles SW of Aberdeen on the A93

Just off the main street, in Dee Street, the award-winning **No. 10 Coffee Shop &
Licensed Restaurant** is a family-run business which provides all its customers
with a warm welcome and friendly personal service. Alice and Ray Parr, together with their daughter Caroline, have been running No. 10 since 1994 and
they specialise in traditional home baking, along with an extensive range of
freshly prepared food. Alice and Caroline are in charge of the kitchen and they
reckon that since opening here they have produced more than 95 different

**No. 10 Coffee Shop & Licensed Restaurant, 10 Dee Street
Banchory AB31 3ST Tel: 01330 822869**

varieties of scones! Their other offerings include muffins, traybakes, Danish pas-
tries, meringues, dough rings, and Passion Cake. No. 10's wide-ranging menu
also offers a good choice of light meals, salads, burgers, and hot dishes cooked
to order. There's a selection of vegetarian meals and a "Hungry Horace" menu
for small children. In addition to the regular menu, Alice and Caroline always
offer several daily specials. Children are welcome at No. 10, there's good wheelchair access, and a conveniently located car park just across the road. The coffee
shop and restaurant is open 7 days a week, from 9.00 to 18.30 in summer; 9.30

to 16.30 in winter. Lovers of Scottish folk music will want to pay a visit to Banchory's little Museum in Bridge Street where an exhibit celebrates local man James Scott Skinner, the famous fiddler and author of such tunes as *The Bonnie Lass o' Bon Accord*. There's also a stone to his memory in the High Street and if you're lucky your visit might co-incide with a meeting of the Strathspey and Reel Society which keeps his memory alive. Another attraction, just south of the town, is the salmon leap at the point where the Dee joins the River Feugh.

About 3 miles east of Banchory, **Crathes Castle** (National Trust for Scotland) is one of the most appealing old buildings in the country. Built between 1550 and 1590, its sturdy outline is sprinkled with fairytale-like turrets and fantastic gargoyles. The interior is no place for claustrophobics but the low ceilings of the small rooms are dazzlingly decorated with wonderful early 17th century paintings. The Nine Muses and Seven Virtues are depicted in the Muses' Room, while the Room of the Nine Nobles portrays great heroes of the past, amongst them Julius Caesar and King Arthur. Outside, the Victorian walled garden has eight themed areas, the extensive grounds contain six woodland walks, and there's an imaginative adventure playground.

Drum Castle (National Trust for Scotland), a few miles further along the A93 towards Aberdeen, has a massive square tower of pink granite, (which was once the property of Robert the Bruce), adjoining a fine Jacobean mansion house. Inside, there's some fine furniture and paintings; outside, a walled garden where the Trust has created a unique Garden of Historic Roses.

STONEHAVEN   MAP 5 REF N8
15 miles S of Aberdeen on the A90

Set around a sheltered bay, this popular holiday resort has a picturesque harbour overlooked by the town's oldest building, the **Tolbooth**. Originally built in the 1500s as a storehouse, it later served as the town jail and is now a museum of local history and fishing. An interesting time to visit Stonehaven is at Hogmanay when the ancient ceremony of **Fireballs** takes place. The townspeople parade along the High Street swinging metal cages full of burning rubbish. This ensures that they will be protected from evil spirits during the coming year.

The High Street links the harbour area to the 18th century New Town set around a Market Square with a striking **Market Hall** topped by an impressive steeple. One of the houses in the square bears a plaque identifying it as the birthplace of Robert Thomson (1822-73), inventor of the pneumatic tyre, the fountain pen and the dry dock.

Handily located in the heart of the town, just a couple of minutes from the A90, the **Queen's Hotel** is a splendid listed building dating back to 1763. The oldest surviving coaching inn in Stonehaven, the Queen's is owned and run by partners Tom and Eleanor Wilson, and David Forbes. When they bought the

Queen's Hotel, 9 Allardice Street, Stonehaven, Aberdeenshire AB39 2BS
Tel: 01569 764993 Fax: 01569 767055

hotel in 1989 it had fallen on hard times: its rooms silent and its windows boarded up for some four years. The partners have restored the grand old building to its former state of grace and today the Queen's Hotel is a lively place with a marvellously friendly atmosphere. The public bar provides an excellent choice of ales, beers and lagers, and to the rear there's an outstanding café/bar serving a wide variety of main courses, Lite Bites, and sweets, as well as vegetarian options and a children's menu. The hotel also offers superb accommodation in 5 outstanding en suite letting rooms, and 2 self-catering suites. All have up-to-date facilities, and are spacious and cosy - a wonderful place to use as a base for exploring this attractive corner of the country.

Occupying a superb position on the quayside overlooking the harbour, **The Ship Inn** is a lively hostelry, frequented by locals and visitors alike. Built in 1771, The Ship has remained a popular eating and drinking place among sailors to this day, their loyal patronage reflected in the many maritime pictures and other memorabilia decorating its walls. Many of the building's original 18th century features have survived, and recently a 19th century Smokehouse was uncovered. It dates from the era during which Stonehaven was home port to a large fishing fleet. When herring catches declined, the Smokehouse was simply covered with panelling and forgotten. These days, The Ship offers a good choice

of value for money food, with different menus for lunch (noon until 14.00) and evening meals, (18.30 - 21.00, booking advisable). For whisky-lovers, The Ship is an absolute paradise, offering a constantly expanding choice of prime malts. There were more than 100 at the last count, ranging from Glen Ury, ("Rare, Strong"), to Rosebank, ("Smooth, Mild"); from Tobermory, ("Heathery"), to Laphraoig, ("Strongly Peaty"). The inn has a useful Malt Whisky Menu providing these brief descriptions but if you would like more comprehensive advice, just ask your friendly hosts, Bill and Sandra Holmes.

The Ship Inn, 5 Shorehead, Stonehaven, Aberdeenshire AB39 2JY Tel: 01569 762617

Just a few minutes drive from the town centre, **Woodside of Glasslaw Guest House** is surrounded by lovely countryside. Aileen and Doug Paton built their attractive house here in 1987 and five years later added purpose-built accommodation for visitors. Because it was built so recently, the facilities at Woodside

Woodside of Glasslaw Guest House, Stonehaven, Aberdeenshire AB39 3XQ
Tel/Fax: 01569 763799

of Glasslaw are all up-to-date and of top quality. All 5 letting rooms are well-equipped, comfortably furnished, and all are en suite with good modern showers. Two of the rooms are doubles, two are twin-bedded, and one is a family room with bunk beds for the children. The accommodation was also designed to be disabled-friendly, so there are no steps at all and ramps are provided where necessary. Aileen and Doug are welcoming hosts and do everything they can to make their guests feel at home. Located a couple of minutes from the A90, Woodside of Glasslaw provides a perfect base for exploring the Kincardine coast and for visiting attractions such as nearby Dunottar Castle.

Dunottar Castle, 2 miles south of Stonehaven, has starred as Elsinore Castle in the film versions of *Hamlet* directed by Mel Gibson and Franco Zeffirelli. Rising menacingly from the top of a sheer-sided crag, the shattered fortress glares defiantly out to sea. Dunottar's grim appearance accords well with its blood-stained history. In 1297, for example, William Wallace set fire to Dunottar, burning alive every man of the English garrison within. Some 400 years later, the castle vaults witnessed the imprisonment and savage torture of 167 Covenanters. Nowhere else in Scotland is the pitiless savagery of those times more powerfully evoked than at Dunottar.

FETTERCAIRN
15 miles SW of Stonehaven on the B966

MAP 5 REF M9

In September 1861, Queen Victoria and Prince Albert paid an unheralded visit to Fettercairn, taking over the local inn, the Ramsay Arms. Their identity having been discovered by the next morning, the royal couple were loyally cheered on their way, and the local people later erected the impressive **Fettercairn Arch** at the entrance to the village. Today, the Arch marks the start of the **Victoria Heritage Trail** linking the many locations associated with the Queen. About a mile to the west, the **Fettercairn Distillery**, the second oldest in Scotland, offers free tours and the usual complimentary sample. **Fasque House**, to the north of Fettercairn, has been the family home of the Gladstones since 1829. The most famous of them, William Ewart, served four times as Prime Minister under Victoria but he was not a royal favourite. The Queen complained that he addressed her like "a public meeting". The interior of the Gladstones' stately Georgian house has changed little since the late 19th century and provides a fascinating insight into the life-style of the upper middle-class in those days.

LUTHERMUIR
8 miles NW of Montrose off the B974

MAP 5 REF M9

Inland from the attractive Kincardine coast lies the fertile **Howe of Mearns**, a broad, shallow valley, (a "Howe"), within the Mearns, an ancient name for the former county of Kincardineshire. The small village of Luthermuir enjoys a peaceful setting in this pastoral landscape.

THE ABERDEENSHIRE HEARTLAND

The distinctive profile of Bennachie (1733 feet) dominates the rural centre of the county, a peaceful landscape of rolling hills, woodland and scattered farms. Although it was the setting for the first known battle in Scottish history, back in Roman times, the county's remoteness spared it from the worst of the constant warfare that plagued most of southern Scotland in the Middle Ages.

Despite this happy state of affairs, the area boasts an extraordinary number of castles and grand houses. The Castle Trail leads visitors from medieval Kildrummy Castle, via the Renaissance flamboyance of Craigievar Castle, to the Georgian elegance of Haddo House and Duff Castle.

The River Don meanders through this unspoilt countryside, dropping from the hillsides of Bennachie in the west and flowing into the sea at Aberdeen. From the estuary, a splendid sandy beach stretches northwards for some ten miles, ending at the Sands of Forvie, a National Nature Reserve noted for its extensive dunes - *"like something out of Lawrence of Arabia"*.

INVERURIE
MAP 5 REF N7

16 miles NW of Aberdeen off the A96

One of the few sizeable communities in the Aberdeenshire heartland, this flourishing farming town hosts the thrice-weekly **Thainstone Mart**, one of the largest livestock auctions in Europe. Over to the west rises **Bennachie**, its tor-like summit a useful point of reference wherever you are travelling in this area. Back in AD 84, it was somewhere near Bennachie that the Romans defeated the Picts in what the historian Plautus called the battle of Mons Graupius, Latin for "Grampian Mountain". This was the most northerly battle fought by the Romans in Britain and also the first to be recorded in Scotland.

The area around Inverurie is also rich in ancient remains with the Pictish **Brandsbutt Stone** and the prehistoric **East Aquhorthies Stone Circle** both close by. And, 4 miles to the northwest, the **Maiden Stone** is a striking 10 feet high monument carved with a Celtic cross and Pictish symbols.

KINTORE
MAP 5 REF N7

13 miles NW of Aberdeen off the A96

This tiny Royal Burgh has an elegant **Tolbooth** of 1740 with a two-winged outside staircase. The town is well-known to archaeologists because of the ancient **Ichthus Stone** in the churchyard which is carved with a fish on one side and what might be an elephant on the other. On the surrounding hills are many prehistoric remains of forts and stone circles, most of which have probably already entered their 4th millennium.

Scottish hoteliers seem to have a special talent for creating country house hotels which combine stately surroundings with a friendly, relaxed atmosphere

The Torryburn Hotel, Kintore, Aberdeenshire AB51 0XP
Tel: 01467 632269 Fax: 01467 632271

for their guests. **The Torryburn Hotel** at Kintore is a perfect example. It's a strikingly grand 19th century building, set in some 3 acres of gardens, the kind of place which, if it were owned by the National Trust for Scotland, you would happily pay a few pounds to visit. Lorraine and Verdun Moar own and run this exceptional property where guests find themselves really pampered. Their 12 letting rooms are all en suite, indulgently comfortable, and equipped with just about every amenity you can think of. The hotel's restaurant is equally satisfying. Whether you are vegetarian or carnivore, you can be sure of finding something on the menu that appeals to your palate. How about a really Scottish dish like Sirloin Caberfiedh, for example - sirloin steak stuffed with haggis and topped with whiskied mushrooms? If you happen to be visiting on special occasions such as Burns' Evening or Mothering Sunday, for example, The Torryburn Hotel pulls out all the stops to make your stay an event to remember.

KEMNAY   MAP 5 REF N7
15 miles NW of Aberdeen on the B993

Just step inside **Bennachie Lodge** and the friendly atmosphere, the cosy bar with its real fire, and the attractive furnishings make you feel instantly at home. The Lodge was bought by Nicky Dalgarno in December 1998 and together with partners Caroline and Iain McDonald he has steadily upgraded the hotel's deco-

Bennachie Lodge, Victoria Terrace, Kemnay, nr Inverurie, Aberdeenshire AB51 5RL Tel: 01467 642789

ration and amenities. Visitors will find quality food available every lunchtime and evening, served in the attractive restaurant and complemented by a good choice of top-notch ales. Bennachie Lodge currently offers guests a choice of 7 letting rooms, (possibly more by the time you read this), all en suite, comfortably furnished and well-appointed. For entertainment, the Lodge hosts regular discos on Friday and Saturday evenings and there are many historic and natural attractions within easy reach. Bennachie, the great granite tor from which the Lodge takes its name, challenges hill-walkers with a fairly stiff 2-hour walk; the East Aquhorthies Stone Circle near Inverurie contains stones weighing up to 20 tons; and a couple of miles south of Kemnay, Castle Fraser is one of the grandest castles in the country.

Begun in 1575, **Castle Fraser** is an authentic example of the original Scottish Baronial style of architecture with stout walls, lots of perky little turrets, and a lofty circular tower. Inside, the austere simplicity of the Great Hall, dominated by its immense fireplace, vividly evokes the atmosphere of past centuries. Fine furniture and paintings inside; a beautiful walled garden, woodland walks and an adventure playground outside are amongst the many attractions.

ALFORD   Map 5 ref M7
27 miles W of Aberdeen on the A944

Alford's main allure for visitors is the **Grampian Transport Museum**, a remarkable collection of vintage road vehicles supported by push-button exhibits and video presentations tracing the history of road travel in the locality. One of the stars of the show is the "Craigevar Express", an extraordinary steam-driven 3-wheeler constructed by a local postman in the 1890s to convey him on his rounds. Back in 1859, the Great North Scotland railway made Alford its western terminus. From the former station, a 2-feet narrow gauge railway carries passengers on a 1-mile trip to **Haughton Country Park**. Within the park's extensive grounds there are riverside Nature Trails, a Visitor Interpretive Centre and a picnic area.

To the south and west of Alford are two more stops along the Castle Trail. **Kildrummy Castle** is an impressive 13th century ruin crowning a hilltop site. At the base of the cliff, beautifully maintained Alpine shrub and water gardens soften the contours of a former quarry.

Craigievar Castle has to be seen to be believed. This exuberant wedding-cake confection in pink granite, dating back to 1626, is so popular with visitors that the National Trust for Scotland sometimes has to restrict the numbers allowed to enter. But you can always enjoy the chocolate-box exterior of the castle from the grounds, for which there is no admission charge.

INSCH   MAP 5 REF M7
25 miles NW of Aberdeen on the B992

Just a couple of miles off the main A96 Aberdeen to Inverness road, the little village of Insch boasts its very own (working) railway station and, directly opposite, an outstanding hostelry, the **Station Hotel**. Dating back to early Victorian times, the handsome old building is part-listed. It's owned by James and Fiona Sutherland, a welcoming, outgoing couple who in the 5 years or so they've

Station Hotel, 1-3 Commercial Road, Insch, Aberdeenshire AB52 6JN
Tel/Fax: 01464 820604

been here have made the hotel a great success. Good food and quality ales are always available and there's a separate restaurant seating about 20 people. The hotel also offers an interesting choice of accommodation. There are 9 ground floor chalet-style rooms, all en suite, while the main building has a further 5 rooms to let. This guest-friendly hotel also welcomes children and pets. The Station Hotel is well-known to lovers of Country & Western music since the Sutherlands present live entertainment every 2 months. These events attract C & W enthusiasts from all over the world, especially when the famous singer Paddy O'Brian is topping the bill, which he does about 4 times a year.

About 2 miles north of Insch, the **Picardy Stone** is a fine example of a Pictish carved symbol stone, dating back to the 7th century. Anyone with an interest in the area's prehistoric treasures will find it rewarding to visit **Archaeolink Prehistory Park**, about 5 miles southeast of Insch, in the foothills of Bennachie. The 40-acre Park includes the remains of a genuine Iron Age fort, and a working Iron Age farm, complete with Iron Age characters and ancient animal breeds. Inside the Archaeodome, there's a Myths and Legends Gallery and the Archtivity Fun Room where young and old can try out ancients crafts such as weaving and arrow making. Archaeolink can even provide you personalised print-outs giving directions to almost 100 of these ancient sites within the region.

West of Insch, the Castle Trail leads to **Leith Hall**, an appealing 17th century mansion house set in the middle of a 286-acre estate. The Leith family who lived here for some 300 years produced a long line of distinguished soldiers and the Hall contains a unique collection of military memorabilia.

HUNTLY

MAP 5 REF M6

33 miles NW of Aberdeen off the A96

The attractive market town of Huntly, surrounded by pleasant, open countryside, also lies on the Castle Trail. The ruins of **Huntly Castle** are beautifully set overlooking a gorge of the River Deveron. Until the mid-1500s, the castle belonged to the "Gey Gordons", a term which was later corrupted into the name of a popular Scottish dance. "Gey" meant prominent or influential which the Gordons certainly were from medieval times until the Civil War when the Marquess of Huntly supported Charles I. He was shot against the walls of his own castle but not before uttering the defiant words "You can take my head off my shoulders, but not my heart from my sovereign".

Located in the heart of the town, **The Gordon Arms Hotel** is a magnificent listed building, parts of which date back to 1746. David and Jennifer Sherriffs bought the hotel in early 1998 and quickly established a reputation for providing their guests with imaginative food, well-tended ales and wines, and top-quality accommodation. The hotel's long history is reflected by a flagstone outside which bears the inscription, "Coaches left from here to Aberdeen", and inside by striking stained glass windows and an attractive spiral wooden staircase. Arriving guests step into a wonderfully relaxed and welcoming environment.

The Gordon Arms Hotel, The Square, Huntly, Aberdeenshire AB54 8AF
Tel: 01466 792288 Fax: 01466 794556

The 14 letting rooms are all en suite, outstandingly well-furnished and deco-rated, and those on the top floor enjoy splendid views over the surrounding hills. The cuisine on offer in the hotel's restaurant is equally satisfying. There's an extensive menu which makes the most of quality ingredients such as prime Aberdeenshire meat, fresh fish from Cullen, and fresh local vegetables in sea-son. (If you have any special dietary requirements, don't hesitate to ask for advice). Children have their own menu, (the Wacky Chicken Waffles seem to be especially tempting to juvenile palates), and for senior citizens with smaller appetites the restaurant offers some of the dishes in more manageable portions. Diners can complement their meal with a sensibly priced bottle of wine, or sample the Australian House Wines by the carafe or glass. The Gordon Arms Hotel also offers its guests the amenities of the Cheers Bar, a stylish café/bar with a relaxing olde-worlde atmosphere. The hotel welcomes party bookings. Groups of up to 20 can enjoy their own private dining area; the upstairs restau-rant can accommodate up to 60 people; and the hotel's spacious function room can seat up to 200 guests.

FISHERFORD   MAP 5 REF M6
30 miles NW of Aberdeen on the B992

From Huntly, the A96 passes through the scenic Glens of Foudland towards Aberdeen. After about 10 miles, follow the signs to the village of Fisherford for a visit to **The Fjord Inn**. Resting in view of Bennachie, one of the north of Scotland's best-loved hills, The Fjord radiates an atmosphere of tranquillity and well-being. The owners, Evelyn and Norman Mundie, are friendly, down-to-earth people who, together with their staff, immediately put guests at their ease. The Inn's comfortable, unfussy furnishings have a warm, homely character which reflects the personality of the owners. Born and bred in Aberdeenshire, Norman is the chef and carefully prepares his dishes using only the very finest and freshest produce. The menu changes regularly, with a variety of main courses

**The Fjord Inn, Fisherford, nr Inverurie, Aberdeenshire AB51 8YS
Tel: 01464 841232**

on offer, all home-cooked, and with fish dishes a speciality of the house. No wonder Norman and Evelyn enjoy a well-earned reputation for consistently producing excellent meals, attractively presented. The traditional yet imaginative Scottish cuisine is available every lunchtime and evening from Wednesday to Sunday. The Inn also has a well-maintained one and half acre Caravan Park, ideal as a base for exploring the surrounding district, abounding as it does with castles, prehistoric sites, country parks, whisky distilleries and golf courses.

ROTHIENORMAN   Map 5 ref N6
28 miles NW of Aberdeen on the B9001

Tucked away in the Aberdeenshire countryside, about 4 miles east of Fisherford, Rothienorman is a small village well worth seeking out for the **Rothie Inn.** It was built in the early 1800s when Rothienorman was a rather more important place, standing as it did on the road used by drovers and coaches. The inn dispensed hospitality to these travellers and almost 200 years later, Laraine and Stuart continue the grand old tradition. They bought the Rothie Inn in 1992 and over the years have steadily enhanced its facilities, most notably in the splendid conservatory restaurant. Both of them cook and their regularly-changing menus offer some distinctly enticing fare. As a starter, for example, you could choose Melon & Smoked Salmon Kebab, followed by a main course of Highland Chicken, (succulent chicken supreme poached in wine and served

The Rothie Inn, Main Street, Rothienorman, Aberdeenshire AB51 8UD
Tel: 01651 821206

with a Drambuie, onion, and cream sauce, along with Stuart's special Turnip Cake), and ending with a home-made Sticky Toffee Pudding. For children, there's an unusually extensive menu of special dishes. (Do note that the kitchen is closed on Wednesdays). If you are staying in the area, the Inn also has three comfortable letting rooms, a double and two twins, both with en suite facilities.

Between Rothienorman and the coast followers of the Castle Trail will find 3 more links in the chain. **Fyvie Castle** (National Trust for Scotland) is perhaps the most perfect example of the Scottish Baronial style of architecture in the country, a winner of the Europa Nostra Gold Medal. Its 5 fanciful towers are said to represent the 5 families who have lived at Fyvie since the original castle was built in the 1400s. Each family made its own additions, most notably the elaborately decorated 17th century south front, and the opulent Edwardian interior where there are major works by Gainsborough and Henry Raeburn. An unusual extra "attraction" is an authentic Victorian earth closet.

Further east, **Haddo House** (NTS) is a magnificent Palladian mansion designed by William Adam and built in 1735. Former home of the Earls of Aberdeen, Haddo has sumptuous Victorian interiors in the 1880s "Adam Revival" style. The lovely grounds were created from wasteland in the early 1800s by the 4th Earl. Finally, there's secluded **Tolquhon Castle** (Historic Scotland) near Pitmedden, a 15th century ruin with an impressive gatehouse richly decorated with sculpted figures and coats of arms. Inside, interesting features include a medieval kitchen and a grim dungeon.

Nearby **Pitmedden Gardens** were laid out in 1675 by Sir Alexander Seton in order to occupy his mind when he was forced into political exile by James VII. Three of the huge geometric flower beds follow designs used at Holyrood House in Edinburgh, the fourth re-creates the Seton family crest in brilliant living colour. Also within the 100-acre estate is the **Museum of Farming Life** which present a vivid picture of the days when the horse was the power in front of the plough.

"THE LAND AT THE BEND IN THE OCEAN"

Otherwise known as **Buchan**, the northeast corner of Grampian presents an open landscape with productive farms nestling between gently rolling hills leading down to the coastal plain. Peterhead and Fraserburgh are both important fishing ports and Peterhead is also home to several other significant industries.

Elsewhere though, you'll only find small country and seaside towns, and a coastline of empty, unspoilt beaches, soaring cliffs and secret coves. Wildlife attractions include the RSPB Visitor Centre near Crimond, the Macduff Marine Aquarium near Banff and, most glorious of all - although sightings are totally unpredictable - the resident population of bottlenose dolphins in the Moray Firth.

PETERHEAD   MAP 5 REF O6
35 miles NE of Aberdeen off the A90

At Peterhead more white fish is landed each year than at any other port in Europe. The harbours are always chock-a-block with shipping and each weekday morning the fish market is frantically busy selling off the previous day's catch.

The town's sea-going history is presented in a lively way at **Peterhead Maritime Heritage** using modern interactive displays, a live relay of the harbourmaster's radio channel and the recorded memories of old fishermen and women.

The town's most ancient building, some 400 years old, is still fulfilling the same purpose for which it was originally built. At **Ugie Salmon Fishings** in Golf Road visitors can watch salmon and trout being smoked over oak chips in the traditional way and purchase the finished product.

BURNHAVEN   MAP 5 REF O6
2 miles S of Peterhead on minor road off the A982

Burnhaven village looks out across Sandford Bay to Buchan Ness, the most easterly point in Scotland. Occupying a scenic position overlooking the bay, **Invernettie Guest House** is a handsome pink-granite building where Scottish hospitality goes hand in hand with a warm Scottish welcome and a hearty Scottish breakfast. Kathleen and Sandy Simpson have lived here for more than 40 years and first began welcoming visitors for bed & breakfast accommodation in the late '50s. They stopped to bring up their family and then re-opened in 1994.

Invernettie Guest House, South Road, Burnhaven, Peterhead AB42 0YX
Tel/Fax: 01779 473530

Their century-old house was formerly a grocer's shop but the Simpsons have added a spacious extension and now they can offer 7 comfortable, well-decorated rooms: 2 twins en suite; 3 singles, also en suite; and 2 singles, one of which is suitable for disabled guests. All rooms have colour television and tea/coffee-making facilities. Breakfasts range from a simple continental breakfast to the more traditional Scottish cooked breakfast and Invernettie Guest House also offers evening meals based on local seasonal produce and tailored to your requirements. An additional attraction is the relaxing residents' lounge which enjoys grand views over the bay.

A few miles south of Burnhaven, the famous **Bullers of Buchan** is an awe-inspiring chasm, 254 feet deep, into which the sea has forced its way by scouring out a natural archway. Great spumes of foam rise from every incoming surge of the sea. Visiting in 1773, Dr Samuel Johnson described The Bullers as "perpendicularly tubulated". Bring his famous Dictionary along with you and try to work out what on earth he meant.

A little further south, the ruins of **Slains Castle** overlooking the sea are said to have inspired Bram Stoker to write his chilling novel, *Dracula*.

FRASERBURGH

Map 5 ref O5

43 miles N of Aberdeen on the A90

A major fishing port, Fraserburgh is also a busy holiday resort boasting several miles of crunchy, sandy beaches. To the north of the harbour stands **Kinnaird**

Head Lighthouse, the first to be built in Scotland, in 1787. Abutting the tower is the purpose-built **Museum of Scottish Lighthouses** which contains an exhibit celebrating the Stevenson family who built so many of them. Two generations of the Stevensons helped to make the seas around Scotland much safer for mariners: their offspring, Robert Louis Stevenson, endowed English literature with a legacy of stirring, well-crafted stories which have never lost their appeal. The museum also houses a fascinating collection of equipment rescued from redundant lighthouses and the guided tours culminate in a tour to the top of the old lighthouse.

Well-known for its wonderful home-made cakes, **The Coffee Shoppe** in Cross Street is housed in a sturdy building of multi-coloured granite. Inside, there's a friendly and welcoming atmosphere, created by sisters Chris Patterson and Ann Thomson, and your eyes go straight to the trolley laden with cakes, scones and slices all of which will have been freshly baked that morning. Pavlovas and other marvellous treats also feature on the tempting bill of fare. The Coffee Shoppe was purchased by a group of local Christians in 1988 and all profits from the shop are devoted to Christian Relief and Mission work in the Third World. So too is the income from The Coffee Shoppe Cookbook which contains many of the recipes for the bakery items on sale here. Children are welcome

The Coffee Shoppe, 30 Cross Street, Fraserburgh, Aberdeenshire AB43 5EQ
Tel: 01346 517355

and there is good access and facilities for the disabled. The Coffee Shoppe, which is non-smoking, is closed on Wednesday and Sunday; on other days it is open from 9.00 until 16.30. If you appreciate top quality home baking, The Coffee Shoppe should not be missed.

ROSEHEARTY   MAP 5 REF N5
4 miles W of Fraserburgh on the B9031

From Fraserburgh an especially scenic route follows the coast, passing en route through the attractive village of Rosehearty. **Pitsligo Castle** dates from 1424 and passed through various hands to the 4th Lord Pitsligo who was equally admired for his generosity to the poor and for his ingenuity in escaping capture after the '45 Rising. Pitsligo was outlawed and his castle left to decay until the 1980s when one his descendants, the multi-millionaire American publisher, partially restored it.

Situated at the bottom of the road from the castle, **The Masons Arms Hotel** is known locally as "Fit o' the Cassa" (at the foot of the Castle) and has a history going back some 200 years to the time when it was a staging inn. Visitors receive a genuinely warm family welcome from Scott Hornal, his girlfriend Fayona, daughter Maxine, and son Scott. Scott senior has owned and personally run the inn since 1992 and his hostelry is well-known for serving excellent food and

**The Masons Arms, 1 Castle Street, Rosehearty, Fraserburgh,
Aberdeenshire AB43 7JJ Tel: 01346 571250**

quality ales. Food is available every lunchtime and in the evening from 20.00, wholesome fare at very reasonable prices. Children are welcome and other attractions here include a large screen television, a pool table, function suite - and a golf course directly across the road! This picturesque coastal village provides a handy base for visitors to the area and The Masons Arms can offer 3 comfortable letting rooms: 2 family rooms upstairs and a single en suite on the ground floor.

PENNAN
9 miles W of Fraserburgh on the B9031

MAP 5 REF N5

This beautiful old smugglers' village stands at the base of mighty cliffs, hidden by the overhang. Pennan was the setting for Bill Forsyth's film, *Local Hero,* in which a small Scottish community hoodwinks a giant American oil company. The culmination of the film involves a call from the traditional pillarbox-red phone box which is still in place and is now a listed historic monument.

GARDENSTOWN
13 miles W of Fraserburgh off the B9031

MAP 5 REF N5

With its busy little harbour and houses rising in tiers, Gardenstown is another in this string of picture-postcard villages. If you take the steps leading up from the harbour to Main Street, you will find the excellent **Brooms** restaurant and tea room. It's housed in an 1845 building which has served over the years as a chandlers, a general store & drapery, and even as a pottery and craft shop. Some three years ago, Barbara and Chris Broom, thoroughly refurbished the old property, and opened their stylish eating-place. Their varied menu is prepared from top quality local produce with bakery items coming from the baker just across the road, meat from the butcher just along the street who hangs his meat in the old-fashioned way. Brooms offers meals, snacks, afternoon and high teas throughout the day, and a more comprehensive menu for dinner in the evening. Children have their own special choices and Brooms stocks an inter-

Brooms, Main Street, Gardenstown
Aberdeenshire AB45 3YP
Tel: 01261 851629 Fax: 01261 851551

esting selection of country fruit wines from Errol in Perthshire. The restaurant is licensed but guests are also welcome to bring their own wine.

Nestling at the foot of steep cliffs, Gardenstown occupies one of the most spectacular settings along this coast. The **Braes O' Gamrie** self-catering holiday homes overlook the old part of the village and enjoy magnificent views over the harbour, Gamrie Bay and clear across the Moray Firth to the hills of Sutherland. There are 5 houses in all, 4 of them with 2 twin and 1 double bedroom, bathroom, lounge and well-equipped kitchen. The fifth has a double bedroom and a

Braes O'Gamrie, 2-10 Garden Crescent, Gardenstown, AB45 3ZJ
For enquiries & bookings, contact owners Charles & Lorna Davidson,
Havenlee, 2 Markethill Road, Turriff AB53 4AZ Tel/Fax: 01888 563827

double bed settee suite in the lounge. All the properties have large front lawns, private off street parking, and are available all year round. Walkers will appreciate the many cliff-top walks, anglers can go salmon fishing on the River Deveron just 10 minutes drive away, and bird watchers will find colonies of puffins, razorbills, cormorants, gannets and other species at nearby Troup Head. And between June and September, schools of dolphins make this favoured area their home.

MACDUFF   Map 5 ref N5
21 miles W of Fraserburgh on the A98

This pleasant fishing port at the mouth of the River Deveron enjoyed a few decades during the 19th century as a popular spa town but nowadays it's the excellent **Macduff Marine Aquarium** that draws visitors to the town. It boasts the deepest aquarium tank in Britain - 400,000 litres of sea water stocked with a unique kelp reef and a wide variety of marine life, including wolf-fish, conger eels and octopi. Don't miss seeing divers feeding the fish!

This corner of Grampian boasts only one stately house of any consequence, but **Duff House** is quite exceptional and one of the not-to-be-missed sights of northeast Scotland. Designed by William Adam in 1730, the house is a breathtaking extravaganza of Georgian Baroque approached by an elegant 7-arched bridge over the River Deveron. The house was commissioned by the enormously wealthy William Braco, later Earl of Fife. Because of a dispute with his respected architect, Braco never set foot in the house and would even close   the curtains of his coach if he was forced to drive by.

In 1835 the house was sold and over the years has served as a hotel, sanatorium, prisoner of war camp but is now the principal outstation of the National Gallery of Scotland. The outstanding collection of paintings on display includes portraits by Allan Ramsay, Sir Henry Raeburn, an El Greco and, dominating the Great Staircase, a copy of Raphael's colossal *Transfiguration*. In the Great Drawing Room a splendid set of Chippendale furniture contrasts with a fine suite of French furniture from the Empire period.

Other attractions include lovely riverside walks, a tearoom housed in the former Servants' Hall, a shop and a mini-cinema where visitors can watch the story of this remarkable house.

BANFF   MAP 5 REF M5
22 miles W of Fraserburgh on the A98

Macduff stands on the east bank of the River Deveron, Banff on the west. An ancient seaport and Royal Burgh, Banff is also a holiday resort with good beaches. The old part of the town has a goodly number of 17th and 18th century houses which the Banff Preservation Society has helpfully labelled with informative plaques. You can glean even more knowledge of the town's buildings and history if you rent a Walkman Tour from the Tourist Information centre.

One of the town's many gracious Georgian houses is now **The County Hotel**, a grand old Grade B listed granite building with a striking fanlight window above its entrance. A plaque placed by the Banff Preservation Society records that the house was built around 1778 for Mr Garden Robinson, a scion of the rich linen-manufacturing family whose members often served as Provosts of the burgh. Tim and Ankie Carins own and run this inviting and welcoming hotel where residents and non-residents alike can sample the quality food available in the downstairs Bistro or upstairs in the elegant à la carte Restaurant which enjoys wonderful views over Banff Bay. (Booking is required for the Restaurant). The menu changes every 3 or 4 weeks but there's always a good choice of grills, seafood, and imaginative chicken dishes such as Skirlie - half a stuffed chicken with traditional skirlie. If you are planning to stay in this attractive

**The County Hotel, 32 High Street, Banff, Aberdeenshire AB45 1AE
Tel: 01261 815353**

little town, The County Hotel with its central location, gardens and ample parking is ideal. It has 5 letting rooms, 4 of them en suite, the other with a private bathroom, all extremely comfortable and well-appointed.

About a mile outside Banff, the **Colleonard Sculpture Park** (free) provides a tranquil garden setting for a unique display of abstract sculptures created from the trunks of trees. Sculptor Frank Bruce began his collection in 1965 and he's usually to be found in the Park.

PORTSOY   MAP 5 REF M5
8 miles W of Banff on the A98

Portsoy is built around a picturesque harbour and much of the town is designated an outstanding conservation area. Many of the houses were skilfully restored in the 1960s, amongst them **Soy House**, built in the 1690s and the oldest in the town. Portsoy Marble, or serpentine, a dark green stone resembling marble, is quarried to the west of the town and has found its way to many stately houses, include the Palace of Versailles.

Occupying a superb position on the Old Harbour, **The Shore Inn** is an historic building, believed to be as old as the harbour itself (1690). There are dark tales of it being used as a smugglers' haunt before becoming a respectable inn around 1864. The interior is as appealing as the outside, with real fires and an abundance of bygones and memorabilia around the walls. The Shore Inn is the

The Shore Inn, The Old Harbour, Church Street, Portsoy,
Banffshire AB45 2QR Tel: 01261 842831 Fax: 01261 842833

place to come to if you are fastidious about your ale. The owners, Kerr and
Sandra Hill, ran and owned the Tring Brewery in Hertfordshire before they moved
to Portsoy in 1997. So you can be confident that the real ales and others on offer
will be served to you in prime condition. The food at The Shore Inn is equally
satisfying. A full menu is available every day from noon until 21.00, and there
are additional daily specials listed on old beer barrel tops. Especially popular are
the huge breakfasts served from 10.00 until 12.30 every day in summer, and on
Saturdays and Sundays only out of season. Children are welcome here and there
is access for the disabled, although the ladies' toilet is upstairs. If you enjoy
traditional folk and jazz music, The Shore Inn hosts live bands on Thursday
evenings from around 20.30.

BOYNDIE   MAP 5 REF M5
6 miles W of Banff on the A98

Set in tranquil countryside just 6 miles from the town of Banff, **Cowfords Farmhouse** provides a wonderfully peaceful setting for a self-catering holiday. It stands
in the grounds of Culbirnie Farm and the owner, Mrs Greenlaw, can give you
directions to a hilltop vantage point where you will get a panoramic view of the
coast from Macduff to Portsoy. On a really clear day you can even discern, far in
the distance, the hills of Caithness. The century-old farmhouse offers visitors
comfortable accommodation for up to 6 people, a lounge with colour televi-

**Cowfords Farmhouse, Culbirnie Farm, Boyndie, nr Banff AB45 3AX
Tel: 01261 843227**

sion, a dining room and kitchenette. Guests are asked to bring their own bed linen and towels, children and pets are welcome, and the quoted price includes everything except electricity which is paid for by a £1 coin meter. Cowfords Farmhouse is available to rent from May to the end of September, the best time of the year to enjoy this unspoilt corner of the country.

BRIDGE OF MARNOCH   MAP 5 REF M6
12 miles SW of Banff on the B9117

One of only 28 hotels in Scotland to have received the AA Red Star award, **The Old Manse of Marnoch** is a truly outstanding establishment. It was also proclaimed Hotel of the Year in 1997 by the *Which? Hotel Guide*. Set in four acres of mature gardens on the banks of the River Deveron, the house is a former Church of Scotland manse. Its oldest part dates back to the late 1700s; the main frontage with its distinctive "cherry-picking" was completed in 1805; the "modern" extension was constructed in 1926; and the hotel's owners, Patrick and Keren Carter, are adding a new west wing. Guests at the Old Manse can be assured of personal attention, luxurious accommodation, and excellent cuisine. Karen is the chef, her superb meals based on top quality Scottish produce complemented by soft fruit, vegetables and herbs from the hotel's acre of kitchen garden which is tended by Patrick. The guest bedrooms are beautifully decorated and furnished, and equipped with just about every amenity you can think of. (The Carters will even provide you with synthetic pillows should you be allergic to feathers). Breakfast at the Old Manse is a really memorable experience. The

**The Old Manse of Marnoch, Bridge of Marnoch, by Huntly AB54 7RS
Tel/Fax: 01466 780873**

extensive choice includes that Edwardian favourite, Devilled Ham, Herring in Oatmeal, Kippers, of course, and the once-ubiquitous but now hard to find Anglo-Indian speciality, Kedgeree. Wonderful!

ABERCHIRDER
MAP 5 REF M6
9 miles SW of Banff on the A97

No one has yet provided a convincing reason why the village of Aberchirder is known locally as Foggie. North Sea mists certainly drift inland from time to time, but they also smother many other communities in this rural corner of the county. Interpreters of Scottish place-names admit that they have only the "Foggie-est" notion about the origins of Aberchirder's alternative name.

TURRIFF
MAP 5 REF N6
11 miles SE of Banff on the A947

In early August, this little town is packed with visitors attending the Turriff Agricultural Show, one of the largest such events in Europe. **Delgatie Castle**, 2 miles to the east, also gets its fair share of visitors. Attractively set amidst parkland and woods, the castle has been the home of the Clan Hay family for almost 700 years. Inside, there are some marvellous painted ceilings from around 1590, a magnificent turnpike stair with 97 steps and some interesting paintings, including one of Mary Stuart who stayed at the castle for 3 days in 1562.

CUMINESTOWN
MAP 5 REF N6

23 miles W of Peterhead on the B1970

When William Robertson came to the **Commercial Hotel** in Cuminestown some 40 years ago, it was run by his parents. William, together with his wife Ena, took over the helm 18 years later and the hostelry has gone from strength to strength. At the rear of the hotel they have added a really impressive function room which can accommodate up to 180 people and has become a popular venue in the area for wedding receptions. The hotel is open all year round, seven days a

**Commercial Hotel, Cuminestown, nr Turriff, Aberdeenshire AB53 5WJ
Tel/Fax: 01888 544205**

week, from 11.00. An excellent choice of food is available at lunchtimes and from 17.00, either at the bar or in the relaxing dining room. (By the way, if you plan to eat here on a Saturday evening, you would be wise to book ahead). Children are welcome in both the Lounge Bar and the dining room, and the Robertsons are always pleased to welcome coach parties. They can also offers visitors to the area 3 letting rooms - two of them double, the third a family room.

MAUD
MAP 5 REF N6

14 miles W of Peterhead on the B9029/B9106

The Aberdeen to Fraserburgh railway that used to run through this small town has been closed for many years but the station buildings still stand and are open to the public. Across the road stands the **Station Hotel** which was converted from a private house around the time the railway was completed. Today the sturdy, granite building is still welcoming visitors and providing first class hos-

Station Hotel, Station Road, Maud, Aberdeenshire AB42 5LY
Tel: 01771 613245

pitality. The owners, Monica and David McLean, offer their customers an extensive choice of good wholesome food, (cooked by Moica), which is available
from 11.00 until 14.30, and between 17.00 and 23.00, Monday to Saturday, and
all day on Sunday. The hotel also offers a selection of at least 5 different ales for
beer connoisseurs to choose from. This quiet little village is a handy base for
exploring the area and the Station Hotel has 6 quality letting rooms at very
reasonable prices. The rooms are available throughout the year; children are
welcome; and the McLeans also offer special breaks.

STUARTFIELD   Map 5 ref O6
12 miles W of Peterhead on the B9030

Built in the early 1800s and previously known as The Commercial Hotel, **The**
Crichie Inn is an attractive black and white-painted building situated in the
heart of the village. Lynn Robertson and her husband took over the Inn from
her parents in 1998 and they have continued to provide visitors with the quality food and ales for which The Crichie Inn was already well-known. The
ever-changing menus offer a good choice of dishes, served in hearty portions
and at reasonable prices. Food is available every lunchtime from oon until 14.00,
and in the evenings from 17.00 until 19.30, except on Tuesdays. Meals can be
enjoyed either in the bar or in the stylishly refurbished dining room with its

The Crichie Inn, Burnett Street, Stuartfield, Peterhead AB42 5DN
Tel: 01771 624214

leather banquettes and elegant furniture. At weekends, it's advisable to book ahead for the dining room. Children are welcome at The Crichie Inn until 20.00, and from time to time there's live music on Saturday evenings from 20.30.

OLD DEER   MAP 5 REF O6
11 miles W of Peterhead off the A950

This attractive little village takes its name from the 13th century Deer Abbey whose sparse remains stand in a lovely setting in the grounds of **Pitfour House** near the South Ugie Water. On the outskirts of the village, **Saplinbrae House Hotel** is a striking old building dating back to 1756 when it was built as a dower house. It is now a gracious country house hotel offering outstanding cuisine and top quality accommodation. Owned and run by Julia and Andy Brown, Saplinbrae House stands in its own grounds and anglers will be delighted to know that the hotel's next door neighbour is a 37-acre Trout Fishery. Dining at Saplinbrae House is a memorable experience: prime ingredients imaginatively prepared and served in an elegant dining room where the tables are covered with crisp linen tablecloths and the windows overlook the gardens. Each month, the Browns hold themed evenings when the food is entirely Italian, Moroccan,

Saplinbrae House Hotel, Old Deer, nr Mintlaw, Aberdeenshire AB42 4LP
Tel: 01771 623515 Fax: 01771 624472

Spanish or drawn from some other exotic cuisine. No wonder the hotel has a Taste of Scotland award. Accommodation at Saplinbrae House is of comparable quality with 7 en suite rooms, all beautifully furnished and decorated. The hotel can also offer more basic accommodation at Cedar Lodge, situated within its grounds, which can sleep parties of up to 25 - ideal for anglers, shooters, walkers, etc.

STRICHEN
MAP 5 REF N6
15 miles NW of Peterhead on the A981

Strichen village has enjoyed a unique position in the history of Buchan ever since it was developed back in 1764 as a model village. The cross-shaped layout of the village devised then by The Laird of Strichen is still in place today. A couple of miles outside the village Mormond Hill, at 759 feet, is the highest point in the Buchan countryside and notable for the famous **White Horse** created in the early 1800s. Believed to be the only one of its kind in Scotland, the figure measures 164 feet from nose to tail, and 14 feet from ear to hoof. This striking feature dominates the Buchan plain and when Marion and Gordon Thom bought The Freemasons Inn in Strichen they decided to re-name it **The White Horse Hotel.**

The hotel is well-known locally for its excellent home cooking, prepared with the finest meat, fish and seafood for which the area is renowned, and served in the intimate dining room. Diners can complement their meal with a choice from the select wine list. The hotel's elegant residents' lounge provides an ideal spot in which to relax, with a favourite book perhaps, whilst the public bar with its traditional wood panelling offers a good range of wines, beers and spirits and a chance to "meet the locals". Guests can also enjoy using the games

**White Horse Hotel, 65 High Street, Strichen, Fraserburgh,
Aberdeenshire AB43 6SQ Tel: 01771 637218 Fax: 01771 637940**

room offering darts and a pool table. All the hotel's 6 guest bedrooms are attractively furnished and equipped with colour television and tea/coffee hospitality tray. In addition, 3 of the bedrooms have full en suite facilities. With a Coastal Trail, Fishing Heritage Trail, Castle Trail, Malt Whisky Trail, Victorian Heritage Trail and many parks and gardens of interest all within easy reach the area has much to offer - including an ideal touring base at The White Horse.

MORAY: "MALT WHISKY COUNTRY"

In 1727, Daniel Defoe described Moray as a *"pleasant country, the soil fruitful, watered with fine rivers, and full of good towns"*. The town of Elgin, in particular, was *"a very agreeable to place to live in"*.

Defoe's praise holds true almost 300 years later. He might also have mentioned the pretty villages sprinkled along the coast. They are especially picturesque because many of the houses follow the local tradition of using colour wherever possible. Not just windows and doors, but cement window surrounds, mortar between the stonework, and soetimes even the masonry itself, it picked out in a variety of shades.

Moray's other distinctive buildings are the pagoda-like roofs of the whisky distilleries. The signposted **Malt Whisky Trail** links half a dozen of them, but in all there are 50 or so distilleries in the area, the largest concentration anywhere in the world.

ELGIN MAP 5 REF L5
35 miles W of Banff on A96

This handsome market town, which developed around the River Lossie in the 1200s, still retains most of its medieval street plan. The bustling High Street gradually widens to a cobbled Market Place where the architectural focus is an elegant neo-classical building, the **Church of St Giles,** erected in 1828. Eight years later, at the top of the High Street, the townspeople of Elgin subsribed funds to build one of the first municipal museums in Britain. The **Elgin Museum** offers a good display of local artefacts, some fine Pictish stoes, pre-Columbian pottery, and also houses an eclectic anthropological collection which includes a shrunken head from Ecuador and a gruesomely grinning mummy from Peru. When the museum first opened, **Johnstons of Elgin Mill** was already well-established. For almost two centuries, Johnstons has been noted for is fine fabrics and finished garments. Modern day visitors can watch the whole process by which raw cashmere from China and Mongolia is transformed into finished garments.

Elgin has a partcular resonance in Scottish history for it was here that Bonnie Prince Charlie spent eleven days in 1746 just before taking to the field of Culloden. During his stay, the Prince visited the ruins of **Elgin Cathedral** which is possibly the most accident-prone ecclesiastical buildig in the country. Founded in 1224, barely fifty years later it was severely damaged by fire. Rebuilt, the Cathedral was described as "the ornament of the district, the glory of the kingdom, and the admiration of foreigners". Then in 1390 the "Wolf of Badenoch", (the epithet applied to the lawless Earl of Buchan), with his "wyld, wykked Helendmen", set fire to the building along with the rest of the town. It was the Earl's way of expressing his displeasure towards the Bishop of Moray who had excommunicated him for leaving his wife. Rebuilt once again, the Cathedral flourished for a century and a half until the Reformation. Then it was stripped of all its priceless treasures, the lead was salvaged from its roof in 1667, and on Easter Sunday 1711, the central tower collapsed. The ruins were cannibalised as a "common quarry" until 1807 when steps were taken to preserve what remained. And what remains is still remarkably beautiful.

To the north and west of Elgin, three historic buildings definitely merit a short diversion. **St Peter's Kirk** near Duffus dates back to 1226, and although only mournful fragments of that original structure remain, the church is worth visiting to see its fine 14th century cross, the exquisite calligraphy on many of the tombstones, and the watch-house built in 1830 to protect the newly-interred from the depredations of grave-robbers. Duffus is also home to **Gordonstoun School,** founded in 1933 by Kurt Hahn, a refugee from Nazi Germany who by manic force of character successfully established a dire educational establishment. Gordonstoun managed to incorporate the wort elements of the English public school ethos Hahn so greatly admired, along with a glorification of physical prowess borrowed from the Nazi regime he so much detested. Prince Philip was happy as a pupil here: his son, Prince Charles, rather less so.

Duffus Castle, about a mile and a half to the southeast of Duffus village, owes its present dramatic appearance tosome Norman builders who didn't get their calculations exactly right. The great earthern mound on which they erected their huge castle eventually gave way under the massive weight of so much stone, undermining the impressive 14th century tower which has sunk, split open, and now leans at an ominous angle. Admission to Duffus Castle is free, but take care which side of the tower you inspect it from.

The third of this group of historic buildings close to Elgin is **Synie Palace** (Historic Scotland). Tacked on to a much older building, the palace was built in the 1460s as a residence for the Bishop of Moray, David Stewart. Taking into account the less-than-respectful attitude of the locals at that time to the established church, the bishop decided that a well-fortified building might be appropriate. The colossal, four-square **David's Tower,** named after him, is the largest tower house in Scotland - a clear indication from His Grace to his flock that in this part of Moray, at least, the meek would not be inheriting the earth for a while

LOSSIEMOUTH   Map 5 ref L5
6 miles N of Elgin on the A941

Four miles north of Spynie Palace is Elgin's nearest seaside resort, Lossiemouth, with two sandy beaches swept by invigorating breezes. Once important for its herring fishing, the town is generally known as Lossie, and its residents as "Lossie loons". The town's most famous loon was Ramsay MacDonald, the first Lbour prime minister, and the house in which he was born in 1866 stands at 1, Gregory Place, identified by a plaque. The interior is not open to the public but, curiously, there is a reconstruction of MacDonald'sstudy in the **Lossiemouth Fisheries & Community Museum** which is otherwise devoted to the town's fishing industry and includes some interesting small scale models of fishing boats.

SPEY BAY   Map 5 ref L5
14 miles NE of Elgin on the B9104

This small village at the mouth of the Spey is nowadays best known for the **Tugnet Ice House** (free), the largest industrial ice house in Scotland. Built in 1890, it's an odd-looking building, rather like three grassed-over Nissen huts. The Ice House is now a museum, telling the story of shipbuilding and salmon fishing on the Spey through models and displays while a video programme takes the visitor on a journey down the river from its source to the mouth.

FOCHABERS
MAP 5 REF L6
9 miles SE of Elgin on the A96

Fochabers is one of many Scottish villages which were re-sited from their original location when an 18th century Laird, embarking on a programe of improving his property, decided to remove his tenants' unsightly hovels from view. Normally, this could be achieved with a few strokes of a lawyer's pen, but at Fochabers the ancient contract of "feu tenancy" involved the Duke of Gordon in a quarter of a century of expensive litigation before he finally removed the last blot on his landscape in 1802. The Duke's gracious Georgan residence, **Gordon Castle**, overlooking the now-sanitised view, is not open to the public.

A century or so after the building of Gordon Castle in 1776, one of the 50 gardeners who tended its extensive grounds made a momentous decision. George Baxter resigned his job, borrowed £100, and together with his wife Margaret, an inspired cook, opened a small grocery store in Spey Street, Fochabers. In the back of the shop, Margaret magicked the fruits of local hedgerows into unbelievably tasty jams and jellies. George's former employer, the Duke of Gordon, was captivated by them. They graced his breakfast and tea tables, and so introduced his many rich and aristocratic friends to these very Scottish specialities. As a result of the Duke's patronage George and Margaret Baxter's business thrived. But it was their daughter-in-law, Ethel, who in 1929 created the firm's most famous product, Baxter's Royal Game Soup, still savoured by gastronomes around the world. Today, the **Baxters Visitor Centre** at Fochabers welcomes almost a quarter of a million visitors each year, drawn here by its historic appeal, its Old Shop Museum, (a re-creation of George Baxter's original establishment in Fochabers), and its constellation of other attractive speciality shops.

KEITH
MAP 5 REF L6
17 miles SE of Elgin on the A96

Keith stands at the northeastern tip of the popular **Whisky Trail**, a 70-mile wander around the area which will guide you to 7 major distilleries and a working cooperage. All the distilleries offer tours, a complimentary dram and, usually, discouts on their products. One of the best known is the **Strathisla Distillery** at Keith, famous for its Chivas Regal blended scotch which is exported all over the world. Founded in 1786, Strathisla is the oldest working distillery in the Highlands and, with its curious twin pagodas servin as vents, one of the most architecturally interesting.

ROTHES
MAP 5 REF L6
9 miles SE of Elgin on th A941

Just outside this little town, the **Glen Grant Distillery & Garden** stands in a sheltered glen surrounded by a beautifully landscaped Victorian garden. The distillery was founded in 1840 by two Grant brothers and produces a light, floral maltwhisky which is quite distinctive. Visitors can enjoy a tour and discover the secrets of the distillery, wander through the delightful garden, and sample a dram from "Major Grant's whisky safe".

CRAIGELLACHIE
Map 5 ref L6

13 miles SE of Elgin on the A941/A95

Four miles south of Rothes,the village of Craigellachie sits on the hillside looking down on the meeting of the bight waters of the Rivers Fiddich and Spey, the latter spanned by the elegant **Iron Bridge** built by Thomas Telford in 1815. The village lies on the Whisky Trail, not because of a distillery, but because of **Speyside Cooperage** where visitors can see highly skilled coopers practising their ancient craft. Each year, they prepare some 100,000 oak casks which will be used to mature many different whiskis. It's like watching an industrial ballet as the coopers circle the casks, rhythmically hammering the iron bands into place.

GLENFIDDICH
Map 5 ref L6

17 miles SE of Elgin on the A96

About 3 miles southeast of Craigellachie, stands another famous distillery **Glenfiddich** (free) which is still owned and managed by the Grant family who built it more than a century ago. They take great ride in the fact that Glenfiddich is the only "château-bottled" malt whisky made in the Highlands. Bottling at the distillery, using a single source of water, gives Glenfiddich, they believe, its unique purity of taste and enables visitors to observe the whole process from *"barley to bottle"*. In the early years of the 20t century, when successive British governments imposed increasingly savage duties on whisky, Glenfiddich cannily advertised the mediinal properties of their malt, *"manufactured under the Careful and Personal Supervision of a Fully Qualified Doctor"*..

Standing beside the distillery, overlooking great piles of whisky barrels, are the substantial and picturesque ruins of **Balvenie Castle** (Historic Scotland), a moated stronghold originally built by the "Black" Comyn Earls of Buchan in the late 1200s and extended during the 15th and 16th century by the Earls of Atholl who added the great round tower which still looks formidable. It was here that Mary, Queen of Scots, stayed during a brief visit in 1562. The castle was stormed by Royalists in 1649, and occupied during both Jacobite rebellions, after which it was abandoned. The grand old fortress steadily decayed until 1929 when its last owner, the 6th Earl and 1st Duke of Fife entrusted its still iposing ruins to the care of the state.

DUFFTOWN
Map 5 ref L6

17 miles SE of Elgin on the A941

A local saying claims that "While Rome was built on seven hills, Dufftown stood on seven stills". Today, this agreeable market town asserts its title to being "Malt Whisky Capital of the World" with some legitimacy since it is surrounded by no fewer than 7 distilleries and exports more of the amber liquid than anywhere else in Britain. Originally named Balvenie, after the nearby castle, Dufftown is elegantly laid out with spacious streets, a legacy of its creation as a new town in 1817 by James Duff, 4th Earl of Fife, wit the aim of creating employment following the Napoleonic wars. Its four main streets converge on an attractive **Clocktower** of 1839 which now houses the town's **Museum** (free) and Tourist Information Centre.

Over to the west from Dufftown, are two more distilleries featured on the Whisky Trail. At the tiny village of Knockando, **Cardhu Distillery** has the distinction of being the only malt distillery pioneered by a woman. In the early days, she would raise a red flag to warn local crofters with their unlicensed stills that the Excise authorities were in the area. Cardhu stands in Speyside, close to the source of its success - the ice-cold fresh mountain spring water. To this day, the art f distilling here is unhurried and unchanging, ith the resulting malt maturing for at least twelve years in old oak casks.

A few miles away, to the south, is **Glenfarclas Distillery** where, since 1836, five generations of the Grant family have been distilling the spirit of Speyside into a premium malt whisky of outstanding character. A professional whisky taster recently declared that a dram of Glenfarclas "goes down singing hymns". (Hymns? Shouldn't that be drinking songs?). The distillery has a cask-filling gallery, gift shop, and picnic area, and your admission fee includes a voucher redeemable in the distillery shop.

About 4 miles southwest of Glenfarclas stands an ancient house which is not just one of the most beguiling in Stathspey, but in the whole of Scotland: **Ballindalloch Castle.** The charm, as always, derives from the fact that the same family has lived here for generations: the Macpherson-Grants who have managed to both preserve their heritage intact while also imaginatively adapting to 20th century economic imperatives. According to family legend, its original builder back in the 16th century, the Laird of Ballindalloch, intended his new castle to crown a nearby hill. But each morning, when his masons returned to their work, they found their previous day's construction strewn across the ground.

So, one stormy night, the Laird, ccompanied by his masons, kept vigil on the hill site. Great gusts of wind swept across them, each blast somehow conveying the repeated message, *"Build it in the coo haugh,* (cow pasture)". Deeply impressed by this wind-borne supernatural advice, The Laird complied and so his new castle was built on a level plain beside the River Spey, a location which also happened to provide one of the most picturesque settings for any inland Scottish castle.

A vigorous stream of supernatural events continued to flow through the castle's history. General James Grant inherited Ballindalloch in 1770, died here in 1806, and was buried in his favourite spot overlooking the River Spey. From his grave, the General, who was a noted *bon viveur*, rises each evening, and "walks to the dungeon passage to refresh himself from his beloved wine cellar". Inside the castle itself, a vaporously beautiful lady, dressed in a pink crinoline gown and wearing a large straw hat, is said to regularly visit the Pink Bedroom. These spectral appearances cannot be guaranteed, but you can certainly see an extraordinary collection of 16th and 17th century Spanish paintings acquired by Sir John Macpherson during his tenure as Secretary of the British Legation in Lisbon. Painted on a small scale, these fine and delicate paintings provide an interesting cultural contrast with the grandiose portraits by Allan Ramsay of George III and Queen Charlotte displayed in the Great Hall of the castle. In the grounds outside roam the famous herd of Ballindalloch Aberdeen Angus cattle, the oldest registered herd of its kind in existence. Other attractions include extensive gardens and grounds; river walks; craft workshops; gift shop, and tea room.

GLENLIVET   Map 5 ref K7
13 miles SW of Dufftown on the B9008

"The celebrated **Glenlivet Distillery**" Queen Victoria called it in her diary after passing its lonely hillside setting one windy autumn day in 1867. Established some 40 years earlier by George Smith, The Glenlivet's much appreciated fragrant single malt whisky swiftly acquired a dedicated following of connoisseurs. Modern-day visitors are welcomed to a guided tour of the production process, given the opportunity to see inside the vast bonded warehouses where the spirit matures for 12 years, and to browse through he multimedia exhibition devoted to The Glenlivet's history. A free lealet, "Discover Glenlivet", provides further details of walks and trails, and historic places of interest close by.

TOMINTOUL   Map 5 ref K7
19 miles SW of Dufftown on the A939/B9008

Surrounded by bleak moorland, Tomintoul, pronounced *Tom*-in-towel, sits 1160 feet above sea level, the highest village in the Highlands although, strangely, not the highest in Scotland. (That distinction belongs to Wanlockhead in "lowland" Dumfries & Galloway). The village was plonked down in this raw countryside by the Duke of Gordon in 1779. Fifteen years later a visitor noted that 37 families lived here, "with not a single manufacture to employ them, but all of them sell whisky and all of them drink it". century later Queen Victoria, passing through, described it as "the most tumble-down, poor looking place I ever saw". She was told that it was the "dirtiest, poorest village in the whole of the Highlands". Things have changed greatly since those days, particularly in recent years when Tomintoul has become a base for skiers on the area nearby known as the Lecht. **The Lecht** provides dry ski-slope-skiing all year and snow-making equipment helps to extend the snow season in winter. In the village itself, the **Tomintoul Museum** (free) features a re-created crofter's kitchen and smiddy, with other displays on the local wildlife, the story of Tomintoul, and the Cairngorms.

At the centre of the village is the 18th century Square and here you will fmd **The Gordon Hotel**, an imposing 4-storey building which was originally a coaching inn. It is now a quality hotel offering excellent food and accommodation. The Restaurant serves a range of traditional Scottish favourites using fresh local produce in a creative manner, complemented by appropriate wines and spirits. A separate bar menu is available within the Grouse's Nest bar which concentrates on home made dishes "just like grandmother used to make". The Gordon

The Gordon Hotel, The Square, Tomintoul, Banffshire AB37 9ET
Tel: 01807 580206 Fax: 580488 e-mail:reservations@whiskytrail.com

also offers a totally separate vegetarian menu, prepared under strict conditions, but this should be pre-booked when making your reservation., Another special feature of the cuisine at The Gordon is its gourmet weekends, usually held during the winter months, when Guest Chefs demonstrate their culinary brilliance. Appropiately, since Tomintoul lies at the heart of Whisky Trail country, one of the two bars offers a fine range of unusual malt whiskies. The hotel has 29 bedrooms, all en suite and well-equipped with useful extras such as a hairdryer and trouser press. The Gordon Hotel's declared aim is that their guests should "be happy and return soon, to sample our traditional Scottish hospitality", an aim it achieves in full.

BRIDGE OF BROWN
MAP 5 REF K7

23 miles SW of Dufftown on the A939

Set on the hillside overlooking the bridge is Graham and Sue Larrington's **Bridge of Brown Tea Room & Craft Shop**, offering visitors an outstanding collection of home baked cakes, tarts, puddings and pies, along with a well-stocked Craft Shop packed with a wide range of pictures, jewellery, pottery, speciality jams,

Bridge of Brown Tea Room & Craft Shop, Tomintoul, Ballindalloch, Banffshire AB37 9HR Tel: 01807 580335

and many other eye-catching items. Dating from about 1800, the Tea Room has served various functions in its time, from a threshing barn to a coffin maker's workshop. Enjoying fine views across the countrside and with a welcoming open fire for days when there's a nip in the air, the Tea Room serves everything from a simple cup of coffee, through light snacks to a full and satisfying meal. Amongst the desserts, Sue's hot bread pudding with cream deserves a very special mention. Graham has a special interest in model engineering, building fine steam models for private and commercial collectors. Ready-built models can also be located and supplied. Graham will also build model aircraft and can teach you how to fly them using his trainer fitted with dual controls - the easy way to learn! Advice and help with models is always available and with something interesting being built or restored in the workshop, the Bridge of Brown Tea Room makes a very pleasant stop.

9 The Highlands

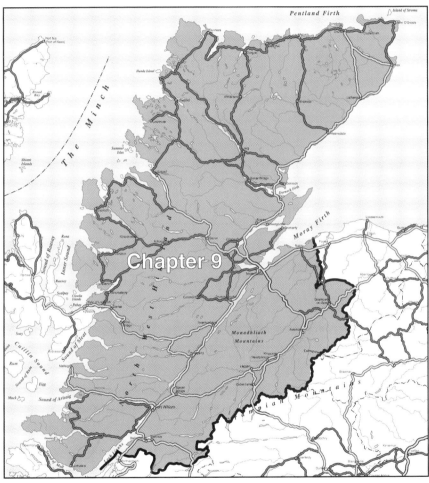

Chapter 9

Covering some fourteen thousand square miles, (almost one-sixth of mainland Britain), the Highlands & Islands of Scotland boasts some of the most varied and spectacular scenery in Europe. There are huge tracts of territory such as the Monadhliath Mountains which are accessible only to the most determined, spellbindingly beautiful lochs and glens, stretches of fertile farmland, a coast-line that ranges from the holiday beaches of the Moray Firth to the fearsome cliffs of northwest Sutherland, and a bewildering choice of literally hundreds of islands with scenery that varies from the dramatic hills of Arran and Skye, to the more gentle landscape of Cromarty and Caithness.

Set within this scenic splendour are countless prehistoric ruins, a wealth of ruined castles and abbeys, grand stately homes such as Dunrobin Castle, appealing market towns, and unspoilt villages. Throughout this vast region there is not a single mile of motorway, (although the main road artery, the A9, is dual carriageway for much of its length), not a single city, and only one really sizeable town, Inverness, with a population of some 40,000.

IN AND AROUND INVERNESS

Long known as the "Capital of the Highlands", Inverness is a cosmopolitan town attractively sited around the River Ness where it flows into Beauly Firth. Its history stretches back to the 6th century when it developed as a trading port serving what was then, and still is, the most populated part of the Highlands. In medieval times, David I elevated the town to royal burgh status and built the first of the three castles which were to occupy the same dominating position above the town.

The present **Inverness Castle** was erected in the mid-19th century, a striking mock-medieval building in red sandstone which today houses the Sheriff Court and during the season hosts the **Castle Garrison Experience**, a novel interactive entertainment in which visitors take on the role of new recruits to the 18th century Hanoverian army. On the terrace outside the castle, the **Flora MacDonald Memorial** commemorates the strong-charactered clanswoman who rowed Bonnie Prince Charlie over the sea to Skye after his defeat at Culloden.

Nearby, the **Town House** is another fine building in red sandstone, built in 1878 in the then- popular Victorian Gothic style and now used as council offices. In September 1921, the Town House was the venue for the first cabinet meeting ever held outside London when Prime Minister Lloyd George called an emergency meeting in response to the Irish crisis. In front of the Town House, the **Mercat Cross** stands above the ancient *clach-na-cuddain*, or Stone of Tubs, a rough block on which women carrying water from the River Ness would rest their buckets. A misty superstition asserts that the continued prosperity of Inverness depends on the stone never being moved.

Across the road from the Town House is the **Inverness Museum and Art Gallery**. The Museum concentrates on Highland and Jacobite history; the Art Gallery is largely devoted to images of old Inverness.

The oldest buildings in the town are to be found around Church Street where the **Steeple**, built in 1791, is notable for having had its spire straightened out after an earthquake in 1816. The most ancient structure is **Abertarff House** (National Trust for Scotland), a laird's town house dating from 1593 and distinguished by its round tower staircase and stepped gables.

Sombre memories are associated with the **Old High Church**, about a couple of hundred yards further north. After the battle of Culloden, any Jacobites who had survived that massacre were brought here and imprisoned before being taken into the churchyard and executed. Bullet marks left on the gravestones by the firing squads can still be seen. Around the corner from the Old High Church, a footbridge across the River Ness leads to **Balnain House,** an immaculately-restored Georgian house which is now home to an innovative, interactive exhibition which traces the development of Highland music from heroic warrior songs to modern Gaelic folk-rock.

A little further out from the town centre, **Cromwell's Clock Tower** is all that remains of his garrison fort which was smartly demolished by Inverness townspeople at the Restoration. Many of the stones from the fort were used to build **Dunbar's Hospital** in Church Street. Founded by Alexander Dunbar in 1668 as an almshouse, it is one of the oldest buildings in Inverness, but it was used as a poor house, or Hospital, for only 16 years of its life. At various times it has been used as offices, workshops, schools and even the town's first fire station. This impressive building with its six dormer windows bearing scriptural quotes now houses an extensive selection of gifts and crafts, the vast majority of them made in Scotland. Anyone of Scottish descent will be interested in the **Clan Tartan Centre** at James Pringle's Holm Mills on Dores Road where traditional tartans and tweeds have been produced since 1798. Visitors can watch the centuries old art of tartan-weaving on impressive Hattersley power looms, trace their own links to a Scottish clan through a data base of more than 50,000 names all fully researched, or browse in a shop stacked with a huge range of woollen clothes. On a similar theme, the **Scottish Kiltmaker Visitor Centre** in Huntly Street is devoted entirely to the kilt and offers audio-visual displays on its history, the opportunity to watch kilt makers at work, and there's even a Kilted Hall of Fame.

BUNCHREW
MAP 4 REF I6
4 miles W of Inverness on the A862

If you drive west from Inverness for about 4 miles along the A862, you will come to the **Ardfearn Plant Centre** at Bunchrew, established in 1987 by the well-known lecturer and TV personality, Jim Sutherland, and his son Alasdair. The nursery produces a fascinating range of shrubs, trees and herbaceous plants and the largest selection of alpines in Scotland. Plants from every continent in the world are raised here with new species continually being introduced.

With its tower and turrets, crow-stepped gables and idyllic position overlooking Beauly Firth, **Bunchrew House Hotel & Restaurant** seems like something from another, more beautiful world. The house was started as far back as 1505 by Alexander of Lovat and enlarged to near its present state by Simon, 8th Lord Lovat, in 1621. Some 50 years later Bunchrew was bought by the Forbes family whose most famous member, Duncan Forbes, was actually born in the house.

Duncan was largely responsible for the defeat of the Jacobite force at Culloden although he strongly disapproved of the subsequent brutalities. It was his father who planted the 20 acres of grounds as they are today, including the magnificent Lebanon Cedar tree opposite the front entrance. This tree is known locally as the "loving tree" and it is said to bring good luck if young couples plight their troth beneath its branches. The House became an hotel in 1986 and was opened by Sir Malcolm Rifkind, then Scottish Secretary of State. Bunchrew has been lovingly restored to preserve its heritage whilst affording guests high standards of luxury and modern-day amenities. Guests can relax in the charm-

Bunchrew House Hotel & Restaurant, Bunchrew, Inverness IV3 8TA.
Tel: 01463 234917 Fax: 01463 710620

ingly panelled drawing room (with its roaring log fires in winter), and rest peacefully in one of the exquisitely decorated suites, two of which feature magnificent full canopied four poster beds. Bunchrew's owners, Graham and Janet Cross, take good food very seriously and their head chef, Walter Walker, offers a superb menu based on prime quality Scottish ingredients. In the evening, you can dine by candlelight to the sight of waves breaking on the shore a few yards away. Incidentally, if you notice something a little strange about Table 2 in the restaurant, don't worry. It's only the benign resident ghost, affectionately known as Isobel, who divides her time between the restaurant and one of the rooms above the older part of the house. Her portrait hangs just inside the front door of this superb hotel.

DAVIOT   MAP 4 REF J6
5 miles SE of Inverness on the B851 towards Croy

A lovely setting, unusual architecture, exceptional food, comfortable accommodation and a warm welcome - **Daviot Mains Farm** offers just about everything you could want in a guest house. The farmhouse and steading was built around 1820 to an unusual design, with 4 wings enclosing a central courtyard. In the whole of Scotland only two other farmhouses adopted this particular defensive layout. The house is surrounded by 365 acres of mixed farmland which has been worked by the Hutcheson family for more than 60 years. Alex and Margaret have been welcoming bed and breakfast guests here since 1982 and their watchword has always been comfort. The 3 (non-smoking) guest bedrooms, named

Daviot Mains Farm, Daviot, Inverness IV2 5ER
Tel: 01463 772215 Fax: 01463 772099 e-mail: farmhols@globalnet.co.uk

after local rivers, are delightfully furnished with sprigged or flowered fabrics and wooden bed heads. The sitting room, where tea and home made cake is offered before bedtime, is furnished with lots of books and deep, sink-into chairs, and the coal-burning stove in the dining room provides a warm setting in which to enjoy Margaret's excellent food. A hearty Scottish breakfast is included in the tariff and evening meals are available by arrangement, Monday to Friday in summer and Monday to Saturday in Winter.

CULLODEN MOOR
6 miles E of Inverness off the B9006

MAP 4 REF J6

At the Battle of Culloden, in August 1746, some 1500 Highlanders were slaughtered. A mere 76 English soldiers died. The casualty figures reflect how hopelessly outnumbered were the forces of Bonnie Prince Charlie against those of the Duke of Cumberland. Culloden became the graveyard for all the hopes of the Stuart dynasty of ever recovering the throne. Immediately after the battle, Cumberland ordered that none of the wounded should be spared, a brutal command that earned him the bitter nickname of "Butcher" Cumberland. Culloden was the last land battle of any significance to be fought in Britain and it marked the end of a distinctive Highland way of life. The clan leaders, forbidden to maintain private armies, became mere landlords, seeking rents rather than service. The English government passed a series of punitive laws designed to obliterate the Highlanders very culture: speaking Gaelic became a crime, wearing the tartan and playing the bagpipes were also banned. The story of this turning-point in Scottish history is vividly presented at the National Trust for Scotland's **Visitor Centre** by an imaginative audio-visual and historical display.

The Centre also houses a reference library and will check the records for you if you think that an ancestor of yours took part in the battle. Next door to the Centre is **Old Leanach Cottage**, outside which 30 Jacobite soldiers were burnt alive in the aftermath of the battle, and the **Well of the Dead** marks the spring where wounded Highlanders were killed as they tried to drink the water. Visitors can walk freely around the battlefield where flags show the position of the two armies, clan graves are marked by simple headstones, and the **Field of the English** marks the mass grave of the four-score English soldiers who died in the battle. Guided tours of the battlefield are available during the summer season and each year in April, on the Saturday closest to the date of the battle, a service is held in the Visitor Centre to commemorate the fallen of both armies.

THE MORAY COAST

Stretching eastwards from Inverness, the coastal strip of the **Moray Firth** is a popular destination for those in search of a seaside holiday. Some 20 miles of sandy beaches run from Nairn to beyond Lossiemouth, and another major attraction is the colony of some 130 bottle-nosed dolphins which has taken up residence here. Known to scientists as *Tursiops truncatus,* this is the largest species of dolphin in the world, with a fully-grown adult attaining a length of 13 feet and weighing between 400 and 660 pounds. Spectacular though they are to watch as they "bow-ride" in front of boats, the **Moray Firth colony of dolphins** has the uncharacteristic and unappealing habit of killing porpoises. Despite this unlovely trait, they are an irresistible sight and several companies run regular dolphin-spotting boat trips, although these are restricted during the dolphins' breeding season between late June and August.

The coastal area alongside the Moray Firth is one of the most fertile in the Highlands, and has always been comparatively well-populated, leading to the growth of attractive small towns such as Nairn. The region also boasts two major castles, Cawdor and Brodie, (both of which are still lived in by descendants of the original builders), and a huge 18th century military base, **Fort George** (Historic Scotland).

Set dramatically on **Ardersier Point**, the fort is a remarkable example of 18th century military architecture and generally regarded as one of the most impressive fortifications in Europe. Its perimeter walls are almost a mile long and enclose an area of 42 acres - Edinburgh Castle would comfortably fit onto its parade ground. Commanding the narrow entrance to the Moray Firth, the fort was designed by Robert Adam and building began in 1748. The fort took 21 years to complete and cost nearly £1 billion in today's money, but has never seen a shot fired in anger. Fort George is still a barracks, manned by the Queen's Own Highlanders whose glorious history is recorded in the **Regimental Museum** here. Bird-watchers will be delighted to find a colony of kittiwakes perched on the fort's roof-tops, and flocks of waders and seabirds on the sands and mud flats below. From the vantage position of the fort's lofty walls, you may even be lucky enough to catch sight of some of the bottle-nosed dolphins who have made the Moray Firth their home.

CAWDOR   Map 4 ref J6

8 miles E of Inverness on the B9090

The lovely conservation village of Cawdor is best known for **Cawdor Castle**, home of the Thanes of Cawdor for more than 600 years. A fairy-tale building of turrets and towers, it must surely be the only castle built around a tree. A family tradition asserts that in a dream the 3rd Thane of Cawdor was told to load his donkey with gold and wherever the beast settled for the night, there to build his castle. The tree still stands, bare and limbless now, in the great vaulted room at the base of the central tower. It was a holly tree, one of the seven sacred trees of Celtic mythology, and has been carbon-dated to 1372. The presence of such a mystic tree was probably intended to ward off evil influences, but in the late Middle Ages it would have needed more than a tree to preserve the Cawdors from the rampant intrigue, murder and mayhem of the time. A typical (and true) story tells of Muriel, the 9th Thaness. She inherited the title at her birth in 1510, her father having died a few months before. As a rich heiress, the infant girl was promptly kidnapped by the most powerful man in Scotland, the Earl of Argyll, and "for future recognition, the babe was branded on the hip by her nurse with a key, and the top joint of her left little finger was bitten off". The rest of Muriel's long life, (she lived to be 77 years old), is strewn with similarly striking incidents.

The castle is well worth visiting for its remarkable collections of tapestries, paintings (Reynolds, Lely, Lawrence, Romney, Stanley Spencer and John Piper amongst them), Chippendale furniture, and a wealth of family memorabilia. The grounds of Cawdor Castle are especially satisfying, with superb gardens (first laid out in the 1720s), a 9-hole mini-golf course, a topiary maze, picnic spots, and several Nature Trails.

Many visitors are still drawn to Cawdor because of its associations with Shakespeare's *Macbeth* although the present castle wasn't built until more than 300 years after Macbeth had died. Still worse, Macbeth never was Thane of Cawdor - the title was retrospectively bestowed on him by the 16th century historian Hector Boethius to give the old story more dramatic spice.

A short walk from the famous castle brings you to "**Limegrove**", Mhairi and Ian Munro's pleasant bed & breakfast establishment which is hidden away in delightful surroundings. (A brown-and-white sign points the way to "Limegrove" off the B9090 in the centre of Cawdor). The house was built by the Munros in 1979 so it has every up-to-date amenity and is also attractively decorated and furnished. There are 3 quality bedrooms, all on the ground floor, and the at-

"Limegrove", Cawdor, Nairn IV12 5RA
Tel/Fax: 01667 404307

mosphere is very homely, peaceful and comfortable. A full Scottish breakfast is included in the tariff and packed lunches are available if required. The Munros do not provide evening meals but there are plenty of good eating places within easy reach. "Limegrove" has a well-tended garden, children are welcome and so too are pets, by arrangement. (The family's own pet, a friendly collie called Bobby, is an energetic creature who is always ready for a lively game of football!) With historic Cawdor Castle almost on the doorstep, the Moray Coast just a few miles to the northeast, Culloden battlefield and Inverness about 10 miles in the other direction, "Limegrove" is very conveniently located for exploring the area's many attractions.

NAIRN

MAP 4 REF J6

16 miles E of Inverness on the A96

An attractive county town of mellow buildings and a popular holiday resort, Nairn has long been regarded as marking the boundary between the Lowlands and the Highlands. This divide was made abundantly clear to King James VI when he visited in the late 1590s. The fishermen, he found, spoke Gaelic; the farmers, English. He boasted sardonically that his kingdom was so extensive that people at one end of a town's main street could not understand those who lived at the other. Nairn marks the beginning of a seaside holiday coast: inviting sandy beaches stretch eastwards some 20 miles or so to Lossiemouth. To clinch the town's appeal as an inviting holiday resort, Nairn can truthfully claim to be one of the driest and sunniest places in all Scotland.

Nowadays, the few fishing boats sheltering in the harbour built by Thomas Telford are vastly outnumbered by pleasure craft, but for an insight into Nairn's maritime past, pay a visit to the tiny **Fishertown Museum** (free) which has an interesting collection of vintage photographs and artefacts connected with the herring fishing industry during the days of steam drifters. On the eastern edge of the town, the **Invernairn Mill Visitor Centre** offers a wide variety of attractions. There's a heritage museum, exhibition centre with working displays by local craftsmen, a working mill wheel complete with all its gearing, a blacksmith's, craft and woollen shops selling high quality Scottish and locally crafted goods, an excellent delicatessen and a restaurant overlooking the Lethen hills.

BRODIE

MAP 4 REF K6

20 miles E of Inverness on the A96

Continuing eastwards along the A96, follow the signs to **Brodie Castle**. The estate was granted to the Brodie family in 1160 by Malcolm IV and, although the house is now maintained by the National Trust for Scotland, the 25th Earl of Brodie still lives here. The present castle, built in a curious Z shape, replaced a medieval structure which was burnt down during the Civil War in 1645. Surrounded by lovely grounds, where each spring a sea of daffodils waves a golden haze, Brodie Castle houses an outstanding collection of porcelain, French furniture, and paintings - amongst them works by Jacob Cuyp and Edwin Landseer. A wood-panelled dining-room, a grandiose Victorian kitchen and austere servants' quarters vividly evoke the disparities between life upstairs and downstairs in those days. Standing in the grounds, **Rodney's Stone** is a well-preserved stone slab sculpted with Pictish symbols on one side and a cross on the other.

STRATHSPEY

One of Scotland's most famous rivers runs through southeast Aberdeen-shire. The Spey is the country's second longest river (110 miles), and its fastest flowing. It is famous for salmon, sea trout and brown trout fishing of the highest quality, and from the start of the season in early February, the Spey salmon fishing intensifies throughout the summer.

The Spey's unpolluted waters are also much appreciated by the producers of malt whisky - half of all Scotland's malt whisky distilleries are located in the surrounding glens. The **Malt Whisky Trail** is a 70-mile route which links up seven of them and a cooperage. They all offer visitors a guided tour, a free dram, and, if they charge an entrance fee, usually part of it can be redeemed against a bottle of whisky from the distillery shop. In addition to these distilleries, there are many others which also welcome visitors.

GRANTOWN-ON-SPEY   MAP 4 REF K7
23 miles SE of Nairn, on the A939

One of Queen Victoria's favourite little towns, Grantown-on-Spey was originally laid out in 1776 with wide, tree-lined streets leading to a central square. This traditional Highland resort grew in stature when doctors began recommending its dry, bracing climate for those "requiring rest and quiet on account of nervous overstrain and debility". The town stands close to several busy tourist routes and is a popular centre all year round: many winter visitors for the skiing at Aviemore preferring Grantown's elegant Georgian and Victorian appeal to the rather functional facilities at Aviemore itself.

Not many hotels have had a piper compose a tune in their honour. **Culdearn House** has, along with a string of more familiar awards from tourist and travel

Culdearn House, Woodlands Terrace, Grantown-on-Spey, Moray PH26 3JU
Tel: 01479 872106 Fax: 01479 873641

organisations, amongst them "Scotlands Hotel of the Year" accolades from both the RAC and the *Which? Hotel Guide* whilst the dining room is acclaimed by "Taste of Scotland" and *AA Best Restaurant Guide*. The proprietors, Alasdair and Isobel Little are both Scottish and they delight in maintaining a distinctive Scottish atmosphere at Culdearn House. Occasionally guests are entertained by a local Pipe Major and a champion highland dancer, and the cuisine, prepared by Isobel, features prime local produce prepared in classic Scots ways. (Dinner, incidentally, is included in the overnight tariff). The Scottish theme continues with a choice of over 70 carefully selected malt whiskies while the extensive and helpfully-annotated wine list draws on quality wines from around the world. The house itself was built more than a century ago by an admirer of granite stone, wood panelling and fine moulded ceilings. The 9 guest rooms, all en suite, have been sympathetically modernised and decorated to offer every comfort, while the dining room and lounge have fine marble fireplaces which burn logs or peat when appropriate. Open from March to October, Culdearn House can truthfully claim to provide "Scottish hospitality at its best".

To the south of Grantown, on the B970, is a rather unusual tourist attraction, **Revack Estate**, where the estate's owner, Lady Pauline Ogilvie Grant, invites visitors to explore its 15,000 acres of splendid Highland countryside. You can wander along trails through wet ground habitats which provide nesting sites for oyster catchers, lapwings, skylarks and curlews, and also attract colourful colonies of butterflies. There's an exotic collection of orchids on display and for sale; a generously equipped Adventure Playground; gift shop; licensed restaurant and cafeteria.

About 6 miles southwest of Grantown, at Skye of Curr, visitors can acquire a living memento of their stay in Scotland at the **Speyside Heather Garden & Visitor Centre** which has more than 300 varieties of heather growing in its landscaped show garden. Its Heather Heritage Centre houses an exhibition on the varied historical uses of the plant in thatching and rope making, for doormats and baskets, as well as in medicine, cooking, drinks, and dyeing wool. In the heather craft shop you can buy the plants themselves and gifts associated with them, (including heather wine).

CARRBRIDGE

MAP 4 REF J7

10 miles SW of Grantown-on-Spey off the A9

The stone bridge that gave Carrbridge its name still survives, an elegant, single high-arched span. It was built in 1717 following the deaths of two men who had drowned here while attempting to cross the treacherous ford over the River Spey. Today, Carrbridge's other prime attraction is its imaginative **Landmark Forest Heritage Park** which has as its focus a striking modern building surrounded by pine trees. Inside, you can watch a dramatic, triple-screen, audio-visual history of the Highlands. Outdoors, you can wander through a sculpture park; trace your way through a woodland maze or nature trail; climb a 65 feet high observation tower; and even, securely raised on timber stilts, strut your stuff along a tree-top-level trail. A great place for children.

With its attractive black and white frontage, **Carrmoor Licensed Guest House** looks especially inviting and once you step inside the atmosphere is equally welcoming. Carrmoor is a family-run business owned by Michael and Christine Stitt. Michael is the chef and Carrmoor's restaurant (non-smoking) is well-known for its excellent cuisine, available either from the à la carte, including vegetarian selections, or table d'hôte menus. All meals are freshly prepared using local

Carrmoor Licensed Guest House, Carr Road, Carrbridge,
Inverness-shire PH23 3AD Tel/Fax: 01479 841244
e-mail: carrmoor.gh@lineone.net

produce where possible; and special diet dishes can also be arranged on request. A small but well-chosen selection of wines is available to complement your meal and after dinner you can retire to the comfortable lounge for coffee and maybe a liqueur. The unspoilt village of Carrbridge enjoys a long tradition as a popular holiday resort and Carrmoor Guest House has 6 letting rooms all en suite, non-smoking and tastefully appointed. The tariff includes a full Scottish breakfast and packed lunches are also available. Well-behaved pets are welcome!

AVIEMORE   MAP 4 REF J7
12 miles SW of Grantown-on-Spey on the A9

Scotland's premier skiing resort was built almost from scratch during the 1960s - Europe's first purpose-built leisure, sports and conference centre. The developers threw in everything they could think of: high-rise hotels, a cinema, a theatre, ice rink, swimming pool, go-karting track, and a dry-ski slope. A more recent addition is a children's amusement park, **Santa Claus Land**, set in the heart of a mature pine forest and offering a range of attractions - amongst them go-karts, a Lego play area, a pets' farm, dinosaur safari ride, craft village, and Techno Land where kids can don a virtual reality helmet and step into an interactive video game.

For adults, Aviemore's most attractive feature, apart from the glorious mountain scenery all around, is the **Speyside Railway** whose steam trains run for some five miles from here to Boat of Garten, along the track of the old Highland Railway which opened in 1863 and closed in 1965. The railway's vintage rolling-stock includes a functioning restaurant car that was once part of the *Flying Scotsman* and, depending on the time of year, there are from five to eight return trips each day. The Aviemore station is worth visiting just to see its engine shed full of burnished locomotives. The shed itself is original, but the other station buildings were imported from Dalnaspidal, and the turntable from Kyle of Lochalsh.

One of Speyside Railway's special offers should not be resisted - an inclusive tour which combines train travel from Aviemore to Boat of Garten with a 4-mile bus journey to the RSPB reserve on the shores of **Loch Garten**. For bird-watchers, Loch Garten is a holy place, the nesting place of one of Britain's rarest birds, the osprey. In the mid-20th century, it was assumed that this fearsome grey-and-white eagle had disappeared for ever from the British Isles. Then, in 1954, a single pair arrived mysteriously and set up home in a tree about half a mile from the loch. Ever since then, a steadily increasing number of ospreys have flown from Africa each spring to nest here. Between late April and August, the RSPB opens a special observation hide where with the aid of powerful binoculars and live television monitoring visitors can watch these magnificent birds in their nests.

Built in the late 1800s, **Ravenscraig Guest House** is an eye-catching building with its red- and-white colour scheme and pink granite stone surrounding the windows. Ravenscraig has been a well-established guest house for some 30 years, with its present owners Jill and Jonathan Gatenby taking over in late 1998. They have tastefully refurbished the house and now offer 12 en suite bedrooms of which 6 are on the ground floor, some are for non-smokers, and all are attractively decorated and furnished. There's also a comfortable residents' lounge. Children are welcome at Ravenscraig and the Gatenbys offer special discounts for holiday breaks. They do not provide evening meals but there are

**Ravenscraig Guest House, 141 Grampian Road, Aviemore,
Inverness-shire PH22 1RP Tel: 01479 810278 Fax: 01479 812742**

plenty of pubs and restaurants within easy reach. Open all year round, the Ravenscraig is located in the heart of this popular skiing resort with the magnificent scenery of the Cairngorm Mountains stretching for miles to the south and east.

COYLUMBRIDGE
Map 4 ref J7
2 miles SE of Aviemore, on the B970

Set amongst towering Caledonian pine trees, the award-winning **Rothiemurchus Camp & Caravan Park** offers sheltered camping in a unique wilderness setting. Open every day of the year, the park has a wide range of Thistle Award cabins for hire and provides a full range of facilities including toilets, hot showers and a launderette. The Park lies within the vast Rothiemurchus Estate which stretches from the River Spey at Aviemore to the granite peaks of the Cairngorm Mountains. In recognition of the quality of its landscape, wildlife and natural beauty, the area has been part of the Cairngorm National Nature Reserve since 1954. Within its boundaries there is an enormous range of recreational activities on offer: bankside or boat fishing, clay pigeon shooting, 4x4 off-road driving, cycling and mountain biking, birdwatching, guided walks with a Rothiemurchus Ranger, or tours of the estate by Landrover. There's far too much going on to give a complete list here, but the Rothiemurchus Visitor Centre will happily provide full information. The Centre is also worth visiting for its Card Shop

which stocks a wide selection of books, maps, cards and much more, and its Old School Shop displaying an excellent range of Scottish craftwork, designer knitwear, quality stone and glass ware, and exclusive jewellery.

Also within the Rothiemurchus estate is **Loch an Eilean**, "Loch of the Island", an island on which stands a picturesque ruined castle. There's a gentle one-hour walk which wanders around the loch: details of this walk and of the many other woodland trails in the area can be obtained from the Rothiemurchus Visitor Centre.

Rothiemurchus Camp & Caravan Park,
Coylumbridge, Aviemore, Inverness PH22 1QU
Tel: 01479 812800

To the west of Rothiemurchus, the **Glen More Forest Park** covers some 4000 acres of the northwest slopes of the Cairngorms. At its heart is **Loch Morlich**, around which Scotland's only free-ranging herd of reindeer have found a congenial habitat, and in winter the Siberian Husky Club hold their races in the surrounding area. Beyond the loch, the road bends south towards the **Cairngorm Ski Area,** and climbs steadily above the forest to the high-level car parks which in winter and early spring service the ski-lifts. The whole year round, a chair-lift operates to the **Ptarmigan Restaurant** which, at 3,600 feet, is the highest building in Britain.

KINGUSSIE
MAP 4 REF J8
12 miles SW of Aviemore on the A9/A86

Southwest of Aviemore, the A9, the B9152, and the railway run alongside each other towards the little resort village of Kingussie, (pronounced King-*yoo*-see). The B9152 will give you better views of **Loch Alvie**, and of **Loch Insh**, where there's a watersports centre, and also bring you to the excellent **Highland Wild-**

life **Park** near Kincraig. The Park is owned and run by the Royal Zoological Society of Scotland, a registered charity which also owns Edinburgh Zoo. Its declared mission is to promote the conservation of animal species and wild places by captive breeding, environmental education and scientific research. Visitors drive around the huge reserve where herds of red deer, secretive roe deer, enormous bison, ancient breeds of sheep, and wild Przewalski horses, one of the world's rarest mammals, all roam freely. The rest of the Park can be explored on foot, wandering through themed habitats such as the Wolf Territory where a raised walkway takes visitors right into the heart of the enclosure

Kingussie, small though it is, can also boast a major visitor attraction, the **Highland Folk Museum.** Across an 80-acre site, this outstanding museum displays a fascinating collection of buildings, amongst them a reconstructed Lewis "black house", an old smokehouse, a water-powered sawmill, a 19th century school, a clock maker's workshop, and a traditional herb and flower garden. Indoors, the farming museum has a stable, barn, dairy, and a large range of old carts, ploughs and other farming implements. On most days during the summer there are also demonstrations of various traditional crafts.

A mile or so away, on the south side of the Spey, stand the substantial remains of **Ruthven Barracks**. Built in 1719 to keep Highlanders in check following the 1715 Rising, the barracks were extended by General Wade in 1734. After the tragedy of Culloden, Jacobite survivors rallied here hoping that Bonnie Prince Charlie might once again take to the field. When they received a brusque message advising that every man should seek his safety in the best way he could, they blew up the barracks and fled. The stark ruins of the once-mighty military outpost they left behind look their best at night when they are floodlit.

A mile or so from Ruthven Barracks is the RSPB reserve at **Insh Marshes,** one of the most important wetlands in Britain. In spring, lapwings, redshanks, and curlews all nest here, and in the winter, when the marshes flood, they attract flocks of whooper swans and greylag geese. The best months for visiting are from November until June.

NEWTONMORE   MAP 4 REF J8
16 miles SW of Aviemore on the A86

This small village is home to the **Clan Macpherson Museum**, one of whose prize exhibits is a black chanter allegedly presented to the Macphersons by the "little people", and to the **Newtonmore Highland Games**, held on the first Saturday in August, when clan members from around the world rally here. A few miles south of Newtonmore, at Laggan, a minor road strikes off westwards alongside the Spey but fizzles out some 10 miles short of the source of this famous river and so puts a full stop to this tour of Strathspey.

Although it's not in Strathspey, you may want to make a short detour to **Dalwhinnie Distillery**, about 7 miles south of Laggan on the A889. The highest distillery in Scotland, Dalwhinnie produces a single malt whisky with a light heather fragrance. Guided tours are available and the admission charge includes a voucher redeemable in the distillery shop against the purchase of a bottle of malt whisky.

THE GREAT GLEN

The single most impressive feature of the Highlands is the Great Glen, a vast geological fault that stretches some 60 miles in a diagonal line from Inverness to Fort William. Two thirds of its length is filled by the waters of Lochs Lochy, Oich and Ness, and the construction of the **Caledonian Canal** in the early 1800s linked them together, creating a navigable waterway running all the way from Fort William to the Moray Firth at Inverness.

Ben Nevis from the Caledonian Canal

The most famous of the three lochs in the Great Glen is, of course, **Loch Ness**, and whether or not a fabulous creature lurks in its depths, the loch is remarkable in itself. Twenty-four miles long, it is fed by eight rivers, its bed lies deeper than anywhere in the North Sea and even much of the Atlantic, and it has never been known to freeze. Because of its great depth and length, the loch is one of Europe's largest freshwater systems, holding more water than all the reservoirs and lakes in the whole of England and Wales. A monstrous creature swimming in its waters was first reported in AD 565 by no less a witness than St

Columba, but the "Leviathan of the Loch" was then not spotted again until the 1930s, a sighting which sparked off huge enthusiasm for tracking down the beast. Echo-sounders, a submarine and devices to obtain a piece of Nessie's skin or flesh have all been employed in the massive search, so far without the slightest success. Various photographs of the monster, including the familiar "Surgeon's" photograph taken in 1934, have all subsequently proved to be fakes. On the other hand, there have been numerous credible witnesses who claim to have seen Nessie, and many respected scientists are convinced that an as yet unknown species of aquatic life, a "bio-mass", does indeed inhabit the loch.

DRUMNADROCHIT   Map 4 ref I7
15 miles SW of Inverness on the A82

Drumnadrochit is, in effect, the headquarters of the "Nessie" industry. This little town has two exhibitions devoted to the elusive monster: the **Original Loch Ness Monster Exhibition** which is little more than a souvenir shop with a half-hearted audio-visual show as an afterthought seemingly, and the **Official Loch Ness Monster Exhibition** which takes its subject rather more seriously with photographs, sonar scans, eye-witness accounts from across the ages, and reconstructions of the various research projects carried out in the loch. Outside, emerging from its own lochan, rears a "life-size" model of a rather mean-looking Nessie. Cruises around Loch Ness can also be booked here.

If you fancy the idea of seeing the monster yourself, the most likely viewpoint apparently is at **Castle Urquhart**, to the east of the town. More sightings of the monster have been reported from this point than from anywhere else on or around the loch. Perhaps significantly, the water here is the deepest in the whole of the loch, reaching some 750 feet in depth. The castle, reached by a

Castle Urquhart, Nr Drumnadrochit

steepish climb up a hundred steps, was built in the 14th century to guard this strategic point in the Great Glen. It is dramatically sited on a bluff and looks particularly splendid at night when it is floodlit. The castle was deliberately blown up in 1692 to prevent it falling into the hands of the Jacobites, but the keep and four-square turrets are still very imposing.

A couple of miles to the south of Castle Urquhart stands the **John Cobb Memorial**, honouring the land-speed record holder who, in 1952, had just established a new water-speed record in his jet-engined craft, *Crusader*, when his boat disintegrated on the loch near this point. Still alive, Cobb was recovered from the wreckage and carried up this hillside. He died a few metres from where the monument now stands.

It was along this road that Dr Johnson and James Boswell made their way in August 1773, the first occasion on which Boswell had seen the bulky doctor on horseback and, he observed, riding well. As they continued southwards to Fort Augustus, they noticed an elderly woman at the door of a wretched hovel, and asked if they might see inside. The house was made of earth "and for a window had only a small hole, which was stopped by a piece of turf that was taken out occasionally to let in light". Johnson was curious to know where the woman slept. A guide translated the question into Erse. "She answered with a tone of emotion, saying, as he told us, she was afraid we wanted to go to bed with her". The exchange gave the good doctor and his biographer much cause for merriment as they resumed their journey. Boswell maintained that it was Johnson who had alarmed the poor woman's virtue. "No, sir" said he. "She'll say, There came a wicked young fellow, a wild dog, who I believe would have ravished me, had there not been with him a grave old gentleman who repressed him". "No, sir" replied Boswell, "She'll say, There was terrible ruffian who would have forced me had it not been for a civil, decent young man who, I take it, was an angel sent from heaven to protect me".

FORT AUGUSTUS
38 miles S of Inverness on the A82

MAP 4 REF H8

The modest village of Fort Augustus takes its imposing name from the military base established here in the wake of the 1715 Jacobite rising. The fortress was built by General Wade and named after George II's younger son, Augustus. At that time, Augustus was a plump lad just 8 years old but he would later be reviled as the Duke of Cumberland, the "Butcher of Culloden". Following that battle, it was at Fort Augustus that the Duke expressed his gratification at receiving the head of Roderick Mackenzie, a young Edinburgh lawyer who had maintained the pretence of being Bonnie Prince Charlie in order to help the real prince escape.

After Culloden, the fort no longer had any useful purpose and in 1876 it was demolished, giving way to a Benedictine Abbey. The Abbey is still a monastery but also houses a particularly lively **Heritage Centre** where, with the aid of a walkman and a sound-and-light show, visitors are provided with an interesting insight into the history and culture of the area with exhibits on Loch Ness and the Great Glen, the Jacobite uprisings, and the story of the old fort. The Abbey has been acclaimed as "one of the finest heritage centres in Britain" and the attractions also include a living museum of 17th century Highland life, staged at the Clansman Centre; peaceful grounds; a gift shop; the Abbot's Table restaurant, and 50-minute cruises around Loch Ness aboard the cruiser *Old Catriona* which featured in the film, *Loch Ness*. You can even take a helicopter ride over the loch and stay overnight in budget accommodation in the Abbey's guest rooms. During the season there are special Highland Gatherings featuring events such as tossing the caber, piping competitions, and Scottish dancing.

Running through the centre of Fort Augustus is the **Caledonian Canal,** linking Loch Ness to Loch Oich with the help of six locks. Designed by the celebrated engineer Thomas Telford, the canal completed a waterway along the Great Glen that provided a 60-mile through route from the Atlantic Ocean to the North Sea, and spared shipping the perilous, perennially storm-tossed route around Cape Wrath.

INVERGARRY   Map 4 ref H8
40 miles SW of Inverness on the A82/A87

South of Fort Augustus, the A82 runs alongside Loch Oich to Invergarry. In medieval times this little town was important as the base for the MacDonnells of Glengarry, staunch Jacobites whose **Invergarry Castle** was destroyed by the Duke of Cumberland after Culloden but not before the fugitive Bonnie Prince Charlie had stayed there the night after the battle. The ruins still stand in the grounds of Glengarry Castle Hotel.

SPEAN BRIDGE   Map 4 ref H9
8 miles NE of Fort William on the A82/A86

There are in fact two bridges at Spean Bridge: Thomas Telford's elegant bridge of 1819, and a couple of miles downstream, the older High Bridge built by General Wade in 1736. One hundred feet high it spans the deep gorge here. In 1913, one of its arches collapsed and has never been repaired. Spean Bridge offers some excellent views of the Ben Nevis range, especially from the **Commando Memorial** atop a hill just outside the village. This much-admired bronze sculpture, designed by Scott Sutherland, shows three soldiers looking west to the Cameron country of Lochiel where they trained during World War II. Spean Bridge has another notable military connection for it was nearby, on August 16th, 1745, that a mere dozen of MacDonald of Keppoch's Highlanders "armed with little more formidable than bagpipes and blood-curdling cries" managed to rout two companies of government troops. The incident is regarded as the first skirmish of the '45 rebellion, formally declared two days later by Bonnie Prince Charlie.

If you would like a souvenir of the Highlands which will last and last, pay a visit to **The Heather Centre** about 200yds from Telford's bridge on the Inverness road. As well as the traditional purple variety, the Centre also has lucky white heathers, and a whole range of golden, orange, or bronze modern hybrids. There's an Exhibition of Scottish plants, many of which, along with imported species, are for sale.

About halfway between Spean Bridge and Fort William, at **Nevis Range**, Britain's only mountain gondola system offers an exhilarating ride up **Aonach Mor** (4006 feet). The gondolas rise up through the forest at the base station to an altitude of 2150 feet in just 15 minutes. The views, needless to say, are staggering.

IN AND AROUND FORT WILLIAM

With its excellent road, rail and waterway links, Fort William has become the business and tourism "capital" of the Western Highlands. It occupies a glorious position overlooking Loch Linnhe, (although an ill-conceived dual carriageway has blocked off access to the shore). The town is the main shopping centre for a huge area and the High Street, with inviting little squares set back from it, gets very busy during the season. The major attraction for tourists is, of course, **Ben Nevis**, at 4406 feet Britain's loftiest mountain and with a base which is said to be 24 miles in circumference. Despite its height, there are several undemanding and well-worn routes to the top. The record time achieved during the annual race to the summit is one and a half hours, but for those walking at a more realistic pace between four and five hours should be allowed. The views from the top are incredible, extending halfway across Scotland to the distant Hebrides.

In the town itself, the **West Highland Museum** has collections covering almost every aspect of Highland life, an extensive and well-presented display. The museum's most famous exhibit is the "secret portrait" of Bonnie Prince Charlie - a meaningless smudge of colour until viewed against a curved mirror when a charming miniature of the Prince, wearing a brown wig and an elaborate satin coat comes into focus. The portrait dates from the time when the penalty for anyone possessing an image of the Prince was death. Another intriguing exhibit is the long Spanish rifle used in the assassination of a local factor in 1752, the notorious "Appin Murder" that inspired Robert Louis Stevenson's *Kidnapped*.

A highly recommended excursion from Fort William is a day trip on the **Jacobite Steam Train** to Mallaig. The 45-mile journey passes alongside Loch Eil and on to the west coast through some of the most spectacular scenery in the country. En route, it crosses the massive **Glenfinnan Viaduct** and makes an extended stop at Glenfinnan Station, allowing time to visit the **Station Mu-**

seum. Drinks, snacks, souvenirs and audio line-guides are available from the on-train shop.

Whisky lovers will undoubtedly want to make their way to the **Ben Nevis Distillery & Visitor Centre** on the A82 just north of Fort William. The major product here is The Dew of Ben Nevis, a distinctive blend of choice whiskies from all over Scotland. Visitors can follow the whole process of whisky making, find out about the "mighty Ben" itself, and discover the part that a legendary hero, big Hector MacDram, played in its creation.

A mile or so to the northwest of the town, at Banavie, is **Neptune's Staircase**. Designed by Thomas Telford in 1822, this is a remarkable feat of engineering - a series of 8 locks which in the course of just 500 yards raise the level of the Caledonian Canal by 72 feet.

ONICH   Map 4 ref G9
9 miles SW of Fort William on the A82

Game Terrine as a starter, Venison Pudding as a main course, Gingered Fruit Pudding as a dessert - that's just one of the combinations you might be tempted to choose from the ever-changing menu on offer at the **Four Seasons Bistro & Bar**, located within the holiday centre of Inchree Chalets near the village of Onich. Should you prefer vegetarian dishes, how about Mushrooms marinated in garlic and white wine, followed by the Vegetarian Dish of the Day? The Four Seasons is a relaxing place where attentive staff, a peaceful ambience and a glowing real log fire all combine to help you wind down. This family-run enter-

Four Seasons Bistro & Bar, Inchree, Onich, by Fort William PH33 6SE
Tel: 01855 821393 Fax: 01855 821287

prise offers a unique combination of well-equipped holiday homes set within an area of outstanding natural beauty and a bistro/bar that attracts lovers of good food and drink from all around the area. The nine comfortable chalets are of traditional design, fully insulated, (a welcome bonus if you are staying here during the cooler months), and supplied with just about every facility you would want in your own home.

BALLACHULISH
15 miles S of Fort William on the A82

Map 4 ref G10

On her way to visit Glencoe, Queen Victoria noted the village of Ballachulish, "where the slate quarries are". The miners had "decorated every house with flowers and bunches or wreathes of heather and red cloth". The slate quarries at Ballachulish had provided a living for the villagers since 1693 and at the time of Victoria's brief visit were at the height of their productive life with some 26 million slates being shaped and shipped in 1875. The quarries finally closed in 1955 but their legacy lives on in the slate gravestones in the churchyard, many of them elegantly engraved, and in the unique loch-side boat sheds constructed almost entirely of slate, their survival guaranteed by preservation orders.

Standing at the gates of the former slate quarry, and opposite the Tourist Information Centre, **The Arches Craft Shop** was originally the village Post Office. It now stocks much more interesting items, most notably its fascinating

The Arches Craft Shop, East Laroch, Ballachulish, Argyll PA39 4JB
Tel: 01855 811866

Wood Exhibition of Ancient Scots Pine Root sculptures by a local craftsman, Brian Dickie. These weird and wonderful creations justify a special trip by themselves, but Margaret Dickie's shop has a great deal more on offer. There are hand-crafted bowls, large and small, carved by Hamish Small of Kinlochleven from Scottish woods, and locally-made jewellery, hand-painted, copper and brass, semi-precious stone and silver. You'll also find unusual Celtic crafts; clothing (with a difference); toys for the tots; exquisite glass; and beautiful cards and gift wrap - in fact, a comprehensive showcase for local crafts from Scotland and around the world. As Margaret says, "There's an awful lot in such a wee shop!" which, incidentally, is open all year round.

On the edge of the town, **Highland Mysteryworld** promises to take you back in time to a world of bogles, kelpies, fachans, and the Blue Man of the Minch, with the help of energetic actors in costume, special effects and lots of models. Children garbed in Viking helmets and cloaks can have great fun in the adventure playground, and there's also a lochside trail, a gift shop specialising in herbal mixtures and books of legends, and a restaurant.

A couple of miles to the west of Ballachulish, on the A828 road to Oban **Craiglinnhe Guest House** enjoys a magnificent position looking across Loch Linnhe to the mountains of Sunart. Backed by wooded hills, the house is an imposing building of light grey Kentallen Granite and dates from 1885 when it was built for the Manager of the famous Ballachulish quarries. It also served as an Isolation Hospital in the early 1900's but has long been established in its

Craiglinnhe Guest House, Ballachulish, Argyll,
Western Highlands PA39 4JX   Tel/Fax: 01855 811270

current role as a friendly and welcoming Guest House. Derrick Armitage and Brian Hitchcock took over here in March 1999 after running a successful guest house in St Andrews and they offer visitors 6 attractive, well-appointed en suite rooms, 3 doubles and 3 twins, with one of the twin rooms on the ground floor. The house is non-smoking. A full Scottish breakfast is included in the tariff and evening meals are also available by arrangement. Craiglinnhe is licensed with a good choice of wines to complement your meal. Glencoe and Ben Nevis are within easy reach and the busy little port of Oban lies about half an hours drive to the south.

GLENCOE   MAP 4 REF G9
17 miles S of Fort William on A82

To the east of Ballachulish opens up one of the starkest and most sombre glens in Scotland, **Glen Coe**. Translated from Gaelic, the name means "Valley of Weeping". Here, in the early hours of February 13th, 1692, during a howling blizzard, some forty men of the Clan MacDonald were slaughtered by soldiers under the command of Campbell of Glenlyon. It was a heinous crime, "murder under trust", since for the previous ten days Campbell's soldiers had been entertained with traditional Highland hospitality by the MacDonalds. The legal pretext for the government-ordered massacre was that the MacDonalds had failed to meet the deadline of New Year's Day, 1692, for signing an oath of loyalty to William III. In fact, the necessary papers had been signed but, because of bad weather, arrived a few days late at Edinburgh. Secretary of State Sir James Dalrymple seized on the opportunity of making an example of the MacDonalds who, besides being notorious for their thievery, were also known Jacobite sympathisers. The MacDonalds may have been unpopular but the treachery of their slaughter outraged the whole country. Three years later, an official enquiry confirmed that the killings were indeed murder. Dalrymple was forced to resign, but no-one else was ever brought to account. The massacre at Glencoe poisoned the history of western Scotland for generations and even now a sign on the door of an inn in the village still proclaims: *"Nae Campbells"*.

Today, most of this gloomy, melancholy glen is owned by the National Trust for Scotland which maintains a small **Visitor Centre** where, along with a gift shop and the usual amenities, you can also watch a video retelling the dreadful events of February, 1692.

KENTALLEN OF APPIN   MAP 4 REF G10
17 miles S of Fort William off the A828

This tiny village was the setting for the real-life "Appin Murder" which captured the imagination of Robert Louis Stevenson and inspired his novel *Kidnapped*. The murdered man was Colin Campbell of Glenure, known as the "Red Fox". In the aftermath of the 1745 Jacobite rising, the Appin lands of the Stewart clan had been forfeited to the Crown. As government factor, the Red Fox had been charged with evicting the Stewarts and replacing them with men of Campbell blood. In May, 1752, Campbell was riding through Kentallen when two rifle shots rang out from a holly tree on the hillside. The Red Fox was killed immediately. A certain Alan Breac Stewart was suspected of the crime but as he could not be found, James Stewart of the Glens was arrested instead. After a travesty of a trial, with a blatantly prejudiced jury, eleven of whose members were Campbells, James was hanged at Ballachulish. Even this outrageous injustice failed to satisfy the Campbells. James' body was hung in chains for two months, and when only the bones remained, the skeleton was wired together and hung up again. The name of the true murderer of the Red Fox was known to leading Stewarts of the time, but for reasons of clan loyalty it has never been disclosed and remains to this day a family secret.

The charming village of Kentallen seems far too pretty for such a gruesome story, enjoying as it does breathtaking views across Loch Linnhe to the mountains of Morven. Sharing this spectacular view is **Ardsheal House**, a magnificent 18th century granite and stone manor set in scenery that is exceptionally beautiful, even for the West Highlands. An earlier 16th century mansion on this promontory of pink marble was destroyed by fire as a result of the 1745 uprising, and the present house was built around 1760. Ardsheal has an inviting country house ambience with spacious public rooms panelled in warm oak, and the six delightful bedrooms are furnished with family antiques and pictures. The feeling that you are visiting a welcoming private house is re-inforced by the owners of Ardsheal House, Neil and Philippa Sutherland. As one noble guest,

Ardsheal House, Kentallen of Appin, Argyll PA38 4BX
Tel: 01631 740227 Fax: 01631 740342
e-mail: info@ardsheal.co.uk website: www.ardsheal.co.uk

Lord Wilson of Tillyorn, remarked, it was "memorable and wonderful to find such accomplished hosts, delicious food and courteous attention". The food, wine, and malt whiskies are indeed memorable. Philippa serves 4-course dinners, with set menus changing daily, in the attractive dining room or the garden fronted conservatory. The innovative cooking makes full use of the abundant local produce, together with vegetables, herbs and fruit from the house garden, all served with home-baked bread. With Ben Nevis, Glencoe and Loch Ness all within easy reach, this outstanding hotel makes a perfect base for exploring the scenic glories of the West Highlands.

FROM INVERNESS TO JOHN O'GROATS

The 110-mile journey from Inverness to John O'Groats offers a wide variety of scenery and visitor attractions that range from some of the finest prehistoric sites in Scotland to a state-of-the-art time travelling museum at Tain. The route passes through the entrancing little town of Cromarty, past the splendid beaches of the Dornoch Firth, and on to one of the grandest houses in Scotland, Dunrobin Castle. Along the way there are powerful reminders of the Highland Clearances and of more agreeable events such as the Kildonan Gold Rush of 1869.

A couple of miles north of Inverness, in the car park of the Tourist Information Centre on the A9, the **Dolphin and Seal Centre** offers a fascinating insight into the lives of these popular residents of the Moray Firth. The Centre has a magnificent view of the Firth - just pick up a pair of binoculars and look out for one of the 130 individually identified dolphins which have made their home here. Measuring up to 4 metres in length, the Moray Firth dolphins are among the largest in the world, and since many of their favoured areas are close to the shore, this is one of the best places in Europe to see them at relatively close quarters. Underwater microphones pick up dolphin, seal and other underwater sounds and relay them to amplifiers in the Centre. Just put on a set of headphones and you can tune into this undiscovered world.

Two miles north of the Dolphin Centre, the **Black Isle Wildlife and Country Park** is another excellent venue for a family outing. Wallabys, llamas, rare sheep and cattle are among the more unusual residents, but there are also plenty of cuddly smaller animals for children to handle.

EASTER KINKELL   Map 7 ref I6
10 miles NW of Inverness on the B9169

Enjoying wonderful panoramic views over the Cromarty Firth to Ben Wyvis and the Wester Ross hills, **Kinkell House** is peacefully situated in 3 acres of its own grounds, surrounded by trees and pasture land. This appealing hotel and licensed restaurant is personally run by the proprietors, Steve and Marsha Fraser, who take great pains to ensure that their guests are very well looked after. The

Kinkell House, Easter Kinkell, Conon Bridge, by Dingwall, Ross-shire IV7 8HY Tel: 01349 861270 Fax: 01349 865902

house is traditionally furnished and offers great comfort, in a relaxed and informal atmosphere which is more like that of a private house than a hotel. The 9 double bedrooms, all en suite, are individually decorated and furnished: one of them, on the ground floor, is suitable for the disabled. Marsha is the chef and offers a daily changing menu which makes the most of prime quality local ingredients with a selection of fine wines to complement the food. (Reservations for lunch and dinner are requested). The restaurant enjoys beautiful views and in the evening captures the setting sun. After your meal, why not settle down in the stylish conservatory-style drawing room with its welcoming log fire.

STRATHPEFFER   Map 7 ref I6
24 miles NW of Inverness on the A834

In its heyday as a spa town during the 19th century, Strathpeffer attracted visitors from all over Europe. They would stroll along the wide streets of the "Harrogate of the North", past elegant villas and hotels to the Pump Room where the sulphurous waters on offer were deemed so disgusting that they must surely be doing one some good. Legend has it that the hot springs that abound in this once-volcanic area were caused by the Devil taking a bath. Wherever the sulphurous waters mingled with those rich in iron, they turned black, a phenomenon attributed to the fact that the Devil was washing his filthy clothes. The Pump Room in the main square has been restored as the **Water Sampling Pavilion** where you may, if you wish, sample the evil-smelling liquid. Good health to you!

Other attractions in the town include the restored Victorian railway station where there are no trains but an interesting collection of craft shops, and a superb museum, the **Highland Museum of Childhood.** It tells the story of childhood in the Scottish Highlands through a series of well-presented displays each exploring a different theme - education, health, home-life, folklore, and recreation. Items on show include toys, games, puppets, cradles, a school desk, slate and strap, as well as a number of rare dolls from the Angela Kellie Collection. Particularly engrossing are the historic photographs of Highland children at work and play from late-Victorian times to the recent past.

A curious tale is attached to the **Eagle Stone** which stands at the end of a lane off the main road. It is carved with an eagle, the crest of the Clan Munro and commemorates their victory over the Macdonalds in 1411. A local visionary, the Seer of Brahan, said that "ships would anchor here" if the stone fell three times. It has fallen twice, so it is now protected. The precaution seems wise, since many other of the Seer's prophecies have come to pass since his death in 1660. He is credited with foreseeing the building of the Caledonian Canal, the Clearances, and World War II, as well as predicting that Strathpeffer "uninviting and disagreeable as it now is, the day will come when crowds of pleasure and health seekers shall be seen thronging its portals".

CROMARTY

MAP 7 REF J5

25 miles NE of Inverness on the A832

No-one travelling in these parts should miss a visit to the enchanting little town of Cromarty, an almost perfect example of an 18th century seaport. Narrow streets and old cottages are intermixed with handsome Georgian houses built during the period of prosperity from the 1770s to the 1840s. In 1772, the Laird of Cromarty, George Ross, founded a hemp mill here in which imported Baltic hemp was spun into cloth and rope. The business was spectacularly successful and the profits helped build some of Scotland's finest Georgian houses. Also dating from those affluent days is the elegant **Cromarty Courthouse** of 1782. It's now a museum which tells the story of the town with the help of an audio guide, films and animated figures. Visitors also receive a complimentary map of the town with suggested walks. One of the places it will lead you to is **Hugh Miller's Cottage** (NTS), a charming thatched building of 1711 where the celebrated geologist and prolific man of letters was born in 1802. The cottage has been restored to its early Victorian character and gives a good sense of what life in Cromarty at that time was like. Three years after Miller's death, a statue was erected adjoining the chapel and in the churchyard there are tombstones carved by him.

If you are travelling north from Cromarty, there's a quaint, two-car ferry service during the summer which will take you the mile or so across the mouth of Cromarty Firth to Balnapaling on the Nigg Peninsula.

TAIN

MAP 7 REF J5

24 miles NE of Inverness off the A9

The most distinctive building in Tain is the **Tolbooth**, built in the 1500s and restored in 1707. It's an attractive sight with its conical spire and corner turrets but at the time of the Clearances this "sharp-pointed house" struck fear into the hearts of local crofters. It was then the administrative centre from which notices of dispossession were issued, and also the jail for anyone who tried to resist the order.

Tain's history stretches back to Viking times when it was the administrative centre for the area, its name a corruption of the Norse word "Thing", meaning a Council. St Duthus was born here around AD 1000, and sixty-six years later Tain became a Royal Burgh. The **900 Roses Garden** commemorates the town's nine centuries of existence.

For a riveting insight into its history during that time, a visit to **Tain Through Time** is absolutely essential. This fascinating complex includes a Museum with a range of displays illustrating Tain's rich and varied past, the ruins of a Chapel destroyed by fire in 1428, and the 14th century St Duthus Church, one of Scotland's most important medieval shrines. This lovely building once housed the relics of St Duthus whose bones, enclosed in reliquaries of gold and silver, were believed to possess miraculous curative powers. (They mysteriously disappeared in 1560 and have never been seen since). King James IV made an annual pilgrimage here every year between 1492 and 1513, combining this pious act with a visit to his mistress, Janet Kennedy, whom he had installed in nearby Moray. Other attractions at this inventive centre include a dramatic sound and light show telling the story of some of St Duthus' miracles; the opportunity for children to dress up as a King's jester or learn the mysterious Ogam alphabet; and a gift shop selling a wide range of unusual gifts and souvenirs.

Just to the north of the town, off the A9, is the **Glenmorangie Distillery** which operated illegally for many years before acquiring a licence in 1843. Tours are available, and there's also a Visitor Centre and Shop.

DORNOCH

MAP 7 REF J4

41 miles NE of Inverness via the A9/A949

With miles of sandy beaches, and near the top of Scotland's listings for hours of sunshine, Dornoch is a trim holiday resort with flowers everywhere and a celebrated championship golf course. The town overlooks the Dornoch Firth with fine views across the estuary to the Tain peninsula. In the spacious main square, **Dornoch Cathedral**, dating back to 1224, dominates the town. The building suffered extensive damage in 1570 when a clan feud led to the Mackays of Strathnaver pillaging the town and setting fire to the Cathedral. Only the tower and its spire were left unscathed. The roofless choir, transept and nave were restored in the 1600s but it wasn't until 1924 that restoration work undertaken as part of the Cathedral's 700th anniversary celebrations revealed the beautiful 13th century stonework that had lain behind plaster for centuries. No fewer than 16 Earls of Sutherland were laid to rest here, and at the west end the 1st Duke, who died in 1833, is commemorated by a fine statue sculpted by Francis Chantrey.

Two other ancient buildings have acquired new roles: the tower of the 16th century **Bishop's Palace** is now part of Dornoch Castle Hotel, while the **Old Jail** currently houses a craft shop and a re-creation of a 19th century prison cell.

Incongruously, this attractive little town witnessed the last burning of a witch in Scotland. The year was 1722 when a misfortunate old woman named Janet Horne was accused of transforming her daughter into a pony, riding her to a witches' coven and having her shod there by the Devil. During her trial, Janet was judged to have confirmed her guilt of these improbable crimes by incorrectly quoting the Gaelic version of the Lord's Prayer. She was sentenced to be roasted alive in a barrel of boiling tar. This gruesome event is commemorated by the **Witch's Stone**, just south of the Square on Carnaig Street.

Two minutes from town centre and Dornoch's superb sandy beach (Blue Flag) is **Achandean,** an attractive stone-built bungalow set back from the road in a sheltered feature garden with private parking, offering excellent bed and breakfast accommodation. Refurbished and redecorated to a high standard, Achandean is the home of Audrey and Basil Hellier whose warm welcome ensure their guests, old and new, have a happy and enjoyable stay. The attractive bedrooms are en suite (one private), and all are fully equipped with colour television, clock radios, welcome tray and, most importantly clean, comfortable beds. There is a comfortable, relaxing sitting room and separate dining-room where you may, on request, enjoy an evening meal. Senior citizens and the disabled are specially welcome. Special rates for OAP's and stays of three or

Achandean, The Meadows, Dornoch, Sutherland IV25 3SF
Tel: 01862 810413 Fax: 01862 810413 e.mail: hellier92.freeserve.co.uk

more days. Achandean is the ideal base for exploring the spectacular northern Highlandsabove Inverness with its colourful history and superb golf courses.

Just north of Dornoch is **Skelbo Castle**, on the shore of Loch Fleet. Originally built in 1259, it is now a dangerous ruin best seen from the roadside. **Loch Fleet** itself is a massive saltwater basin at the mouth of the River Fleet, a Scottish Wildlife Trust Reserve and home to many seals, ducks and waders.

SPINNINGDALE

MAP 7 REF I4

38 miles N of Inverness via the A9 and A949

Some enterprising hotelier built **The Old Mill Inn** at Spinningdale around 1745 to provide overnight food and accommodation for the drovers hustling their cattle southwards to English markets hungry for prime Scottish beef. By chance or by intent, the unknown founder of The Old Mill Inn placed his hostelry at a location which enjoys superb views over Dornoch Firth to the Ross-shire hills, an ever-changing panorama of skyscapes. Lesley Elizabeth Phelps' welcoming and friendly inn also enjoys clear views of the dramatic ruins of Dempster's Cotton Mill, built in 1793 and the only one of its type in the Highlands. Open from dawn to dusk, The Mill as it is affectionately known to locals, offers a good

The Old Mill Inn, Spinningdale, Sutherland IV24 3AD
Tel: 01862 881219

choice of accommodation with some rooms providing en suite facilities. Meals are available all day from either the bar menu or in the restaurant where you can select the table d'hôte or the à la carte menus, both of which offer an excellent selection of traditional Scottish Fayre from local sources and include vegetarian options. Families are especially welcome at The Mill: there's a special menu for younger guests and a baby-listening service is also available. More than 250 years after it was founded, The Old Mill Inn is still maintaining the highest traditions of Highland hospitality.

GOLSPIE
Map 7 ref J4
58 miles SW of Wick on the A9

Returning to the coast, the A9 continues northwards to the straggling red-sandstone village of Golspie, the administrative centre for Sutherland and the "capital" of the Dukes of Sutherland who still own vast tracts of northeast Scotland. Above the village, atop **Beinn a'Bragaidh** (1293 feet high, and also known as Ben Vraggie), stands a colossal **Monument**, 100 feet high, to the 1st Duke. It was this Duke who evicted some 15,000 crofters from his land during the infamous Clearances of the early 19th century. However, the inscription on his monument, "erected by a mourning and grateful tenantry", refers only to "a judicious, kind and liberal landlord who would open his hands to the distress of the widow, the sick and the traveller". For several years, campaigners have been trying to have the monument destroyed and another erected in memory of the Duke's dispossessed tenants. The Sutherland presence is also clear in Golspie's 17th century church where the finely carved and panelled **Sutherland Loft**, complete with its own retiring room, was installed for the then Earl in 1739.

A mile or so north along the A9 from Golspie is **Dunrobin Castle,** set beside the sea and surrounded by woodland. The hereditary home of the Earls and Dukes of Sutherland, Dunrobin has a late-13th century square Keep, but most of the castle was built in the 19th century to a design by Sir Charles Barry in the exuberantly mock-medieval Scottish baronial style so popular at the time. Queen Victoria described it very accurately as "a mixture of an old Scotch castle and a French château". The treasures on show include paintings by Landseer, Allan Ramsay, Reynolds, and Canaletto; some exquisite Mortlake tapestries; Louis Quinze furniture; a wonderfully ornate ceiling in the drawing room; and a library lined with sycamore wood. The castle is the largest house in the Northern Highlands with no fewer than 189 furnished rooms in all, although visitors only get to see 17 of the grandest ones. In the grounds, there are magnificent formal gardens to explore, modelled on those at Versailles, and a museum housed in a gracious 18th century building. It contains an astonishing collection including archaeological remains and hunting trophies from all over the world, Pictish stones, one of John O'Groats' bones, a "picnic gong from the South Pacific", and mementoes of Queen Victoria who was a great chum of the 3rd Duke and Duchess.

Nearby, **Dunrobin Castle Station** is one of the most exclusive railway halts in Scotland. It was built as a private stop for the Duke and his guests and last used regularly in the 1960s.

BRORA
Map 7 ref J4
47 miles SW of Wick on the A9

The little town of Brora used to be described as "the industrial capital of Sutherland" because of the once-thriving coal mines in the area. The town has a good sandy beach, and a mile or so north of the town the **Clynelish Distillery** (free) will provide you with a guided tour and a complimentary dram. **Hunters Woollen Mill**, known throughout the world for its tweeds and woollens, also welcomes visitors.

In Gaelic, **Ar Dachaidh** means "Our Home" - an appropriate name for Kath MacDonald's peaceful and welcoming house about a mile outside Brora village. Situated at the end of a single track road that wanders through the crofting area of Badnellan, Ar Dachaidh is a traditional Croft House set in 1/2 an acre of garden. Kath is an outstanding cook whose culinary skills have earned her an entry in the "Taste of Scotland" book, one of very few bed and breakfast establishments to be included. Breakfast options include genuine oatmeal porridge, and Jugged Kipper, along with home made bread, Scottish Pancake or Potato Scone. Kath's 3-course dinners offer traditional cooking with an Italian twist,

Ar Dachaidh, Badnellan, Brora, Sutherland KW9 6NQ
Tel/Fax: 01408 621658

using the very best of local produce and crowned by a delicious home made dessert. Vegetarians are catered for, children are welcome, and packed lunches are available. Ar Dachaidh has 3 guest rooms, (1 double, 1 single, 1 twin), a residents' lounge and separate dining room, and provides an excellent base for touring this wonderfully unspoilt corner of the country.

Three miles north, on the seaward side of the A9, **Kintradwell Broch** is an impressive example of these circular, prehistoric forts, with an interior measuring some 30 feet in diameter. During excavations in 1880, a macabre memento of ancient ways of dealing with criminals was uncovered in the form of two headless skeletons. A little further north, in a lay-by near Lothbeg, **The Wolf Stone** marks the spot where the last wolf in Sutherland was killed, around 1700.

HELMSDALE   Map 7 ref K3
37 miles SW of Wick on the A9

This small coastal town of grey stone was largely built during the Clearances to house the crofters evicted from Strath Kildonan. These unfortunates were much luckier than most since their enforced removal to a windswept seaside location co-incided with the great herring boom of the 19th century and, seizing the opportunity, they thrived off this harvest from the sea. The great shoals of the silvery fish have now disappeared but Helmsdale is still a working port, its harbour busy with fishermen off-loading their catches. And the River Helmsdale which runs into the sea here is famed as one of the most prolific of the northern salmon rivers. There's also a fine sandy beach here and a shoreline where semi-precious stones such as amethyst and jasper are often found. Thousands of visitors each year make their way to the outstanding **Timespan Heritage Centre** where state-of-the-art displays and a video presentation tells the story of Helmsdale and its environs from prehistoric times to the present. You will learn about the Castle that once stood here, Vikings, Picts, the Clearances and the Kildonan Gold Rush. In 1869, gold was found in Kildonan Burn, about 10 miles inland, and a few lucky prospectors did make respectable sums. Tiny amounts of gold are still found every year and if you want to try your hand at panning, you can pick up a free licence and the necessary equipment from the gift and fishing-tackle shop across the road from Timespan.

North of Helmsdale, the A9 winds up the hill to a plateau which ends at the sea in a striking rock called the **Ord of Caithness** (1300 feet). There are wonderful views along the coast. It's said that men of the Sinclair clan will never cross the Ord on a Monday because it was on that day, in 1513, that a large party of Sinclairs marched through here on their way to the Battle of Flodden. Not one of them returned.

A little further north, at Ousdale, a footpath leads from a lay-by to the ruined crofts of **Badbea**. This lonely coastal settlement was founded by tenants evicted from the inland straths during the Clearances. An old tradition asserts that the spot was so exposed that children and cattle had to be tethered to prevent them being blown over the cliffs.

DUNBEATH   Map 7 ref K3
20 miles SW of Wick off the A9

This village was the birthplace of the novelist Neil Gunn (1891-1973). In books such as *The Grey Coast* and *Morning Tide* he drew on his intimate knowledge of the Caithness area and its people to create highly readable tales. His life, and the natural and social history of the region, are presented in a lively way at the **Dunbeath Heritage Centre**.

Enjoying a quiet location in this coastal village, the **Dunbeath Hotel** is an attractive white-painted building with colourful red-and-white awnings, looking out across open countryside. The building dates back to around 1850 when it served as a mail coach inn and for the past 25 years or so has been owned and run by Neil and Pat Buchanan who offer visitors a warm Highland welcome, comfortable accommodation in 6 en suite rooms, and a stylish restaurant serv-

Dunbeath Hotel, Dunbeath, Caithness KW6 6EG
Tel: 01593 731208 Fax: 01593 731242

ing good Scottish fare. Food is available every lunchtime (noon until 14.00) and evening (17.00-21.00) with a wide choice of dishes supplemented by daily Chef's Specials. The hotel is a perfect place to relax, with many places of interest to visit in the area. Nearby is the birthplace of Neil M. Gunn, author of *Silver Darlings* and *Highland River*, whose statue overlooks the harbour where the quayside is stacked with lobster pots. From Dunbeath a scenic road runs 6 miles inland through crofting areas to heather moorland where peat for winter fires is still cut and red deer, or even the occasional golden eagle, can be seen.

About 10 miles north of Dunbeath, along the A9, turn left on a minor road just past the village of Lybster, and after 7 miles you will come to the **Grey Cairns of Camster**, generally regarded as amongst the finest prehistoric sites in Britain and definitely not to be missed. Dating back to around 4000 BC, these two monumental chambered cairns are approached by way of passages so low that at some points you have to crawl. The Round Cairn is 55 feet in diameter, and 12 feet high: the Long Cairn 200 feet long and 65 feet wide.

Two miles north of Lybster, just off the A9, there are yet more ancient remains near East Clyth. From the village a path leads to the **Hill O'Many Stanes**, an early bronze age construction with some 200 standing stones arranged in 22 rows running north to south. Archaeologists haven't yet worked out what their purpose was, but they do know that originally there were 600 stones in place.

IN AND AROUND WICK

In Old Norse "Vik" means a bay, and Wick is indeed set around a bay although its spread of dull grey houses makes the setting far from picturesque. Robert Louis Stevenson was scathing about Wick, describing it as "the meanest of man's towns, situated on the baldest of God's bays". Like Budapest, Wick is really two towns, with the original settlement standing on the north bank of the Wick River, and Pulteneytown on the south.

The latter was named after the president of the British Fisheries Society which in 1806 commissioned Thomas Telford to design a new town to house crofters who had been evicted during the Clearances. The Society was motivated by the humane intention of providing work for them as fishermen and the herring boom of the mid-1800s more than fulfilled their wish. Wick became the busiest herring port in Europe with more than 1,000 boats registered here, exporting tons of the silvery fish around the world. Today, the derelict net-mending sheds, storehouses, and cooperages of Pulteneytown provide a forlorn testimony to those years of prosperity.

The town's chequered history is well-presented at the **Wick Heritage Centre** which, amongst many other interesting exhibits, displays an excellent collection of photographs dating back to the 1880s. The town's major visitor attraction, though, is **Caithness Glass** where you can watch glassmakers demonstrating their skill in this most tricky of processes, and purchase the finished products.

About 3 miles north of the town, on a windswept promontory, stand the theatrical ruins of **Sinclair and Girnigoe Castles**, in medieval times the twin residences of the Earls of Caithness. It was at Girnigoe Castle that the 4th Earl, suspecting that his son was plotting against him, imprisoned him between 1570 and 1576, and then left him to die of starvation.

KEISS

MAP 7 REF L1

8 miles N of Wick on the A99

About halfway between Wick and John O'Groats is the quaint little fishing port of Keiss, (pronounced Keese), the main centre in Caithness for crab fishing. Just a few minutes walk from its picturesque harbour where you can watch fishermen off-loading their catch of crabs, lobster and other shellfish is the **Sinclair Bay Hotel.** Visitors to this charming old coaching inn are assured of a warm welcome from its owners, John and Judith Mowat. They offer first-rate bar lunches and evening meals as well as comfortable accommodation, all at reasonable

Sinclair Bay Hotel, Keiss, by Wick, Caithness KW1 4UY
Tel: 01955 631233

prices. Most of the rooms have grand sea views over Sinclair Bay and children and pets are especially welcome. Close by stand the ruins of medieval **Keiss Castle** and all along the coastline here are glorious safe and sandy beaches. John will gladly arrange sea, river, or loch fishing, golf or shooting for you. And photographers and painters will be enchanted by the area with its breathtaking seascapes.

About 3 miles north of Keiss, the **Northlands Viking Centre** at Auckengill features displays on the archaeological history of Caithness, especially the brochs, and on John Nicolson, a Victorian antiquarian who lived in the village.

JOHN O'GROATS
MAP 7 REF L1

17 miles N of Wick on the A99/A836

It's a mystery why John O'Groats has become accepted as the northern starting-point for the innumerable journeys made by walkers, cyclists, and even people pushing baths, traversing the 874 miles southwards to Land's End. Dunnet Head, over to the west, is a clear 3 miles further north and the itinerary "Dunnet Head to Land's End" surely has just as good a ring to it as the more familiar "John O'Groats to Lands End". But it seems unlikely that a tradition that began in mid-Victorian times is going to change.

The village takes its name from a Dutchman, Jan de Groot, who in 1496 paid a handsome sum to James IV for the exclusive right to run a ferry from here to the Orkney Islands. The business prospered but Jan, it seems, was burdened with a dysfunctional family - eight sons who constantly quarrelled over who should take precedence after his death. In an inspired attempt to secure domestic harmony, Jan built an octagonal house so that each of his fractious children could enter by his own door and sit at (his) head of the table. A much less appealing version of the story is that Jan erected an eight-sided shelter for his ferry customers to protect them from the North Sea's gusting winds, whatever their direction. Whichever interpretation is true, a mound with a flagstaff marks the supposed site of the house/shelter and nearby is a much-photographed sign pole, its arms pointing in all directions, each inscribed with the number of miles from John O'Groats to far-flung places.

Living up to its name, most of the guest rooms at the **Seaview Hotel** do indeed have striking views across the turbulent Pentland Firth to the Island of Stroma and the southernmost of the Orkney Islands. This comfortable, family-run hotel is under the personal direction of Andrew Mowat who makes every effort to ensure that guests have a relaxing and comfortable stay. Open all year, the Seaview Hotel serves food all day with fresh, local seafood a speciality and

Seaview Hotel, John O'Groats, Caithness KW1 4YR
Tel: 01955 611220

another special attraction is its regular music evenings. The hotel is just a quarter of a mile from John O'Groats' modern harbour, built in the 1970s with the help of European funds, which has led to a revival in the traditional fishing for crabs and lobsters, one of the mainstays of the local economy and the basis of many an outstanding meal at the Seaview Hotel. And if you want to claim that you have visited the most north-easterly point, (not the most northerly), on mainland Britain, just travel the couple of miles to Duncansby Point where the headland is crowned by a 1920s lighthouse guarding the eastern end of the Pentland Firth.

In the sea to the east of John O'Groats stand **Duncansby Stacks**, a remarkable series of rocks sculpted by North Sea storms into stark pinnacles, arches and bridges, as well as two spectacular narrow inlets with perpendicular sides, known locally as "goes". This is a seabird haven, a veritable paradise for birdwatchers. Puffins, shags, fulmars, kittiwakes, all kinds of gulls and many more species nest on the rock ledges in their thousands, whilst offshore stately gannets can often be seen diving on to an unwary fish.

About 20 miles northwest from John O'Groats, **Dunnet Head** is the most northerly point on the British mainland and actually nearer to the Arctic Circle than it is to London. Near the lighthouse, a viewfinder identifies the far distant mountains of Ben Loyal and Ben Hope, (visible on clear days), the Old Man of Hoy, off Orkney, and it's also an excellent spot to watch the ships in the busy shipping lanes of the Pentland Firth.

THE NORTHWEST COAST

In parts of west Sutherland "you have as much chance of coming across a golden eagle as you do a petrol station". This is magnificent wilderness country with no towns and with its few villages often many miles apart. "There is a sense of vastness" wrote Matthew Arnold more than a century ago, "miles and miles of mere heather and peat and rocks, and not a soul". Little has changed since then. The majestic mountains and the sea lochs biting deep inland have reminded many travellers of the Norwegian fjords, an appropriate comparison since the Vikings ruled the area for some two hundred years.

DURNESS
69 miles NE of Ullapool on the A838

Map 6 ref H1

Durness is the most northwesterly village on the British mainland, a crofting village which was originally settled by the Picts around 400 BC. It's a popular base for walkers preparing to tackle the daunting hike to **Cape Wrath**, a huge craggy bulkhead jutting out into the Atlantic Ocean. Less energetic visitors can take a ferry and bus for the 12-mile journey to the Cape and its sturdy lighthouse which was built in 1828. Also well worth visiting while in Durness is

Balnakiel Bay with its white sandy beach, and the astounding **Smoo Cave**, a vast limestone cavern easily reached by a path from the car park.

SCOURIE   MAP 6 REF G2

43 miles N of Ullapool on the A894

It's something of a surprise to find palm trees growing around this scattered seaside village. They are believed to be the most northerly specimens in the world. The superb sandy beach and the safe bathing here have made this remote spot popular as a family holiday resort. Scourie lies at the heart of a famous brown trout fishing area and fishermen around the world know the **Scourie Hotel**, famous for providing connoisseurs of game fishing with some 25,000 acres of Loch, River and Hill Loch fishing. The hotel has 36 fishing beats held exclusively for its guests, as well as 3 boats on Loch Stack and 1 boat on Loch More for sea trout and salmon. Built by the 2nd Duke of Sutherland as a coaching inn, the hotel stands on the site of an old fortified house looking towards the sheltered waters and white sands of Scourie Bay. In the shieling below nestle the gable-stepped houses of Scourie village. Beyond spreads the famed empty quarter

Scourie Hotel, Scourie, Sutherland IV27 4SX
Tel: 01971 502396 Fax: 01971 502423

of western Sutherland, a lunar landscape of lochs and mountains rising into a wilderness sky. The 20 guest rooms, and 1 fishermans chalet, most of which have views to Scourie Bay or the distant tops of Ben Stack, Foinaven and Arkle, are all comfortable and well appointed: 2 are very large family rooms with mesmeric views. The hotel has 2 comfortable lounges, a cocktail bar and public bar. Meals are table d'hôte and prepared from fresh local produce - salmon and trout from loch and river, venison from the hill, fresh langoustine and a variety of fish from Kinlochbervie or Lochinver. The cellars date back to the 17th century and some very interesting wines lurk in their depths!

A few miles northwest of Scourie is **Handa Isle**, a Scottish Wildlife Trust bird sanctuary reached by a short ferry ride from the picturesque hamlet of Tarbet. The island is crowded with breeding colonies of puffins, kittiwakes, fulmars, Great and Arctic skuas, and guillemots, who use every nook and cranny of the sea cliffs to make nests for their eggs. The Laxford sea cruise, sailing out of Fanagmore daily, displays this magnificent sight from another angle out at sea, where the knowledgeable boatman knows all the best spots for photographs.

ACHILTIBUIE   Map 6 ref G4
25 miles NW of Ullapool on minor road off the A835

Reached by a scenic single track road, the village of Achiltibuie is a straggle of white cottages gazing over the bay at the Summer Isles and beyond to the Hebrides. Here visitors discover one of the most unusual Hidden Places in Scotland, the **Hydroponicum**. Robert Irvine built this "garden of the future" - a garden without soil. Within its three distinct climates, (Hampshire, Bordeaux and the Canaries), bananas, passion fruit, lemons and vines all thrive, along with more familiar fruits and vegetables. There's a sub-tropical café where you can sample the produce and a gift shop where you can buy hydroponic growing kits.

The Achiltibuie Smokehouse offers produce of a more traditional Scottish nature. Here you can watch the process of curing salmon, fish, meat and game and stock up from the Smokehouse shop.

Occupying a wonderful position in this old crofting village, the **Summer Isles Hotel** has established itself over the years as an oasis of civilisation hidden away in a stunningly beautiful landscape. Mark and Geraldine Irvine run this

Summer Isles Hotel, Achiltibuie, Ross-shire IV26 2YG
Tel: 01854 622282 Fax: 01854 622251

individual but sophisticated hotel which has been in the family since the late 60s. The ambience is undemanding so that people relax easily and soon find they are among friends. Nearly everything you eat here is home produced or locally caught. Scallops, lobsters, langoustines, crabs, halibut, turbot, salmon, venison, big brown eggs, wholesome brown bread fresh from the oven - the list of real food is endless. With such wonderfully fresh ingredients the chef, Chris Firth-Bernard, invariably produces delicious and healthy fare. "There is a marvellous amount of nothing to do in Achiltibuie" say Mark and Geraldine who will be happy to advise you about the opportunities for fishing, walking, birdwatching and sub-aqua diving. Alternatively you could join the *Hectoria* for a cruise around the islands to see the seals and rare birds, or simply relax on the sands of Achnahaird, just down the road.

MOREFIELD   MAP 6 REF G4
1 mile NW of Ullapool on the A835

Anyone who has fallen under the spell of Scottish music will be charmed by the work of Murdo Urquhart who, together with his wife Joan, runs **Strathmore House**, a delightful bed and breakfast establishment enjoying stunning views over Loch Broom. A fisherman by trade, Murdo fishes for prawns and white fish. He is also a talented writer and composer and has produced a CD and tape of songs which celebrate his native Ullapool, its people and its way of life. They provide a wonderful souvenir of this beautiful corner of Wester Ross. Strathmore House is a modern, well-equipped building with 6 quality guest rooms, all doubles and all en suite, with one room on the ground floor. All the rooms are attractively furnished and provided with lots of thoughtful little extras. Children are welcome, vegetarians and those on special diets can be catered for, and

Strathmore House, Morefield, Ullapool, Ross & Cromarty IV26 2TH
Tel: 01854 612423

packed lunches are available by arrangement. A non-smoking house, the Strathmore is open from Easter to October.

ULLAPOOL Map 6 ref G4
59 miles NW of Inverness on the A835

The most northerly settlement of any size on the northwest coast is Ullapool, embarkation point for ferries to Stornaway. This appealing little town was pur-pose-built in 1788, to a design by Thomas Telford, by the British Fisheries Society which hoped to capitalise on the herring boom of the time. Ullapool's streets are laid out in a grid design, their regularity enlivened by brightly-painted houses and a wonderful variety of busy little shops. Despite its smallness, the town has the feeling of a cosmopolitan port: your next-table neighbours in one of its cosy pubs may well be speaking in strange tongues - fishermen from eastern Euro-pean countries as likely as not, celebrating their catch of Atlantic fish. Wildlife flourishes around Ullapool.

The only inhabitants of the **Summer Isles**, (to which there are frequent boat trips during the summer season), are colonies of seabirds, and in the surround-ing waters, dolphins and porpoises can be seen larking about, there are seals greedy for travellers' tit-bits, and if you are really lucky, you may get a sighting of an elusive otter. The town's comparatively short history, a mere two centu-ries, is amply recorded in the **Ullapool Museum**, housed in the old parish church, which has exhibits on crofting, fishing, and a more unsettling display chroni-cling the devastating effects of the 18th century Clearances when thousands of evicted crofters passed through the town on their way to a dubious future in the remote territories of Canada, Australia and New Zealand.

South of the town, **Corrieshalloch Gorge** is one of the most spectacular, and accessible, sights in the Highlands. A mile long and 200 feet deep, this awesome ravine is additionally watered by the **Falls of Measach** which plunge 150 feet down the hillside. The best view of the Falls is from the Victorian suspension bridge strung across the gorge, but do take note of its prominent warning that no more than two people at a time should stand on its vertigo-inducing boards.

LAIDE Map 6 ref F4
32 miles SW of Ullapool on the A832

It was marauding Norsemen who, exhausted by their rape and pillage of the western Highlands, settled on the shores of "Grunna Fjord", (shallow fjord), now known as Gruinard Bay. The Bay lies in one of the most beautiful areas of the Highlands, has a safe sandy beach and sea fishing provides excellent sport in the bay. Occupying a prime location in this idyllic spot, **The Old Smiddy Guest House** enjoys marvellous mountain views to the east and offers genuine, friendly hospitality. The charming whitewashed building is crammed with travel trophies, family memorabilia, books and paintings by local artists. Best of all

The Old Smiddy Guest House, Laide, nr Gairloch, Highlands IV22 2NB
Tel: 01445 731425 Fax: 01445 731425

perhaps is the cuisine, outstanding food using prime ingredients from Scotland's natural larder. As a result the Guest House is a member of the "Taste of Scotland" and in addition Catherine Macdonald was a finalist in the "AA landlady of the year" competition. Guests can enjoy the spectacular scenery of majestic mountains, dramatic coasts, wilderness and its varied wildlife by day, returning to innovative, candlelit dinners. Then sink happily into crisp cotton linen at night!

POOLEWE   MAP 6 REF F5
40 miles SW of Ullapool via the A835/A832

Just to the north of Poolewe, **Inverewe Gardens** (NTS) are one of the "mustnot-miss" attractions of the Highlands. In 1862, young Osgood Mackenzie inherited a huge, 12,000 acre estate from his stepfather, the Laird of Gairloch. The legacy wasn't as valuable as it sounds since almost all of those sprawling acres were barren, covered with beach gravel and sea grass. A dedicated botanist, Osgood made it his life's work to make this desert bloom. He purchased tons of the rich soil which Irish ships carried as ballast to Gairloch and smothered his arid domain with inches-deep layers of this unusual import. He planted a protective break of trees and began his project by filling a walled garden, (which is still the centrepiece of the gardens), with plants from all over the world. Over the course of more than half a century until his death in 1922, he transformed this infertile peninsula into one of the great gardens of the world. Thanks to the mild influence of the Gulf Stream, the gardens are ablaze with exotic plants from the Far East, South America, Australasia and the Himalayas. Mid-May to mid-June is the time to see the rhododendrons and azaleas in their full glory; during July and August the herbaceous garden is at its most colourful. There's a mighty eucalyptus tree, the largest in the northern hemisphere and, close by, a Ghost Tree, so-called because it's an example of the earliest species of flowering trees. The **Visitor Centre** (open mid-March to October, daily) has an informative display about the history of the gardens, and is the starting point for guided walks which leave here every weekday at 13.30.

Poolewe itself is a picturesque crofting village, set around the pool formed where the River Ewe tumbles into the loch of the same name. **Loch Ewe** is as pretty as any in Scotland but blemished in parts by bunkers, pillboxes and gun sites, an unlovely legacy of World War II when the loch was a loading base for convoys to Russia.

Fortunately, nothing mars the attractiveness of **Waterside of Poolewe** where even the names of the two cottages have a magical ring to them: Dóbhran and Corra-bhàn - the Gaelic words for Otter and Heron. The owners, Dee and Derek Murton, can't guarantee that you will see a wild otter with its family, but on a good day between October and April you might see as many as five at once. And on most days you should see at least a couple of seals hunting right below your cottage. If you take time for a leisurely stroll along the shore to Inverewe Gardens, you will almost certainly catch sight of oyster catchers, herons, cormorants, mallards, Great Northern Divers, eider ducks, and if you're reasonably lucky,

Waterside, Poolewe, Achnasheen, Wester Ross IV22 2JX
Tel/Fax: 01445 781482 e-mail: waterside@poolewe.inuk.com
Website: www.poolewe.inuk.com

white-tailed sea eagles, wild deer, and even Golden Eagles. One of the cottages sleeps 4 people, the other up to 6, and both are comprehensively equipped with a fridge, microwave, toaster, auto washer, tumble dryer and electric coffee maker, and the bathrooms have power showers, and also a bath for those long, lazy soaks. Staying at these cottages you can revel in the utter peace and quiet of unspoilt wilderness as you relish the thought of lunch or dinner either in your own home or at one of the excellent licensed restaurants in Poolewe. Children over 12 are welcome at Waterside, as are pets.

Travellers in this part of the country come to expect stunning views to open up at almost every turn, but the vistas of Loch Maree and the Isle of Skye from the viewpoint on the A832 just south of Poolewe are quite unforgettable.

GAIRLOCH
MAP 6 REF F5
57 miles SW of Ullapool via the A835 & 832

The busy little fishing port of Gairloch has been one of the main resorts of the north-west since Victorian times, with visitors of those days greatly appreciating its superb location, fine sandy beaches and scenic coastal walks. The village faces west, enjoying stunning views to distant Skye and the Torridon mountains and of wonderful sunsets. There are facilities for almost every kind of outdoor activity from golfing to windsurfing and should the weather be inclement, the **Gairloch Heritage Museum** provides plenty of interest. Amongst the many fascinating items on display at the Museum are two sturdy fishing-boats constructed locally around the turn of the century; the huge lantern from Rudha Reidh lighthouse just up the coast; and an illicit still. This appealing museum, housed in a former farm steading, was established by local volunteers in 1977 and since then has garnered no fewer than seven National Awards. Since virtually all the exhibits have been collected in Gairloch parish, a visit to the Museum is an excellent way of finding out what life was like in a typical West Highland parish in the past.

KYLE OF LOCHALSH
MAP 6 REF F7
78 miles W of Inverness on A87

Until the Skye Bridge was opened in 1995, Kyle of Lochalsh was a busy little place with a constant stream of traffic rolling in to line up for the ferry to the fabled Isle of Skye. The elegant new bridge has put the old ferry boat out of business, much to the annoyance of islanders who resent paying the steep toll, (currently £5.60), for crossing the bridge. There is an alternative, a vehicle ferry taking about 10 minutes to cross from Galtair on the mainland to Kylerhea on Skye, but it only operates during the summer months. The swooping Skye Bridge bypassing their small town has been bad news for shopkeepers in Kyle of Lochalsh; the good news for visitors is that the traffic-clotted streets of the past are no more. It's now an inviting place to stay before setting off to explore the Isle of Skye.

Parts of the **Kyle Hotel** are so old that they were built even before roads reached this traditional "Gateway to the Isle of Skye". The hotel looks across to the dramatic hills of An t-Eilean Sgitheanach ("Island of the Men of Skye") and from its spacious car park at the rear there's another striking sight to be seen during the summer months - vintage steam locomotives puffing into the station here. Kyle Hotel has been owned since 1991 by Maureen Duffin and she ensures that not only will guests feel genuinely welcome but will also find the very best in food and accommodation. The spacious and elegant restaurant is a

Kyle Hotel, Main Street, Kyle of Lochalsh, Ross-shire IV40 8AB
Tel: 01599 534204 Fax: 01599 534932

pleasant place for morning coffee or afternoon tea when you can sample the home baking. Dinner, served from 18.00 until 21.30, offers menus based on fresh local produce, including seafood and game, followed by wonderful home-made sweets. Complement your meal with wine, mostly from the New World and available by the glass, carafe or bottle. The hotel has 31 tastefully furnished guest rooms, all en suite and provided with such home comforts as colour television, hairdryer, radio alarm and a direct dial telephone, while the freshly-stocked hospitality tray enables you to make a hot drink whenever you please.

ERBUSAIG
MAP 6 REF F7

1 mile N of Kyle of Lochalsh on minor road off the A87

A mile or so north of Kyle of Lochalsh, the **Tingle Creek Hotel** is situated in one

Tingle Creek Hotel, Erbusaig, by Kyle of Lochalsh, Ross-shire IV40 8BB
Tel: 01599 534430 Fax: 01599 534315

of the world's great beauty spots. Close to the Skye Bridge, it lies on the road to the picturesque village of Plockton and enjoys magnificent views across the water to the mountains of Skye and the Isle of Raasay. Close by is the famous "Kyle Line" which provides one of the most scenic railway journeys of the globe.

Cherry and Tommy Dougherty have owned and run the Tingle Creek since 1990 and have firmly established its reputation for excellent food and accommodation. The cuisine here is quite outstanding - the very best of Highland meat, game and seafood is provided, including steaks, local prawns, scampi, crab and lobster to order. It is served in an attractive, intimate restaurant and the menu also includes some tasty vegetarian options. In addition to an exceptionally comfortable lounge bar, the public bar offers pool, darts and other games with snooker also available on a full sized table. The oldest part of the hotel was a croft house but it has expanded greatly since then and the Doughertys now have 14 guest rooms, 12 of them en suite. They strive to ensure that the interior of the hotel is in keeping with the requirements of today's discerning clientele, so all the comfortable bedrooms have private facilities, colour television, direct dial telephone and tea/coffee makers. Open all year, the Tingle Creek is centrally heated throughout. Perhaps the centrepiece at the Tingle Creek, however, is the outstanding modern Function Suite with its attractive brass decor and sunken dance floor. Catering to 150 for weddings and functions, this popular venue offers entertainment all year round. By the way, don't bother to search the neighbourhood for a creek called Tingle: the hotel actually takes its name from a famous racehorse of that name.

10 | The Islands

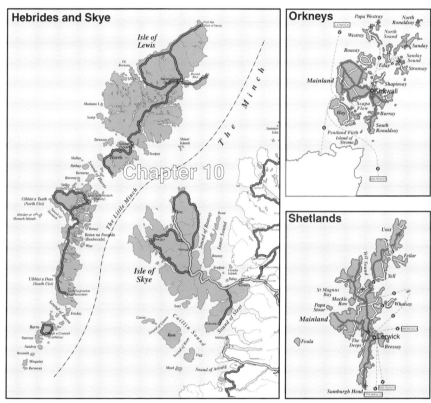

Hebrides and Skye

Isle of Lewis

Gt. Bernera

Broad Bay

Mealasta I.

Scarp

The Minch

Taransay

Shiant Islands

Scalpay

Summer Isles

Harris

Shillay

Pabbay

Berneray

Vallay

Sound of Harris

Uibhist a Tuath (North Uist)

Heisker or Monach Islands

The Little Minch

Ronay

Beinn na Faoghla (Benbecula)

Wiay

Uibhist a Deas (South Uist)

Rona

Sound of Raasay

Inner Sound

Raasay

Scalpay

Crowlin Islands

Pabay

Isle of Skye

Sound of Scalpay

Soay

Cuillin Sound

Sound of Sleat

Eriskay

Sound of Eriskay

Barra

Vatersay

Sandray

Pabbay

Canna

Sound of Canna

Rum

Sound of Rum

Eigg

Muck

Sound of Arisaig

Mingulay

Berneray

Orkneys

Papa Westray

North Ronaldsay

LERWICK

Westray

North Sound

Sanday

Rousay

Sanday Sound

Eday

Stronsay

Mainland

Shapinsay

KIRKWALL

Scapa Flow

Hoy

Burray

South Ronaldsay

Pentland Firth

Island of Stroma

ABERDEEN

Shetlands

Unst

Yell Sound

Fetlar

St Magnus Bay

Yell

Muckle Roe

Whalsay

Papa Stour

Mainland

ABERDEEN

Foula

The Deeps

Lerwick

Bressay

Sumburgh Head

ABERDEEN

STROMNESS

© MAPS IN MINUTES ™ (1998)

ISLE OF SKYE

Skye is the best known and, at 50 miles long and up to 25 miles wide, one of the largest of the islands of Scotland. The **Skye Bridge** (toll) now links the island to the mainland, although the vehicle ferry from Mallaig makes for a much more picturesque approach. The landscape of Skye is dramatic and beautiful whatever the season, but two areas deserve special mention. In the southwest, the spectacular peaks of the **Cuillin Hills** rise more than 3000 feet and offer a serious challenge to climbers, but there are also many good walks of varying difficulty for which Sligachan is a good starting point. North of Portree, the lonely **Trotternish Peninsula** is remarkable for its bizarre rock formations and its associations with Flora Macdonald.

Skye is flooded with visitors in the summer months but, as so often in the Highlands and Islands, once you are away from the main tourist centres it seems you have the Isle almost to yourself. We begin our tour of Skye in the southeast corner of the island.

BROADFORD
MAP 8 REF E7

8 miles SW of Kyle of Lochalsh on the A87

Broadford has the distinction of being Skye's largest crofting township. It's a long straggling village set beside the bay of the same name, and surrounded by dramatic hills - **Beinn na Cailleach** (2403 feet), the Red Hills, and Applecross. The village is well-placed for exploring south Skye and has a number of good shops selling gifts or souvenirs.

The **Claymore Restaurant** in Broadford is highly regarded for its excellent food but it should perhaps also be listed under "Art Galleries". Step inside and you will find that the whole of one wall is covered by a superbly executed mural, by Skye man Angus Macphee, encapsulating the history of Skye in 18 brilliantly conceived vignettes. In the bottom right hand corner, Dr Johnson and James Boswell are seen crossing a packhorse bridge; to their left, a crofter

Claymore Restaurant, Broadford, Isle of Skye IV49 9AQ
Tel: 01471 822333 Fax: 01471 820017

tills the soil with a primitive foot-plough, a "cas-chrom", (literally, "bent foot"); Viking warriors invade the island from top left, and dominating the centre of the mural is a Sgiathanach, (Gaelic for a "Man of Skye"), resplendent in full Highland dress. Donald and Seonaid Nicolson, ably assisted by their daughter Anne, own and run this understandably popular restaurant. Naturally, fish takes pride of place on the menu and it includes the local delicacy, Squat Lobsters, (tails only, tossed in Garlic Butter), but there's also a good choice of meat and poultry dishes. And if you enjoy desserts, you may find yourself pondering for some time over a menu that offers such home made treats as Meringue Chantilly, Banoffee Tartlet and Crème Brûlée.

ARMADALE
MAP 8 REF E8

On the SW tip of the Isle of Skye, on the A851

Armadale lies on the **Sleat Peninsula** (pronounced "Slate") in the southwest corner of Skye. This is the most fertile part of the island, an area which also goes by the name of "The Garden of Skye". An attractive village, Armadale is strung along the wooded shore and during the summer is linked to Mallaig on the mainland by a regular vehicle ferry.

The village is also home to **Skye Batiks** which for two years running has been voted the Best Craft Shop in Scotland. After a few minutes browsing around their display of dazzlingly colourful scarves and skirts, shirts and fishermen's

Skye Batiks, Armadale, Ardvasar, Isle of Skye IV45 8RS
Tel: 01471 844396 Fax: 01471 844496

smocks, bathrobes and cushion covers, it's easy to understand why. Theresse and Gavin Major opened their shop in Armadale in 1987 and almost immediately hit a problem. The problem was that they couldn't keep up with the demand, partly because the drying time on Skye can sometimes be measured in *months*. In their words, "The solution was simple. We moved the workshop down the road (7000 miles) to Theresse's back garden in Sri Lanka". Today, eighteen of Theresse's family and friends are making batiks for the Armadale shop and its sister outlet in Portree. In Skye, there are eight sewers working all year round making the smocks and jackets, much of the cutting out and design work being done in the Armadale shop. At Skye Batiks, the centuries-old Oriental craft of batik and mystical Celtic designs have been creatively blended to produce something quite unique.

SLIGACHAN
Map 8 ref E7

9 miles S of Portree on the A87

Unrivalled scenery, outstanding food, comfortable modern accommodation - those are just a few of the many good reasons for visiting the **Sligachan Hotel**. The hotel is beautifully set at the head of a sea loch, and commands a magnificent view of the Sound of Raasay and the mighty Cuillin Hills. One of the best centres from which to explore the Isle of Skye, The Sligachan is owned and run by business partners Iain Campbell and Norrie MacLeod. The main part of their

The Sligachan Hotel, Sligachan, Isle of Skye IV47 8SW
Tel: 01478 650204 Fax: 01478 650207

hotel dates back to around 1830 and has been in Iain's family for some 70 years. Here you'll find the John McKenzies Bar, (named after the world's first mountain guide), a friendly atmospheric place with its own log fire. In the Seumes' Bar you'll a selection of no fewer than 70 malt whiskies, along with 8 real ales and a specially brewed MacKenzie's Ale. The Collie Lounge boasts the finest view of the Cuillins from any window on Skye, while the Cairidh Restaurant serves prime Scottish beef, lamb, seafood and game dishes as well as offering a range of vegetable cuisine. Children are most welcome at the Sligachan which provides them with a games room, kiddies play room and an adventure playground. The hotel is open all year round with 22 very comfortable en suite rooms available on either a bed & breakfast, or a dinner, bed & breakfast basis.

CARBOST   MAP 8 REF D7
18 miles SW of Portree on the B8009

The only distillery on Skye is at Carbost where the **Talisker Distillery** produces a very peaty, smoky malt and welcomes visitors during the season. A few minutes walk from the distillery **The Old Inn** at Carbost stands on the shore of Loch Harport with the Cuillin Hills rising dramatically to the south. As you sit on the patio looking out across the loch to the hills it would be difficult to imagine a more peaceful setting. Originally an inn, The Old Inn had its licence removed in the 1920s and this was not restored until 1979. The building has of course been much modernised since those days, but every effort has been made to retain its original charm. Deirdre Morrison and her son Angus are "mine

The Old Inn, Carbost, Isle of Skye IV47 8SR
Tel/Fax: 01478 640205

hosts" at this genuinely welcoming inn, open all year round, where they serve food in the cosy atmosphere of the bar from lunchtime until 10 o'clock in the evening. With the spectacular Cuillin Hills just a few miles away, the Inn is an ideal base for walkers and climbers, or indeed anyone who wishes to enjoy the scenic beauty of Skye. There are 6 en suite bedrooms in the adjoining Lodge, a self-contained family unit, and for walking or other groups a Bunkhouse which can accommodate up to 24 people. "We welcome children and dogs" says Deirdre, "and are not averse to adults!"

PORTREE
MAP 8 REF E6

34 miles NW of Kyle of Lochalsh on the A87

With a population of around 2000, Portree is the largest community on the island and its administrative centre. It's an attractive little town, enclosed by wooded hills with a deep, cliff-lined harbour busy with fishing boats and with whitewashed buildings all around. The harbour is well-protected by the bulk of the Isle of Raasay, easily reached by one of the regular boat trips available.

Right on the quay here is **The Lower Deck Seafood Restaurant**, an appropriate location for this outstanding restaurant which specialises in locally-caught seafish, salmon and white fish. It enjoys a fine view of the busy little harbour with the raucous cries of seagulls always in the background. Should you happen

**The Lower Deck Seafood Restaurant, The Harbour, Portree,
Isle of Skye IV51 9DD Tel: 01478 613611**

to be on the quay at the right time, you can watch your lunch or supper being landed, gleaming fresh fish the best of which will find their way to Dan Corrigall's kitchen at the Lower Deck. His restaurant is built in traditional style on the site of an earlier seafood restaurant called The Upper Deck. Inside, the Lower Deck is uniquely decorated in nautical style, featuring photographs of the old MacBrayne fleet of steamers and with ships' souvenirs and memorabilia all around. It's a suitable setting in which to enjoy the fruits of the sea, carefully prepared, attractively presented and complemented by a wine list which is both well-chosen and reasonably priced.

Standing on the waterfront of the sheltered harbour, **The Rosedale Hotel** enjoys impressive and unique views across the Bay towards Ben Tianavaig and the Isle of Raasay. The original buildings here, some of them dating back to the reign of William IV, were homes for Portree fishermen. From the hotel's first-floor restaurant diners have a good view of today's fishermen unloading their catch, some of which may well appear on the menu tomorrow. The Rosedale's excellent reputation for high standards of cuisine relies on the kitchen using as

**Rosedale Hotel, Beaumont Cescent, Portree, Isle of Skye 1V51 9DB
Tel: 01478 613131 Fax: 01478 612531**

much local, fresh produce as possible. This policy has earned the hotel a whole clutch of awards, including an AA Rosette, a 4-Crowns Highly Commended rating from the STB, along with recommendations from Ashley Courtenay, Les Routiers and Egon Ronay. After your meal, there's a comfortable lounge with a good selection of Highland malt whiskies, (including the locally distilled Talisker), available from the cocktail bar. Rosedale has 23 bedrooms, all en suite and well-equipped, and most of them enjoying the impressive view across Portree Bay. The rooms have been skillfully converted, retaining a pleasing variety of indi-vidual character and size. Some of the rooms are located in Beaumont House, 100m further along the waterfront, where there's a beautiful harbourside gar-den to settle down in and watch the colourful, ever-changing scene.

In Gaelic, *Port an Righ* (now Portree) means Port of the King, a name the town assumed after James V came here in 1540 to settle a feud between the Macleod and Macdonald clans. A more melancholy royal visitor to Portree was

Bonnie Prince Charlie preparing to leave for France and lifelong exile. Taking his leave of Flora Macdonald, the Prince rather optimistically remarked "For all that has happened, I hope Madam that we shall meet in St James' yet". The room at McNab's Inn where he bade her farewell is now part of the Royal Hotel.

Even on this island of enchanting views, few can rival the vista from the garden terrace of the **Green Acres Guest House** on the southern outskirts of Portree. This modem, apricot-coloured detached dormer house is set well back in its own immaculately-kept grounds overlooking Portree Harbour and the Sound of Raasay. Ewen and Marie MacRae bought Green Acres in 1991 and have gone to great lengths to furnish and decorate the house to the very highest standards. There are 8 comfortable and attractively-fumished guest rooms, 6 of

Green Acres Guest House, Viewfield Road, Portree, Isle of Skye 1V51 9EU
Tel: 01478 612605

them en suite, with 4 on the ground floor. The same care has been taken in the pleasant dining-room where a full Scottish breakfast is served, and in the residents' lounge with its elegant Conservatory looking out across the sea. The MacRacs do not provide evening meals but Green Acres is conveniently placed for the town centre where there are many good pubs and restaurants. The Guest House is centrally heated throughout and open all year, but please note that Green Acres is a non-smoking establishment.

One of the oldest buildings in Portree is **Meall House**, the former jail and courthouse. Until fairly recently it housed the Tourist Information Centre with the manager's office located in what used to be the condemned cell. From here, those sentenced to death would be taken to **The Lump**, overlooking the harbour. On this steep peninsula a flagpole marks the site of the gallows to which as many as 5000 people would flock for the free entertainment of a public execution.

Much more pleasant entertainment, (albeit for a modest charge), can be found at the **Aros Heritage Centre,** about a mile south of the town, where a variety of dioramas and videos recount the turbulent history of the island. And just to the east, housed in a converted fever hospital, **An Tuireann Arts Centre** (which *is* free) puts on exhibitions and concerts.

A little further afield, some 6 miles north, is the extraordinary **Old Man of Storr,** a 160 feet pinnacle of rock that looks as if one vigorous push would topple it. It's actually part of a massive landslip from the face of the Storr mountain (2358 feet) which still occasionally sheds huge blocks of stone. The Old Man can be reached by an easy 30-minute walk from the car park on the A855. There are many other spectacular and eccentric rock formations to the north, most notably the **Quirking** (pronounced Crooking) with its outlandish forest of huge pinnacles and tortured rocks.

Self-catering holidays are increasingly popular throughout the area, although renting a holiday cottage can be a chancy business. However, if you book through **Islands and Highlands Cottages,** based in Portree, you can feel confident that all their properties, large or small, new or old, are furnished and equipped to the highest standard, are excellent value for money, and most importantly, provide a welcoming home from home atmosphere. Each property has been personally visited and the agency's informative full-colour brochure includes comprehensive details along with photographs of each location. The brochure lists scores of holiday homes chosen to suit all tastes and pockets. They range from grand old mansions to trim Alpine lodges, from shoreside cottages where you can enjoy your supper whilst watching otters and seals, to comfortable town centre

Islands & Highlands Cottages, Bridge Road, Portree, Isle of Skye IV51 9ER
Tel: 01478 612123 www.ihc.ndirect.co.uk

apartments. On the magnificent island of Uist, the agency can even offer you a choice of horse-drawn gypsy caravans, a wonderful way of experiencing an old fashioned "life on the open road" holiday. Islands and Highlands Cottages specialise in those places most people only dream about, surrounded by awesome scenery and offering breathtaking sunsets, miraculous dawns and an abundance of wildlife.

From the Quirking, the A855 continues around the **Trotternish Peninsula**, passing Flodigarry where Flora Macdonald lived. Her cottage has been restored, and is now part of Flodigarry House Hotel. About 4 miles further on, the road passes the dramatically sited but minimal remains of **Duntulm Castle**, and after another couple of miles arrives at the village of **Kilmuir**. In the burial ground here, a tall Celtic cross stands above **Flora Macdonald's Grave**, and nearby is a well-preserved crusader's slab. Also in Kilmuir is the **Museum of Island Life**, housed in a group of old cottages and exhibiting an interesting collection of old documents and photographs. The A855 continues down the western side of the peninsula to the attractive little port of **Uig** which has vehicle ferries serving the islands of Harris and North Uist.

SKEABOST BRIDGE
Map 8 ref D6

40 miles NW of Kyle of Lochalsh, on the A850

About 4 miles north of Portree, the road forks and if you take the left fork (the A850) you will soon come to a bridge across the River Snizort at Skeabost. On an island just below the bridge, reached by stepping stones, are the remains of a chapel reputedly connected with St Columba. A diligent search of the neglected cemetery will reveal memorials to three crusaders. Close by, on a minor road leading to the hamlet of Tote, stands **Clach Ard**, the "Stone on the Hill", which is engraved with Pictish symbols.

GRESHORNISH
Map 8 ref D6

18 miles NW of Portree on minor road off the A850

Continue along the A850 for about 14 miles to the hamlet of Upperglen where a minor road to the right leads to the enchanting **Greshornish House Hotel**. The Isle of Skye provides all the ingredients for a perfect holiday: peace, tranquillity and some delightful places to stay - like this historic hotel. Once an 18th century Scottish Highland mansion, Greshornish has been tastefully converted into a private country house hotel, secluded in its own 12 acres of picturesque grounds. This 3-Star Commended establishment offers its guests a real escape from the busy outside world. Immerse yourself in the gracious olde worlde charm that still lingers in these elegant surroundings. Each guest room has been individually tailored to meet your every need, complete with central heating and private facilities and there is even a 4-poster bedroom for those special occasions. Your hosts for your stay are Campbell and Sandra Dickson, a

Greshornish House Hotel, Greshornish, Isle of Skye IV51 9PN
Tel: 01470 582266 Fax: 01470 582345 Website: www.skye.co.uk
e-mail:campbell@greshornishhotel.demon.co.uk

couple who offer their guests true Scottish hospitality, right down to Campbell's kilt and his tradition of piping all his visitors to dinner in the evening! All the food is freshly prepared using only the best local ingredients and is served in an elegant atmosphere with crystal glasses, mahogany tables, silver candelabra and silver tableware. The dining room is spacious and comes complete with open log fires that burn brightly in the colder months: they are also the main feature in the drawing room and attractive cocktail bar which is the perfect place to relax with a warming glass of whisky after that superb meal.

DUNVEGAN
22 miles NW of Portree via the A87/A850

MAP 8 REF D6

Returning to the main road, the A850 leads to Dunvegan and the island's most imposing and historic building, **Dunvegan Castle.** For centuries the only way of reaching the castle was by sea, landing on the stony beach and entering beneath the portcullis of the sea-gate. Arriving by this route, friend and foe alike were presented with Dunvegan's most forbidding aspect, a daunting fortress surmounting a rocky crag. This spectacular site overlooking Loch Dunvegan has been fortified for more than a thousand years, for the last 750 of them as the stronghold of the Chiefs of Macleod. The present owner, John Macleod of Macleod, is the 29th chief in an uninterrupted line.

The oldest part of the castle is the Keep, built around 1340 by the 3rd Chief, Malcolm. The gruesome dungeon here, 16 feet deep and just 6 feet wide, and covered by a heavy flagstone is a chilling memorial to medieval justice. Malcolm figures in one of the oldest of the Macleod legends. Returning from a clandes-

Dunvegan Castle

tine visit to a neighbour's wife, he was confronted by a mad bull. Armed only with a dirk, he killed the beast and cut off one of its horns. Thereafter, the Macleod crest was emblazoned with a bull's head and the horn, rimmed with chased silver, was fashioned into a drinking vessel. Clan tradition requires that the Chief's heir, on coming of age, must take a full horn of claret - equivalent to a good bottle and a half, and drink it at one draught "without setting down or falling down". This traditional ceremony was last observed in 1965 when the present Chief drained the 10th century horn in 1 minute 57 seconds. The horn is on display at the castle, but even more treasured is the *Am Bratach Sith MhicLeoid*, the **Fairy Flag.** Experts agree that this tattered banner of faded yellow silk was made in the Middle East sometime between the 4th and 7th centuries AD, but its provenance remains a mystery. Tradition asserts that if the flag is waved on the battlefield, it will bring victory to the MacLeods; if spread on the marriage bed, the Chief will be blessed with a male child; and if unfurled at Dunvegan, will charm herring into the loch.

The tower in which the flag used to be housed was consequently named the **Fairy Tower,** a dainty name for a building with massive walls 10 feet thick in places, and still exactly as they were when built in 1500 by the 8th Chief, Alasdair "Crotach", or hunchback. The Chief's deformity resulted not from a birth defect, but from having an axe driven between his shoulder-blades in battle.

Little changed at Dunvegan over the next 300 years, but towards the end of the 18th century, the 23rd Chief, Gen. Norman MacLeod, began a thorough overhaul of the castle in order to make it more inviting for his young second wife, Sarah, fresh from the pampered life of colonial India. He remodelled the

Great Hall into an elegant Georgian drawing-room, acquired some fine paintings by Ramsay and Raeburn, and generally transformed an uncompromising fortress into a gracious home. Half a century later, his grandson put the finishing touches to the castle as we see it today, adding battlements and the dummy pepperpot turrets that give this sprawling building its remarkable unity.

Dunvegan also offers visitors boat trips to the nearby seal colony, sea cruises, sea & loch fishing, a camp site and caravan park, craft shops, the "St Kilda Connection" woollens shop, a restaurant and a bistro.

THE OUTER HEBRIDES

Also known as the Outer Hebrides, the Western Isles stretch for 130 miles, a string of islands which in most places rise no more than a few hundred feet and are battered by the full force of Atlantic storms. Westwards, the nearest landfall is Labrador, some 4000 miles away. It sounds desolate but there are miles upon miles of empty beaches with dazzling white sands, unbelievably clear water and breathtaking sunsets. There is also a fascinating range of flora and fauna here with most islands having at least one Nature Reserve. The islands have been inhabited for over 6000 years and there are numerous prehistoric remains, most notably the **Callanish Standing Stones** and the **Carloway Broch**. The area is a stronghold of Gaelic speech and culture melded with strong Scandinavian influences - the Vikings ruled the islands from the 9th century until 1280 and many place names are of Norse origin, especially in the north. Much more of a culture shock to visitors is the Sabbatarianism of the Free Church, the "Wee Frees", which imposes a strict observance of Sunday as a day of rest. Shops, pubs, garages, and public transport all close down and even the swings in the children's playgrounds are padlocked.

STORNOWAY (STEORNABHAGH) MAP 9 REF D3
East Coast of Isle of Lewis on A859

With around 8000 inhabitants, Stornoway is by far the largest community on the islands, the political and commercial centre of the Western Isles. Its harbour is no longer busy with the thousand or more fishing boats registered at Stornoway a century ago, but there are regular ferries to and from Ullapool and a small active fishing fleet whose catches are sold at the fish markets on Tuesday and Thursday evenings. The town's architecture is generally functional rather than attractive but there are two notable exceptions. One is **Lews Castle**, a mid-19th century mock Gothic pile, now part of the University of the Highlands and Islands, with attractive wooded grounds for which thousands of tons of soil had to be imported. The other is the former town hall, built in full-blooded Scottish Baronial style, which now houses the **An Lanntair Art Gallery**, a showcase for the work of local artists. Also worth a visit is the **Museum nan Eilean** (free) which has some interesting temporary exhibitions and a CD-ROM presenting the story of the famous Uig Chessmen, 12th century Viking chess pieces carved from walrus ivory which were unearthed in 1831 by a grazing cow near the village of Ardroil. The pieces themselves are occasionally on display here but otherwise divide their time between the Edinburgh Museum of Antiquities and the British Museum in London. And at the **Lewis Loom Centre** in Cromwell Street you can see how the islands' most famous export, Harris Tweed, is created.

TOLSTA CHAOLAIS
MAP 9 REF E2
15 miles NE of Stornoway on the B895

The old white croft house known as **The Willows Vegetarian Guest House** sits alone by a loch where otters play in the early dawn amongst flocks of Whooper swans. This could be the smallest vegetarian guest house in Britain, offering just one suite comprising a comfortable twin room, bathroom and living/dining room. The perfect retreat, The Willows is also a wonderful base for those questing for history and mystery, being within a couple of miles of the Callanish

**The Willows Vegetarian Guest House, 19, Tolsta Chaolais,
Isle of Lewis HS2 9DW Tel: 01851 621321**

stone circles and many other historical sites, some of them actually on the miles of golden sands of the island. There are no fanatical beansprout-eaters here! Debbie Nash, the owner, is known for her sumptuous cooking and has never been beaten by a special diet yet. Non-vegetarians are also welcome - it's just that The Willows doesn't serve anything that would prefer to be walking or swimming around to being on your plate. Debbie and her husband David are interesting folks - sometimes musicians, artists and craftspeople. Their guests are made to feel genuinely welcome and they always have time for a chat and a glass of the *uisge beatha*.

CARLOWAY
MAP 9 REF D2
25 miles NW of Stornoway on the A858

Located within a short drive of the magnificent sands of Dalbeg Bay, the **Doune Braes Hotel** offers its visitors comfortable accommodation and fine food. The hotel occupies a spectacular lochside position and most of the well-appointed bedrooms, (all equipped with TV and beverage-making facilities), enjoy lovely views. A former schoolhouse, Doune Braes is owned and run by Eileen Macdonald who offers her guests a mouth-watering menu of the best of Scottish cuisine,

Doune Braes Hotel, Carloway, Isle of Lewis HS2 9AA
Tel: 01851 643252 Fax: 01851 643435
e-mail: hebrides@doune-braes.co.uk

including delicious seafood dishes using local produce wherever possible. After a meal in the comfortable dining room visitors can relax with a fine single malt in the friendly bar or enjoy good conversation in the spacious lounge. The hotel is ideally placed for experiencing the fascinating history and atmosphere of this lovely island. Carloway Broch, a fine example of these ancient fortified circular buildings, lies close by and a few miles to the south the awe-inspiring standing stones of Callanish form an impressive prehistoric monument - the Stonehenge of northern Britain.

ISLE OF BARRA
MAP 9 REF B8
South of Isles of Lewis and Harris

Despite its small area, just 4 miles wide and 8 miles long, Barra has been described as being the "Western Isles in miniature". There are sandy beaches and mountain peaks which rise to 1260 feet, prehistoric relics and even a ruined medieval fortress, **Kisimul Castle**. It stands on a small island in the bay and is the ancestral home of the MacNeils, once notorious for their piracy and vanity. After years of neglect, the 45th chief of the MacNeil clan bought back the castle in 1937 and it has since been restored to its original appearance. The castle is reached by ferry from **Castlebay**, the only settlement of any size on the island and the proud possessor of the only airfield in Britain that disappears under water twice a day - scheduled flights to the tiny island land on the beach here.

ORKNEY

For more than 400 years, the Orkney and Shetland archipelagos were governed by Norsemen and the islands still have strong links with Scandinavia. Many of the place names are pure Norse and the ancient Norn language was still in use on Shetland until about one hundred years ago. Even today, the local accent is much closer to Scandinavian rhythms and inflections than it is to Scottish English.

Orkney has some 70 islands, although only 17 of them are inhabited. But they have been inhabited for more than 5000 years and can boast Northern Europe's greatest concentration of prehistoric monuments to prove it. **Skara Brae** on the **Mainland** (the largest island, some 20 miles long), is one of the best-preserved Stone Age settlements in Europe and across the islands there are literally hundreds of chambered tombs, stone circles and Iron Age brochs.

Whaling and fishing have been the most important industries of the Orkney Islands and Orcadians at one time were the preferred employees of the Hudson's Bay Company. During both World Wars the naval base at Scapa Flow brought much-needed prosperity, a role performed nowadays by the North Sea oil industry. The generally flat and treeless but fertile land provides an abundance of wildflowers in the summer, and along with magnificent coastal scenery, the towering cliffs support a huge bird population during the breeding season.

On Orkney, says the local tourist board, "the commonplace is frequently extraordinary". Where else would you find a road sign asking you to give way to otters, or discover that your beach picnic has been raided by a seal? Killer whales patrol the surrounding waters and on Hoy colonies of mountain hares study passers-by with an inquisitive interest. As the Orcadian poet, Edwin Muir, recorded:

> *"The Orkney I was born into was a place*
> *Where there was no great distinction between*
> *the ordinary and the fabulous; the lives of*
> *living men turned into legend".*

KIRKWALL
East Coast of Mainland

Map 10 ref T3

The most imposing building in Kirkwall, Orkney's capital, is the **Cathedral of**

St Magnus, founded in 1127 in honour of Magnus, Earl of Orkney, who had been assassinated by his cousin in 1117. As Magnus was buried, a heavenly light irradiated the sky, divine confirmation it was thought of the Earl's sanctity. The Cathedral attracted pilgrims from across the extensive Earldom of Orkney, their donations helping to fund the building of this immensely impressive church with its pink, sandstone columns and arches of exposed brickwork. During restoration work back in 1911, a skull and some bones were found concealed in one of the pillars. The skull was cleft as if by an axe: exactly the way Magnus was said to have met his death. These relics are now on display in the Cathedral, along with a monument to the dead of the *Royal Oak* (torpedoed in Scapa Flow in 1939 with the loss of 833 men), and a collection of 16th and 17th century gravestones engraved with cheerful inscriptions such as "Remember death waits us all, the hour none knows".

A mere 100 yards away is **Earl Patrick's Palace** which has been described as one of the finest pieces of Renaissance architecture to have survived in Scotland. Built around 1600 by the tyrannical Earl Patrick Stewart, the palace is now roofless but the superb central hall, the colossal fireplaces and the dismal dungeons evoke a powerful impression of upper-class Orcadian life in the early 17th century.

Standing in its own courtyard opposite the Cathedral with an ornamental garden behind, **Tankerness House** is a fine 16th century town house, considerably enlarged in the early 1700s, and now home to an interesting and wide-ranging museum celebrating some 5000 years of Orkney history. Look out for the Pictish board games, an Iron Age bone shovel, and antique bowls made from the vertebrae of whales. More specialised interests are catered for at the **Orkney Wireless Museum**, a tiny building chock-a-block with every conceivable kind of radio equipment, and the **Highland Park Distillery** where you can tour the lovely old buildings and enjoy a complimentary dram.

HOY   MAP 10 REF T4
Southwest of Mainland

Hoy is the second largest of the Orkney Islands and scenically the most dramatic. Most of the north-west corner of the island lies within the **RSPB North Hoy Reserve**, home to a wide variety of birds amongst which are merlins, kestrels, peregrine falcons, and the largest colony of Great Black-backed Gulls in the world. The rest of the island is spectacularly under-populated with a mere 400 permanent residents.

Hoy provides some splendid walks. Amongst them is one leading to the unique **Dwarfie Stane**, a 5000 year old rock tomb cut from an isolated block of red sandstone; another will take to one of Orkney's most famous landmarks, the 450 feet high sea stack known as the **Old Man of Hoy**.

SHETLAND

Sixty miles to the north, Shetland is closer to Bergen in Norway than it is to Edinburgh, the Arctic Circle nearer than Liverpool. In midsummer there is scarcely any night, just a dimming of the sky around midnight, a phenomenon known locally as "simmer dim". The islands' northerly location is rewarded with one of the most spectacular light shows on earth - the **Aurora Borealis**, or Northern Lights, which shimmer across the night sky in September and October.

The sea is part of everyday life in Shetland, Britain's northernmost islands and such was the reputation of the Shetlanders' sea-faring skills that 3000 of them were serving with Nelson's fleet during the Napoleonic wars. Today, around 24,000 people live in the islands, but they are greatly outnumbered by some 30,000 gannets, 140,000 guillemots, 250,000 puffins, 300,000 fulmars and at least 330,000 sheep. Despite lying so far north, Shetland enjoys the benefit of the Gulf Stream which creates a temperate, oceanic climate. It doesn't however protect the islands from ferocious winter storms which have battered the coastline into a frazzled hem of caves, blow-holes and rock stacks. The best months to visit are from June to September which are usually marked by long, dry sunny spells and, in June and July, almost continuous daylight making it possible for midnight golf tournaments to be held.

As in Orkney, the principal island is called Mainland, with Lerwick as the capital. The name Shetland is derived from the Norse word "Hjaltland", meaning high land, and for the most part the island is upland peat bog and grass or heath moor with countless small lochs of a brilliant blue. Some 50 miles long, Mainland is so indented that it varies in width from 20 miles to just a few yards and nowhere on the island is more than 3 miles from the sea.

Shetland is, of course, the home of the hardy ponies of that name, and the distinctive black and brown native sheep, said to be descended from a Siberian breed, are everywhere. Until the 1970s most Shetlanders were either fishermen or crofters but with the arrival of North Sea oil the economic pattern has changed dramatically. Most of the development though has been contained within the Sullom Voe area in the north of Mainland so those seeking unspoilt scenery, peace and quiet will not be disappointed.

LERWICK   MAP 10 REF T7
East coast of Mainland

The only town of any size in Shetland and the centre of all transport and communications, is Lerwick, "da toon" to locals, where around one third of Shetlanders live. Its busy **Harbour** is always thronged with craft of all kinds: ferries, oil-rig supply boats, cruise liners, yachts, fishing and naval boats, even an occasional tall ship. (In 1999, the port is the venue for the Cutty Sark Tall Ships Race). There's also a replica Viking longship, "Dim Riv", which is available for visitors to row and sail.

Behind the harbour, the compact old town built in stone has some striking buildings, most notably the neo-Gothic **Town Hall** (free) with its stained glass windows depicting Shetland's history, and **Fort Charlotte** (free) originally built between 1665-67 during Charles II's war with the Dutch. The fort was attacked and burnt down by them in 1673 and not rebuilt until 1782 when it was named after George III's queen. There are some grand views from the battlements.

Also well worth a visit is the **Shetland Museum** (free) which documents the history of the islands from the earliest times to the present day. Amongst the treasures on display is the exquisite Gulberwick Brooch, a 9th century Viking cloak pin which, according to local legend, was about to be melted down by the young boy who found it when his father intervened.

Shetland's wealth of neolithic, Iron Age and Viking remains are too numerous to record in any detail but there are major sites at **Jarlshof**, where there's evidence of more than 4 millennia of continuous occupation, **Clickimin Broch** near Lerwick, and the **Broch of Mousa** near Sumburgh Head on the southern tip of Mainland.

Also pagan in origin is the boisterous event known as **Up Helly Aa** which takes over the town of Lerwick on the last Tuesday in January. Dressed in a bizarre motley of costumes and carrying flaming torches, up to one thousand islanders march through the town behind a replica Viking longship. In a field on the outskirts they toss their torches into the longship, creating a huge bonfire which marks the start of the evening celebrations.

UNST   Map 10 ref U5
Northeast of Mainland

Of Shetland's 15 inhabited islands, Unst is the most northerly and packed into an area just 12 miles long by 5 miles wide you'll find some of the most spectacular scenery in Shetland - stupendous cliffs, sculpted sea stacks, sheltered inlets, golden beaches, heather-clad hills, freshwater lochs, fertile farmland, and even a unique, sub-arctic stony desert. Unst also offers standing stones, brochs, ruined **Muness Castle** (built in 1598), two important National Nature Reserves, **Hermaness** and **Keen of Hamar**, as well as an abundance of wild-life: freeroaming Shetland ponies, sea-birds, seals and porpoises, even, if you're lucky, sightings of otters or killer whales. It seems fitting somehow that in Robert Louis Stevenson's *Treasure Island* the map showing where the treasure is hidden closely resembles the shape of Unst. The author visited the island in 1869, following in the footsteps of his father, Thomas, who built the spectacularly-sited lighthouse on **Muckle Flugga** rocks in 1857-8.

The main settlement on Unst is Baltasound which has shops, a post office, marina, leisure centre with heated swimming pool and, nearby, the island's airport. It also boasts an excellent hotel occupying a lovely position overlooking the sea: the **Baltasound Hotel** which claims the distinction of being the most northerly hotel in Britain. Stone-built, with a Scandinavian-style wooden

Baltasound Hotel, Baltasound, Unst, Shetland ZE2 9DS
Tel: 01957 711334 Fax: 01957 711358 e-mail: balta.hotel@zetnet.co.uk

extension and pine log chalets in the garden, this welcoming hotel is family-owned and run by Jean Ritch, her son Geoffrey, and daughter Desley. They also have their own salmon farm, so fresh salmon is always on the menu along with free range organic eggs and other local produce whenever possible. The Ritchs are happy to cater for special diets - vegan, gluten or sugar-free, just let them know. Drinks on offer include the local ale, "Auld Rock", brewed at the Valhalla Brewery on Unst which, of course, is the most northerly in Britain. The Baltasound has 25 guest rooms, (of which 22 are en suite), some in the main hotel building, others in the attractive chalets. There's a comfortable residents' lounge, lined with mellow pine and stocked with a selection of Shetland books and magazines. The hotel is just 2 minutes from the new pier in Baltasound's harbour and a 5-minute walk will take you to the Keen of Hamar National Nature Reserve, a dramatic moonscape which nevertheless supports a number of rare plants, including Edmondston's Chickweed found nowhere else in the world. With free access all across the island, Unst is especially popular with walkers and all visitors appreciate the peace of an area which is crime free, where children are safe, and where residents happily leave their doors unlocked and the keys in their cars.

A couple of miles north of Baltasound, Haroldswick is home to Britain's most northerly Post Office; the fascinating **Unst Heritage Centre** (free) which has permanent displays on the island's geology, genealogy and Unst's famous fine lace knitting and spinning, and the **Unst Boat Haven** (free) which houses a unique collection of traditional Shetland fishing craft. A little further north, a walk through the Hermaness National Nature Reserve will bring you to a cliff top panorama overlooking the **Muckle Flugga** rocks and **Out Stack**, the very last speck of northern Britain.

TOURIST INFORMATION CENTRES

Centres in **Bold** are open all the year around.

Aberdeen Tourist Information Centre
St Nicholas House, Broad Street, Aberdeen AB9 1DE
Tel: 01224 632727

Aberfeldy Tourist Information Centre
The Square, Aberfeldy, Perthshire PH15 2DD
Tel: 01887 820276 Fax: 01887 829495

Aberfoyle Tourist Information Centre
Main Street, Aberfoyle, Stirling
Tel: 01877 382352

Abington Tourist Information Centre
Motorway Service Area, Junction 13, M74, Abington, South Lanarkshire ML12 6RG
Tel: 01864 502436 Fax: 01864 502765

Aboyne Tourist Information Centre
Ballater Road Car Park, Aboyne, Royal Deeside
Tel: 013398 86060

Aden Tourist Information Centre
Aden Country Park, Mintlaw, Aberdeen-shire
Tel: 01771 623037

Alford Tourist Information Centre
Railway Museum, Station Yard, Alford, Aberdeen-shire
Tel: 019755 62052

Alva Tourist Information Centre
Mill Trail Visitor Centre, Alva, Clackmannanshire FK12 5EN
Tel: 01259 769696

Anstruther Tourist Information Centre
Scottish Fisheries Museum, Harbourhead, Anstruther, Fife KY10 3BA
Tel: 01333 311073

Arbroath Tourist Information Centre
Market Place, Arbroath, Angus DD11 1HR
Tel: 01241 877883 Fax: 01241 878550

Ardgarten Tourist Information Centre
Arrochar, Ardgarten, Dunbartonshire
Tel: 01301 702432

Auchterarder Tourist Information Centre
High Street, Auchterarder, Perthshire PH13 1BJ
Tel: 01764 663450 Fax: 01764 664235

Aviemore Tourist Information Centre
Grampian Road, Aviemore, PH22 1PP
Tel: 01479 810363 Fax: 01479 811063

Ayr Tourist Information Centre
Burns House, Burns Statue Square, Ayr, Ayrshire KA7 1UP
Tel: 01292 262555. Fax: 01292 269555

Ballachulish Tourist Information Centre
Albert Road, Ballachulish, Argyll PA39 4JR
Tel: 01855 811296 Fax: 01855 811720

Ballater Tourist Information Centre
Station Square, Ballater, Royal Deeside
Tel: 013397 55306

Balloch Tourist Information Centre
Balloch Road, Balloch, Dunbartonshire
Tel: 01389 753533

Banchory Tourist Information Centre
Bridge Street, Banchory, Aberdeenshire AB31 3SX
Tel: 01330 822000

Banff Tourist Information Centre
Collie Lodge, Banff, Aberdeenshire AB45 1AU
Tel: 01261 812419

Bettyhill Tourist Information Centre
Clachan, Bettyhill, by Thurso, Sutherland KW14 7SS
Tel/Fax: 01641 521342

Biggar Tourist Information Centre
155, High Street, Biggar, South Lanarkshire ML12 6DL
Tel: 01899 221066

Blairgowrie Tourist Information Centre
26, Wellmeadow, Blairgowrie, Perthshire PH10 6AS
Tel: 01250 872960 Fax: 01250 873701

Bo'ness Tourist Information Centre
Union Street, Bo'ness, West Lothian
Tel: 01506 826626

Bowmore Tourist Information Centre
Isle of Islay
Tel: 01496 810254

Braemar Tourist Information Centre
The Mews, Mar Road, Braemar, Royal Deeside
Tel: 013397 41600

Brechin Tourist Information Centre
St Ninians Place, Brechin, Angus DD9 7AH
Tel: 01356 623050

Broadford Tourist Information Centre
The Car Park, Isle of Skye IV49 9AB
Tel: 01471 822361 Fax: 01471 822141

Brodick Tourist Information Centre
The Pier, Brodick, Isle of Arran KA27 8AU
Tel: 01770 302140 Fax: 01770 302395

Buckie Tourist Information Centre
Cluny Square, Buckie, Moray
Tel: 01542 834853

Burntisland Tourist Information Centre
4, Kirkgate, Burntisland, Fife
Tel: 01592 872667

Callander Tourist Information Centre
Rob Roy & Trossachs Visitor Centre, Ancaster Square, Callander, Stirling
Tel: 01877 330784

Campbeltown Tourist Information Centre
Mackinnon House, The Pier, Campbeltown, Argyll PA28 6EF
Tel: 01586 552056

Carnoustie Tourist Information Centre
High Street, Carnoustie, Angus DD7 6AN
Tel: 01241 852258

Carrbridge Tourist Information Centre
Main Street, Carrbridge, Inverness-shire PH32 3AS
Tel/Fax: 01479 841630

Castlebay Tourist Information Centre
Main Street, Castlebay, Isle of Barra
Tel: 01871 810336

Castle Douglas Tourist Information Centre
Markethill Car Park, Castle Douglas, Dumfries & Galloway
Tel: 01556 502611

Coatbridge Tourist Information Centre
The Time Capsule, Buchanan Street, Coatbridge, North Lanarkshire
Tel: 01236 431133

Coldstream Tourist Information Centre
Town Hall, High Street, Coldstream, Borderss TD12 4DH
Tel: 01890 882607

Craignure Tourist Information Centre
Isle of Mull
Tel: 01680 812377

Crail Tourist Information Centre
Crail Museum & Heritage Centre, 62-64 Marketgate, Crail, Fife KY10 3TL
Tel: 01333 450869

Crathie Tourist Information Centre
Car Park, Balmoral Castle, Royal Deeside
Tel: 013397 42414

Crieff Tourist Information Centre
Town Hall, High Street, Crieff, Perthshire PH7 3HU
Tel: 01764 652578 Fax: 01764 655422

Cullen Tourist Information Centre
20, Seafield Street, Cullen, Moray
Tel: 01542 840757

Cupar Tourist Information Centre
The Granary, Coal Road, Cupar, Fife
Tel: 01334 652874

Dalbeattie Tourist Information Centre
Town Hall, Dalbeattie, Dumfries & Galloway
Tel: 01556 610117

Dalkeith Tourist Information Centre
The Library, White Hart Street, Dalkeith, Midlothian
Tel: 0131 663 2083 / 660 6818

Daviot Wood Tourist Information Centre
Picnic Area (A9), by Inverness IV1 2ER
Tel: 01463 772203 Fax: 01463 772022

Dornoch Tourist Information Centre
The Square, Dornoch, Sutherland IV25 3SD
Tel: 01862 810400 Fax: 01862 810644

Drymen Tourist Information Centre
Drymen Library, The Square, Drymen, Stirling
Tel: 01360 660068

Dufftown Tourist Information Centre
Clock Tower, The Square, Dufftown, Moray
Tel: 01340 820501

Dumbarton Tourist Information Centre
Milton, A82 Northbound
Tel: 01389 742306

Dumfries Tourist Information Centre
Whitesands, Dumfries DG1 4TH
Tel: 01387 253862

Dunbar Tourist Information Centre
143, High Street, Dunbar, East Lothian
Tel: 01368 863353

Dunblane Tourist Information Centre
Stirling Road, Dunblane, Stirling
Tel: 01786 824428

Dundee Tourist Information Centre
7-21, Castle Street, Dundee DD1 3AA
Tel: 01382 527527 Fax: 01382 527550

4, City Square, Dundee DD1 3BA
Tel: 01382 434128 Fax: 01382 434665

Dunfermline Tourist Information Centre
13/15 Maygate, Dunfermline, Fife KY12 7NE
Tel: 01383 720999 Fax: 01383 625807

Dunkeld Tourist Information Centre
The Cross, Dunkeld, Perthshire PH8 0AN
Tel/Fax: 01350 727688

Dunoon Tourist Information Centre
7, Alexandra Parade, Dunoon, Argyl, PA23 8AB
Tel: 01369 703785

Durness Tourist Information Centre
Sango, Durness, by Lairg, Sutherland IV27 4PN
Tel: 01971 511259 Fax: 01971 511368

Edinburgh Tourist Information Centre
Edinburgh & Scotland Information Centre, 3, Princes Street, Edinburgh EH2 2QP
Tel: 0131 557 1700

Edinburgh Airport Tourist Information Centre
Tourist Information Desk
Tel: 0131 333 2167

Elgin Tourist Information Centre
17, High Street, Elgin, Moray IV30 1EG
Tel: 01343 542666

Ellon Tourist Information Centre
Market Street Car Park, Ellon, Aberdeen-shire
Tel: 01358 720730

Eyemouth Tourist Information Centre
Auld Kirk, Market Square, Eyemouth, Borders TD14 5HE
Tel: 01890 750678

Falkirk Tourist Information Centre
2-4 Glebe Street, Falkirk
Tel: 01324 620244

Forfar Tourist Information Centre
40 East High Street, Forfar, Angus DD8 2EG
Tel: 01307 467876

Forres Tourist Information Centre
116 High Street, Forres, Moray
Tel: 01309 672938

Fort Augustus Tourist Information Centre
Car Park, Fort Augustus, Inverness-shire PH32 4DD
Tel: 01320 366367 Fax: 01320 366779

Fort William Tourist Information Centre

Cameron Centre, Cameron Square, Fort William, Inverness-shire PH33 6AJ

Tel: 01397 703781 Fax: 01397 705184

Forth Road Bridge Tourist Information Centre

By North Queensferry, Edinburgh

Tel: 01383 417759

Fraserburgh Tourist Information Centre

Saltoun Square, Fraserburgh, Aberdeen-shire

Tel: 01346 518315

Gairloch Tourist Information Centre

Achtercairn, Gairloch, Ross-shire IV22 2DN

Tel: 01445 712130 Fax: 01445 712071

Galashiels Tourist Information Centre

3, St John's Street, Galashiels, Borders TD1 3JX

Tel: 01896 755551

Gatehouse of Fleet Tourist Information Centre

Car Park, Gatehouse of Fleet, Dumfries & Galloway

Tel: 01557 814212

Girvan Tourist Information Centre

Bridge Street, Girvan, Ayrshire KA26 9HH

Tel: 01465 714950

Glasgow Tourist Information Centre

11, George Square, Glasgow G2 1DY

Tel: 0141 204 4440 Fax: 0141 221 3524

Glasgow International Airport Tourist Information Centre

Paisley PA3 2ST

Tel: 0141 848 4440 Fax: 0141 849 1444

Glenrothes Tourist Information Centre

Rothes Square, Kingdom Centre, Glenrothes, Fife

Tel: 01592 754954/610784

Glenshiel Tourist Information Centre

Shielbridge, Glenshiel, Ross-shire IV40 8HW

Tel/Fax: 01599 511264

Gourock Tourist Information Centre

Pierhead, Gourock, Inverness-shire

Tel: 01475 639467

Grantown-on- Spey Tourist Information Centre
54, High Street, Grantown-on-Spey, Moray PH26 3EH
Tel/Fax: 01479 872773

Greenock Tourist Information Centre
7a, Clyde Square, Greenock, Inverclyde PA15 1NB
Tel: 01475 722007 Fax: 01475 730854

Gretna Green Tourist Information Centre
Gateway to Scotland, M74 Service Area, Gretna Green,
Dumfries & Galloway DG16 5HQ Tel: 01461 338500

Old Blacksmith's Shop, Gretna Green, Dumfries & Galloway
Tel: 01461 337834

Hamilton Tourist Information Centre
Road Chef Services, M74 Northbound, Hamilton, South Lanarkshire ML3 6JW
Tel: 01698 285590 Fax: 01698 891494

Hawick Tourist Information Centre
Drumlanrig's Tower, Tower Knowe, Hawick TD9 9EN
Tel: 01450 372547. Fax: 01450 373993

Helensburgh Tourist Information Centre
The Clock Tower, Helensburgh, Argyll & Bute
Tel: 01436 672642

Helmsdale Tourist Information Centre
Coupar Park, Helmsdale, Sutherland KW8 6HH
Tel/Fax: 01431 821640

Huntly Tourist Information Centre
7a The Square, Huntly, Aberdeen-shire
Tel: 01466 792255

Inveraray Tourist Information Centre
Front Street, Inveraray, Argyll
Tel: 01499 302063

Inverness Tourist Information Centre
Castle Wynd, Inverness IV2 3BJ
Tel: 01463 234353 Fax: 01463 710609

Inverurie Tourist Information Centre
Town Hall, Market Place, Inverurie, Aberdeen-shire
Tel: 01467 620600

Irvine Tourist Information Centre
New Street, Irvine, Ayrshire KA12 8BB
Tel: 01294 313886. Fax: 01294 313339

Islay Tourist Information Centre
White Hart Hotel, Port Ellen, Isle of Islay
Tel: 01496 810254

Jedburgh Tourist Information Centre
Murray's Green, Jedburgh, Borderss TD8 6BE
Tel: 01835 863435/863688. Fax: 01835 864099

John O'Groats Tourist Information Centre
County Road, John O'Groats, Caithness KW1 4YR
Tel: 01955 611373 Fax: 01955 611448

Keith Tourist Information Centre
Church Road, Keith, Moray
Tel: 01542 882634

Kelso Tourist Information Centre
Town House, The Square, Kelso, Borders TD5 7HF
Tel: 01753 223464

Kilchoan Tourist Information Centre
Pier Road, Kilchoan, Acharacle, Argyll PH36 4LH
Tel: 01972 510222

Killin Tourist Information Centre
Main Street, Killin, Stirling
Tel: 01567 820254

Kilmarnock Tourist Information Centre
62, Bank Street, Kilmarnock, Ayrshire KA1 1ER
Tel: 01563 539090. Fax: 01563 572409

Kincardine Bridge Tourist Information Centre
Pine 'n' Oak, Kincardine Bridge Road, Airth, by Falkirk
Tel: 01324 831422

Kingussie Tourist Information Centre
King Street, Kingussie, Inverness-shire PH21 1HP
Tel: 01540 661297

Kinross Tourist Information Centre
Turfhills, Junction 6, M90, Kinross KY13 7NQ
Tel: 01577 863680 Fax: 01577 863370

Kirkcaldy Tourist Information Centre
19, Whytescauseway, Kirkcaldy, Fife KY1 1XF
Tel: 01592 267775 Fax: 01592 203154

Kirkcudbright Tourist Information Centre
Harbour Square, Kirkcudbright, Dumfries & Galloway
Tel: 01557 330494

Kirkwall Tourist Information Centre
6 Broad Street, Kirkwall, Orkney KW15 1DH
Tel: 01856 872856

Kirriemuir Tourist Information Centre
Cumberland Close, Kirriemuir, Angus DD8 4EF
Tel: 01575 574097

Kyle of Lochalsh Tourist Information Centre
Car Park, Kyle of Lochalsh, Ross-shire IV40 8AQ
Tel: 01599 534276 Fax: 01599 534808

Lairg Tourist Information Centre
Ferrycroft Countryside Centre, Lairg, Sutherland IV27 4AZ
Tel/Fax: 01549 402160

Lanark Tourist Information Centre
Horsemarket, Ladyacre, Lanark, South Lanarkshire ML11 7LQ
Tel: 01555 661661 Fax: 01555

Langholm Tourist Information Centre
High Street, Langholm, Dumfries & Galloway
Tel: 01387 380976

Largs Tourist Information Centre
The Promenade, Largs, Ayrshire KA30 8BG
Tel: 01475 673765. 01475 676297

Lerwick Tourist Information Centre
The Market Cross, Lerwick, Shetland ZE1 0LU
Tel: 01595 693434

Leven Tourist Information Centre
The Beehive, Durie Street, Leven, Fife
Tel: 01333 429464

Linlithgow Tourist Information Centre
Burgh Halls, The Cross, Linlithgow EH49 7EJ
Tel: 01506 844600

Lochboisdale Tourist Information Centre
Pier Road, Lochboisdale, Isle of South Uist
Tel: 01878 700286

Lochcarron Tourist Information Centre
Main Street, Lochcarron, Ross-shire IV54 8YD
Tel: 01520 722357 Fax: 01520 722324

Lochgilphead Tourist Information Centre
Lochnell Street, Lochgilphead, Argyll
Tel: 01546 602344

Lochinver Tourist Information Centre
Kirk Lane, Lochinver, by Lairg, Sutherland IV27 4LT
Tel: 01571 844330 Fax: 01571 844373

Lochmaddy Tourist Information Centre
Pier Road, Lochmaddy, Isle of North Uist
Tel: 01876 500321

Lochranza Tourist Information Centre
Isle of Arran
Tel: 01770 830320

Mallaig Tourist Information Centre
TIC, Mallaig, Inverness-shire PH41 4SQ
Tel: 01687 462170 Fax: 01687 462064

Mauchline Tourist Information Centre
National Burns Memorial Tower, Kilmarnock Road, Mauchline,
Dumfries & Galloway Tel: 01290 551916

Melrose Tourist Information Centre
Abbey House, Abbey Street, Melrose, Borders TD6 9LG
Tel: 01896 822555

Millport Tourist Information Centre
28, Stuart Street, Isle of Cumbrae KA28 0AJ
Tel: 01475 530753

Moffat Tourist Information Centre
Churchgate, Moffat, Dumfries & Galloway
Tel: 01683 20620

Montrose Tourist Information Centre
Bridge Street, Montrose, Angus DD10 8AB
Tel: 01674 672000

Motherwell Tourist Information Centre
The Library, Hamilton Road, Motherwell, North Lanarkshire
Tel: 01698 267676

Musselburgh Tourist Information Centre
Brunton Hall, Musselburgh, East Lothian
Tel: 0131 665 6597

Nairn Tourist Information Centre
62, King Street, Nairn, Nairnshire IV12 4DN
Tel/Fax: 01667 453753

Newtongrange Tourist Information Centre
Scottish Mining Museum, Lady Victoria Colliery, Newtongrange, Midlothian
Tel: 0131 663 4262

Newton Stewart Tourist Information Centre
Dashwood Square, Newton Stewart, Dumfries & Galloway
Tel: 01671 402431

North Berwick Tourist Information Centre
Quality Street, North Berwick, East Lothian
Tel: 01620 892197

North Kessock Tourist Information Centre
Picnic Site, North Kessock, Ross-shire IV1 1XB
Tel: 01463 731505 Fax: 01463 731701

North Queensferry Tourist Information Centre
Queensferry Lodge Hotel, St Margaret's Head, North Queensferry, Fife KY11 1HP
Tel: 01383 417759

Oban Tourist Information Centre
Argyll Square, Oban, Argyll, PA34 4AR
Tel: 01631 563122

Oldcraighall Tourist Information Centre
Granada Service Area (A1), Musselburgh, East Lothian
Tel: 0131 653 6172

Paisley Tourist Information Centre
Town Hall, Abbey Close, Paisley, Renfrewshire
Tel: 0141 889 0711

Peebles Tourist Information Centre
High Street, Peebles, Borders EH45 8AG
Tel: 01721 720138. Fax: 01721 724401

Pencraig Tourist Information Centre
A1 by East Linton, East Lothian
Tel: 01620 860063

Penicuik Tourist Information Centre
Edinburgh Crystal Visitor Centre, Eastfield, Penicuik, Midlothian
Tel: 01968 673846

Perth Tourist Information Centre
45, High Street, Perth PH1 5TJ
Tel: 01738 638353 Fax: 01738 444863

Caithness Glass, Inveralmond, Perth PH1 3TZ
Tel: 01738 638481

Peterhead Tourist Information Centre
54 Broad Street, Peterhead, Aberdeen-shire
Tel: 01779 471904

Pitlochry Tourist Information Centre
22, Atholl Road, Pitlochry, Perthshire PH16 5BX
Tel: 01796 472215/472751 Fax: 01796 474046

Portree Tourist Information Centre
Bayfield House, Bayfield Road, Portree, Isle of Skye IV51 9EL
Tel: 01478 612137 Fax: 01478 612141

Ralia Tourist Information Centre
A9 North, by Newtonmore, Inverness-shire PH20 1BD
Tel/Fax: 01540 673253

Rothesay Tourist Information Centre
15 Victoria Street, Rothesay, Isle of Bute PA20 0AJ
Tel: 01700 502151

St Andrews Tourist Information Centre
70, Market Street, St Andrews, Fife KY16 9NU
Tel: 01334 472021 Fax: 01334 478422

Sanquhar Tourist Information Centre
Tolbooth, High Street, Sanquhar, Dumfries & Galloway
Tel: 01659 50185

Selkirk Tourist Information Centre
Halliwell's House, Selkirk, Borders TD7 4BL
Tel: 01750 20054

Spean Bridge Tourist Information Centre
TIC, Spean Bridge, Inverness-shire PH34 4EP
Tel: 01397 712576 Fax: 01397 712576

Stirling Tourist Information Centre
Dumbarton Road, Stirling FK8 2LQ
Tel: 01786 475019/479901

Royal Burgh of Stirling Visitor Centre, Castle Esplanade, Stirling
Tel: 01786 462517

Pirnhall (March-November) Tourist Information Centre
Motorway Service Area, Junction 9 (M9), Pirnhall, Stirling
Tel: 01786 814111

Stonehaven Tourist Information Centre
66 Allardice Street, Stonehaven, Aberdeen-shire
Tel: 01569 762806

Stornoway Tourist Information Centre
26 Cromwell Street, Stornoway, Isle of Lewis
Tel: 01851 703088

Stranraer Tourist Information Centre
1 Bridge Street, Stranraer, Dumfries & Galloway
Tel: 01776 702595

Strathaven Tourist Information Centre
Town Mill Arts Centre, Stonehouse Road, Strathaven,
Tel: 01357 29650

Strathpeffer Tourist Information Centre
The Square, Strathpeffer, Ross-shire IV14 9DW
Tel: 01997 421415 Fax: 01997 421460

Stromness Tourist Information Centre
Ferry Terminal Building, The Pier Head, Stromness, Orkney
Tel: 01856 850716

Strontian Tourist Information Centre
TIC, Strontian, Argyll PH36 4HZ
Tel/Fax: 01967 402131

Tarbert Tourist Information Centre
Harbour Street, Tarbert, Argyll
Tel: 01880 820429

Tarbert Tourist Information Centre
Pier Road, Tarbert, Isle of Harris
Tel: 01859 502011

Thurso Tourist Information Centre
Riverside, Thurso, Caithness KW14 8BU
Tel: 01847 892371 Fax: 01847 893155

Tobermory Tourist Information Centre
Caledonian MacBrayne Ticket Office, Main Street, Tobermory, Isle of Mull
Tel: 01688 302182

Tomintoul Tourist Information Centre
The Square, Tomintoul, Moray
Tel: 01807 580285

Troon Tourist Information Centre
South Beach, Troon, Ayrshire KA10 6EF
Tel: 01292 317696

Turriff Tourist Information Centre
High Street, Turriff, Aberdeen-shire
Tel: 01888 563001

Tyndrum Tourist Information Centre
Main Street, Tyndrum, Stirling
Tel: 01838 400246

Uig Tourist Information Centre
Ferry Terminal, Uig, Isle of Skye IV51 9XX
Tel/Fax: 01470 542404

Ullapool Tourist Information Centre
Argyle Street, Ullapool, Ross-shire IV26 2UB
Tel: 01854 612135 Fax: 01854 613031

Wick Tourist Information Centre
Whitechapel Road, Wick, Caithness KW1 4EA
Tel: 01955 602596 Fax: 01955 604940

INDEX OF TOWNS, VILLAGES AND PLACES OF INTEREST

G

INDEX OF PLACES TO STAY, EAT, DRINK & SHOP

THE HIDDEN PLACES
ORDER FORM

To order any of our publications just fill in the payment details below and complete the order form *overleaf*. For orders of less than 4 copies please add £1 per book for postage and packing. Orders over 4 copies are P & P free.

Please Complete Either:

I enclose a cheque for £ .... made payable to Travel Publishing Ltd

Or:

Card No: ☐☐☐☐ ☐☐☐☐ ☐☐☐☐ ☐☐☐☐

Expiry Date: ☐☐ ☐☐

Signature: ....

NAME: ....

ADDRESS: ....

....

....

POSTCODE: ....

TEL NO: ....

Please send to: Travel Publishing Ltd
7a Apollo House
Calleva Park
Aldermaston
Berks, RG7 8TN

THE HIDDEN PLACES ORDER FORM

	Price	Quantity	Value
Regional Titles			
Cambridgeshire & Lincolnshire	£7.99	....	....
Channel Islands	£6.99	....	....
Cheshire	£7.99	....	....
Chilterns	£7.99	....	....
Cornwall	£7.99	....	....
Devon	£7.99	....	....
Dorset, Hants & Isle of Wight	£7.99	....	....
Essex	£7.99	....	....
Gloucestershire	£6.99	....	....
Heart of England	£4.95	....	....
Highlands & Islands	£7.99	....	....
Kent	£7.99	....	....
Lake District & Cumbria	£7.99	....	....
Lancashire	£7.99	....	....
Norfolk	£7.99	....	....
Northeast Yorkshire	£6.99	....	....
Northumberland & Durham	£6.99	....	....
North Wales	£7.99	....	....
Nottinghamshire	£6.99	....	....
Peak District	£6.99	....	....
Potteries	£6.99	....	....
Somerset	£6.99	....	....
South Wales	£7.99	....	....
Suffolk	£7.99	....	....
Surrey	£6.99	....	....
Sussex	£6.99	....	....
Thames Valley	£7.99	....	....
Warwickshire & West Midlands	£6.99	....	....
Welsh Borders	£5.99	....	....
Wiltshire	£6.99	....	....
Yorkshire Dales	£6.99	....	....
Set of any 5 Regional titles	**£25.00**	....	....
National Titles			
England	£9.99	....	....
Ireland	£9.99	....	....
Scotland	£9.99	....	....
Wales	£8.99	....	....
Set of all 4 National titles	**£28.00**	....	....

*For orders of less than 4 copies please add £1 per book for postage &
packing. Orders over 4 copies P & P free.*

THE HIDDEN PLACES
READER COMMENT FORM

The *Hidden Places* research team would like to receive reader's comments on any visitor attractions or places reviewed in the book and also recommendations for suitable entries to be included in the next edition. This will help ensure that the *Hidden Places* series continues to provide its readers with useful information on the more interesting, unusual or unique features of each attraction or place ensuring that their stay in the local area is an enjoyable and stimulating experience.

To provide your comments or recommendations would you please complete the forms below and overleaf as indicated and send to: The Research Department, Travel Publishing Ltd., 7a Apollo House, Calleva Park, Aldermaston, Reading, RG7 8TN.

Your Name:

Your Address:

Your Telephone Number:

Please tick as appropriate: Comments ☐   Recommendation ☐

Name of *"Hidden Place"*:

Address:

Telephone Number:

Name of Contact:

THE HIDDEN PLACES
READER COMMENT FORM

Comment or Reason for Recommendation:

....

....

....

....

....

....

....

....

....

....

....

....

....

THE HIDDEN PLACES
READER COMMENT FORM

The *Hidden Places* research team would like to receive reader's comments on any visitor attractions or places reviewed in the book and also recommendations for suitable entries to be included in the next edition. This will help ensure that the *Hidden Places* series continues to provide its readers with useful information on the more interesting, unusual or unique features of each attraction or place ensuring that their stay in the local area is an enjoyable and stimulating experience.

To provide your comments or recommendations would you please complete the forms below and overleaf as indicated and send to: The Research Department, Travel Publishing Ltd., 7a Apollo House, Calleva Park, Aldermaston, Reading, RG7 8TN.

Your Name:

Your Address:

Your Telephone Number:

Please tick as appropriate: Comments ☐   Recommendation ☐

Name of *"Hidden Place"*:

Address:

Telephone Number:

Name of Contact:

THE HIDDEN PLACES
READER COMMENT FORM

Comment or Reason for Recommendation:

....

....

....

....

....

....

....

....

....

....

....

....

....

MAP SECTION

The following pages of maps encompass the main cities, towns and geographical features of Scotland, as well as many of the interesting places featured in the guide. Distances are indicated by the use of scale bars located below each of the maps

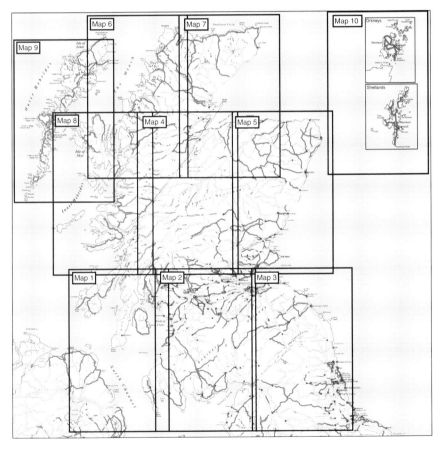

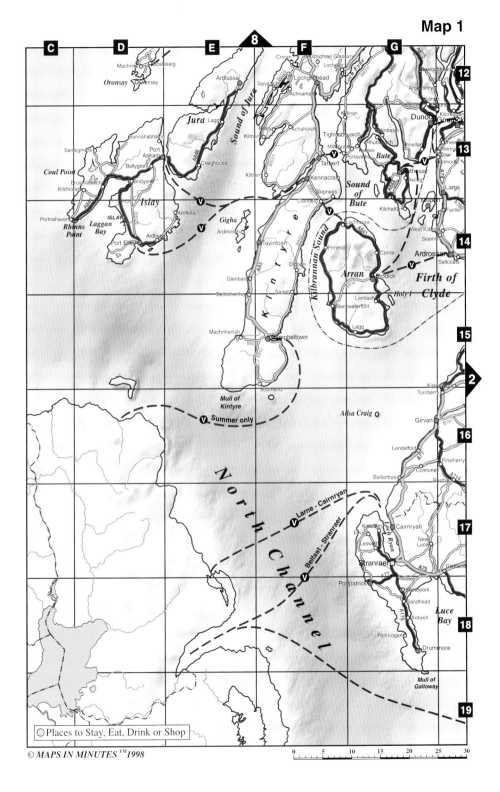

Map 1

Map 2

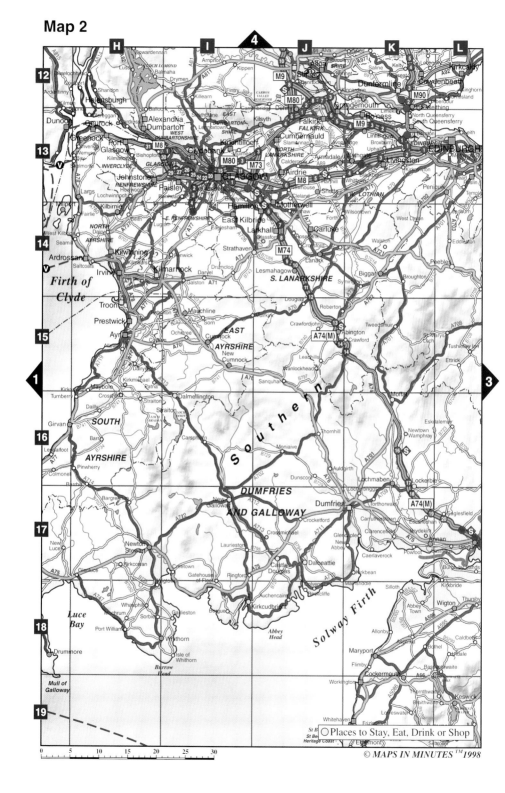

Places to Stay, Eat, Drink or Shop

© MAPS IN MINUTES ™ 1998

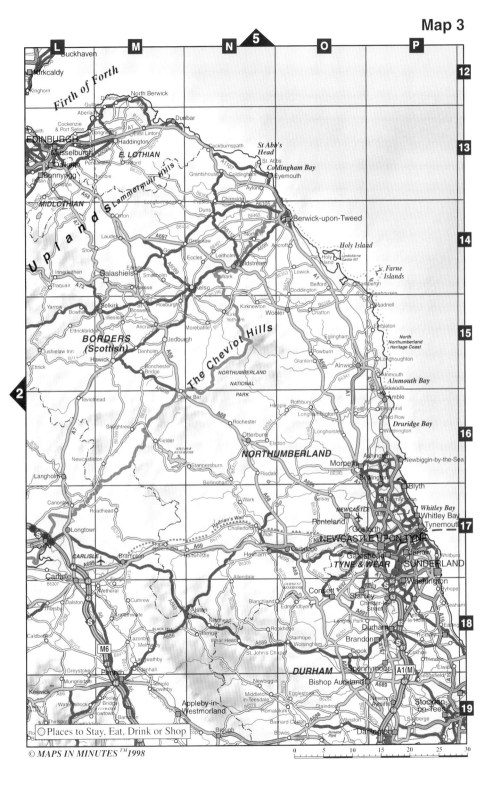

Map 3

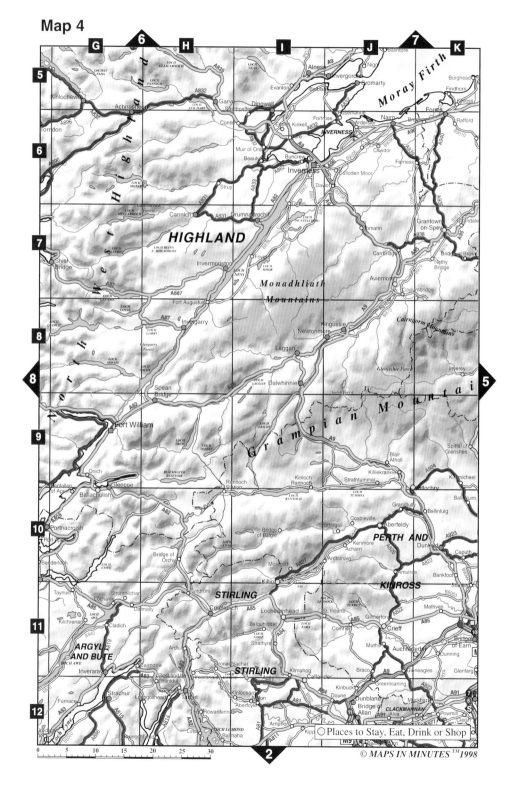

Map 4

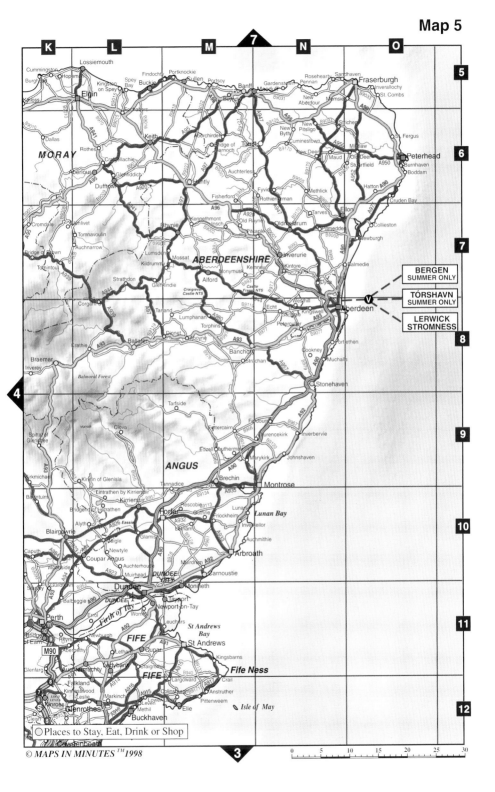

Map 5

Map 6

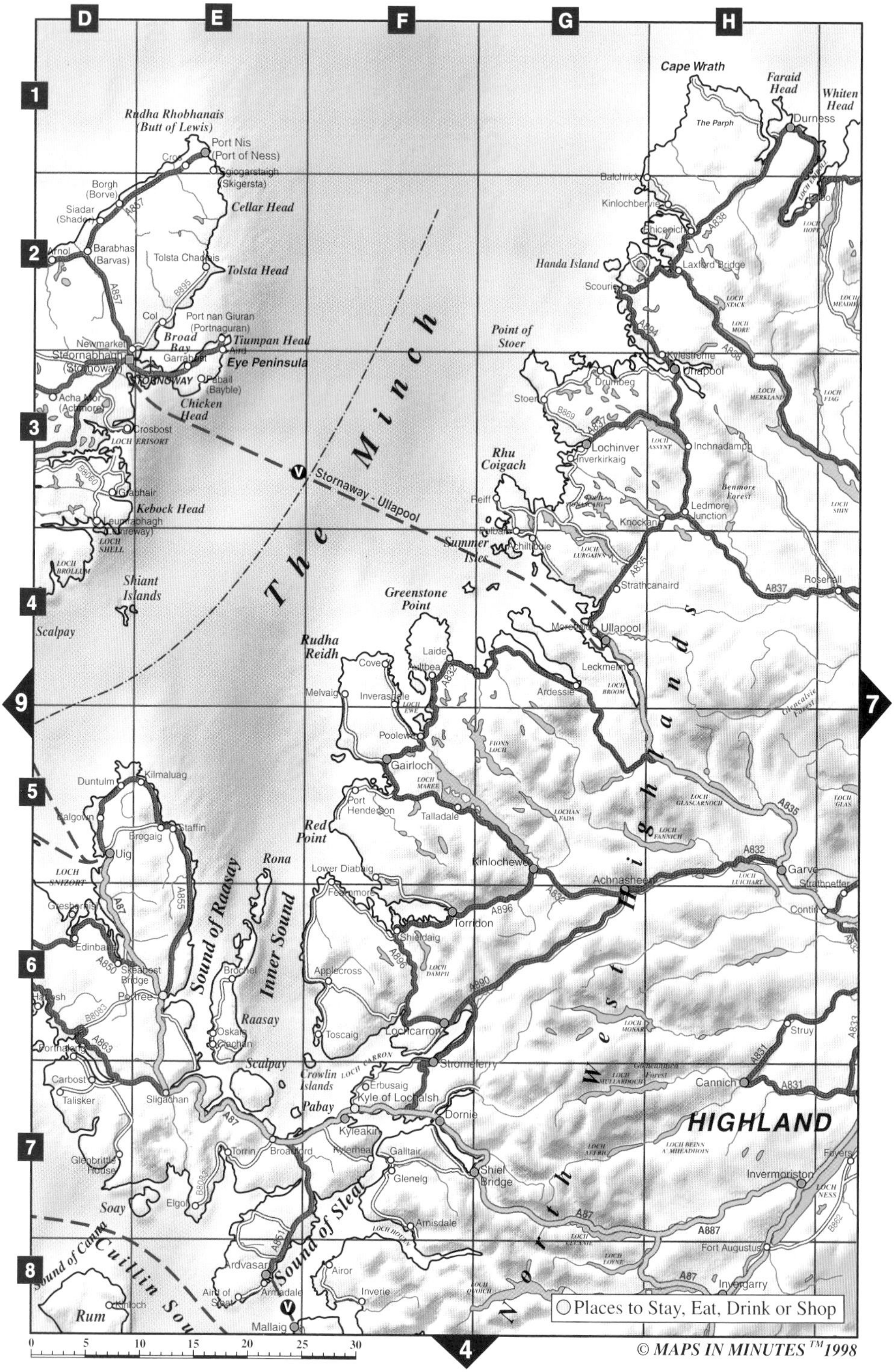

D E F G H

1

Cape Wrath
Faraid Head
Whiten Head
The Parph
Durness

Rudha Rhobhanais
(Butt of Lewis)
Port Nis
(Port of Ness)
Cross
Sgiogarstaigh
(Skigersta)

Borgh
(Borve)
Siadar
(Shader)
Cellar Head

Batchrick
Kinlochberrie
Rhiconich

2

Arnol
Barabhas
(Barvas)
Tolsta Chaolais
Tolsta Head

Handa Island
Scourie
Laxford Bridge

LOCH STACK
LOCH MORE
LOCH MEADHOII

Col
Port nan Giuran
(Portnaguran)
Broad Bay
Tiumpan Head
Garrabost
Eye Peninsula
Newmarket
Steornabhagh
(STORNOWAY)
Bayble
(Bayble)
Chicken Head

Point of Stoer
Kylesku
Kylestrome
Unapool
Drumbeg
Stoer

LOCH MERKLAND
LOCH FIAG

3

Acha Mor
Achmore
Crosbost
LOCH ERISORT
Grabhair
Kebock Head
Leurbost
(Lemreway)

Rhu Coigach
Lochinver
Inverkirkaig
Inchnadamph
LOCH ASSYNT

Benmore Forest
Ledmore Junction
LOCH SHIN

4

LOCH BROLLUM
Shiant Islands

LOCH SHELL

Scalpay

Greenstone Point

Rudha Reidh
Cove
Laide
Aultbea
Melvaig
Inverasdale

Reiff
Achiltibuie
Summer Isles
Knockan
LOCH LURGAINN
Strathcanaird
LOCH SIONASCAIG

Rosehall
A837

Stornaway - Ullapool

The Minch

9 ◆   ◆ **7**

Poolewe
FIONN LOCH
Ardessie
Leckmelm
Ullapool
More
LOCH BROOM

The West

5

Duntulm
Kilmaluag
Gairloch
LOCH MAREE
Talladale
LOCHAN FADA

Balgown
Brogaig
Staffin
Port Henderson
Red Point
Rona

LOCH GLASCARNOCH
LOCH FANNICH
A835
LOCH GLAS

Uig
LOCH SNIZORT
Geisgeil
Lower Diabaig
Fearnmore
Kinlochewe
Achnasheen
Garve
Strathpeffer
A832
LOCH LUICHART
Contin

6

Edinbane
Snizort
Sgarbost
Bridge
Uinish
Portree
Braes
Shieldaig
Applecross
Torridon
LOCH DAMPH
A896
Sound of Raasay
Inner Sound
Achnasheen
LOCH MONAR
Struy
A831

Oskaig
Suardalan
Raasay
Toscaig
Lochcarron
Scalpay
Crowlin Islands
Stromeferry
Glenmore Forest
Cannich
A831

Dunvegan
Carbost
Talisker
Sligachan
Erbusaig
Kyle of Lochalsh
Pabay
LOCH LONG
Dornie

7

Glenbrittle House
Soay
Torrin
Broadford
Kylerhea
Galltair
Kyleakin
Glenelg
Shiel Bridge
Invermoriston
LOCH NESS
LOCH BEINN A MHEADHOIN

HIGHLAND

Elgol
Armadale
Airor
Inverie
Arnisdale
A87
A887
Fort Augustus
Invergarry

8

Sound of Canna
Cuillin Sound
Rum
Ardvasar
Aird of Sleat
Armadale
Sound of Sleat
Mallaig

Places to Stay, Eat, Drink or Shop

0 5 10 15 20 25 30

◆ **4**

© MAPS IN MINUTES ™ 1998

Map 7

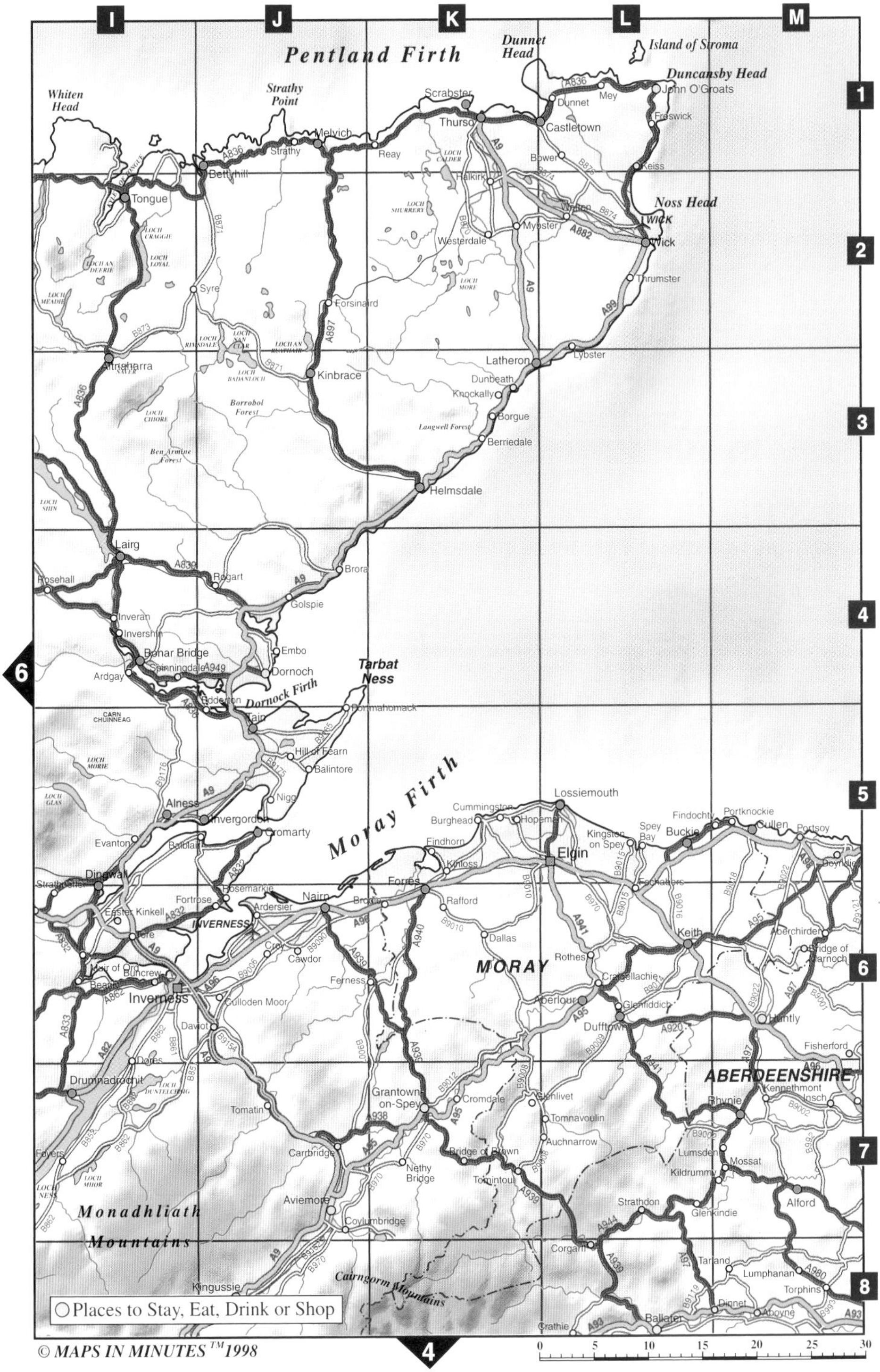

I J K L M

1

2

3

4

5

6

7

8

Pentland Firth

Dunnet Head

Island of Stroma

Duncansby Head

Whiten Head

Strathy Point

Scrabster

Mey

John O'Groats

Dunnet

Freswick

Melvich

Thurso

Castletown

Strathy

Reay

Bower

Keiss

Bettyhill

Halkirk

LOCH CALDER

LOCH SHURRERY

Tongue

Noss Head

Wick

LOCH CRAGGIE

Westerdale

Mybster

Wick

LOCH AN DHERIE

LOCH LOYAL

Thrumster

LOCH MEADIE

Syre

Forsinard

LOCH MORE

Altnaharra

LOCH RIMSDALE

LOCH NAN CLAR

LOCHAN RUATHAIR

Latheron

Lybster

LOCH BADANLOCH

Kinbrace

Dunbeath

Knockally

Borrobol Forest

Langwell Forest

Borgue

LOCH CHOIRE

Berriedale

Ben Armine Forest

Helmsdale

LOCH SHIN

Lairg

A836

A839

Rogart

A9

Brora

Rosehall

Inveran

Golspie

Invershin

Embo

Bonar Bridge

Spinningdale

A949

Dornoch

Tarbat Ness

Ardgay

CARN CHUINNEAG

Bridgend

Dornoch Firth

Edderton

Tain

Portmahomack

Hill of Fearn

Balintore

LOCH MORIE

Nigg

LOCH GLASS

Alness

Cummingston

Lossiemouth

Findochty

Portknockie

Evanton

Invergordon

Cromarty

Burghead

Hopeman

Kingston on Spey

Spey Bay

Buckie

Cullen

Portsoy

Balblair

Moray Firth

Findhorn

Elgin

Strathpeffer

Dingwall

Rosemarkie

Nairn

Kinloss

Forres

Conon Bridge

Fortrose

Brodie

Rafford

Keith

Aberchirder

Easter Kinkell

Ardersier

MORAY

Dallas

Rothes

Bridge of Warnoch

Muir of Ord

Cawdor

Ferness

INVERNESS

Croy

Rothiemurchus

Aberlour

Craigellachie

Glenfiddich

Balloch

Beauly

Inverness

Culloden Moor

Dufftown

Huntly

Davoit

Fisherford

Dores

Drumnadrochit

ABERDEENSHIRE

INVERFARIGAIG

Grantown-on-Spey

Cromdale

Tomatin

Glenlivet

Rhynie

Insch

Foyers

Carrbridge

Bridge of Brown

Tomnavoulin

Auchnarrow

Lumsden

Mossat

LOCH MHOR

Nethy Bridge

Tomintoul

Kildrummy

LOCH NESS

Aviemore

Strathdon

Glenkindie

Alford

Monadhliath Mountains

Coylumbridge

Corgarff

Tarland

Lumphanan

Kingussie

Cairngorm Mountains

Torphins

Dinnet

Aboyne

Crathie

Ballater

○ Places to Stay, Eat, Drink or Shop

0 5 10 15 20 25 30

© *MAPS IN MINUTES* ™ 1998

4

Map 8

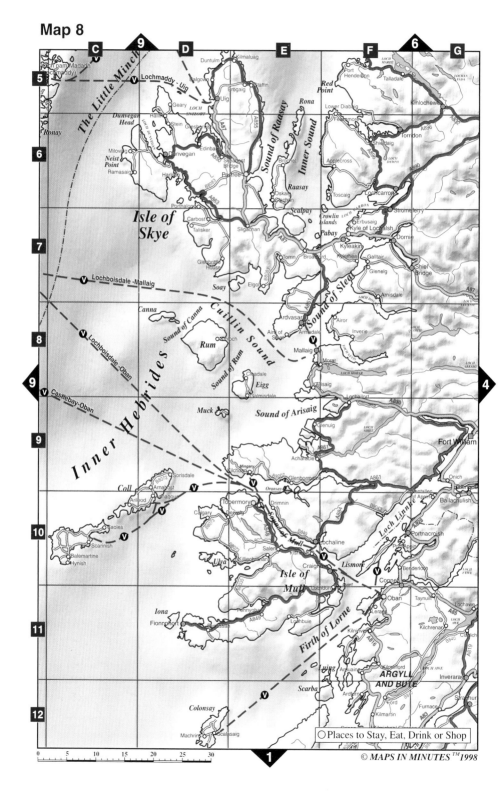

Map 9

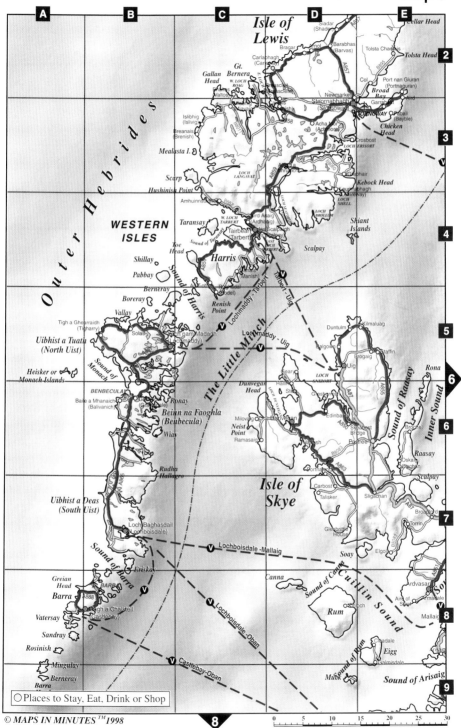

Map 10

Orkneys

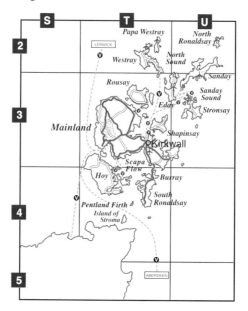

Shetlands

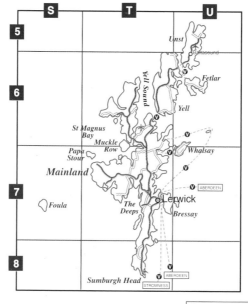

○ Places to Stay, Eat, Drink or Shop

© *MAPS IN MINUTES* [TM]*1998*